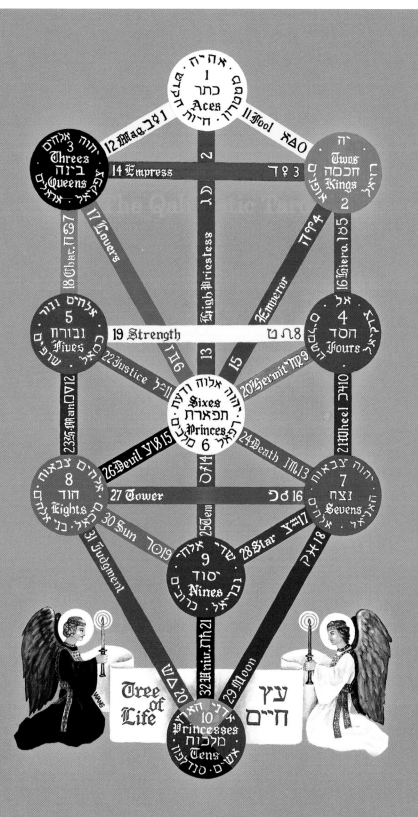

BY THE SAME AUTHOR

The Golden Dawn Tarot (78 Illustrated Cards
—With Israel Regardie)
The Jungian Tarot (78 Illustrated Cards)
An Introduction to the Golden Dawn Tarot
The Secret Temple
Tarot Psychology
The Jungian Tarot and Its Archetypal Imagery
Perfect Tarot Divination
The Rape of Jewish Mysticism by Christian Theologians:
(How the Modern Occult Movement Grew out of
Renaissance Attempts to Convert the Jews)

The Qabalistic Tarot

A Textbook of Mystical Philosophy

Revised Edition

Robert Wang

Marcus Aurelius Press

ILLUSTRATIONS

CONTENTS

THE MAJOR ARCANA ON THE TREE OF LIFE

"...The Tarot, the most satisfactory of all systems of divination, rises from and finds its explanation in the Tree and nowhere else. That may seem a dogmatic statement to the scholarly historian searching for traces of the origin of these mysterious cards, and, we may add, most lamentably failing to find it; but when it is realized that the initiate works the Tarot and the Tree together, that they dovetail into each other at every imaginable angle, it will be seen that such an array of correspondences could be neither arbitrary nor fortuitous."

Dion Fortune

"The only theory of ultimate interest about the Tarot is that it is an admirable symbolic picture of the universe, based on the data of the Holy Qabalah."

Aleister Crowley

"Without the Tarot the magic of the ancients is a closed book, and it is impossible to penetrate any of the great mysteries of the Kabbalah."

Eliphas Lévi

"...the activities of French and English occultists contributed nothing and only served to create considerable confusion between the teachings of the Kabbalah and their own totally unrelated inventions, such as the alleged kabbalistic origins of the Tarot-cards."

Gershom Scholem

PREFACE TO THE SECOND EDITION

When I wrote this book twenty years ago, it was during a period when serious historical studies of the occult movement and of the wonderful picture book called "Tarot" were in their infancy, and when, as Dion Fortune commented, scholars were lamentably failing to find the origins of the cards and of the movements which embraced them. Today, however, there have been tremendous strides among academics, and a great many of the early claims about the history of Tarot have been unequivocally shown to be pure nonsense.

But the truth about the roots of Tarot imagery is actually far more interesting than the various myths surrounding the cards. Over a period of hundreds of years a set of pictures created as a game in some Italian castle, and representing a courtly world as then known, was turned first into a device for telling fortunes, and then into a repository for some extraordinary and complex metaphysical principles.

In this regard, there is a very interesting parallel between the development of Christianity and that of Buddhism. Both Siddhartha and Jesus were seekers of truth whose ideas were twisted into formal and complex religions that provided a framework for theocratic societies. Historians understand today that long after the death of the Buddha, Tibetans grafted a baroque pantheon of gods, demons and formal practices onto his simple teachings. The same happened with the ideas of Jesus. Even those miracles attributed to Jesus in the synoptic gospels, have been demonstrated, by brilliant scholars at the Claremont School in California, to be the embellishment of a zealous Roman writer. In this history there is certainly a lesson about the tools of inner search available to us.

Some, especially Jewish scholars, have been quite hostile toward an attachment of Qabalistic ideas to the Tarot, which is completely understandable. But what we find, when we look into the pedigrees of both Christianity and Judaism, is a sociopolitical core and layer upon layer of complex ideologies added by rabbis and theologians. Starting from scratch, organized belief systems are created and may eventually become archetypal "paths" for inner development. Indeed, Christian and Jewish mystical exercises are profound and effective because they promote a search for simple spiritual principles which transcend cultus. The same may be said for the use of Tarot images, although this path (which some criticize as "occult" in the most negative sense), is quite recent.

To these comments, let me add that when I wrote *The Qabalistic Tarot*, the utility of relating Tarot images to Qabalistic principles was only beginning to emerge from the supposedly "secret teachings" of a number of esoteric fraternities, and was not well-understood by most people. Today previously secret uses of the Tarot, especially the use of Tarot cards as gateways into inner worlds, a process which Carl Jung described as "active imagination," are becoming more and more common.

We are living in a most excellent new era.

Robert Wang
Washington D.C. 2004

PREFACE TO THE FIRST EDITION

The purpose of this book is to demonstrate the relationship between the Qabalah, a time-honored mystical system, and the Tarot. To do so is to pointedly disagree with some very great Jewish scholars, who state that no such relationship exists.

What I have attempted to do in this work is to integrate some of the very complex threads of Qabalistic symbolism and interpretation, emphasizing the relationship of the *Tree of Life* (primary symbol of the Qabalah) and the Tarot as taught in the tradition of the Hermetic Qabalah. I must emphasize that I am not writing on the Hebrew Qabalah, but on a separate and distinct system also based on Hebrew texts. In my opinion, the Hebrew scholars have been mistaken in their perception of late nineteenth century occult developments as merely a romantic and misunderstood pastiche of mystical Hebrew lore.

Moreover, I have attempted to demonstrate that the principles of the Qabalah are appropriately applied to any ordinary Tarot deck. To that end this work reproduces four entire decks, including *The Marseilles Tarot*. Very little discussion is accorded that work, chosen as a comparison with the more symbolically concise modern decks because it is the most common and popular of the decks crystallizing the cards' early imagery. *The Marseilles Tarot* is a "standard" deck, the other three decks used here are those related to the nineteenth century occult fraternity, The Hermetic Order of the Golden Dawn. Those decks are *The Golden Dawn Tarot, The Thoth Tarot* and *The Rider-Waite* deck. One other deck, not shown, but which I recommend very strongly, is that of the late Paul Case and his organization, The Builders of the Adytum. This is a deck to be hand colored by each student.

Besides this deck, Case produced some exceptionally good Tarot literature to which I have devoted considerable attention. His correspondence courses on Tarot, written more than forty years ago, are still being distributed. And, since distribution is restricted, I must quickly note that I am in no way associated with that organization, having been provided a complete set of his courses by sympathetic friends.

Case was a brilliant teacher who must be credited as the first to apply the terms of modern psychology to the cards, an approach very much like that of Carl Jung. I consider Case to be the first great modern scholar on the Tarot, unrecognized as such generally because his major works have been available only to corresponding students of the Builders of the Adytum, who are asked that they be kept confidential.

I have found his ideas, which have influenced my approach, very profound, but with reservations. I question his dogmatic reliance on Gematria (Qabalistic numerology), as well as some of his interpretations of Waite's symbolism. Moreover, at the time Case was writing, our psychological language was in a state of development, and his courses do not reflect today's more precise terminology. A student must "read between the lines," considering forty years of publications on the occult since Case wrote his courses. A great deal of what Case did not say to his corresponding students has been published explicitly by Regardie, Butler, and others.

Such criticism does not apply to his small work entitled *The Book of Tokens,* written in 1934. If there is one single book which I would recommend, it is that collection of poetic essays on the Hebrew letters. It is a milestone of philosophical literature, showing the Tarot to be a key part of the Western Mystery Tradition.

A comment might also be in order here about my frequent reference to the works of Aleister Crowley, considered by many to be one of the twentieth century's great fiends, and by others to be the torchbearer of the religion of the future. It is very difficult to be objective about Crowley, but in making the attempt I have been impressed by the profundity of his writings on the Tarot. His work remains instructive despite criticisms which may be leveled against his personal behavior. I suspect that history will view Crowley as very much a representative of the early twentieth century, a period which espoused the aesthetic of the *avant garde:* What was new and shocking was better, by definition, than what was old. This idea actually underlies all of modern art, music and literature, not to mention the behavior patterns of the artistic elite of London, Paris and New York during the nineteen twenties and thirties. Crowley's behavior fits this pattern, as does the very style of his cards, which is essentially Cubist, the most important and avant garde of all styles of modern art during his prime.

It is important to appreciate this conceptual difference, imbedded in the Crowley deck versus the others. The Order of the Golden Dawn (1888-1900) was created at a period when an idea was revered according to its antiquity. Thus the leaders claimed that their order's history traced deep into the past of mankind, and invoked the monolithic ideological structure of the gods of Egypt. Crowley, on the other hand, says that a new age has arrived (of which he is, not coincidentally, the prophet). Old may be good, but new is better.

I may well be criticized for staying too close to traditional symbolic lines in this work, particularly since the climate today is one of rather sweeping reorganization of symbol systems. A number of books have recently appeared in which the traditional placement of Tarot cards on the Tree of Life has been radically altered. And, frankly, there are several keys which I might assign differently were I starting with no prior conceptions about where the cards should be placed.

But the system, while drawing vitality from gentle modification, does not graciously suffer radical overhaul at the hands of any single individual. It appears intended to develop slowly, each authority incorporating some socially based alteration, making the discipline of greater value to the contemporary society. A system, whether cult, religion or meditative program, is an access pattern into inner worlds, one agreed upon and strengthened by generations of use. It is a path into the unknown paved with culturally-determined, though universally applicable, symbols. And within any given school, the symbols may be manipulated and variously applied. Certainly, I have no quarrel with those who have virtually turned the Tree of Life upside down with their combinations and permutations of ideas. But to do so mitigates the powerful group effort called "tradition," and potentially creates a new Path. Expressed in another way: It is the agreement over time on the meaning of a set of symbols which makes a system a Path. To this end I have given only those attributions which are now commonly accepted. This is not to imply that such attributions are immutably correct, rather to suggest that their accepted interlock is of greater immediate utility to the student than some of the many divergencies.

In this regard, Gareth Knight makes a profound observation. In his *Experience of the Inner Worlds* he describes the workings of a group using the Tarot cards as psychic doorways. He states that "From a formal Qabalistic point of view it was found possible to start any Path working from virtually any Tarot trump—which suggests that the sacrosanct and rigid application of Tarot correspondences to the Tree of Life is of little real importance."[1]

Thus, one must always approach these materials with the attitude that no matter how specific the system, it is only one means of approaching an inner reality. My own style of approach involves building a solid intellectual foundation for the ideas of each Tarot card, yet doing so with full understanding that every tower of ideas must eventually fall, and a new tower built in its place. Each of us builds our own Qabalah, which changes as we learn. What this means is that we all begin with the same concepts, which we personalize and incorporate into our own systems, so that they take on real meaning. And the more we learn, the more we see the original concepts in a different light than when we began.

In attempting to present a basic framework for study, I have tried to show how concepts have been derived wherever possible. Most of all this means a frequent repetition of the Tree of Life illustration, applying different sets of corresponding symbols. To understand the Hermetic Qabalah means to draw literally hundreds of Trees of Life, until the myriad interrelationships begin to make sense. What I have done here is to provide examples of my own manipulation of Qabalistic ideas, i.e., those ideas which when seen graphically, have led to special insights. A work such as this can only be a record of its author's learning process. I must add that this work focuses entirely on the philosophy, rather than on the practical exercises involving the Tarot. Those exercises, both meditative and ritual, have been so extensively discussed by others that there is no need to repeat them here. Of course, I have cited the most important books in which these procedures are to be easily found.

Let me say, finally, that this book has been extremely difficult to write, and I doubt that it will be much easier to read, although I have done my best to simplify abstract concepts wherever possible. The irony is that the baroque and convoluted system of ideas called Qabalah, that impossibly complicated intellectual exercise which is the topic of this book, leads to an inner reality of such beauty and simplicity that it could be explained to a child. Yet it is the very complexity of this exercise of approach that makes the inner simplicity meaningful and comprehensible.

Robert Wang
Washington, D.C. 1982

INTRODUCTION

Modern Tarot Studies
A Nineteenth Century Legacy

This is a book of philosophy, of metaphysics, describing a profound system of self exploration imbedded in seventy eight simple pictures known as the Tarot. And while these cards have long been publicly associated with odd cults and gypsy fortune tellers, they are increasingly capturing the attention of serious students, who view the cards as a repository of a very complex system for the development of inner knowledge.

Perhaps the inventors of the Tarot cards intended that they should be understood as a graphic summation of the principles of the Qabalah, or perhaps not. At least there is no written evidence to suggest this, and the great Jewish scholar of the Qabalah, Gershom Scholem, is probably correct in his assertion (however deprecatory) that the connection was made by late nineteenth century English and French occultists. One way or the other, the interlock of modern Tarot interpretation and Qabalah is so precise that the systems are mutually explanatory. And actually, the likelihood that the two systems developed independently gives far greater authority to the ideas of both because it points toward their mutual roots in universal Truth.

Yet, a great deal of nonsense has been written about both the Tarot and the Qabalah, the sale of a large percentage of occult literature being a tribute to the public's gullibility. Thus, we should be grateful for the scholarly works of the past few decades. Scholem pioneered studies on the Jewish Qabalah, while the western trends have been admirably researched by scholars such as Frances Yates, D.P. Walker, Francis King and Ellic Howe. Serious research is increasingly disabusing us of incorrect notions about the roots of modern esotericism, and we should not be disturbed to see sand castles tumbling. If a system has inner merit it will remain unscathed. We must also appreciate that what is known as

"The Mysteries" have apparently, until very recently, been transmitted through a secret oral tradition.

Despite increased public interest, surprisingly little attention has been paid to the Tarot by academia, though the cards are a veritable gold mine of art history and metaphysical philosophy. They should be of great interest to any medievalist, being clearly of the same temperament which produced the sculptural programs of the Gothic cathedrals. It is likely, also, that the cards in some way relate to the medieval books of *Emblemata* and to those delightful, and supposedly historical, narratives called the *Chansons de Gestes*.

What the Tarot represents is an allegorical journey, each card being the experience of something (a universal energy) along the way, rather like the episodes in Dante's *Divine Comedy*, Bunyan's *Pilgrim's Progress* or even Tolkien's *Trilogy of the Ring*. And the idea of an adventuresome and perilous journey through unknown territory was typical of medieval literature. The analogy here is that to travel in the Middle ages was as dangerous and difficult as to travel the inner paths of the Mysteries. So one might agree with the monk who in 1377 suggested that the Tarot was a mirror of fourteenth century society, saying that the cards represented "...the state of the world as it is now most excellently described and figured."[2] Early decks show many of the virtues and liberal arts so important to the iconographic programs of Gothic Humanism, some of which remain in today's standard Tarot keys: *Temperance* is Prudence, *Strength* is Fortitude, Justice remains Justice, etc. All of these cards are female, as the virtues and liberal arts were always represented.[3]

Even an emperor was visible in the real society. That had been especially true since 800, when the Pope crowned Charlemagne Holy Roman Emperor in an attempt to strengthen Christianity by aligning it with a great secular power. And when we come to *The High Priestess*, we find that tradition related her to the legend of a "Female Pope,"[4] circulating at just this time in history. The evidence for the fourteenth century origin of the cards is convincing, and hopefully some historian of medieval art history will pick up these fascinating threads and provide us with the real historical answers.

On the other hand a considerable number of well trained esotericists insist that the cards are of very ancient origin, which some claim to be an encounter of these individuals, through the Tarot, with the shadows of other systems which have been used to approach the same universal energies. Such differentiation may be extremely difficult on an inner plane and if so might explain why the experiences of so many students contradict historical evidence. Of course, if the Tarot can be of use to us in something so important as the development of inner understanding, study of its origins is little more than a pleasant side trip. The same is true for the very question of an original link between Qabalah and the Tarot, although we are not here proposing that such a link was originally intended between Tarot and the Hermetic Qabalah on which this present book is based.

That system, developed in Europe from the time of the Renaissance, is a westernized Qabalah. It grew from the improbable attempts of fifteenth century philosophers to incorporate the essence of Jewish mysticism into Christian thought. The history of the modification of these ideas by the philosophers of the sixteenth, seventeenth and eighteenth centuries is particularly interesting. But it is the nineteenth century developments which are most important for us. During that time the Hermetic Qabalah, largely dechristianized, reached its fullest expression with the Hermetic Order of the Golden Dawn. The leaders of that fraternity performed the remarkable task of unifying the disparate elements of the Western Mystery Tradition (Qabalah, Hermeticism, Astrology, Neoplatonism, Dee's Enochian Magic, etc.) in such a way that it formed a coherent method of inner exploration for the fin de siècle temperament. There are few modern schools of western esoteric thought which have not been affected in some way by the developments of that group. And as one discusses Hermetic Qabalism, one of necessity refers to the Golden Dawn as its primary modern expression. Hermetic Qabalah and Golden Dawn must be considered virtually synonymous.

Nor is it significant whether the esoteric tenets of this group were handed down secretly for generations, or if they were meticulously culled from ancient manuscripts in the British Museum. The authority of any group derives entirely from its inner contacts. The "Secret Tradition," "The Mysteries," or whatever this may be called, can be tapped into by anyone. An individual or group becomes a part of an ancient tradition by contacting inner teachers in that tradition, and it would certainly appear that the decks used to illustrate this book are the result of such inner contact.

The three key decks of the modern era were all produced by members of that fraternity: *The Golden Dawn Tarot* (designed by MacGregor Mathers), The *Rider-Waite Deck* (designed by A.E. Waite), and the Thoth Tarot (designed by Aleister Crowley). A fourth major deck, already mentioned, is that of Paul Case for the BOTA. His version is an excellent development of that issued by Waite.

The Waite deck, one of the most popular ever published, seems to have been designed with such concern for oaths of membership in the Order that it remains entirely exoteric. It is included in the hope that those who may have chosen to study the deck may find its (often admirable, occasionally unacceptable) symbolism more useful when considered from the standpoint of the Hermetic Qabalah.

The Golden Dawn Tarot is an esoteric deck, intended for the private use of members of the Order. Crowley's deck is also esoteric, in that it conceals the nineteenth century Order's symbolism. Certainly, Crowley's Thoth Tarot is the most original recent contribution to Tarot studies.

Unfortunately neither Crowley nor Mathers has received appropriate credit for their work with the Tarot. And because of their occasionally outrageous behavior, both men have been fair game for social historians. Moreover, their scholarly limitations have made them the object of jokes by meticulous researchers on the Hebrew Qabalah. But a study of any mystery tradition, unless it be purely historical, requires that preconceived notions be set aside, and that the system be judged solely on the merit of its efficacy. One must use the word efficacy because that is the only valid measure of a metaphysical system. Does it work? But how do we establish whether it works or not? The answer to these questions is certainly not to be found through the present methods of the sciences, or of the humanities, which are predicated on those of science; data is collected and analyzed empirically. And since those ideas known as "The Mysteries" do not lend themselves to this sort of attack, being in high degree irrational, they may be denigrated even by historians. Many knowledgeable scholars perceive late nineteenth century Hermetic Qabalism as only a romantic and fanciful offshoot of Hebrew Qabalism, unworthy of the sort of research devoted to esoteric Judaism. And the social toning of the materials as "occult" adds to the wall of preconceptions and prejudgments.

The problem arises in that to study any aspect of the Mysteries the investigator must himself or herself become a part of the system. A person must evaluate it from the inside, which may make it appear that one has abrogated investigative objectivity. Today's academicism does not allow for the acquisition of knowledge through intuition and psychism, an attitude placing it in paradoxical contradiction to a high proportion of those great thinkers whom the humanities study and purport to revere. In the humanities, the universities have deteriorated into observers of, rather than participants in, the development of mankind's creative and intellectual faculties.

A more serious problem, in terms of the cautious dissemination of occult ideas, is that any proofs which may emerge are valid only for the investigator himself. Carl Jung expressed this by stating that "only the psyche can know the psyche."

The fact is, however, that those who travel the inner paths (using any given system) have parallel experiences. The encounter of, for example, the energies symbolized by *The Universe* card, theoretically produces the same basic experience for everyone. It should be quickly added, however, that through what is known as the astral level of consciousness, one functions within the confines of a *cultus*. A Catholic mystic will learn the same lessons through the symbolism of Christianity that a Qabalist learns through the symbolism of the Tree of Life. The universal energies are actually formless, yet we perceive them in the guise of our chosen system.

It is at the level of the Christ/Buddha/Krishna Intelligence that the unity of all systems becomes apparent, and we are freed into pure consciousness. Thus, in these terms, one may appreciate that when the question is asked, "Does the system work?", it means: is the symbolic structure of the system representative of universal truths sufficient to carry one beyond the system itself? In the case of the Hermetic Qabalah and its practical tool, the Tarot, there can be no doubt. This is an extremely potent system, particularly in that it may be incorporated into any school of thought or religion in which the student chooses to function. Of course, no one is asked to accept this statement on face value. Blind acceptance of anything whatsoever is contrary to the Qabalistic method.

The Search for "Truth"

The chances are good that most readers of this book are disillusioned with both organized religion and science. Neither seems to provide the insight into our human condition demanded by an increased and world wide sophistication. We have learned so much through the wonders of technology and modern communications, that the explanations of our fathers appear more placebo than panacea.

Many of those so disillusioned turn to occultism and mysticism in the hope of finding broader meaning and truth. They do so in the essential belief that direct knowledge of the cosmic order, enlightenment, is possible.

The mystery schools teach that what we can see, touch and feel presents us with only a relative reality. Beyond that which is considered "real" by most people are worlds of an even greater reality, which every individual has the capacity to explore. Enlightenment means emergence from the darkness of our limited sense perceptions and thought framework into a consciousness of the greater reality. It is of that from which we are born, and into this that we shall return at the end of our brief life cycle. The Qabalah is a system once traditionally claimed (prior to the work of Scholem) to have been given to Adam by God, to have been the province of a few chosen adepts until it became "Hellenized" by the Greeks and began to form a sub-current of Western civilization. The value of the system is that it divides the universe into specific categories, allowing for the establishment of correspondences between all cults and religions. The Tarot cards, also, may be equated with the major aspects of most religious systems.

Esoteric tradition, as represented by the Tarot, makes some very basic statements about man and the nature of the universe which is our immediate environment. It says that there is a perfect order which one has the capacity to perceive, and that there is no such thing as an accident. For every movement of every leaf on every tree there is a reason, and every movement of every thing is interrelated. Separateness is a myth. We are all part of one great unity.

These principles have been expressed for thousands of years, and in thousands of ways. And somehow, as expressed, they are always so simple. The concept that All is One and we are All has a certain poetry to it. It may strike a deep rooted chord and then be quickly forgotten. But there is a feeling that the statement has merit. The words of prophets may imbue us with a strange and momentary silence, as if our minds are straining to recall something.

Students may respond in this way to a small book from 1912, called *The Kybalion*. This work involves all of the key principles of Tarot, and purports to sum up ancient Hermeticism. The ideas here are actually the same sorts of Gnostic thought that produced the Qabalah. Hermeticism and Qabalah both date from the period of earliest Christianity. When we describe the Hermetic Qabalah we mean the later amalgam of the principles of both.

The Kybalion gives seven Hermetic Principles.[5] These are, quite literally, a distillation of the universal principles on which the Tarot is based, and deserve to be the subject of every student's meditation. They are:

1. *The Principle of Mentalism:* "The All is Mind; The Universe is Mental."
2. *The Principal of Correspondence:* "As Above, so below; as below, so above."

3. *The Principle of Vibration:* "Nothing rests; everything moves, everything vibrates."
4. *The Principle of Polarity:* "Everything is Dual; everything has poles; everything has its pair of opposites; like and unlike are the same; opposites are identical in nature, but different in degree; extremes meet; all truths are but half truths; all paradoxes may be reconciled."
5. *The Principle of Rhythm:* "Everything flows, out and in; everything has its tides; all things rise and fall; the pendulum swing manifests in everything; the measure of the swing to the right is the measure of the swing to the left; rhythm compensates."
6. *The Principle of Cause and Effect:* "Every Cause has its Effect; every Effect has its Cause; everything happens according to Law; chance is but a name for Law not recognized; there are many planes of causation, but nothing escapes the Law."
7. *The Principle of Gender*: "Gender is in everything; everything has its Masculine and its Feminine Principles; gender manifests on all planes."

The doctrine that our universe is so precisely ordered is basic to the Tarot, as is the idea that the Tarot images accurately symbolize the very framework of the universe. As MacGregor Mathers stated: "I have not only transcribed the symbolism, but have tested, studied, compared and examined it both clairvoyantly and in other ways. The result has been to show me how absolutely correct the symbolism of the *Book T* [meaning Tarot] is, and how exactly it represents the occult forces of the universe."[6]

Eliphas Lévi described the Tarot in even more flamboyant terms: "...although it is popular in a sense and may be found everywhere, this is of all most occult and unknown, because it is the key to the rest... It is, in truth, a monumental and extraordinary work, strong and simple as the architecture of the pyramids, and consequently enduring like those—a book which is a summary of all sciences, which can resolve all problems by its infinite combinations, which speaks by evoking thought, it is an inspirer and moderator of all possible conceptions, and the masterpiece perhaps of the human mind. It is to be counted unquestionably among the great gifts bequeathed to us by antiquity."[7] Lévi was among the first to claim publicly that the Tarot was more than merely a quaint device for telling fortunes, and that it was virtually the key to all occult science.

Clearly, for one to take this approach to the Tarot requires a considerable amount of faith. But this should be a faith which is understood to represent merely a suspension of judgment. One who fails to exercise rational judgment, or who accepts any esoteric principle unquestioningly, is a poor candidate for inner development. We must engage our every capacity, and the capacity to reason is our greatest protection against being led astray in these matters. One might also suggest that the methods of the Hermetic Qabalah will be particularly attractive to those who are natively intellectual, artistic, or both. These methods are not for everyone, and to study them efficiently requires a significant commitment. The pursuit of any specific method of spiritual development represents a choice. And herein lies another important principle. This principle is frequently encountered in popular literature, couched in aphoristic terms such as "We are masters of our own destiny," or "The Stars impel, they do not compel." We are, in fact, the authors of our every experience, from the non-accident of our birth and the parents whom we choose, to the very time and circumstances of our death. Some of the inspired religious literature of the West hints at this idea. It is a principle which has been stated openly and explicitly in Eastern religions for thousands of years.

This is not an easy concept to accept, because it lays full credit or blame for all that occurs in our lives squarely on our own shoulders. But this does not imply that we are necessarily aware of the decision making process. That is the province of the Higher Self, that spiritual part of ourselves which endures, while the personalities molded for each successive incarnation dissipate and cease to be (save as they represent experience assimilated by the Higher Self). The pursuit of enlightenment is the pursuit of the "Knowledge and Conversation of the Holy Guardian Angel," aspect of the Higher Self. This means the development of a conscious awareness of, and contact with, an innermost spiritual nature which is the essence of God. The goal is a lofty one. The decision to pursue it seriously, as well as the means of pursuit, pivotal choices. And here one must not lose sight of the fact that whatever the chosen path, whether that be Tarot or Yoga or Catholic mysticism, it is a means of self exploration, and not an end in itself. Yet as Jung points out, some people try to escape into a system:

> People will do anything, no matter how absurd, in order to avoid facing their own souls. They will practice Indian Yoga in all its exercises, observe a strict regimen of diet, learn theosophy by heart, or mechanically repeat mystic texts from the literature of the whole world all because they cannot get on with themselves and have not the slightest faith that anything useful could ever come out of their own souls.[8]

It is a sad fact that many disturbed people are attracted to all forms of occult work. These are people who look for an escape, but do not find it. An unbalanced personality, unable to cope with its own earthly environment, will find little solace in the Tarot or in any other facet of the Mysteries. Instead, such persons may find esoteric research very disconcerting, as they discover themselves required to face aspects of their personalities with which they cannot cope, or increasingly immersed in their own fantasies and losing touch with reality. The dawning awareness of the truth of the universal order is difficult for the most balanced personality, because it involves concepts that totally refute what most people believe themselves to be. There is a cause and effect here, which is the

reason that so many esoteric works include a warning. Anyone can learn to manipulate the Kundalini forces of their own body, and open the channels by which
Light descends. The methods are basically very simple, and are openly described
in works such as Regardie's *Middle Pillar* and in his *Foundations of Practical
Magic*.[9] Yet if the basic preparatory work has been ignored, or done casually, the
result may be a systemic imbalance, rather than balance and increased vitality
and awareness. These dangers are one reason that the Mysteries maintained
strict secrecy for so many centuries.

Tradition states that the Mysteries maintained secrecy as a matter of keeping sacred ideas from the profane, although we appreciate that in some ages past
secrecy has also kept the metaphysician from being burned at the stake. But
those who have been the guardians of the orally transmitted Mystery Tradition
over the centuries have also understood the responsibility of conveying practical techniques to those who might misunderstand or misapply the principles of
their use.[10]

Even today one could argue reasonably that the practical esoteric techniques should be kept secret, although so much has now been published that
the point is purely moot. And the fact is that there are no real "secrets," as most
people understand the word. Herein lies the crux of all occultism, mysticism
and esoteric religion. In fact, one important "secret" is so simple that it can be
conveyed in a single paragraph:

What is called enlightenment depends on the physical opening of channels
so that the consciousness of the personality can directly contact the consciousness of the greater universe. What this means is a manipulation of vibrations
within the body and a subtle change in physiochemistry. It is all a form of yoga,
where one experiences what feels like an electromagnetic current in the body.
Everyone has felt this current and anyone can learn to manipulate it. Moreover,
this has nothing whatsoever to do with the school of mysticism or occultism in
which one operates. The directive "Inflame thyself with prayer," meaning to
excite the inner currents of the body, is the practical essence of Christianity,
Judaism, Buddhism, Hinduism and every legitimate form of mystery religion or
cult. To the technique of manipulation of body energies, the Hermetic Qabalah
adds a program of inner visualization. One begins by imagining an inner scene,
a tightly created and directed daydream. Soon, however, one discovers that what
is happening is not an invention.

The Tarot is, of course, ideal for this kind of visualization, known as "path
working" or "rising on the planes." To focus on any given Key is to turn attention to a specific intelligent energy as anthropomorphized in a card. This very
focus of attention tends to effect an unconscious link with the energy which
the card symbolizes. This is not to suggest, however, that the Tarot offers any
shortcuts, for it does not. One who chooses to study the Tarot by the Qabalistic
method must do so with discretion, sensitivity, completeness and acceptance of a
certain disciplined boredom until positive results are obtained, which may take
years. Those who make the system work do so by pursuing strict meditative
exercises, without concern for result.

But results do come, and one begins to perceive the entire system very differently, appreciating the fluidity with which the cards must be interpreted. A Key may have several possible interpretations (some even apparently contradictory), particularly when it represents a Path on the upper levels of the Tree of Life. Thus, the values inherent in a card can never be attributed to a few catch phrases easily memorized. Aleister Crowley, in his *Book of Thoth,* makes the point that what he can say about a card may either represent a small part of its meaning, or may not necessarily appear to make sense. Often, in that work, Crowley finds a card so profound that he must resort to the word symbols of poetry to approach its most serious implications. He was also uniquely honest in his assertion, published in *The Confessions of Aleister Crowley*, that he did not completely understand all of the cards. He wrote:

> "The true significance of the Atus of Tahuti, or Tarot Trumps, also awaits full understanding. I have satisfied myself that these twenty two cards compose a complete system of hieroglyphs, representing the total energies of the universe. In the case of some cards [presumably referring to his own deck] I have succeeded in restoring the original form and giving a complete account of their meaning. Others, however, I understand imperfectly, and of some few I have at present obtained no more than a general idea."[11]

Certainly, the Tarot offers us great potential for self deception. We can believe we have understood some aspect of the study, yet still be working within a very personal and distorted framework. For this reason, it is best to refer, at every step of the learning experience, to the time honored documents on the subject. For the Tarot, this means the *Sepher Yetzirah*, a very brief work by which we relate the Hebrew letters to the Tarot Keys. Another great work is the source book of the Jewish Qabalah, *The Zohar*, a mystical commentary in many volumes which has never been fully translated into a European language.

Some claim that the greatest Qabalistic work of all is the Pentateuch of Moses, the first five books of the Bible. The study of the first four books, in Hebrew, and on the basis of numerology, is the essence of Jewish Qabalah.

On the surface all of this may seem unapproachably complex. But the intellectual Qabalah, as opposed to the practical work, is easily understood by anyone willing to consider it with the intensity and diligence that one would apply to the learning of a new language. The Qabalah is essentially artificial. It is a defining pattern imposed on qualities which would otherwise be too impossibly fluid to grasp. By example, one could cite the idea of periodization in history. There is, obviously, no line of demarcation between the centuries. But to place blocks of ideas and social styles within the brackets arbitrarily established as the eighteenth, nineteenth or twentieth centuries is useful.

The Golden Dawn

It is no coincidence that the three most important Tarot decks of the modern era, those of Waite, Crowley and the Golden Dawn, were produced by members of the Hermetic Order of the Golden Dawn. That fraternity, the intellectual heir of the Renaissance Qabalists and Baroque Rosicrucians, placed greater emphasis on the Tarot than any other group whose activities have yet been made public. Their attitude that the Tarot synthesizes the principles of the Hermetic Qabalah has been pivotal to modern esoteric studies.

The Hermetic Order of the Golden Dawn, particularly insofar as it represented a social phenomenon, is best viewed against the backdrop of its own period. London today is a sprawling and sophisticated metropolis, a center for international trade and communications. Even the traditional reserve of the English themselves does not serve to mask the vitality and rapidity of life there. London of the 1890's was more tranquil and picturesque. One imagines streets lined with trees and quaint shops, horse drawn carriages moving leisurely across cobblestoned streets carrying ladies in long gowns and gentlemen in tophats. The tranquil quality of some of London's streets however, was in sharp contrast to the squalor of the same city's slums, or to the factory areas of the emerging industrial nation ruled by Queen Victoria. This was a time and place of great polarities.

This was the society which acted as a crucible for the ideas of the modern Hermetic Qabalah, a society very different in tone and quality from that which we know today. The Order of the Golden Dawn emerged during one of the most interesting periods of modern history, the Fin de Siècle, La Belle Époque. It was a time when people were beginning to assess and place in perspective a great deal of knowledge gained in previous decades.

Many historians view the extraordinary interest in occultism at that time as a reaction against industrialization and its concomitant materialism. There was definitely a fear in some quarters that machine technology might overwhelm and destroy individuality. Others tend to view the interest in esoteric matters as the result of politically based contact with eastern ideas, relating to England's involvement in India and the subsequent birth of Theosophy. Yet, however one may choose to assess the development of occultism in the late nineteenth century, like the other threads of the social fabric, it represented the fruit of generations of exploration. The same may be said at this time for the sciences, for politics, for industry, and for all phases of the arts.

Expressed in another way, there was more change in human lifestyle and philosophy at the turn of that century than at any other time in history. It was overwhelming, it was rapid, but it did not happen overnight. An analogy could be made with a balloon that fills with air slowly, but bursts suddenly. The Golden Dawn was a stylish bursting forth of pressure that had begun to build in the Qabalistic philosophies of the Renaissance.

Those who criticize the Golden Dawn for its theatricality should appreciate that it emerged from much the same social forces which were producing the modern theatre, to say nothing of modern literature, modern art and modern music. This was the age of Ibsen, of Stravinsky, of Henri Bergson (Mrs. Mathers' brother), of William Morris, of Oscar Wilde, of Rimbaud and Verlaine, of Van Gogh and Gauguin.

It is in this light that the Order is best understood. What the Order did, essentially, was to collect, focus and expand upon all of the previous experience of the Western Mystery Tradition. The elements of the Hermetic Qabalah were very different after undergoing the refinements and critical definitions of the Golden Dawn.

In 1888 the Order was founded under the joint leadership of William Wynn Westcott, S.L. MacGregor Mathers and W.R. Woodman. Its "authority," as well as its claim to have descended from Christian Rosencreutz (father of Rosicrucianism) was based on a mysterious set of "Cypher Manuscripts" which came into Westcott's hands in 1887.

The story is very complicated, and made even more so by the likelihood that at least some of the materials issued to the members by Mathers, *et al.*, and claimed by them to be of great antiquity, were their own invention.[12]

The "Ancient Cypher Manuscripts" were (suspiciously) in English, translated into a very simple cypher for letter code invented by the Abbot Trithemius (patron of Agrippa) in the sixteenth century. These pages outline the rituals and grade structure of an occult fraternity, and supposedly originated in Germany. And while there is a serious question about the authenticity of these documents, they were definitely written by one with a profound knowledge of occult tradition.

It was, in any event, on the basis of the claimed laying on of hands from the past that members were solicited for the new order. They came from a wide range of pursuits and included, by 1890, William Butler Yeats, Annie Homiman and the actress Florence Farr. A.E. Waite was a member of the group for somewhat more than a year. Later he rejoined but eventually wrote disparagingly of his experiences with the fraternity.

In 1892 Mathers became sole Chief, and the Second, or Inner Order (offering the grade of Adeptus Minor) was established. Mathers was a skillful organizer, though perhaps addicted to small deceits aimed at aggrandizing his own image, or adding to the lustre of the order in the eyes of its members. Serious problems began to appear in 1895, stemming largely from Mathers' autocratic leadership. While Mathers claimed to be in contact with three "Secret Chiefs," unseen Masters who guided the course of the order, the members had become increasingly reluctant to accept Mathers' statements on faith. Aleister Crowley joined the Order in November of 1898 and was soon apprenticed to the legendary Alan Bennett. He also earned the respect of Mathers for his intelligence and talent for esoteric work. But the same qualities of investigative independence, albeit genius, which so attracted Bennett and Mathers, tended to be viewed as abrasive by other members. In 1899, after MacGregor and Moina Mathers had moved to Paris to establish a continental branch of the Order, the leaders of the

London Temple decided to reject Crowley's application for membership in the Second Order. That decision led ultimately to the final disintegration of the order as it had been originally.

In Paris, Mathers unilaterally conferred the Adeptus Minor degree on Crowley. But this incurred the wrath of the London members, who refused to accept the initiation as valid, and voted to expel Mathers himself. Undaunted, Mathers proceeded to found a new group. Others, including Crowley, eventually did the same, each claiming that his fraternity was authentic, and in contact with the Secret Chiefs. Thus, the teaching of the Order was disseminated around the world, as splinter groups formed in England, America and other countries. The methods of the order became public knowledge between the years 1937 and 1940 when Israel Regardie's four volume *The Golden Dawn* appeared.[13] This work contains all of the order's significant lectures and rituals, as well as a very thorough explanation of their underlying principles.

The Golden Dawn Tarot

There is only one known, published, reference to the origin of the Golden Dawn Tarot. This appears in the 1945 autobiography of Irish artist and poet, Ella Young. In the book, *Flowering Dusk,* she describes a visit to the home of the Mathers, having been brought there by Maud Gonne, a member of the order. Maud Gonne had herself been brought into the group by William Butler Yeats, who courted her unsuccessfully for many years. Ella Young describes having been attracted to some large illustrations of Egyptian Gods executed in paper mosaic, and claimed by MacGregor Mathers to have been done by him in one night.

> "When we are in the quiet street again, I say to Maud Gonne, 'How can he expect us to believe that he did those mosaics in one night?' "
> "I think it quite likely that he did."
> "But to cut those strips of paper, sort the colours, glue them into position: to say nothing of designing and drawing the figures it seems to be impossible!"
> "He can do things like that. One time he made up his mind that the society should have Tarot cards. At headquarters he took a packet of white cards, asked a member to mark them, went into an inner room for a little while, and came out with those marked cards. The Tarot signs were painted on them. The cards used by the society are copied from the pack.' I had seen those cards. To produce them at short notice 'while you wait' was a feat equaling the mosaics."[14]

It appears that a finished deck was painted by Mrs. Mathers, a very accomplished artist. Her deck was subsequently lent to members of the Inner Order who were required to copy it by hand. This was the procedure followed by the late Golden Dawn lodge to which Israel Regardie belonged, the Stella Matutina, although by that time preparation of a Tarot deck was optional.

Photographs of Regardie's deck (the original having been stolen) were the basis of The Golden Dawn Tarot, painted by Robert Wang under Regardie's direction, and published in 1978.

The Rider-Waite Deck

In 1910 Arthur Edward Waite and the artist Pamela Colman Smith produced what has become the most popular Tarot deck in history, generally called The Rider Deck after his publisher, William Rider & Son. The production of this deck is discussed by Waite in his autobiography, *Shadows of Life and Thought*:

> "*The Secret Tradition in Goetia* was my first considerable work bearing the Rider imprint, but it was preceded in 1910 by a delightful experiment with the so called Tarot Divinatory Cards, otherwise denominated the *Book of Thoth* in the high fantasia of my old friend Eliphas Lévi. Now, in those days there was a most imaginative and abnormally psychic artist, named Pamela Colman Smith, who had drifted into the Golden Dawn and loved its ceremonies—as transformed by myself—without pretending or indeed attempting to understand their sub-surface consequence. It seemed to some of us in the circle that there was a draughtsman among us who, under proper guidance, could produce a Tarot with an appeal in the world of art and a suggestion of significance beyond the Symbols which would put on them another construction than had ever been dreamed by those who, through many generations, had produced and used them for mere divinatory purposes. My province was to see that the designs—especially those of the important Trumps Major— kept that in the hiddenness which belonged to certain Greater Mysteries, in the Paths of which I was travelling. I am not of course intimating that the Golden Dawn had at that time any deep understanding by inheritance of Tarot cards; but, if I may so say, it was getting to know under my auspices that their Symbols—or some at least among them—were gates which opened on realms of vision beyond occult dreams. I saw to it therefore that Pamela Colman Smith should not be picking up casually any floating images from my own or another mind. She had to be spoon fed carefully over The Priestess Card, over that which is called The Fool and over The Hanged Man...If anyone feels drawn in these days to the serious consideration of Tarot Symbolism they will do well to select the codex of coloured cards produced under my supervision by Miss Pamela Colman Smith."[15]

Imbedded here are two ideas which may help to explain Waite's early estrangement from the Order of the Golden Dawn. He suggests that he not only "transformed" the Golden Dawn ceremonies, but that it was he who introduced the members to the real meaning of Tarot.

Such pronouncements made him few friends, and stimulated Aleister Crowley to publish some very vitriolic comments. One article in *The Equinox* was a tongue-in-cheek obituary of the still very much alive Waite, complete with heavy black borders on every page. The title of the article was "Dead Weight." It began: "It is with the deepest feeling that we record the passing over of...the aged saint known on earth as Arthur Edward Waite." The article continues with a mock life story. "The career of Arthur Edward Waite was largely determined by his father's fine perception. 'Ned, my lad,' said he when the future saint was barely six years of age, 'brains are not your long suit, I can see. But it doesn't matter. If you can't be wise, look wise!' "[16]

Crowley was a bitter adversary, a thorn in Waite's side for decades. But Waite may actually have had the last laugh, for in his lengthy autobiography, he has not mentioned the name of Crowley even once.

Aleister Crowley's Thoth Tarot

The Crowley deck has had a long and complex history. Not only did it take Lady Frieda Harris five years to paint the cards, but the completed work remained unpublished for twenty five years.

The first (and little known) printing was done privately by Carr Collins and his Texas based Sangrael Foundation. This was a very poor printing, in one color. It was not until 1969 that an American publisher of occult books arranged for the first color edition, the actual printing being done in Hong Kong. Undoubtedly, Lady Harris, who had insisted that only the English printer of government postage stamps would be allowed to produce the deck, would have been very disappointed (if not sickened) by these editions.

In 1979 the cards were finally published in an edition conforming to the highest standards of reproduction. Yet it was not without serious obstacles that the cards appeared. In the interim, between the Sangreal and the corrected edition, the curator of the collection of Crowley documents housed at the Courtauld Institute in London, refused to allow the original paintings to be photographed. The large collection of Crowleyana, donated to the Courtauld by Gerald Yorke, had been the object of numerous thefts and the museum was becoming increasingly cautious about allowing access to these materials. It was more than two years after negotiations began between Samuel Weiser publishing company and the Courtauld, that an expertly produced Thoth Tarot finally appeared. The project of painting the cards was begun in 1938, and was completed in 1943, as Lady Harris described in a lecture to the Tomorrow Club which remains the only public statement of her role in developing the deck:

> In despair of arriving at any lucidity I will tell you how it
> happened that I painted these cards. I was interested in the Tarot
> after reading Ouspensky's book, *The Model of the Universe.* I

could find very little information or research about it until I met A.C. He had studied the cards seriously for 40 years... I asked him to help me and with great patience and courtesy he did so and we tottered along for 5 years wrestling with the accumulated mass of tradition emanating from sources such as Freemasons, Alchemists, Rosicrucians, Kabalists, Magicians, Geometricians, Gematricians, Mathematicians, Symbolists, Diviners, Numerologists, Druids, Spiritualists, Psychologists, Philologists, Budhists [*sic*], Togas, Psychoanalysts, Astrologers, even Heraldry, all of whom have left traces on the symbols employed. From these multitudes, we endeavoured to reinstate the cards in their original sacred, simple forms and, in addition, indicate the New Aeon of Horus, a terrifying apparition...The cards push me off my feet and I get into a train of thought that can only be expressed in gasps and hiccups...I have never tried to paint them with the help of automatic writing, trances, seances, mediums, autosuggestions, drugs, absent treatment, Yoga, meditation, mysterious masters or any other emotional approach of inspiration.They are the result of hard work, honest investigation and common sense, which I believe are the true magics and were done in the open air and sunshine of the country.[17]

Lady Harris' comments reflect the deep inner exploration necessary to produce an occult work of this magnitude. Indeed, any artist who has painted an entire Tarot deck would agree with one of her more frustrated comments: "Sometimes when I am sufficiently crushed by all these meanings I say in the words of Alice in Wonderland 'Who cares for you. You're nothing but a pack of cards.' "[18]

Book "T"

The Golden Dawn, Waite, and Crowley decks are agreed in their conceptual dependence on the principles of *Book T*, a set of Tarot papers issued to members of the inner lodge of the Order of the Golden Dawn. The principal suggestion of the papers is that the key to the Tarot is the Qabalah and the Tree of Life. Certainly, without some basic knowledge of the symbols of the Qabalah the modern decks illustrated here would be incomprehensible. One must also know the Hebrew alphabet, since in its use for esoteric studies, each Hebrew letter is a symbol, embodying a block of concepts. All that is implied by the symbolic picture of *The Fool* is also implied by the Hebrew letter Aleph. It is one of the peculiarities of the Mysteries that many aspects of the study are so profound that one symbol can be explained only in terms of another, and a student buys into the circle with the symbol which he or she best understands.

Book T, a complex presentation of Tarot symbols, elaborates a formula originally given in the *Cypher Manuscripts*. This includes the order of Trumps and the relationship of the Trumps to Hebrew letters. Most significant is the extraordinary reverence accorded the Tarot. It was believed that *Book T,* the Tarot, is the secret key not only to the Hermetic Qabalah, but to all of Western esotericism.

The book begins:

> HRU THE GREAT ANGEL is Set over the operations of the Secret Wisdom. "What thou seest write in a Book, and send it unto the Seven Abodes that are in Assiah." "And I saw in the right hand of Him that sat upon the Throne a book sealed with Seven Seals." "And I saw a strong Angel proclaiming with a loud voice: 'Who is worthy to open the Books and to loose the seals thereof?' "[19]

The passage with which *Book T* is prefaced certainly represents the attitude of the order toward its Tarot deck. The lines are from *The Apocalypse* of Saint John, chapter five. The Saint, having risen into the celestial realm, is shown a scroll, and is told that none on the earth is worthy to open it. The Lamb of God, however, having sacrificed his blood for mankind *is* deemed worthy.

The suggestion is that the Tarot is the book spoken of in *The Apocalypse,* and is the key to the universe. Of course, it is not the Tarot deck, *per se,* that constitutes what is called *Book T.* The implication, rather, is that the key to the Cosmos is our perception of the underlying pattern of which the Tarot deck is an external symbol.

But this "book," or set of universal patterns, is open to no one of this earth. It can be opened only by the Lamb of God, who is Christ/Buddha/Osiris in this context. Only those who have been initiated into the Christ center of the Qabalah (Tiphareth) can fully understand the Tarot. Here the initiation of Tiphareth may be understood as a "sacrifice of man's blood" in that it involves a losing of the "Personality Self" as it has been previously known.

Moreover, we find that it is described in the Rosicrucian documents as having been found in the hand of Christian Rosencreutz when his body was discovered perfectly preserved in the Vault. The Order of the Golden Dawn claimed a direct line of descent from Rosencreutz, and apparently wanted to suggest that they were in possession of the greatest secret of the original Rosicrucians. One must therefore conclude that the Order viewed the Tarot as the symbolic receptable of its primary and most secret teaching.

The member received information on Tarot (as well as almost everything else of importance) after initiation into the grade of Adeptus Minor. This grade related to Tiphareth, the center of Christ and other sacrificed Gods. Thus, it was not until the member assumed the nature of the Lamb of God (even being symbolically crucified in the ritual) that he was deemed worthy of opening the seals on the Scroll of the Apocalypse, *Book T*, the Tarot, or whatever the patterns of the Cosmos might be called. What is important is not the books themselves, but one's ability to read them. That is the breaking of the seals.

THE QABALAH

As understood today, the word Qabalah means a tradition or that which is received. It also means a very specific system of metaphysics. But in earlier centuries "Qabalah" had a more general meaning, that of *The Law*. It could mean an oral law or it could be the law of Moses in the first five books of *The Bible*, *The Torah* (called the *Pentateuch* in Greek). It was not until the twelfth century that the term assumed today's precise meaning.[20]

There are two separate schools of Qabalah, that of Judaism and that which is the product of Italian Renaissance thought, termed the Hermetic Qabalah. A difficulty may arise here in that in any form of Qabalism God names are those of the *Old Testament*, Hebrew is the essential language and the primary texts are those of the Jewish tradition. Nevertheless, while Jewish and Hermetic Qabalah refer to the same literary sources, there are striking differences in both textual interpretation and practical work.

The most significant difference has to do with pictorial representation. Mosaic law forbids showing the human form: "It is likewise forbidden to draw a picture of a man, even only the face of a man...However, only a full face is forbidden, that is, when it has two eyes and a nose, but a profile is not forbidden."[21] Idolatry of any sort was a sacrilege, which may explain the reluctance of some Jewish scholars to use even the Tree of Life in their publications.[22] But more important, when a Christian mystic or Hermetic Qabalist will produce a pictorial vision as a "stepping off" point for inner exploration, the Jewish mystic seeks a direct experience of pure consciousness

There are, of course, myriad other differences between Jewish and Hermetic Qabalah, not the least of which is the way in which the Divine Names are applied. All of these differences are best understood in terms of the historical development of western occultism. It was around the second century C.E. that the Western Mystery Tradition began to emerge, although presumably based on elements handed down from a very ancient, and secret, oral tradition.

Origins of the Qabalah

A great many Qabalistic works, even today, make the claim that the Qabalah was a body of esoteric knowledge given to Moses on Mount Sinai, thus linking it to the very inception of Jewish Law. The suggestion is that God dictated the five books of *The Bible* to Moses, and then provided a secret key for their interpretation.

Another tradition (popularized in the fifteenth century) and the one taught by the Golden Dawn to its members, stated that the Qabalah was first provided by angels to Adam, as the means of return after the Fall. MacGregor Mathers quoted from Christian Ginsburg in his introduction to *The Kabbalah Unveiled:*

> "The Kabbalah was first taught by God himself to a select company of angels, who formed a theosophic school in Paradise. After the Fall the angels most graciously communicated this heavenly doctrine to the disobedient child of earth, to furnish the protoplasts with the means of returning to their pristine nobility and felicity. From Adam it passed over to Noah, and then to Abraham, the friend of God, who emigrated with it to Egypt, where the patriarch allowed a portion of this mysterious doctrine to ooze out. It was in this way that the Egyptians obtained some knowledge of it, and the other Eastern nations could introduce it into their philosophical systems. Moses, who was learned in all the wisdom of Egypt, was first initiated into the Qabalah in the land of his birth, but became most proficient in it during his wanderings in the wilderness when he not only devoted to it the leisure hours of the whole forty years, but received lessons in it from one of the angels. By the aid of this mysterious science the law-giver was enabled to solve the difficulties which arose during his management of the Israelites, in spite of the pilgrimages, wars, and frequent miseries of the nation. He covertly laid down the principles of this secret doctrine in the first four books of the Pentateuch, but withheld them from Deuteronomy."[23]

It is perhaps sad, but this charming story bears no relationship to historical fact, the Qabalah having emerged as the result of a long and complex developmental sequence beginning with Merkabah Mysticism.

Merkabah, meaning "chariot," was the earliest form of Jewish mysticism, preceding the Qabalah.[24] The chariot was that which carried the Throne of God as described by the Prophet Ezekiel—the Throne World, to which the Jewish mystic aspired being the counterpart of the early mysteries of Hermeticism and Christian Gnosticism.[25] The second century witnessed the merger of a great many trends, and Scholem states flatly that: "The Kabbalah in its historical significance, can be defined as the product of the interpenetration of Jewish Gnosticism and Neoplatonism."[26]

In the late-Roman/early-Christian period were found Christian Gnosticism, Jewish Gnosticism, Neoplatonism, Neopythagoreanism, Hermeticism (pseudo-Egyptian religion) and many obscure cults, all interpenetrating in subtle ways. Jewish mysticism of this time is discussed by Scholem in his pioneering study, *Major Trends in Jewish Mysticism*, while the Christian developments have been chronicled, in a readable way, by Elaine Pagels in *The Gnostic Gospels*.

These scholars trace the actual sources of ideas, disputed for generations, which are the basis of the modern Hermetic Qabalah. What is important to recognize is that one need not invoke the smoke screen of "secret oral tradition" in most aspects of the Mysteries. The majority of those who have contributed to the Qabalah have been very explicit about their work and its sources. There is very little in any modern system for which historical precedent cannot be found.

The Sepher Yetzirah (Book of Formation)

This book of six very brief chapters, dating from some time between the third and the sixth centuries C.E., is the cornerstone of Qabalistic literature, and the document in which the word Sephiroth first appears. It is a work which describes the creation of the universe in terms of the letters of the Hebrew alphabet, and in terms of symbolic number undoubtedly related to Neopythagoreanism. *The Sepher Yetzirah* is apparently a summation of earlier ideas in Jewish mysticism, similar in form to Gnosticism and the *Pistis Sophia.*

The precise origin and intention of *The Sepher Yetzirah* is a matter of speculation. One writer of the early nineteen hundreds, with all good intentions, even suggested that this mystical text was no more than a book of grammar and "as the earliest Hebrew grammar contains not only the fundamental rules of Hebrew orthography, but also an account of the origin of letters and numerals."[27] Of course, this theory is not to be taken seriously, but it does demonstrate the extremes of interpretation to which Qabalistic documents have been subjected. On the other hand, *The Sepher Yetzirah* is a very difficult and obtuse work, so abstract that it demands an approach atypical of that taken to most literature. And, when used in concert with the Tarot, the work becomes remarkably useful

Ideally, *The Sepher Yetzirah* should be read in the original Hebrew, but a number of translations have been made into English. It should also be noted that a later document entitled *The Thirty-two Paths of Wisdom* is usually included with *The Sepher Yetzirah.*[28]

Medieval Qabalism

The Sepher Yetzirah set the stage for much later Jewish mysticism by amalgamating various mystical currents into a Jewish context. Called the "earliest extant Hebrew text of systematic, speculative thought,"[29] its ideas were built upon by later scholars. For example, where the very word Sephiroth was originally used to mean simply numbers or numerical stages in creation, in the Middle Ages that word came to mean a specific system of Divine emanation. [30]

One of the most important ideas to be added by late medieval scholars was that numerological links could be found between words (and thus between concepts) using *Gematria*. The introduction of Gematria served two purposes. First, it helped to assure that scribes would spell names precisely as received; second, it tended to serve as an incentive for serious meditation on the Names.

Sometime between 1150 and 1200, in Southern France, another very important Qabalist work appeared. This was the *Sepher-ha-Bahir*, supposedly an ancient work, but more likely edited from several works of either German or Eastern origin.[31] *The Bahir* contains the first reference to a "Secret Tree," and is the first to describe the Sephiroth as the vessels of Divine Light. An English translation of the work, by Aryeh Kaplan, has recently been published [32]

The thirteenth century was especially pivotal for the Jewish Qabalah. It was during this time that Isaac the Blind, a scholar from Narbonne, wrote his comments on *The Sepher Yetzirah*, first describing it as involving a systematic development of Sephiroth. He also built upon some of the ideas expressed in *The Bahir*,[33] as did others in his day. The result of study of *The Sepher Yetzirah* in terms of *The Bahir* was that scholars began to discuss the Ten Sephiroth and the Thirty-two Paths together.

Another major idea, appearing at this time in France and Spain, was that there were evil Sephiroth existing as exact counterparts to the good. [34] This concept was extensively developed by some of the members of the Golden Dawn fraternity.

It was in this climate of mystical-intellectual fruition that the greatest of all Qabalist treatises appeared. *The Zohar* was the work of Moses de Léon, between 1280 and 1286.[35] It is a series of commentaries on *The Bible* and on mystical cosmology.

For generations *The Zohar* was believed to be an ancient work. The text itself purports to have been written by a second century rabbi, Simeon ben Yohai. Moreover, *The Zohar* is written primarily in ancient Aramaic, a language which is the root of both Hebrew and Arabic. Presumably, Moses de Léon felt that his work would be taken more seriously if attributed to an ancient author. He was probably correct, for *The Zohar* quickly assumed major proportions as *the* document of Jewish mysticism. It should be added that between approximately 1500 and 1800 the Qabalah was widely considered to be the true essence of Jewish theology,[36] rather than the curiosity that it is today among Jews.

Unfortunately, *The Zohar* has never been translated completely into a European language. The five volume English set by Maurice Simon and Harry Sperling[37] is competent, but represents only about 35% of the work. The translators chose to eliminate those parts which they believed to be later additions, or unduly obscure. Three of those omitted texts are, however, to be found in *The Kabbalah Unveiled*[38] translated from Knorr von Rosenroth's latin *Kabbalah Denudata* of 1677 to which a modern introduction was added by MacGregor Mathers. Recently, a brilliant and readable three volume anthology of *Zohar* texts in English has appeared. It is *The Wisdom of the Zohar* by Isaiah Tishy, published by Oxford University Press.

There is only one complete translation into a modern language and that is Hebrew. The twenty-one volume translation and commentary, by the late Yehuda Ashlag is described by Scholem as "an extremely literal translation (but not without many textual misunderstandings)."[39]

The Renaissance:
Hermeticism and Christian Qabalah

The key to the modern Hermetic Qabalah is the Renaissance mind which blended Jewish Qabalah and Hermetic Mysteries. During this period of intense intellectual activity, philosophers encountered previously hidden currents of Jewish mysticism, and attempted to adapt these ideas to a Christian framework. It was even asserted that through the Qabalah one could most effectively prove the divinity of Christ.

The Renaissance was a time when man considered himself the jewel in a universal crown. He was the "measure of all things," rather than the lowly sinner atoning for the Fall as had been insisted by medieval dogma. Thus, intellectual and creative activity, a constant questioning of principles, came to be of greater importance than the institutionalized values of the past. In more basic terms, one can say that what had been a church dominated society became secularized. The beliefs and feelings of the medieval period were supplanted by the call for a more rational overview of the human condition. The society was nominally Christian, but theologians and philosophers had a very free hand.

This freedom to doubt and explore some of the most basic principles of Christianity reached its high point at the Medici Academy in Florence. In fact, virtually all modern occultism can be traced back to the developments of scholars in that time and place.

The Medici were a family of immense wealth, ruling Florence from the fifteenth century until 1737. Their primary contribution was as patrons of the arts, a program begun by Cosimo, the first of the great Medici, and continued by Lorenzo "the Magnificent," patron to Leonardo, Michelangelo and Machiavelli. Cosimo de Medici was the founder of the Platonic Academy, dedicated to the study of Greek philosophy, and a center of Neoplatonic ideas. This was an open "think tank," much like today's Institute for Advanced Studies at Princeton University.

Cosimo was a passionate collector of manuscripts and when in 1460 a Greek manuscript of the *Hermetica* came to him from Macedonia, he judged it to be of unique importance. The reputation of Hermes Trismegistus' work as providing a key to all knowledge was so considerable that Cosimo instructed Marsilio Ficino, director of his Academy, to put aside Plato's *Republic* and *Symposium* and translate the Hermetica first.[40]

Early Renaissance philosophers believed that in these documents they had the core ideas of the most ancient Egyptian religion, which would lead them to the very source of illumination.[41] Their awestruck approach, and belief in the utter integrity of these papers, was the foundation of Renaissance magic and a whole school of Neoplatonism. It was these ideas which preceded the Qabalistic philosophy soon after flowing into the Medici Academy.

What is known as the Christian Qabalah was also a development of the Medici Academy, and the primary accomplishment of Pico della Mirandola, one of the court's intellectual luminaries. It was Pico who had the major Qabalistic texts translated into Latin. And it was Pico who, in his *72 Qabalistic Conclusions* (part of his *900 Theses*) made the claim that "no science can better convince us of the divinity of Jesus Christ than magic and the Kabbalah."[42] Pico's fourteenth Qabalistic principle stated that adding the Hebrew letter שׁ (shin) to the Divine name יהוה (yod, heh, vau, heh), and producing יהשוה Jeheshua, Hebrew name of Jesus, made it possible to pronounce the unpronounceable name of God. And, from the standpoint of the modern Hermetic Qabalah and the Golden Dawn, this is of special significance. Perhaps the most important single principle emphasized by today's Hermetic Qabalah is that all things are four elements activated by a fifth, which is Spirit. Yod is Fire, Heh is Water, Vau is Air, Heh final is Earth and Shin is Spirit.

Pico inspired the work of Johannes Reuchlin, the first non-Jew ever to write on the Qabalah. His premise was that the history of mankind is based on three periods. In the first period God revealed himself to the Jewish patriarchs through the three-fold name שׁדי, Shaddai. The second period was that of Moses and the Talmud, when God appeared as the four-lettered name, יהוה (the Tetragramaton). Finally, came the period of man's redemption through Christ, when God revealed himself as the five-lettered יהשוה, Jeheshua.

Thus Pico della Mirandola and Johannes Reuchlin became the founders of the philosophical aspects of Christian Qabalism. The first practical work of their school was produced by Henry Cornelius Agrippa, whose *De Occult Philosophia* of 1531 was widely read.[43] It is, however, Agrippa who is responsible for the very negative association of Qabalah with witchcraft and sorcery, a belief held by many even today.

All of these literary works had been stimulated by social developments in the West. Much of the intellectual current of the fifteenth century can be traced to the conquest of the Byzantine Empire by the Turks in 1453, and the subsequent migration of Greek scholars to Italy. A similar trend occurred in 1492 when the Jews were expelled from Spain and many Jewish scholars also settled in Italy, moving onto ground prepared for them by Pico with his *900 Theses* of 1486.

There was widespread interest in Hebrew mysticism by the end of the century, and advocates of the Christian Qabalah included important Catholic prelates and theologians who viewed the Qabalah as a vehicle for the intellectual renewal of the faith. Thus the Christian Qabalah, merged with elements of Hermeticism, came to be the primary occult current of the Italian Renaissance.[44]

The Renaissance attitude toward the Hermetic sciences was jolted sharply approximately one hundred years later when Isaac Casaubon declared the *Hermetica* to be an early Christian forgery rather than an ancient Egyptian document. He stated that the books were written by a Christian or semi-Christian in an attempt to make these doctrines acceptable, to gentiles.[45] Casaubon's work brought about a significant decline of interest in magic, a generally acceptable Renaissance pursuit until his revelations. Today it is understood that the Hermetic documents are not specific forgeries, but that they were produced even later than Causaubon believed.

Despite Causubon's overwhelming evidence, some writers, including Robert Fludd and Athanasius Kircher, chose to ignore historical reality, and continued to declare the Hermetic fragments the work of an ancient Egyptian adept named Hermes Trismegistus.[46]

Magus to the Queen

The next important figure we encounter is Dr. John Dee (1527-1608), the great Elizabethan philosopher who, with Edward Kelly, developed the system of Enochian Magic later expanded by MacGregor Mathers. Dee shared the ideas of men such as Pico della Mirandola and Agrippa, and could be considered their English counterpart. Moreover, like the Italian metaphysicians, he enjoyed the protection of the royal court, being an advisor and confident to Queen Elizabeth.[47]

Dee produced two works of major importance in the history of occultism. The first was his *Hieroglyphic Monad*, an obtuse treatise of spiritual Alchemy and mathematics. The second was his *True and Faithful Relation* in which he records his work with Edward Kelly as they are "given" the Enochian system by spirits. This is a surprisingly fresh and interesting book despite its ponderous seventeenth century style, and includes such gems as the decision of the two researchers to exchange wives.

Both works were important to the development of the modern Hermetic Qabalah. *The Hieroglyphic Monad* provided the philosophical foundation for the ideas of Johann Valentine Andrae, author of at least one of the Rosicrucian allegories (to which the Golden Dawn traced its beginnings). And the ideas of the *True and Faithful Relation* were tremendously expanded by Mathers, who went so far as to develop an Enochian chess set. This latter is virtually unknown, but is deeply linked with the Tarot, and is considered by some to be the most potent divinatory device ever invented. Mathers used Egyptian God forms on four boards derived from the tablets illustrated by Dee, thus incorporating Hermetic ideas (probably through Fludd) into Dee's system.

Rosicrucianism

Rosicrucianism, developed in Bohemia in the early seventeenth century, appears to be the direct result of John Dee's travels through Germany in 1589.[48]

There are three key works of Rosicrucian philosophy. The first of these works is the *Fama Fraternitas* written in German, and originally published (though circulating in manuscript for perhaps four years earlier) in 1614. *The Fama Fraternitas* or *A Discovery of the Fraternity of the Most Noble Order of the Rose Cross*, tells the story of a mysterious Christian Rosencreutz and his fraternity, dedicated to healing the sick. The text particularly describes the discovery of Christian Rosencreutz's tomb, the "vault" which was the inspiration for the *sanctum sanctorum* used by the Hermetic Order of the Golden Dawn (Paul Foster Case had such a vault painted for his BOTA, and many others may still exist today). The legend states that his body was found perfectly preserved, holding the Book 'T,' which has been symbolically connected with the Tarot.[49]

A second work, expanding on the *Fama Fraternitas*, appeared two years later in 1616. This was the *Confessio Fraternitas* or *The Confession of the Laudable Fraternity of the Most Honorable Order of the Rosy Cross, Written to all the Learned of Europe*. Unlike the *Fama*, which appeared in the vernacular German, the *Confessio* is in Latin, and clearly aimed at a more intellectual reader. Also, unlike the *Fama*, it is quite boring.

The author of these two works is unknown. However a third major work, closely connected with the *Fama* and the *Confessio* was written by Johann Valentine Andrae. A cloud has long covered the *Chemical Wedding* of 1616 due to Andrae's later claim that this work of his youth was only a joke. Confusion may arise in that the text is unquestionably a serious and enlightened religious tract. As Rudolph Steiner wrote on his essay on the *Chemical Wedding*: "Anyone who knows what the human soul experiences when it has opened the gates into the spiritual world, need only read a few pages of the *Chemical Wedding* of Christian Rosencreutz of the Year 1459 to recognize that the descriptions given in this book are based upon genuine spiritual experience. "[50]

Frances Yates tries to clear up the mystery with a few words. She notes that in discussing his work, Andrae used the Latin word *ludibrium*, which means a mockery or a sport. He spoke of "the ludibrium of the vain Fama," or the "ludibrium of the fictitious Rosicrucian fraternity." But Yates proposes that in the seventeenth century the word could also mean a play, or a comic fiction, and that Andrae was suggesting that Rosicricianism was theatrical in a positive and educational sense.[51] Our intention here is not to inundate the reader with the weighty theorums of literary research, only to make clear the controversy which surrounds so many of the occult documents which have contributed to the system of Hermetic Qabalah.

Later "Rosicrucians"

Robert Fludd, as we have mentioned, was one of those who insisted on promulgating the Renaissance idea of Hermes Trismegistus as ancient Egyptian adept (another was the German Michael Maier). Fludd significantly furthered the idea that an actual Rosicrucian brotherhood existed, and seems to have believed it himself, though admitting that he had never actually met a Rosicrucian.[52] Fludd combined Hermeticism and Qabalism in the light of the Rosicrucian manifestoes and the developments of John Dee. He is therefore, one of the major precursers of Mathers and the modern Hermetic Qabalah.

Hermetic Qabalistic Deceptions

The question of purposeful deception about the origins of many esoteric manuscripts is a serious and difficult one, usually judiciously avoided by writers on the occult who wish to cast their beliefs in the most positive light. But the tally of literature for which antiquity is falsely claimed is so great that the very consistency of such claims becomes intriguing:

> *The Hermetica*, written by a Greek and widely dated (third century to the Renaissance) by scholars, but claimed to be the original documents of ancient Egyptian religion.

> *The Zohar*, purported to be the work of a rabbi in the early Christian period, yet actually by a thirteenth century writer whose claim of antiquity for it gave the books greater importance.

> *The Rosicrucian Manifestoes*, an invention of Johann Valentine Andrae and others. Neither a Christian Rosencreutz nor the mysterious Rosicrucians ever existed.

> The *"Ancient Cypher Manuscripts"* of the Golden Dawn, a fragmentary system of supposedly ancient rituals, but an unquestionable forgery.[53]

To this list one might certainly add some of Blavatsky's work including the infamous *Mahatma Letters* and perhaps the *Stanzas of Dyzan* on which she based her massive work, *The Secret Doctrine*.

In all such cases of fakery, deception, or whatever it may be called, we find authors under pressure of the public's essential belief that the more traditional a work, the more valid it is. On the other hand, every one of those works which we have listed here as having fraudulent origins claimed for it, stands on its own as enlightened. These are the inspired works of men and women who have known.

Manifestations of the psychology involved occurs repeatedly in all aspects of the study of the Mysteries, even with Paul Foster Case. When *The Book of Tokens* appeared in 1934, Case prefaced it saying: "We do not know the name of the author. Internal evidence in the text suggests that he may have been one of the later Qabalists. Perhaps he knew the Tarot, perhaps not."[54] Today, Case's organization publishes the *Book of Tokens* as Case's own work, responding to inquiries about the discrepancy in attribution of authorship that Case was a very modest man. But if history is any indicator, it is more likely, that Case felt that the work of some anonymous "later Qabalist" would be received more positively than a work of his own.

The point we are trying to make here is that rather than running from the obvious fact that the Hermetic Qabalah is based on many fabricated claims, history should be faced directly. Indeed, the very fabrications are a pattern which, ironically, tends to point us toward the inner legitimacy of the works. Those who remain unconvinced that a work of spurious pedigree might have great spiritual worth should look very closely at the history of Christianity, as well as that peculiar amalgam of heterogeneous texts, *The Bible*.

Hermetic Qabalah and the Golden Dawn

In view of the evidence that Rosicrucianism, though high spiritual allegory, was a seventeenth century myth, the Golden Dawn "history lesson" incorporated into its Adeptus Minor ritual of initiation is interesting. It begins: "Know, then, O Aspirant, that the Mysteries of the Rose and the Cross have existed from time immemorial, and that the Rites were practiced, and the Wisdom taught, in Egypt, Eleusis, Samothrace, Persia, Chaldea and India, and in far more ancient lands. "[55] The ceremony continues to directly paraphrase the description of the life of Christian Rosencreutz in the *Fama Fraternitas*.

It is probable that most of the members of the Order believed that Christian Rosencreutz had been an actual person, and that the Golden Dawn was in a direct line from his fraternity. Whether Mathers and Westcott understood the real history is another matter entirely.[56] There are many instances of both having accepted traditional misattributions of mystical literature. Westcott for example, wrote an introduction to *The Chaldean Oracles* of Zoroaster, describing them as embodying "many of the principle features of Chaldean philosophy."[57] We know that the Oracles were actually written by Julianus, a contemporary of Marcus Aurelius,[58] but the conclusions about authorship on many such works is quite recent.

What is most important, however, is that we are able to uncover so many of the order's historical tracks. Thus, its leaders are understood to have built carefully on a known traditional framework. The Hermetic Qabalah today bears the marks of Westcott and Mathers. Even the spelling of the Hebrew word Qabalah (as opposed to "Kabbalah," or "Cabala"), was chosen by Mathers as being more consistent with the original language (קבל). And the Qabalistic correspondences found in Aleister Crowley's *777* appear to be based largely on Mathers' work. It is with the Order of the Golden Dawn that the modern system of Path colors on the Tree of Life (see reference section) and other attributions first appear. The order developed an elaborate system of teaching based on ritual, although the extent to which the well-known Banishing Rituals may be theirs is uncertain. At least such rituals are not found in Agrippa, Barrett or other magical treatises prior to the Golden Dawn. Here again, the ways in which an oral tradition may have been involved cannot be determined. Historical evidence notwithstanding, the story of Christian Rosencreutz unquestionably taps into some inner tradition. It certainly relates to the same universal patterns symbolized by the Tarot.

The "Hermetic" emphasis of the Golden Dawn on the Egyptian Gods was partly social, and partly traditional. In late nineteenth century England there was great curiosity about anything mysterious and obscure, the science of archaeology being still in its infancy (in 1900, for example, no Greek art prior to the Parthenon was known). Emphasis on the Egyptian Gods served to separate the participants in ritual from the daily routines of Victorian life. It also effected a separation from Christianity. The Hermetic Order of the Golden Dawn affirmed the pure Renaissance Hermeticism of Ficino.

Philosophically, the system of Egyptiang Gods is very comfortably equated with the Qabalah. Despite the apparent proliferation of Gods and Goddesses, Egyptian religion was monotheistic. All of the Gods were aspects or modifications of one ultimate and original deity. Moreover, like the Qabalah, the Egyptian pantheon shows different aspects of the same God under different circumstances. For example, there are many forms of Horus, all of which have the name Heru imbedded in its Egyptian name, such as "Horus the Child," or "Blind Horus (Horus at the Head of Sightlessness)" or "Horus of the two Horizons," whom the Greeks called Harmachis as opposed to Harpocrates.

Horus is the Child who is the center of our known universe in the Qabalah, and to whom we refer in a variety of ways. And as the Child appears in a variety of ways, so do the Great Father and the Great Mother. All of this was clearly understood by the Golden Dawn, who found considerable utility in the Egyptian system of Gods. These Gods express universal relationships better than any other Pantheon. Today, however, the order's dependence on Egyptian Gods is viewed by many students as s only a curiosity of the past.

The Tree of Life

The Tree of Life (Figure 1) is intended to symbolize the entire universe, a proposition so vast in its implications that some may doubt that such a symbol is even possible. It is a deceptively simple diagram composed of ten spheres called Sephiroth, and twenty-two connecting lines called Paths. Collectively, the Sephiroth and Paths are called the *Thirty Two Paths of Wisdom*.

The Ten Sephiroth are:

1. KETHER, כתר *The Crown*
2. CHOKMAH, חכמה *Wisdom*
3. BINAH, בינה *Understanding*

Between Binah and the next Sephira is an invisible Sephira known as Daath, or Knowledge. It is not represented on the Tree, because it is a bridge, built by each individual across the Abyss existing between the upper Sephiroth and those below.

4. CHESED, חסד *Mercy*
5. GEBURAH, גבורה *Severity*
6. TIPHARETH, תפארת
   Beauty
7. NETZACH, נצח *Victory*
8. HOD, הוד *Splendor*
9. YESOD, יסוד *Foundation*
10. MALKUTH, מלכות *Kingdom*

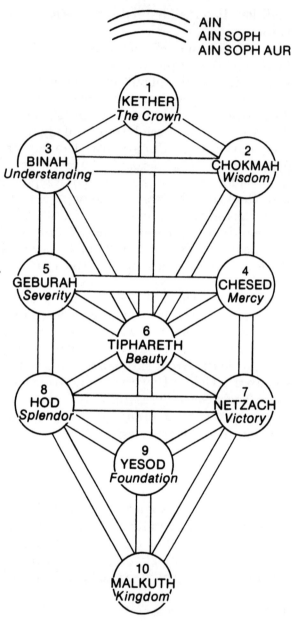

The Tree of Life used by modern Hermetic-Qabalists, was first published in Kircher's *Oedipus Aegypticus* in 1652 (Figure 2A). And while this Tree must have undergone a lengthy development, its historical roots appear buried in the secret past of mystery religions. Moreover, a general developmental sequence is difficult to establish as Jewish Qabalists espoused different forms of the Tree.

The first reference to a "Secret Tree" is in *The Bahir*, appearing in France around 1200. If, however, one were to draw a Tree on the basis of that text, only eight of the ten Sephiroth, Binah through Malkuth, would be included, since the Tree is stated to grow as it is watered by Wisdom (Chokmah). Something of the amorphous spirit of that first Tree is found in the diagram published by Robert Fludd in 1617 (Figure 2B). Yet is is curious to find that a glyph of one hundred years earlier (Figure 2C) is far more conceptually developed and sophisticated.

Moreover, we find that a Jewish illustration from as late as 1708 (Figure 2D) takes a different approach, indicating its dependence on *The Sepher Yetsirah*.

Figure 1. The Ten Holy Sephiroth
on the Tree of Life

Tl   t the Tree of Life has evolved
over th   ral interest and, not coinci-
dentall   ry philosophy. The full color
two-din   s the most developed expression of   . If the evolutionary pattern
continu   Life (cover illustration) is the
form u   considered in generations to
come.   ple of five: four balanced elements,

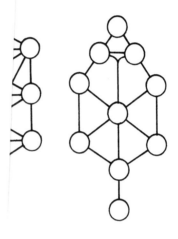

7   D 1708

gram. A) Form of the Tree in
apted from Robert Fludd,
Porta Lucis, Ausburg, 1516.
Rimmon, 1708.

Con

evolved organically and sequen-
tially, following the *Path of the Flaming Sword* (Figure 3). From a mysterious
"Unmanifest" emerged Kether then Chokmah then Binah. These three formed
the *Supernal Triangle*, a spiritual height bridged by the invisible Sephira, Daath.
Chesed, Geburah and Tiphareth formed the *Ethical Triangle*. Finally, with
Netzach, Hod and Yesod, the *Astral Triangle* (Figure 4) was created. Malkuth,
it will be seen, stands alone at the base of the Tree, conspicuously removed from
the rest, particularly when Daath is imagined at the upper point opposite Yesod.

Malkuth is the recipient of the influences of all the other Sephiroth, containing the reflected perfection of Kether, while at the same time being the product of what is described as the Fall.

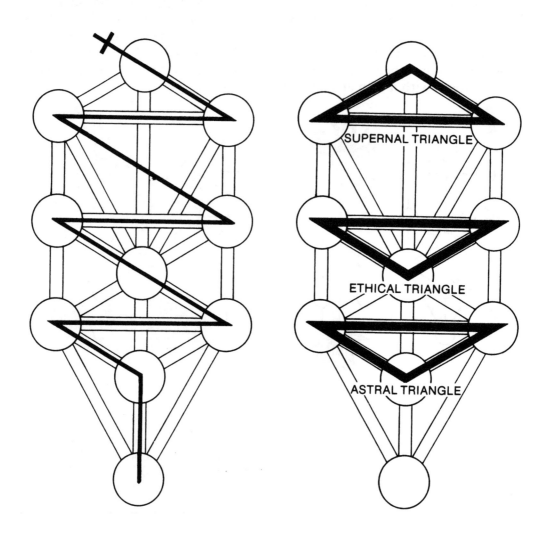

Figure 3. The Path of   Figure 4. The Triangles
the Flaming Sword   of the Tree of Life

The Tree of Life is divided into three Pillars (Figure 5). The Sephiroth on the right side are on the *Pillar of Mercy*, those on the left, the *Pillar of Severity* and those at the center, the *Middle Pillar*. Each Sephira is perfectly balanced by its opposite. Moreover, each Path is the perfect balance between the two Sephiroth which it connects, and of the Path opposite it. This *glyph* is a compound symbol which may be considered at two levels: It is the individual, the *Microcosm* (God in miniature) and the *Macrocosm*, the Greater Universe

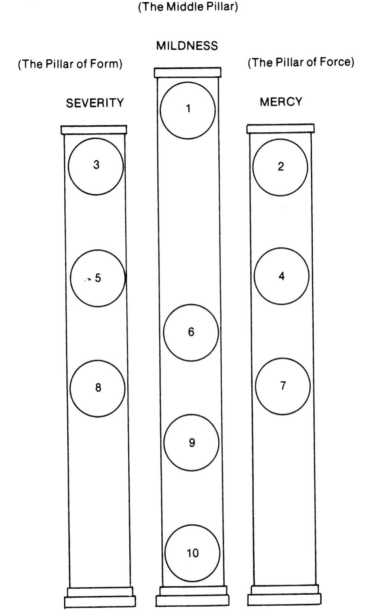

(The Middle Pillar)

MILDNESS

(The Pillar of Form)   (The Pillar of Force)

SEVERITY   1   MERCY

3   2

5   4

6

8   7

9

10

Figure 5. The Pillars on the Tree of Life

in the image of which the individual is created. Each Sephira is related to some part of the human body, and with a corresponding part of a greater Divine Body. The principle involved is expressed by the axiom which we will often repeat, "As above, so below."

There are a number of areas of traditional Qabalah which may be some-what confusing, but which are actually very simple. One of these areas is the application of "man" to the Tree, and involves two separate concepts. The first concept is that of *Adam Kadmon* ("The Grand Old Man of the Zohar"). Adam Kadmon is all ten Sephiroth, a great organic unity, a spiritual body in which each of us might be considered a single cell carrying all of the potential attributes of the whole.

Adam Kadmon should not be confused with *Arik Anpin* or *Zauer Anpin*, the other two personifications covering more than one Sephira. Arikh Anpin means the *Vast Face* or Countenance; Zauer Anpin means the *Lesser Face* or Countenance. Arik Anpin is Macroprosopus an anthropomorphization of the Sephiroth of the Supernal Triangle. Zauer Anpin is Microprosopus, the five Sephiroth around Tiphareth. Together they illustrate the principle of "As above, so below."

To reiterate, Adam Kadmon means the whole Tree of Life pictured as a man. Arikh Anpin is the man above; Zauer Anpin is the man below.

The idea of each part of the human body having some Divine correlate is perhaps more readily comprehensible to an easterner than a westerner. The yogin has no difficulty dealing with the concept of certain centers of spiritual activity within the physical body. The Solar Plexus is the Sun center in man, a link between the individual and the solar powers of the universe. The physical center has the potential to be enervated, consciousness transferred to it, and the individual brought into direct contact with the pure energy which is, in the Qabalistic system, called Tiphareth.

An important part of practical work with the Hermetic Qabalah involves the exercise of the Middle Pillar,[59] where the energies of the Sephiroth are purposely invoked and built up within the individual. In this exercise the Sephiroth are reversed, *i.e.*, Chesed is at the left shoulder, and Geburah is at the right, since they are considered subjectively within the body rather than being viewed from outside.

Practical work on the Tree also involves travelling the Paths connecting the Sephiroth, the objective centers of energy. The Paths are the subjective experience of passing from one Sephira to the next. But insofar as there is a constant flow and motion within the universe, there is a constant flow as energy passes down from one Sephira to another and up again. The universe is like a gigantic circuit, where power flows into Kether from the Unmanifest, down through the Tree and up again. There is a continual renewal of energy. Thus, when viewed from another frame of reference, the Paths may be considered objective. They are subjective for us, yet they are objective in that they carry a constant flow of energy of such specificity as to be expressible as the Major Arcana of the Tarot. In other words, we can study the Tree of Life intellectually, or build it in ourseves. We can approach the Tarot cards symbolizing the Paths from within or without.

When the cards are used individually for astral projection, they are graphic and subjective symbols of that which is experienced on the Paths between the Sephiroth. Here they might also be described as that which is required to pass from one Sephira to another. They define stages of personal development. On the other hand, when the Trumps appear in a divination, they are viewed from without, and are objective forces affecting the question. A large number of these Trumps, appearing in a spread, shows forces entirely beyond the control of the Querent.

"Path working," particularly when it involves the Tarot cards, has a high degree of mystery and romance attached to it (as does all astral projection), but the experiences are very practical. To be of any use, the inner lessons must be applied to our every day lives.

The whole process of spiritual development involves a bringing into balance of the component parts of the personality, so that it may function in conscious cooperation with the Higher Self. But when this process is described by the mystery schools in terms of the Four Elements, Fire, Water, Air and Earth, it may sound remote and mysterious. It is not. We grow by learning perfect control over ourselves within our chosen environment, to the point that we are no longer at the mercy of that environment. This is a spiritual suicide mission for the personality, and for the whole concept of "self" as it exists within an incarnation. This is a process which is natural to everyone, but which is accelerated by focusing attention on it.

The Tree of Life imposes a defining pattern on qualities of the personality and work of personal development which is already in progress. Thus, one feels affinities or antagonisms toward certain Tarot cards, depending upon the extent to which their lessons have already been learned. By purposely studying and using the Paths, we take hold of our own spiritual learning process, forcing attention to many important Paths which we might otherwise choose to avoid.

The fact that the Qabalah demands attention to all parts of a given whole, makes it an ideal system for intentionally affecting spiritual growth. It demonstrates that we exist in a rational and graded system. It suggests where we come from and where we go. There is none of the vagueness of other systems. And, as the symbolic parts of the human body are related to the Tree, so are the various aspects of the soul (Figure 6). We go from the lowest aspect of manifestation to the highest, the Yechidah of Kether, the Primal Point to which we aspire.

All major religions teach that it is our heritage to return to some Primal Point from which we evolved. This is expressed as "heaven," or "nirvana," or whatever is the ultimate happy state promised by the faith. But of all the metaphysical systems available in the west, only the Qabalah suggests the extent to which we progress through a natural course of development, as if through a school, moving from one grade to another.

In the Order of the Golden Dawn, the members were graded according to the highest Sephira to which they had been ritually advanced. 0=0 meant that the candidate was initiated into basic membership; 1=10 meant that he or she had taken the first initiation of the tenth Sephira, Malkuth and the spiritual Element of Earth; 2=9 signified initiation into Yesod, the ninth Sephira and the realm of Air; 3=8 meant the initiation of Hod and the Element of Water; 4=7 meant initiation into Netzach and Fire. These four ritual steps symbolized the introduction of the candidate into the Mysteries of matter. Theoretically, each

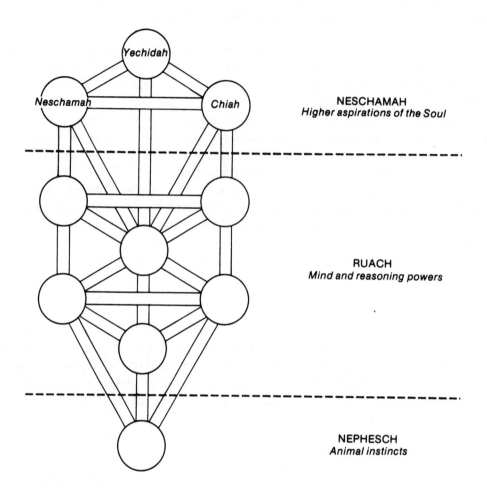

NESCHAMAH
Higher aspirations of the Soul

RUACH
Mind and reasoning powers

NEPHESCH
Animal instincts

Figure 6. The Divisions of the Soul. Note here that the Neschamah of Binah defines the entire Supernal Triangle, in the same way that Binah's planet, Saturn, is also taken to mean the three upper Sephiroth. The scheme above is that taught by the Golden Dawn. Later writers such as Fortune and Case perceived a problem in that the "animal instincts" given to Malkuth were better related to Yesod. Ruach, *i.e.* Microprosopus, Lesser Countenance, was divided into Upper and Lower, Higher Self and Personality.

new initiation meant control over one of the key aspects of the Personality. 5=6 was the initiation into the Inner Order, and the Mysteries of Tiphareth. This also (theoretically) heralded the true enlightenment of the seeker.

Such initiatory rituals demonstrate the process by which the Higher Consciousness unfolds, and may be related to the very symbol of mankind, the Pentagram (Figure 7). The four lower arms are the balanced forces of the Elements. The topmost point is the Spirit functioning through the Elements.

It should not, of course, be supposed that an initiatory ritual always brings a miraculous change in the individual. The real changes are the result of a sacrament within, stimulated by the sacrament without. And it might be safe to assume that very few members of the Order of the Golden Dawn were really adepts in the true sense of the word.

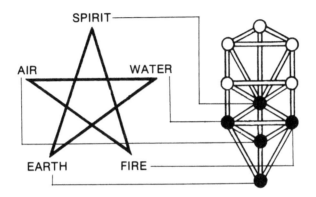

Figure 7. Attribution of Elements to the Pentagram

"Secret" Paths

The idea of Paths which are "secret," or "hidden" seems to have been introduced (or at least popularized) by Paul Case.[60] There is no evidence of the Golden Dawn having schematized any Paths other than the traditional thirty-two. Actually, the Secret Paths are nothing more than the connection of every Sephira with every other Sephira (Figure 8), suggesting that it is possible to move directly from any form of consciousness to any other. This theory is a mitigation of the idea implied in the usual Tree of Life diagram, that we must pass through one Sephira before we encounter another.

The concept of Secret Paths definitely expands the possibilities of the Tree. It also allows us to see certain relationships which would not be obvious otherwise, such as the derivation of the Unicursal Hexagram from the Tree itself. This figure was first published by Aleister Crowley, who undoubtedly derived it in this way. In a Tree of Life drawn by Crowley, and published in the 1955 Neptune Press edition of *777*, we discover that Crowley has shown all of the additional lines between Sephiroth required to make that figure.[61]

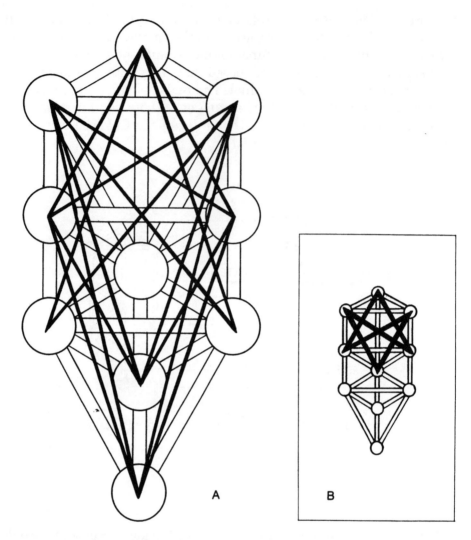

Figure 8. The "Secret Paths." These Paths connect each Sephira to each other. Tiphareth already has atraditional Path to every Sephira except Malkuth. A) The "Secret"Paths on the Tree of Life. B) The Unicursal Hexagram derived from the Tree.

Negative Limitless Light

Qabalistic teachers repeatedly stress that the Tree of Life represents our manifest universe. This emphasis is placed to express the idea that behind even the most exalted aspects of our universe lies an Unmanifest, which is the ultimate source of all, and which cannot be known to us. The Unmanifest is symbolized by the words Negative Limitless Light, or in Hebrew *Ain Soph Aur*. It is shown on the Tree of Life, above Kether, as three curves of radiating light. The outer curve is Ain, the middle Ain Soph, and the innermost Ain Soph Aur. These are understood to be veils separating the outpouring of our universe from That from which it emerged. From behind these veils energy flows constantly down to us through Kether.

While there are points of reference to all aspects of the Tree of Life in the Tarot, no such reference is made to the Ain Soph Aur. The Tarot, whose letters are frequently transposed to form the word Rota, shows the Wheel of the Manifest Universe.

The Four Worlds

The Qabalah describes the universe as divided into four separate "Worlds," (Figure 9), each of which is represented by one letter of the Divine Name, or *Tetragrammaton* (יהוה). The first is *Atziluth*, the Archetypal World, the world of Pure Spirit which activates all of the other worlds which evolve from it. Here are attributed the Gods of the Sephiroth, and the letter Yod, *Primal Fire*. The second world is *Briah*, the Creative World, the level of pure intellect, of the Archangels and of Heh, *Primal Water*. The third is Yetzirah, called the Formative World because here are found the subtle and fleeting patterns behind matter. It is the realm of angels and of *Primal Air*, symbolized by the letter Vau. The final World is Assiah, the active world containing both the physical world of sensation and the unseen energies of matter. It is the realm of the Cherubim, the final Heh of the Divine Name and *Primal Earth*.

Each of these worlds generated the energies beneath it, with the universe becoming increasingly dense as it evolved from nothingness to matter. The Unmanifest produced the Kether of Atziluth, and following the Path of the Flaming Sword sequentially, from Sephira to Sephira, from one world to the next, completion was reached in the Malkuth of Assiah, creating forty Sephiroth in all.

Purists, those who insist that the earlier ideas on the Qabalah are more legitimate than those of more recent Qabalists, tend to espouse a one Tree attribution (compare the methods in Figure 9). However, this is an excellent example of the ways in which the Qabalah has grown as a descriptive system over the centuries. The four Tree attribution is the best for Tarot interpretation.

Four color scales, one for each World, are accepted by the Hermetic Qabalah: The King, Queen, Emperor and Empress, answering respectively to the sequence of the Worlds and the Tetragrammaton. The notion of color is pivotal to the study of Tarot, and painting the Four Worlds in their appropriate colors will provide special insights about the cards. The Golden Dawn Tarot, as published, includes the traditional Tree of Life used for practical work. Here are shown the colors of the Atziluth Paths, and the Sephiroth colors of Briah. There must always be a balance of masculine and feminine in representation involving the Tree, and this is accomplished by combining the two scales in one glyph.

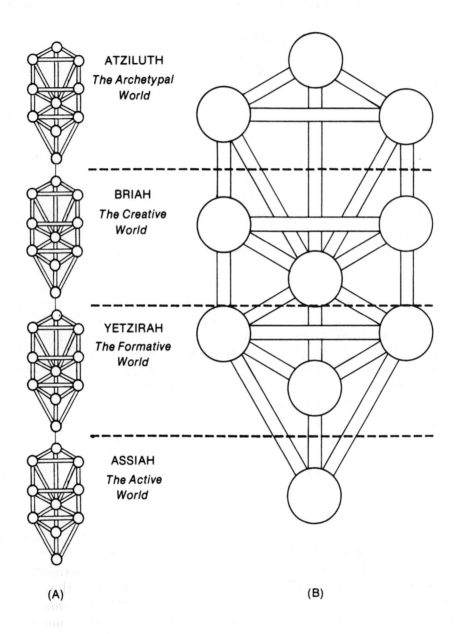

ATZILUTH
*The Archetypal
World*

BRIAH
*The Creative
World*

YETZIRAH
*The Formative
World*

ASSIAH
*The Active
World*

(A)

(B)

Figure 9. The Four Worlds A) Scheme of Separate
Trees B) Attribution of a Single Tree

In our discussion of the Four Worlds we have chosen the term Primal to describe Fire, Water, Air and Earth symbolized by the letters of the Tetragrammaton in the Four Worlds, in an effort to distinguish these energies from other forms of Elements described on the Tree. But in each individual World (Yod) Fire is also attributed to Chokmah, (Heh) Water to Binah, (Vau) Air to Tiphareth and (Heh Final) Earth to Malkuth. We propose to describe these subdivisions of the Primal Elements as *Specific Elements*. Thus, in Atziluth, Primal Fire, are four such Specific Elements: a Fire (Specific) of Fire (Primal); A Water (Specific) of Fire (Primal), an Air (Specific) of Fire (Primal), and an Earth (Specific) of Fire (Primal). In Briah, the World of Primal Water, there is a Fire of Water, a Water of Water, an Air of Water and an Earth of Water. The pattern follows through Yetzirah and Assiah, and is the basis for attributing the Court Cards to the Tarot. For example, the entire suit of Wands describes Atziluth, the Archetypal World. Wands, therefore are Primal Fire, the Primal Yod. This Primal Fire is divided into four aspects, personified by the Tarot: The King of Wands, related to Chokmah in Atziluth, is Fire of Fire. The Queen of Wands, related to Binah in Atziluth, is Water of Fire. The Prince of Wands, related to Tiphareth in Atziluth, is Air of Fire. And the Princess of Wands, related to Malkuth in Atziluth, is Earth of Fire.

There is also an important tertiary application of the Elements, found on the Paths where different Hebrew letters, called *Maternals* by the *Sepher Yetzirah*, are applied. Since all other letters and energies are derived from these three Maternals, the Elements attributed to them will be called *Transitional Elements*. *The Fool*, is the letter Aleph and Air. But this is not the same as that which is represented overall by Vau of Briah (Primal Air) or the Vau of Tiphareth (Specific Air). The Elements of the Paths are Transitional in that they are in a constant state of flow between two Sephiroth.

Having subjected the reader to a bombardment of terms, the suggestion that there are yet three more types of Elements may be less than welcome. However, this is an area of Qabalistic studies which has not been generally explored, and which is a source of constant confusion. Let us quickly consider the other types of Elements, and then attempt to reach some coherent overview of them all.

The Elements, the fourfold division found throughout the Tree of Life, are rooted in Kether. Here they are undefined and unexpressed, and are *Primordial Elements*. Another application of the term Elements is made to the four lower Sephiroth, Fire to Netzach, Water to Hod, Air to Yesod and Earth to Malkuth. These are *Astral Elements*. Finally in Malkuth are the *Base Elements* which are the ultimate expression of those first found in Kether in their primordial state.

In every single application of this fluid term "element," the formula of the Yod Heh Vau Heh applies. Wherever Yod appears it has fiery outgoing qualities; wherever Heh appears it has enclosing and fluid qualities of Water; wherever Vau appears it is the airy result of the combination of the Yod and Heh; wherever Heh Final appears, it is the solidified end result of the actions of the Yod Heh and Vau. This pattern is really the only thing to remember, since it is applied to a variety of very different qualities.

To reiterate those terms which may be applied to the so-called Elements (Figure 10):

1) *Primordial Elements.* Found in Kether. Undifferentiated
   potential.
2) *Primal Elements.* The Yod Heh Vau Heh applied to the Four
   Worlds.
3) *Transitional Elements.* The Yod, Heh and Vau which are Maternals on the Paths of the Tree of Life.
4) *Specific Elements.* The Yod Heh Vau Heh as applied to Chokmah, Binah, Tiphareth and Malkuth in any of the
   Four Worlds.
5) *Astral Elements.* The Yod Heh Vau Heh applied to the four
   Lower Sephiroth.
6) *Base Elements.* Found in Malkuth, blended. The ultimate
   expression of the outpouring of the universe into matter.
   Taken together, the base elements are a subdivision of
   Astral Earth.

This is an admittedly complicated scheme, but it is presented to under-score the fact that different types of energies are symbolized by the Fire, Water, Air, Earth scheme on the Tree of Life. The Yod of Atziluth is not commensurate with the Yod applied to the Path of Shin, or Yod applied to a sequence begun in Netzach. Yet these are all described by the word "Fire." Again, what is re-ally important is the sequence represented by the Tetragrammaton. We might arbitrarily say, for example, that Apple is Fire, Orange is Water, Pear is Air and Lemon is Earth. In this case we would be applying a formula to describe a rela-tionship between Apple, Orange, Pear and Lemon. If, then, the same underlying pattern is found beneath Swing, Chair, Sofa and Footstool, it should not be sup-posed that because both Apple and Swing begin the sequence they are exactly equivalent. A description of different energies in the same way seems to be a trap set by the early Qabalists.

Qabalistic Symbolism

A symbol is of value in that it suggests something which cannot be ad-equately expressed in language (although language is itself a form of symbol-ism). More important, however, is that while on our plane of existence sym-bols are abstractions, they are realities on other planes. In the astral realms a symbol can be a powerful device for attracting or for repelling spiritual en-tities. It can be a call or a protection, in that it affirms the power of a dei-ty governing a particular form and level of energy. When used in this way, a symbol could be defined in the same terms as a talisman on our own plane: it is essentially "charged with the force which it is intended to represent."

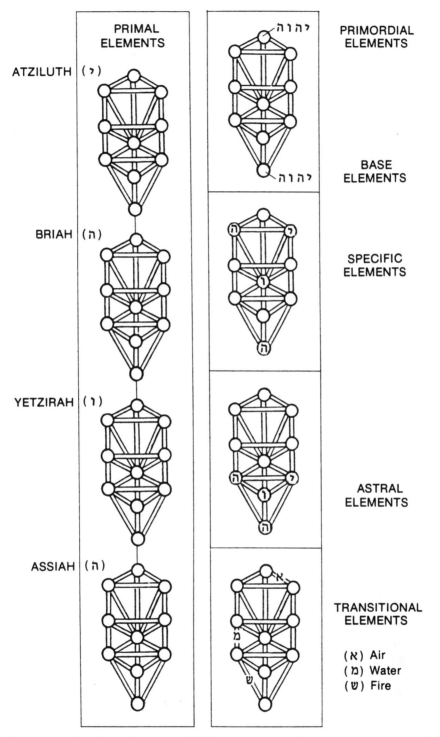

Figure 10. The Four Elements (יהוה) as they describe various aspects of the Tree of Life. Left: The Four Worlds. Right: The Elements as applied to any single Tree. While יהוה relates to the Sephiroth, א, מ, and ש relate to Paths.

There is a vast complex of symbols attached to the Sephiroth and Paths. For example, Kether may be described mathematically as *The Point*, in that it is the First Emanation. As Chokmah emerges from Kether a Line is formed, and with the development of Binah there is a Triangle. And so, one may progress down the Tree applying geometric figures according to the number of the Sephira. Chesed is a Square, Geburah a Pentagram, Tiphareth a Hexagram, etc. These are the most basic and in some respects the most profound of the symbols attached to the Tree. The most complicated symbols are the Hebrew letters and the Divine Names written in those letters.

Some may have an intuitive grasp of the extent to which the Hebrew alphabet is more than just letters. Many years ago the artist Ben Shahn published a book called *Love and Joy About Letters*, in which he described his own feeling toward that alphabet as a child: "I loved to draw and contemplate the big flowing letters; I was most at home with them and could make them long before I could do anything else with my hands. It was such a pleasure to copy them from the prayer-book because in each letter there was some subtle part of the others, and as one learned to make the new ones he discovered those familiar parts that he already knew."[62]

A Hebrew letter, taken by itself, or in conjunction with others as it forms a God Name, is as much a symbol as a geometric figure (letters and words are often visualized in practical work). To each Hebrew letter is assigned a number, and words have special meaning according to numbers derived by what is known as Qabalistic Addition (to be discussed later). Suffice it to say here that insofar as Hebrew letters are assigned to each of the Trump Cards, those cards may even be used to pictorially spell Divine Names, and give insight into the nature of the deity This exercise serves to demonstrate the extent to which the Qabalistic system is composed of precisely interrelated parts.

One important point which must be made has to do with the constant use of color in the Hermetic Qabalah. Most people consider color symbolic, but it is not. Colors are the actual forces, not merely symbols of those forces. The same may be said for pure tone.

The Sephiroth and Their Symbols

In the Tarot, the Sephiroth are represented by the ten numbered cards of each suit (Figure 11) and by the Court Cards which are placed on the Sephiroth according to the principle of the יהוה. Any Ace pertains to Kether, any two to Chokmah, any three to Binah, etc. The Court cards, as we have indicated, are placed with the Kings (י) in Chokmah, the Queens (ה) in Binah, the Knights (ו) in Tiphareth and the Princesses (ה) in Malkuth. Actually, however, the Court Cards relate to the entire Tree, and not just to selected Sephiroth (Figure 11).

The Hebrew alphabet is based on the form of the letter Yod (י). This refers to the idea that the entire universe derives from that which is symbolized by the Yod. Yod ultimately relates to Kether, an idea which Mathers suggests as Yod I. But it is not until the formation of the Sephira Chokmah that what we understand as the outpouring Yod force of the universe, the fiery masculine energy, is separated out and activated. Thus, for practical purposes, the Yod is attributed to Chokmah, and the Heh, the watery feminine principle, is attributed to Binah. Vau is referred to Tiphareth, but it actually encompasses all of the Sephiroth under the Supernal Triangle, except Malkuth, *i.e.*, those six Sephiroth to which Tiphareth is central, Geburah, Chesed, Netzach, Hod and Yesod. And when the hidden Sephira, Daath, is considered, a perfect circle is formed around Tiphareth.

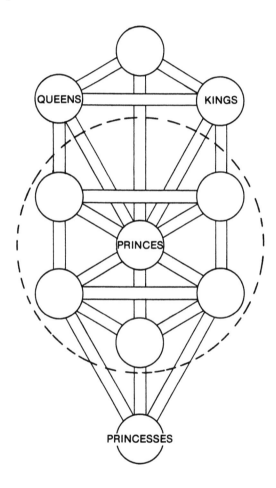

Figure 11. The Court Cards on the Tree of Life

By this point it should be obvious that applying the Tarot to the Qabalistic Tree of Life involves some difficult stretches of language, but the effort to understand these attributions will be well rewarded. While one may feel frustrated, if not inundated, by all of these definitions, it is important to realize that definition is what the Qabalah is all about. It is a very clear and precise system, verbal smokescreens of the early Qabalists notwithstanding.

Insofar as the numbered and Court Cards of the Sephiroth are called the Minor Arcana (Arcana means secret), they may appear to be of less importance than the Major Arcana or Trump cards. They are, however, of the greatest significance in that they symbolize the real potencies in ourselves and in the universe, with which we strive to come into conscious contact.

If the Suits (Sephiroth) appear subordinate to the Trumps (Paths), it is for two reasons. First the Tarot, viewed philosophically, is a teaching device intended to assist in the subjective journey of consciousness from one objective center

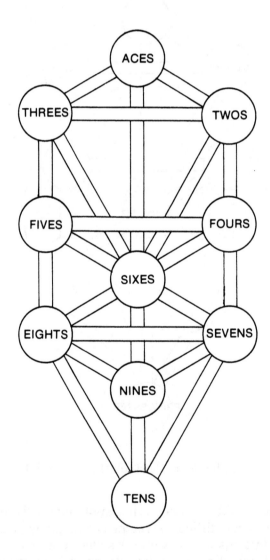

Figure 12. Attribution of the Minor Arcana to the Tree of Life

of energy to another. It may be the chariot which carries us down the road from one inner city to the next. Thus the Paths, while ultimately less important than the Sephiroth, are the primary focus of the Tarot deck. Second, as the cards are used for divination, they describe forces in transition which have brought about past events, function in the present, and have the potential to create future events. This might best be understood by considering the idea that we are all in a continual state of travelling the Paths. It is an unconscious process for most, but a conscious one for those pursuing the Mysteries. Moreover, we are unconsciously travelling many Paths at the same "moment." Our limiting concepts of time, space and form do not apply.

As has been previously suggested, the choice of consciously travelling the Paths, one by one, has the effect of speeding up what would otherwise be a normal course of development. It also has the effect of speeding up the course of karmic action, so that one who becomes involved with the Tarot for the purpose of developing self-knowledge, of exploring an inner universe, may suffer some serious personal problems at the onset. The reason for this is that a number of karmic debts are paid off at once and the "board cleared" of some major impediments to understanding.

The Tarot is best used for divination about mundane matters. It is not particularly well-suited for furnishing answers of an important spiritual nature because it is rooted in Yetzirah, although one brings down insight from higher worlds in interpretation.

The Minor Cards

The Aces relate to the Primordial Elements found in Kether, and the very root of the יהוה. As Crowley stated, "The point to remember is that, both in their appearance and in their meaning, the Aces are not the elements themselves but the seeds of those elements." When the Tree of Life is projected into a solid sphere, they are placed at the North Pole, above the Princesses, which are called the "Thrones" of the Aces. The Golden Dawn taught that the Aces govern the revolution of the universe, and act as a link between Yetzirah, the Formative World, and our material plane.

Casual readers of the original Golden Dawn documents on Tarot may be confused by the order in which the cards, numbered two through ten, are presented. Unlike other systems, which describe these cards in a simple numerical sequence, the Golden Dawn described them in terms of the Decans of the Zodiac. This was an astrological scheme developed by Ptolemy in ancient Egypt.

The Zodiac, a flat disc (360°), is divided into 36 sections of 10° each. Thus, each of the twelve houses of the Zodiac has three Decans, and each Decan is a minor card of the Tarot. These same divisions are days of the year, so that each individual may be assigned one of the Minor cards on the basis of birth date.

The primary symbolism of the Zodiac is of Houses, and Planets. The Houses are simply 30° divisions of the Zodiac, each of which has one of the twelve

Signs naturally attached to it (Fig. 13). Aries is the first House, Taurus the second House, Gemini the third, etc. So, each Sign has three Decans, each ruled by a different planet. The activity of a Planet in a Sign is so specific as to be illustrated as a Tarot card.

♈ ARIES
♉ TAURUS
♊ GEMINI
♋ CANCER
♌ LEO
♍ VIRGO

♎ LIBRA
♏ SCORPIO
♐ SAGITTARIUS
♑ CAPRICORN
♒ AQUARIUS
♓ PISCES

Figure 13. The Signs of the Zodiac in the Twelve Houses

Another confusing element is that the Decans may begin, not with the first Sign, Aries, but with Leo. The first degree of Leo relates to the star Regulus, sometimes called *Cor Leonis* ("The Royal King Star of the Heart of the Lion"). The Golden Dawn taught that the commencement of the Zodiac at 0° Aries was arbitrary, and returned to the very ancient system where the Zodiac begins at 0° Leo. Thus, the first of the Decans is the *Five of Wands*, a dynamic, fiery card.

Moreover, the system of only seven Planets (referred to as the "Old Planets") was developed before the discovery of Neptune, Uranus and Pluto, and considered the Moon, itself, a Planet. This latter idea may be dismissed as representing the ignorance of ancient science. But in terms of the profound and subtle influence exerted by the Moon on our Earth, it is an appropriate description. Planets are attributed to the Decans in a sequence repeated five times: 1) Mars, 2) The Sun, 3) Venus, 4) Mercury, 5) The Moon, 6) Saturn, 7) Jupiter. Yet there is one difficulty. To quote from the *Book T*: "There being only 36 Decanates and only seven Planets, it follows that one of the latter must rule over one more decanate than the others. This is the Planet Mars which is allotted the last Decan of Pisces and first of Aries, because the long cold of the winter requires a great energy to overcome it and initiate spring." Figure 14 shows the Minor cards as they relate to these astrological configurations.

The Minor cards carry two interchangeable sets of symbolism. They represent Planets in the Signs of the Zodiac; they also represent aspects of individual Sephiroth in the Four Worlds.

To each Minor Card and Decan is attributed a pair of angels, one of whom rules the day and the other the night. So each card represents a duality. Here again we return to the idea that the cards are rooted in Yetzirah, the world of Angels, as opposed to the Archangels of Briah or to the Gods of Atziluth.

The cards are Astral images, illustrating the world of matter below, and symbolically reflecting the worlds of mind and spirit above. For example, the *Two of Wands* relates to Chokmah in Atziluth, as does the *King of Wands*. But neither card is precisely the same as the Chokmah in Atziluth upon which one calls with the God Name *Ja*. The *Two of Wands* may be said to represent the effect in Yetzirah of the power of Chokmah in Atziluth, as the *King of Wands* personifies the action of Fire of Fire in Yetzirah. Yetzirah is the Formative World through which higher principles pass down into our lives. It is a world of images reflected from above and below, which explains why the Tarot works so well for divination.

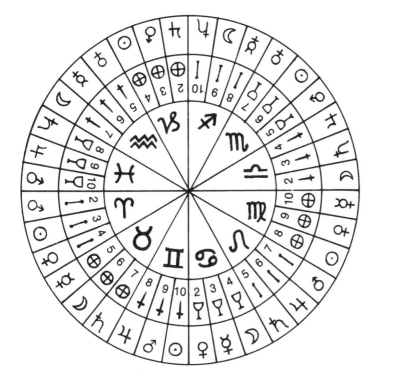

♂ MARS
☉ SUN
♀ VENUS
☿ MERCURY
☽ MOON
♄ SATURN
♃ JUPITER

Figure 14. The Decans, subdivisions of the Signs of the Zodiac. Outermost ring: the small cards of the Tarot applied to the Decans; Intermediate ring: Planets applied to the Decans, rulership of the small cards.

No doubt many will be completely lost at this point. But the Qabalah involves a necessarily complex shuffling of words. The more deeply one goes into the definitions, sub-definitions, super-definitions, pluperfect and platitudinal definitions, the more one is touching on areas where no words can apply. The very effort to find meaning in this maze of ideas is important because it is an expression of commitment. The greatest protection of the Mysteries today, the methods of which have been published openly, is that the early intellectual and meditational exercises are inordinately boring. Few will ever be so serious about the Qabalah as to wade devotedly through its sea of convoluted words. Most will give up quickly, a point thrown here as a gauntlet for those who enjoy real challenges.

Having said this, a further complication will be added, which is the fact that each of the forty Sephiroth of the Four Worlds contains a complete Tree of Iafe of its own, so that there are actually four hundred Sephiroth in all.

Finally, relative to the Minor Cards, it should be understood that the two angels of each numbered card are specific to that card, and the administration of its specific energies. To skry with one of these cards, using the Golden Dawn system, one would first invoke the protection and guidance of the God and Archangel of the related Sephira, then the Angels.

The Court Cards

MacGregor Mathers described the Court Cards as being not on the Sephiroth, but beside them. Here he apparently intended to suggest that these cards are not purely integral to the Sephiroth, but are extensions of their qualities. The Court Cards represent the Elemental powers of the Tetragrammaton, יהוה, in the Four Worlds. They personify the attributes of the Specific Elements (refer again to Figure 10) and, as such, generally represent real people when they appear in a divination. Where this is not the case, they mean an event or situation having a certain personality. It may also be said that the Court Cards represent decision, on our own part or on the part of others. It is the decision of individuals (or the result of situations brought about by individual decision) which bring into effect the forces represented by the cards of the Tarot numbered two through ten. So that when a Court Card comes up in a divination, it suggests a human controlling factor. The Trumps usually represent *karmic forces* also influencing the situations of the numbered minor cards. To reiterate: In divination the Court Cards are the choices of men, the Trumps are the choices of the Gods (although at a more complex level, these are our own choices too) and the small cards are the forces brought into play. Of course any card of the deck may be a clear reference to an individual.

Like the Minor Cards, the Court Cards may also be referred to the Zodiac. The Kings, Queens and Princes stand behind the Decans, while the Princesses are said to "link together the Signs." The Aces through Tens and the Court Cards may be placed on a composite diagram (Figure 15), but this scheme is a simplistic attempt to show relationships which are actually three dimensional, and refer to the Earth and its two magnetic poles. The complete system of attribution of the Tarot to the Tree of Life in a Solid Sphere (shown on this book's front cover) is to be found in Regardie's seminal book, *The Golden Dawn*.

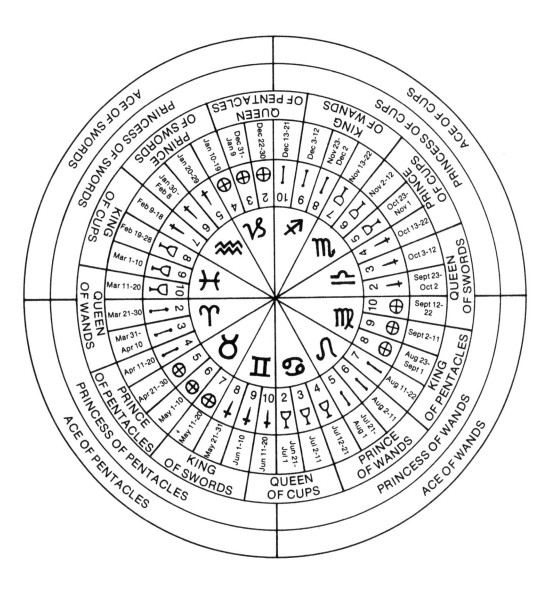

Figure 15. Atribution of the Minor Cards and the Court Cards to the Zodiac. Innermost circle: The Signs and Houses of the Zodiac; Second Ring: Small cards of the Tarot; Third ring: days of the year attributed to the Decans; Fourth ring: Kings, Queens and Princes on the Zodiac; Fifth ring: technically, in three dimensions above the Kings, Queens and Princes; Outer ring: the Aces. These are, when this scheme is considered in a three dimensional sphere, at the North Pole of the earth above the Princesses.

PATTERNS OF THE SEPHIROTH

1. Kether: The Crown
The Four Aces

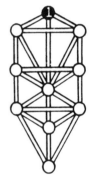

- ◈ All That Is; the Breath of That
  Which Is Not
- ◈ The Source of Energy from the
- ◈ Infinite Unmanifest
- ◈ The First "Motion"
- ◈ God the Creator
- ◈ That from Which We Come, and
  to Which We Shall Return

Symbols: Crown, Point, Swastica
Color: White

In Kether is the Divine White Brilliance, the scintillation and cor-
ruscation of the Divine Glory—that light which lighteth the Uni-
verse—that light which surpasseth the glory of the Sun and beside
which the light of mortals is but darkness, and concerning which
it is not fitting that we should speak more fully. And the sphere
of its operation is called Rashith ha-Gilgalim, *the beginning of*
whirling, the Primum Mobile or First Mover, which bestoweth the
gift of life in all things and filleth the whole Universe. And Eheieh
is the name of the Divine Essence in Kether; and its Archangel is
the Prince of Countenances, Metatron, *he who bringeth forth oth-*
ers before the face of God. And the Name of its Order of Angels is
called Chaioth ha-Qadesh, *the Holy Living Creatures which are*
also called the Order of Seraphim.[63]

All of the Sephiroth must be approached intellectually before some intuition about their natures begins to develop. One begins with a study of the symbols attached to each Sephira. Such symbols transcend language. Moreover, one symbol may suggest something about another symbol, thus creating a general picture of the energy in question. It is impossible to know Kether, as it is said that man cannot look upon the face of God and live. Yet we can establish some principles about Kether through its symbols, such as the Point. It may be said that Kether is the Point, and that is true. But the point is not Kether, it is merely an idea, a focus of reference for our thoughts about Kether.

The interrelationship of symbols provides the best instruction, for each symbol describes a specific aspect of a Sephira. In Kether, these are the *Crown,* the *Point* and the *Swastica.* This latter is one of the oldest symbols of the Ultimate Godhead, unfortunately attached to the positive evil of Nazism in an age past.

The first symbol of Kether is the Crown. Our anthropomorphic perspective may lead us to the idea that the directing force is within our heads, but the Qabalah places that force above. The distinction is a significant one, indicating that the Holy Guiding Spirit is a crowning glory to which we may aspire, and an energy to which the mental processes of our brain are subordinate. The Crown, in the microcosm, is our Essential Spirit. In the Macrocosm it rests above the head of Adam Kadmon, the Archetypal Man of *The Zohar* who symbolizes the entire manifest Universe. Kether is the Crown above creation, but it is also that from which all creation springs. For this reason, another of its prime symbols is the Point.

The Point is complete unto itself, without dimensions or external definition. It represents total unity. It is the seed from which the Universe grows. Ultimately, all is Kether, and each of the Sephiroth emanating successively from Kether are crystallizations of the latent aspects of the One. The journey of manifestation begins and ends with Kether. It is the Kether of Atziluth to which we aspire, and into which the manifest Universe will eventually withdraw.

We begin the process of accelerating our own spiritual development, or return, by the invocation of our own Kether. This Kether unconsciously guides and directs us. The very act of calling attention to the "Light above our heads" brings about a subtle activity on the Inner Planes. It is a conscious affirmation of the Personality in manifestation of its mutability, and that the source of all true life is above. As the very Universe begins and ends with Kether, so all work of spiritual development, whether meditative or ritualistic, must begin with an invocation of the Highest.

The God name in Kether is *Eheieh* (אהיה), meaning "I Will Be," a name which has been likened in its sound and meaning to breath.

To the Point is attributed the number 1 which, mathematically, has the potential for all numbers, by simple addition. If we take the number 1 and place another number 1 beside it, we have 2. If we take a third 1, we have three ones, i.e., 3. This idea may appear so obvious as to be inane, until we begin to meditate on the concept of simple numbers and simple geometry. What do we know, for example, that could be considered *pure one,* which is totally indivisible? Numbers are the most pure form of symbol and are of great importance in the Qabalistic scheme of things. No student who has pursued Ouspensky's *Tertium Organum*[64] through its profound discussion of dimensions would dispute that.

While Kether is symbolized by the Point and the number One, it is not static. In Assiah (the material world) it is also the "First Swirlings" of manifestation. So a third descriptive idea is attached. That is the *Swastica* representing vital, swirling motion around the point. It is self-contained, but in motion.

The Swastica has four arms, representing the four latent aspects of the יהוה in the Primordial Elements. It is not trinitarian. These are the energies which, unified in Kether, are finally differentiated into the four Base Elements of Malkuth, called the *Bride of Microprosopus*. Malkuth is Kether on the lowest arc, and defines the principle of "As above, so below." The Swastica is the perfect symbol for the Primordial Elements because if the arms are imagined in motion, like the blades of a fan, each is indistinguishable from the other. As the Elements are represented in Malkuth they are sharply defined.

"As above, so below" is a principle which states, in essence, that Malkuth, the densest development of the Universe, is equally holy as the source. Fundamentalists, finding the physical world evil, *per se*, are misguided extremists.

This question of evil is best approached in dealing with Kether because this is the sole area of the Tree of Life where no evil exists. It is the Holy of Holies, having no opposing energies within it.

Evil is unbalanced force. It is a by-product of evolution, resulting from a stage of temporary imbalance in one Sephira prior to the mitigating emergence of another. That is the Qabalistic theory: at each point of evolution is left an extreme of a specific energy.

Evil is an extreme. It attempts to pull to one side, making balance impossible. Unity is the ultimate good, and unity is the result of the balance of two opposites. For example: Geburah is dynamic strength and its opposite, Chesed, is Mercy or Love. The extreme of Geburah is hideous cruelty. The extreme of Chesed is the worst kind of weakness manifesting as bigotry and hypocrisy.

Dion Fortune makes the point that there are two kinds of evil, positive and negative. Negative evil is not so much a matter of choice as unbalanced temperament. But positive evil involves willfully espousing an unbalanced force for some sort of self-gain.[65]

Each Sephira has its unbalanced aspect, and a system of named demons, as it has its God Names and angelic forms, known as the *Qlippoth*. These are extremes which are also found in each individual, in varying degrees, and which the Qabalah serves as a method of first defining, and then bringing under control. It is for this reason that a system such as that of Abramelin invokes both the good and evil forces. One is viewed as no better than the other, since they are both an integral part of All. There is no value judgment, only the desire to understand and bring under the control of balance. This is the meaning of the warring families of the *Bhagavad Gita*. They are the component parts of the personality which is, literally, at war with itself until the battle is resolved through the intermediary of the Higher Self (Krishna in this work) and peace restored.

The ultimate peace and unity of Kether is represented by a special an-thropomorphic symbol known as a *Magical Image.* Such an image is given for each of the Sephiroth, and has been built up over the centuries by meditative work on the inner planes. These images are, along with the applicable symbols, points of contact with the energies of the Sephiroth. In the case of Kether, the image is that of an *Ancient Bearded King Seen in Profile.* This is a crowned and white-bearded head, seen from the right side, its left being unknown to us, as it borders on the Unmanifest.

As the Aces are attributed to Kether, they represent the most pure forms of energy, subject to elaboration as the Sephiroth (symbolized by the other num-bered cards of the Tarot) consecutively emerge to form a complete World. Each is unique and distinct in the degree of its density and in its specific type of en-ergy. Thus, when any Ace appears in a divination, it stands for great power.

Finally, it must be reiterated that while the Kether, which is the source of all, is a quality which cannot be known to us, it is a quality which we can symbol-ize to some extent. It is intriguing to consider the idea of *eternity,* an effort which tends to underscore the very frailty of the system of definitions within which we necessarily function. We may be able to deal with the idea that the division between matter and spirit is artificial, or even a concept of intelligence which is totally formless; but our concept of time falls hard. We suppose that if God is not finite, he must be infinite. And yet, we are told that none of our human concepts cannot begin to apply to Kether, and infinite is a human concept. There is a large degree of faith required here, and an open mind which asks questions fearlessly until answers emerge.

The Aces

> *First in order of appearance are the four Aces, representing the*
> *force of the Spirit acting in, and binding together the four scales*
> *of each element and answering to the Dominion of the Letters of*
> *the Name in the* Kether *of each. They represent the Radical or*
> *Root-Force. The Four Aces are said to be placed on the North Pole*
> *of the Universe, wherein they revolve, governing its revolution,*
> *and ruling as the connecting link between Yetzirah*
> *and the Material Plane of the Universe.*[66]

Note: This sequence of illustrations-Golden Dawn (1890), Crowley (1944), Waite (1910), and Marseilles (1748) decks is followed throughout the text.

THE ACE OF WANDS, Root of the Powers of Fire (ʼ).

This card represents the primary outpouring energy of the Universe. It is the Kether of Atziluth, the influence of Kether on the level of pure Spirit. In the Golden Dawn card an angelic hand holds what is basically an inverted root

of three sections (possibly influenced by the Tree of Life diagram published by Fludd). The ten root sections are painted with bands in the colors of the ten Sephiroth in the Four Worlds. The sigils on the three parts are drawn from the *Rose Cross Lamen,*[67] using the letters אש (Aesch, Fire), מים (Maim, Water) and רוה (Ruach, Air). The twenty-two Yods are the Paths on the Tree of Life. The Marseilles deck is perhaps the source of these Yods, although there the number seems arbitrary.

The Golden Dawn card shows the club as living and bearing leaves, a reference which is intentionally phallic. Crowley's Ace abstracts the flaming Yods into the form of the entire Tree of Life, thus continuing the Golden Dawn symbolism of the Ace of Wands as the source of All.

Here it may also be observed that the entire Tree is a glyph of the power of Fire, when manifestation is symbolized as the יהוה, *permeated* by ש). Yod and Shin are, to some extent, used interchangeably.

THE ACE OF CUPS, Root of the Powers of Water (ה).

The Ace of Cups is Kether in Briah, the influence of Kether on the mental level. This is an all-encompassing Maternal Force, symbolized by Water which in the Golden Dawn and Waite cards pours dynamically from the cup but becomes calm and stable beneath. The Golden Dawn represents the unfolding of Divine Consciousness with the Lotus colored red to suggest that the origin of this consciousness is in Fire. Waite, on the other hand, shows thecup as the perfection and formalization of the יהוה evolving toward matter. The twenty-six drops of water coming from the cup mean the יהוה, a number derived by Gematria, as we shall later demonstrate. The dove here is a symbol of Venus as the Great Mother, beneath which is the circle and equal armed cross of the earth which she produces. This symbol was incidentally, adopted by Dion Fortune to represent her Society of the Inner Light.

Crowley's version of the card emphasizes the wave action characteristic of physical water, but here meaning the activity which encloses and directs pure consciousness. The cup emerges from the Lotus itself.

The Marseilles Ace is the most basic of the three versions, and appears to be nothing more than a simple chalice. Yet the suggestion of Gothic architecture tells us that what is intended is *The Church,* as Holy Mother. In the fourteenth century the Virgin Mary was often referred to as the Church itself, the very building which enclosed the faithful. That symbolism is completely consistent with the meaning of the Ace of Cups.

THE ACE OF SWORDS, Root of the Powers of Air (ו).

The card is Kether in Yetzirah, the influence of Kether in the Astral World, the world of fleeting forms. This is a potent card which can be either extremely good or extremely evil. It represents force which is *invoked,* rather than the natural force of the *Ace of Wands.* This is a force called upon.

When the Kether energies are seen on the Astral level they are both dynamic and erratic, having the potential to be applied at will to different situations. Thus, this is described as the "Sword of Good or Evil," of "Whirling force and strength through trouble. It is the affirmation of justice upholding

Divine Authority; and it may become the Sword of Wrath, Punishment and Affliction."[68]

The style for most versions of this card relates to the Marseilles version, showing the Sword of Air, passing through the Crown of Kether. Dual possibilities for action are implied in the palm of suffering, and the olive branch of peace. The six Vaus above the Golden Dawn crown mean Tiphareth, the *Ruach* (Air) center of the Tree of Life.

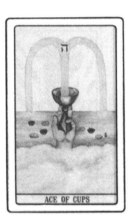

THE ACE OF PENTACLES, Root of the Powers of Earth (ה). This Ace represents Kether in Assiah, the influence of Kether in the World of Matter. It is a card of materiality which may, like the *Ace of Swords*, be either good or evil. It is not necessarily a card of wealth, and should be compared with the *Ten of Pentacles*.

The Marseilles card is extremely simple, and relates to the ancient suit of Coins, money being considered the essence of material things. Waite's version also features a coin, but this is really a *Pentacle,* magical symbol of Earth, held above a flowing garden of pure lilies. The hand floats in the air, suggesting that it is that which brings about the fruition of matter, rather than being matter itself.

In the Golden Dawn card an angelic hand holds a rose tree surmounted by a Pentacle of five concentric circles. The outermost circles are in the colors of Malkuth: citrine, olive, russet and black. These are the four Base Elements, shown to be in perfect balance by the red equal-armed cross. The twelve white rays are the forces of the Zodiac, expressed through the Elements of Earth. The four roses also represent the Elements, but the addition of two buds implies the very fertility of these Elements in their subtle earthly balance. The winged red cross refers to the Primordial Elements of Kether. It is winged to show that the Elements pass through the state of Spiritual Air before manifesting into matter. Crowley's card apparently represents the wings of the four Archangels (Michael, Gabriel, Raphael and Auriel) whose powers serve to balance one another, and create stability. At the center is Crowley's personal phallus symbol and the

number of the Beast of Revelation, 666, with which he identified. In the wheel
are Greek words meaning "to the mark of the beast," another indicator that
Crowley chose this particular card as his own.

2. Chokmah: Wisdom

The Four Twos
The Four Kings

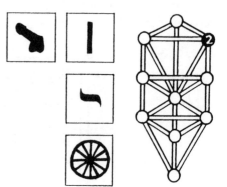

◈   The Supernal Father
◈   The Will to Force
◈   Dynamic Outpouring Energy,
◈   Unorganized and Uncompensated
◈   The Great Stimulator
◈   The First Positive

Symbols: The Phallus, the Line,
        Yod.
Astrological Reference: The
        Sphere of the Zodiac
Color: Grey

*In Chokmah is a cloud-like grey which containeth various colours
and is mixed with them, like a transparent pearl-hued mist, yet radiating withal, as if behind it there was a brilliant glory. And the
Sphere of its influence is in* Masloth, *the Starry Heaven, wherein
it disposeth the forms of things. And* Yah is *the Divine Ideal Wisdom, and its Archangel is* Ratziel, *the Prince of Princes of the
knowledge of hidden and concealed things, and the name of its
Order of Angels is* Auphanium, *the Wheels or the Whirling Forces
which are also called the order of Kerubim.*

Many of our present-day notions of sexuality are still rooted in the Victorian era, when sex was considered almost unnatural. It was, at best, not to be
discussed in polite company. Today we are coming, increasingly, to understand
that what has been described as the "mystery of sex" is aptly termed, and that
the ability to manipulate the sexual currents in one's own body was among the
greatest secrets of the ancient magicians. It is no coincidence that the ecstasies
of visionaries such as Saint Theresa or Saint John of the Cross are described in
words that seem explicitly sexual and orgasmic.

Sexual repression, or discomfort with one's own sexuality (and here we are
neither discussing nor advocating any particular pattern of behavior) is a serious impediment to any understanding of the inner worlds.

The male generative organ (The *phallus,* or *lingham)* is the key symbol of
Chokmah, and the first differentiation of the One. It is the primary quality of
maleness at the most abstract level, and representative of the *Supernal Father*

emanating from the Godhead. From Chokmah emerges Binah, the *Supernal Mother.*

Students of scripture will quickly note the parallels here with the story of Adam and Eve as described in the *Book of Genesis.* God created first man, by molding him from dust and breathing his own breath into his creation. Eve, the first woman, was created from the rib of the first man. The uniting of male and female gave rise to the human race after they were driven from the Garden of Eden.

One can, symbolically, take the Garden of Eden to be the Supernal Triangle itself. The male and female energies, balanced against each other, evolve in increasing density as they develop toward the lowest aspects of the Tree of Life, far from the Supernal Heights. The first book of the Bible has been described as an extremely complex Qabalistic *cryptogram,* where every letter of every Hebrew word, as well as its numerical value, has a specific and hidden meaning. But interpretations of this sort are more the appropriate concern of the theologian. Few students possess the language and research skills to deal with the Qabalah in this way. Nor is this a practical necessity, since understanding the Qabalah (though the study begins with the intellect) is ultimately a spiritual process. As we focus our intellectual attention on the signs and symbols of the Tree of Life we find that we are developing an intangible appreciation of the energies which are described. And, as we have indicated, number is among the most important of the symbols with which we have to be concerned. In the case of Chokmah, that number is two.

The number two symbolizes the balance of opposites underlying all of material existence. Thus does "Perfect Harmony" describe the Chokmah of Atziluth, the *Two of Wands.* Chokmah is the impetus for all manifestation, as opposed to Kether, from which that impetus derives and which is the "Root." In the Mundane Chakra, it is the *Sphere of the Zodiac,* as Binah is the planet *Saturn.*

While Kether is ultimately androgynous, Chokmah is the idea of maleness and Binah is the idea of femaleness. We use the term *idea* here since at the exalted realm of the Supernal Triangle, there can be no sexuality as we understand it in our sphere of sensation. Maleness is described as a vital outpouring energy, which is organized, i.e., limited or formalized, by the qualities of femaleness. In the Qabalah these principles are referred to the Yod (Male) and the Heh (Female). Their offspring is the Vau of the Divine Name, attributed to the six lower Sephiroth to which Tiphareth is central.

There are so many interchangeable symbols in the Qabalah that the system may appear to be more complicated than it actually is. But this concept of vital outpouring energy which, in intercourse with an organizing force, produces something else, is essential. For example, the Hebrew letter Heh applies to Binah, but as the oldest of the Planets is also applied, another suggestion is involved. For Saturn "devours its children." The meaning here is two-fold: first that death is implicit in birth; second, and at a deeper level, that the Universe itself, the pattern of interwoven energies resulting from the balance of Chokmah and Binah, will eventually withdraw inwards along the same course through which it evolved.

The mysteries of the number two must be viewed as the interaction between opposites, found throughout the Tree of Life, and originated in the opposition of Chokmah and Binah. This involves fluid polarities, such as anabolism and catabolism (building up and tearing down), waxing and waning, life and death, etc. However, these opposites are not static. They are not pure and immobile positive against pure and immobile negative held opposite one another in a sort of celestial checkmate. There is a constant growth and movement. As change occurs in the energy of one Sephira, there is a natural balancing response in its opposite, an effect which is seen dramatically as the Sephiroth are applied to aspects of the Microcosm. There is a continual interchange which might be likened to the breathing in and out suggested by the Divine Name of Kether, Eheieh, which sets the pattern for all beneath it.

The key to all systems, and to the universal pattern, is Chokmah, which may be considered the only "reality" as opposed to Kether, which *is not*. One can conceptualize the Universe as non-being (Kether) and being (Chokmah). It is rather like an electrical switch which is turned off in Kether and turned on in Chokmah. The power is potential in Kether, but it does not begin to function until the switch is turned on.

To understand how this works, let us imagine ourselves "switched on" in Chokmah, in a state of deep meditation, with the reality of our current existence welling up in our minds. We dream ourselves, yet that which is dreamed is unaware of the dreamer. Here is what is meant by the Chinese story of a man who dreams he is a butterfly, but on waking wonders if he is actually a butterfly dreaming that he is a man.

That we meditate ourselves, like a dream inside out, is the ultimate fact of our earthly existence. The inner "I" dreams what we perceive ourselves to be in life; we, as such, do not exist, an idea which may be very frightening to some and exhilerating to others.

Now this dream of life of ours has some very specific dimensions, or whatever they may be called. Such dimensions are usually described in spatial terms because that is our best frame of reference. The Qabalah describes an evolution downwards from Chokmah, and various levels of the self-dream which are the symbolic Sephiroth. Other systems explain these levels of self as sheaths developing *outward* from the "I" (Monad, Supreme Spiritual Self, etc.) which does the meditating. Some of the most complex discussions of these sheafs are given by Alice Bailey. Another who attempts an explanation is Dion Fortune, author of *The Cosmic Doctrine*. Such systems, however, appear so obtuse as to be unapproachable by all but a very few.

Yet when the universal patterns are glibly called "so simple that they could be explained to a child," two ideas are intended: First, what we have described as dreaming our own existences. And second, that we are all, collectively, what is known as *God*, but are not aware of it. The loss of our sense of oneness with the Divine, however this may have happened, is the symbolic *Fall* (again, a spatial reference to going "downwards").

These two concepts are, at first, understood intellectually (the "Vision of the Machinery of the Universe" of Yesod). Then the intellectual work turns into a profound inner understanding. We surpass thought and begin to function consciously with our inner dream-maker. Here it may be appreciated that when the dreamer and the dreamed (as we know ourselves) begin to cooperate, we acquire a control over what happens to our lives that is truly extraordinary. We can have anything we want... anything. But what happens is that we want nothing at all, because we have learned what matters and what does not.

The Twos

The Four Deuces symbolize the Powers of the King and Queen: first uniting and initiating the Force, but before the Prince and Princess are thoroughly brought into action. Therefore do they generally imply the initiation and fecundation of a thing.

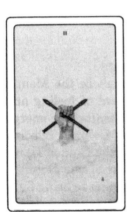 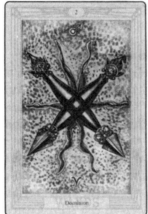  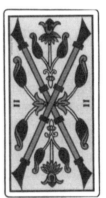

TWO OF WANDS, Lord of Dominion (Mars in Aries).
Angels of the Decan: Vehooel (והואל) and Deneyal (דניאל).

Chokmah in Atziluth is the influence of Chokmah in the World of Pure Spirit. In the Atziluthic realm, the fiery male force is on its own ground, so to speak, and is in a completely harmonious state. The fiery planet Mars rules the fiery sign Aries, a tremendous force which Crowley symbolizes with two crossed *Dorjes,* Tibetan symbol of the thunderbolt. Here we understand that the energies are balanced making this powerful card one of stable strength and dominion.

To the crossed wand pattern, established by the Marseilles deck, the Golden Dawn added an angelic hand. The original Golden Dawn cards included the astrological signs found on the Crowley cards, here Mars and Aries, the decision having been made to eliminate them for publication.

Waite's card shows a man surveying his kingdom, a mnemonic device intended to benefit those who are using the cards primarily for divination, showing only one aspect of the card's meaning, *Dominion.*

TWO OF CUPS, Lord of Love (Venus in Cancer).
Angels of the Decan: Ayoel (איעאל) and Chabooyah (חבויה).
   This is Chokmah in Briah, the influence of Chokmah in the Mental World. Cancer is a watery sign, so Cups apply. This is a card of feeling and romance (particularly in material things) which has the potential for energy misspent. Fish generally refer to the Goddess Venus, the dolphin relating more specifically to Neptune and the Sun God Apollo.[69] On the Golden Dawn card the solar (male) symbolism is implicit in the gold color of one dolphin, while the silver in the other is lunar (female). They work together to bring light to our world, which is also the nature of the sign Cancer, and reinforces the meaning of the card as a harmony of male and female. The water springs from a pure source, the upper lotus, and pours down into the cups, ultimately reaching our material earth. The idea is that Water (ה) can only flow through the energy provided by the Chokmah-Fire (י). It is a joyous and loving partnership.
   The Crowley card is based entirely on that of the Golden Dawn. And in the Marseilles card we find the apparent design roots of both. In his exoteric version, Waite emphasizes the divinatory meaning of love, marriage and partnership.[70]

TWO OF SWORDS, Lord of Peace Restored (Moon in Libra).
Angels of the Decan: Yezalel (יזלאל) and Mebahel (מבהאל) .
   This is Chokmah in Yetzirah, the influence of Chokmah in the Astral World. Swords are generally negative and destructive, but the balancing effect of Chokmah makes this a positive card. Swords, which might otherwise be clashing, hold together a flower in both the Golden Dawn and Crowley cards: The Golden Dawn uses the Venusian red rose of peace; Crowley chose a five petaled lotus. Balance is affirmed by the cross of light behind which, on Crowley's card, implies that this is the balance of active energies.
   The divinatory meaning is suggested by the position of the Moon in Libra. The Moon is a very changeable and erratic planet which assumes some stabil-

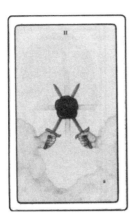 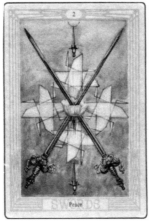  

ity in Libra. The effect is one of subtlety, grace and compromise. So in divination, this card means a *quarrel made up and arranged, the restoration of peace.* Waite's card implies all of this, but also indicates the underlying tension which Crowley shows in his swirling forms behind the Swords. The truce here may be somewhat tenuous.

TWO OF PENTACLES, Lord of Harmonious Change (Jupiter in Capricorn). *Angels of the Decan:* Lekabel (לכבאל) and Veshiriah (ושריה).

This is Chokmah in Assiah, the influence of Chokmah in the material world. Jupiter, a very benevolent planet in traditional astrology, is not well placed in the Sign of Capricorn, meaning that its good influence can only be exerted as an organizer. It assures the harmony of an interaction of dualities inherent in the Chokmah energy as it applies to earth. What was a perfectly unified energy in Atziluth, is now a completely expressed duality; energies in alternation.

Once more it appears that the Marseilles card is the pattern for the three

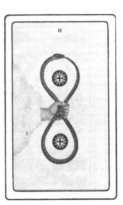 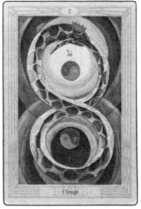  

modern cards, the later versions having simply closed the "S" shape into a perfect symbol of infinity. The snake with its tail in its mouth, the *Uroboros,* is a very ancient symbol of *wisdom* (meaning of the Hebrew word *Chokmah).* But this serpent is in the form of a figure eight, the same infinity sign found over the head of *The Magician.* In divination it means *the harmony of change.* But in esoteric studies, it suggests the underlying patterns of alternation within matter, and the profound relationship between opposites.

The Kings

> *The Four kings or figures mounted on steeds* [Golden Dawn and Crowley versions] *represent the Yod forces in the name of each suit, the Radix, Father and commencement of Material Forces. A Force in which all the others are implied and of which they form the development and completion. A force swift and violent in action, but whose effect soon passes away, and therefore symbolized by a figure on a steed riding swiftly, and clothed in complete armour.*

KING OF WANDS, Lord of the Flame and of the Lightning, King of the Spirits of Fire, King of the Salamanders. (Last Decan of Scorpio, first two Decans of Saggitarius). The King of Wands is Fire of Fire, Specific Fire in Primal Fire on the Tree of Life.

The Marseilles King is seated on a throne, and holds a wand in his right hand. Waite's King is also seated, and holds the same fertile wand found in the Rider Ace of Wands. His crown indicates flames, as the Serpents behind and on his robe refer to Chokmah.

The Golden Dawn and Crowley cards symbolize the dynamic, outrushing, pattern of this energy with the Moorish (Arabian) black horse which leaps through the flames. The King's crest is a winged horse head. Like all of the

Golden Dawn court cards, he is in armor, implying that the qualities of the Elements which they symbolize do life's battle for us. In his hand he carries the same wand found on the Ace, showing that he is the motive vehicle for the Fire Force.

KING OF CUPS, Lord of the Waves and of the Waters, King of the Hosts of the Sea, King of Undines arid Nymphs (Last Decan of Aquarius—first two Decans of Pisces). The King of Cups is Specific Fire in the World of Primal Water. It is a personification of the force which motivates the currents of the unconscious mental world symbolized by water, an idea found in Waite's King, whose heavy throne seems to ride effortlessly on the water as does the Golden Dawn figure. That King carries a cup from which issues a Crab, symbol of the Sign Cancer (Cardinal Water) which, ruled by the Moon, directs the flow of tides. The Crab also relates to Isis, the Great Mother, *Stella Maris*, Star of the Sea.[71] The peacock, found as the crest of the Golden Dawn King, enlarged and abstracted by Crowley, is variously attributed as a symbol of wisdom (i.e., Chokmah) and as a bird whose flesh is incorruptible. It was also related to the phoenix, a bird which died in flames every five hundred years and then rose from its own ashes.[72]

THE KING OF SWORDS, Lord of the Winds and Breezes, King of the Spirit of Air, King of Sylphs and Sylphides (Last Decan of Taurus—first two Decans of Gemini). The King of Swords is Specific Fire in Primal Air. It is a personification of the activating Force behind the World of Astral images and ideas. It is a violent and aggressively cutting power, an idea shown best by Crowley, and not at all by the Waite and Marseilles cards. Crowley's mounted King is the dynamic energy of the charging bull of Taurus, but being predominantly Gemini he turns easily in one direction or the other. Gemini is also implied in the Golden Dawn King's crest, the hexagram which is a merging of opposites.

To this King is attributed a subtleness and craftiness, as Air refers to the conscious mind.

KING OF PENTACLES, Lord of the Wild and Fertile Land, King of the Spirits of Earth, King of the Gnomes (Last Decan of Leo—first two Decans of Virgo). The King of Pentacles personifies Specific Fire in Primal Earth. It is the most dense manifestation of the Elemental Yod Force, and is the energy which brings about material fruition and growth as Waite has shown here in a very effective card. His King is the very essence of the energy underlying earthly growth. The Golden Dawn and Crowley Kings use the emblem of a stag, an animal to whom great regenerative powers are attributed. The stag mythically eats the serpent (absorbs wisdom) and in so doing sheds its skin, as well as any illness, weakness and old age. It is totally regenerated.[73] Thus, it is a fitting symbol for Fire of Earth. It moves fleetingly, as fire, but also represents the cyclic rebirth of the earth. This same fruition is indicated by the corn (symbol of Isis-Ceres) in the foreground. It is clear that Mathers was a student of medieval bestiaries, where the animal legends are collected.

3. Binah: Understanding
The Four Threes
The Four Queens

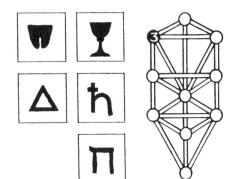

❖ The Supernal Mother
❖ The Organizer and Compen-
    sator
❖ The Bright Fertile Mother
❖ The Great Sea

Symbols: The Yoni, the Triangle,
    the Cup, Heh
Planet: Saturn
Color: Black

*In Binah is a thick darkness which yet veileth the Divine Glory in
which all colours are hidden, wherein is mystery and depth ' and
silence, and yet, it is the habitation of the Supernal Light. There is
the Supernal Triad completed. And the Sphere of its Operation is
Shabbathi, or rest, and it giveth forms and similitudes unto cha-
otic matter and it ruleth the sphere of action of the planet Saturn.
And Jehovah Elohim is the perfection of Creation and the Life of
the World to Come. And its Archangel is Tzaphqiel, the Prince of
the Spiritual Strife against Evil, and the Name of the Angels is
Aralim, the strong and mighty Ones who are also called the Order
of Thrones.*

The key symbol of Binah is the yoni, or female generative organ, indicating
that this Sephira is the energy from which all life emerges. It is the Great Womb,
the Supernal Mother to which all religions make reference in some way. It is also
the completion of the Supernal Triangle, which began as the point in Kether,
emanated to Chokmah as the line, and emerged with Binah as the triangle.

Two questions generally arise when first considering "sexuality" as it is
philosophically described in these upper realms of the Tree of Life. The first
relates to the fact that the primary female Sephira, Binah, stands at the head of
the Pillar of Severity, while the primary male Sephira, Chokmah, is at the head
of the Pillar of Mercy.

This fact reflects the Qabalistic definition of maleness and femaleness as
qualities, rather than as static characteristics, as well as the ultimate bisexuality
of the soul. In the Supernal Triangle, maleness is pure outgoing energy, merciful
in that it is unrestricted; femaleness is a limiting quality, and thus severe. Moving down through the Tree of Life on the Pillar of Severity we find that Geburah
destroys, while Hod again builds up (anabolism and catabolism). And on the
Pillar of Severity we find that Chesed builds up while Netzach has destructive
qualities.

The second question which inevitably arises throughout the Tree of Life is the extent to which there is an interchange of masculine and feminine deities as we know them. Although the key God figure of Binah is Isis, the male Gods Saturn and Chronos are also attributed to it. Moreover, at the base of the Pillar of Severity, beneath Binah, we find the male God Mercury in the Sephira Hod. At the base of the Pillar of Mercy we find the female Goddess Venus in the Sephira Netzach. The answer is that our concepts of gender are insufficient to describe the subtle polarities and interchanges of energy in the Universe. Aspects of a female deity often best describe aspects of a primarily masculine Sephira. Moreover, it will be appreciated that the Pantheons with which we are most familiar in the West are anthropomorphic. We have created the Gods in our own image with a certain fundamentalistic, though comforting naiveté.

Binah is restriction. It is the *will* to form, a discipline imposed on the pure force of Chokmah. At the same time it is the Great Sea from which life emerges, a concept implying a primordial unconscious. Water had always been viewed by poets and philosophers as harboring the deepest mysteries of our existence. Indeed, in the Mundane Chakra, theories of evolution propose that life, as we know it, may have emerged from the sea.

The image of dark and deep waters is a very profound one which, as it rises in our consciousness, cannot help but affect us in some curious way. As the Golden Dawn knowledge lecture states: "In Binah is a thick darkness which yet veileth the Divine Glory in which all colours are hidden, wherein is mystery and depth and silence, and yet it is the habitation of the Supernal Light." In this sense, Binah is described as the Outer Robe of Concealment, an idea which might most readily be understood by considering the extent to which our physical forms conceal our inner realities from others.

In the sense that Binah is the giver of life, she is the Bright Fertile Mother. But in the sense that she restricts and disciplines (in effect, is the first lawgiver), she is called the Dark Sterile Mother. This duality is also found in Yesod (the Moon), which reflects the light of the Sun into Malkuth. The Moon is represented both by *Diana* and by *Hecate*. One is the obverse of the other, bright and dark.

Throughout the Sephiroth and the Paths, the qualities of Binah and Chokmah are given different names, depending on their degree of density, i.e., their placement on the Tree of Life relative to its completion in Malkuth. Thus, we may speak of Isis in Binah, or on the Path of *The Empress* or *The High Priestess* Or we may discuss Venus, Diana, Hecate, or even Ceres in other Sephiroth, knowing that these are aspects of the same Divine Energy. The *Jah* of Chokmah and the *Jehovah Elohim* of Binah wear many robes throughout the Universe.

One of the most important attributions of Binah is *Chronos,* oldest of the Gods and called "Father Time." The concept of time is highly restrictive, and appropriately related to Binah. Time measures the process of aging, the migration from birth through life, toward death, which is the ultimate result of the gift of life which passes through Binah.

Binah, Understanding, is called the *Sanctifying Intelligence,* and the "Parent of Faith." It may be taken to represent the structure underlying established religion of any sect, without which a "church" could not exist. Students of the history of art may recall the iconographic theme where the Mother Mary is shown as a large figure within a church, but where it is understood that Mary is the church, in all of its organization, structure and sanctity.

But Binah is called the "Parent of Faith," rather than faith itself which is belief. Binah is the discipline of organization behind faith. Reason, science and intellectuality, all disciplines of organization, are the fullest development of the Binah energy, found in Hod at the base of the Pillar of Severity. Intuition, feeling and artistic creativity are the ultimate product of the energy of Chokmah, found in Netzach at the base of the Pillar of Mercy.

The Threes

The Four Threes, generally, represent the realization of action owing to the Prince having been produced. The central symbol on each card. Action definitely commenced for good or evil.

THREE OF WANDS, Lord of Established Strength (Sun in Aries).
Angels of the Decan: Hechashiah (הההשיה) and Aamamiah (עממיה).
This is Binah in Atziluth, the influence of Binah in the World of Pure Spirit. The three crossed wands on the card means the balance of Chokmah and Binah which has given forth Tiphareth (the Queen has given birth to the Prince, and growth begins), shown by Crowley as the blossoming of the Lotus. Astrologically, the entrance of the Sun into Aries heralds the Spring. The Sun illuminates Aries, the sign of Cardinal Fire, ruled by Mars. The result is great strength in individual expression, but also egocentricity which may manifest as pride and conceit. Waite's card shows the divinatory meaning of *Established force, pride and arrogance, power sometimes.*

THREE OF CUPS, Lord of Abundance (Mercury in Cancer).
Angels of the Decan: Rahael (ראהאל) and Yebomayah (יבמיה) .

This is Binah in Briah, the influence of Binah in the mental world. Cancer is under the rulership of the Moon, and is Cardinal Water. It is, thus, in perfect affinity with Binah. The gifts of Mercury overflow in this sign, as is indicated by the rushing water crossing the stems of the lotuses of the Golden Dawn card in a way suggestive of a caduceus. Crowley modifies this theme of water flowing from dual lotuses. The water in his card arises from one single lotus, "the dark calm sea characteristic of Binah."[74] His cups are pomegranates, the fruit of Persephone to whom, with Demeter, the card is attributed.

To represent the meaning of *plenty, hospitality, abundance, etc.,* Waite uses a motif of three dancers (the Graces) popularized during the Renaissance.

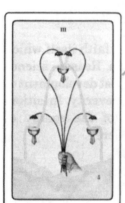

THREE OF SWORDS, Lord of Sorrow (Saturn in Libra). *Angels of the Decan:* Harayel (הרהאל) and Hoqmiah (הקמיה).

This is Binah in Yetzirah, the influence of Binah in the Astral World. Saturn is a very powerful planet, sometimes called "The Great Destroyer," and sometimes "The Great Initiator." Its presence usually means pain and hardship but this should not be taken as evil. It is through suffering, and through encounter with the *Dark Sterile Mother* that we learn life's most important lessons. Saturn throws the scales of Libra off balance in order that they may be rebalanced in a better way. Waite's card of *unhappiness and sorrow* shows a heart pierced by three, swords, while the Golden Dawn swords tear apart the Rose of five Petals as does Crowley's version.

THREE OF PENTACLES, Lord of Material Works (Mars in Capricorn). *Angels of the Decan:* Yechevah (יחוה) and Lehachiah (ליהחיה).

This is Binah is Assiah, the influence of Binah in the material world. The effect of Mars on the earth sign Capricorn is to bring great control and discipline, in material things. The idea of *employment, business, constructive building* is

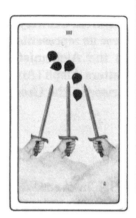  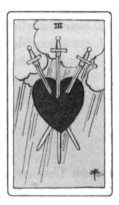 

shown by Waite as a medieval artisan at work in a church. Crowley's card shows material manifestation based on the pattern of three as represented in various symbol systems: Mercury, Sulphur and Salt to the Alchemists; Sattvas, Rajas and Tamas to the Hindus, and the maternal letters Aleph (Air), Mem (Water) and Shin (Fire) in the Qabalah. The pyramid arises in the Great Sea which is Binah.

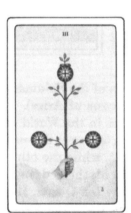   

The Queens

Are seated upon Thrones, representing the Forces of Heh *in the Divine Name of each suit, the Mother, and bringer forth of material Force, a Force which develops and realizes the Force of the King. A Force steady and unshaken, but not rapid though enduring. It is therefore symbolized by a figure seated upon a Throne, but also clothed in armour.*

QUEEN OF WANDS, Queen of the Thrones of Flame, Queen of the Salamanders or Salamandrines (Last Decan of Pisces—first two Decans of Aries).

The Queen of Wands is Water of Fire, Specific Water in the World of Primal Fire. Both the Golden Dawn and Crowley cards show a Queen enthroned above steady flames. In one hand she carries the Fire wand, while the other rests on the head of a leopard, also the symbol of her crest in Mathers' design. This animal represents the extreme ferocity of Fire tamed by the Queen. Her hand on the animal's head shows the power under her control; the wand shows that she is able to direct this force. And here we recall that the wand is also a symbol of the will.

Waite's card appears to stress the warmth and attractiveness of this Queen when she is well-aspected, while also suggesting that she has the potential for violence and tyranny.

QUEEN OF CUPS, Queen of the Thrones of the Waters, Queen of Nymphs and Undines (Last Decan of Gemini-first two Decans of Cancer).

The Queen of Cups is Water of Water, Specific Water in the World of Primal Water. In the Golden Dawn version her right hand holds a cup from which a crayfish emerges, while her left hand rests a lotus upon the head of an ibis. Crowley's card is an abstraction of the same symbols.

The Crayfish relates to the Moon.[75] In fact, one of the characteristics of this totally watery card is that its flow changes according to the influences around it, more so than other cards of the deck. The Ibis is a bird traditionally associated with Thoth-Hermes who is, in one aspect, the Moon God.[76] In mythology the bird eats the eggs of the snake (a reference here to Chokmah) and the corpses of the dead. Thus, in the Water aspect of Binah is the reference to the Great Sea from which life flows out, but which also flows inward in death. The lotus, which has been equated with the rose itself, is sacred to Isis, the Great Mother. It is, thus, through the intermediary of the lotus (rather than a direct touch of the hand) that the Great Mother causes the ibis to do its work. But this is a card as tranquil as the waters flowing before the Queens on the three modern versions. These waters, on which lotuses float, are a means of *transmission* of forces.

QUEEN OF SWORDS, Queen of the Thrones of Air, Queen of the Sylphs and Sylphides (Last Decan of Virgo-first two Decans of Libra).

The Queen of Swords is Water of Air, Specific Water in Primal Air.

The Marseilles and Waite versions are tame compared to those of the Golden Dawn and Crowley. In these latter cards, the image of a head, newly severed by the sword of the Queen, is undoubtedly the most gruesome to appear in any Tarot deck. The Golden Dawn papers do not elaborate on this symbolism, which may seem oddly placed with the crest, a winged child's head. Crowley, however, explains this image as the "clear, conscious perception of Idea, the Liberator of

the Mind."[77] As Yetzirah is the realm of deception, we are to understand that keen observation and perception are the sword which protects us, slicing away all fantasy and unreality. The child alone is innocent and unfettered by sterile concepts and useless ideas. It is the very head of man, the thinking center, which is severed. The principles of the *Queen of Swords* relate to the ways in which we are deceived by thought, and teach us how to transcend it.

QUEEN OF PENTACLES, Queen of the Thrones of the Earth, Queen of the Gnomes (Last Decan of Sagittarius-first two Decans of Capricorn).

The Queen of Pentacles is Water of Earth, Specific Water in the World of Primal Earth. In all versions of this card she holds a symbol of her rulership over earth. In the Golden Dawn card she also holds a sceptre topped by a cube, a six-sided solid referring to the Altar of the Mysteries. She is the uppermost part of this altar (a double cube), the base being the *Princess of Pentacles*. Mathers, Crowley and Waite all agreed that the goat was the appropriate animal symbol for this card because it represents Capricorn.

DAATH: KNOWLEDGE

Daath is called the "Invisible Sephira" in that it does not appear in any representation of the Tree of Life. And, in terms of pure Qabalistic doctrine, it is not actually a Sephira at all. As the *Sepher Yetzirah* states: "Ten is the number of the ineffable Sephiroth, ten and not nine, ten and not eleven."

But an experience of what is called Daath is required to cross the *Abyss,* the great gulf between the Supernal Triangle and all beneath. This is the area of demarcation between *Macroprosopus* and *Microprosopus,* the potential and the actual.

The important idea associated with the Abyss is that there is a vital and distinct separation between the energies of the Supernal Triangle and the seven Sephiroth beneath it. Kether, Chokmah and Binah are totally abstract, and beyond comprehension. Through the meditation of Binah, the energy of Chokmah pours across the Abyss and becomes a realized pattern in Chesed. But again, the Abyss symbolizes the vast separation between the creators and the created. The Supernals are potential separated from their realization by a chasm bridged by Daath.

It is said that the level of Daath is as far as the Higher Self can rise, which requires a definition of terms. Students of the mystical arts often describe a simple dichotomy between the Personality in Incarnation and the Higher Self which controls and directs its personality projections through various incarnations. Strictly speaking, however, the make-up of the individual is quadripartite, and an even more pure form of energy directs and controls the Higher Self.

First there is our *Material Body* (Assiah), then the conscious mind, which is the *Personality* (Yetzirah), then the *Higher Self,* the unconscious (Briah) and finally there is the *Essential Spirit,* the Primal Life Spark (Atziluth).

On the single Tree of Life, The Essential Spirit refers to Kether. The Higher Self, one aspect of which is called the *Holy Guardian Angel* to underscore its protective capacity for the Personality in incarnation, is referred to Chesed, Geburah and Tiphareth.

The Personality, created anew for each specific incarnation, belongs to Netzach, Hod, and Yesod. This is the normal waking consciousness, and the aspect of the individual which must be put in perfect balance before it can directly contact the Higher Self (the ultimate intent of initiatory rituals or meditative work). The physical vehicle is in Malkuth.

When the perfect balance of the elements of the Personality has occurred, the Light of Tiphareth can descend into the lower Temple of Self, and bring a new level of consciousness. This is the "Knowledge and Conversation of the Holy Guardian Angel." The experience is known as "adepthood" or "enlightenment," and it is the introduction to Inner Truth which may ultimately lead to the greater initiation of the Essential Spirit above the Abyss. To pass through Daath, and the Abyss, means to wilfully relinquish the powers of adepthood which one has earned, an experience which has been described as a more over-whelming and solitary one than human imagination can conceive.

It will be noted that the *Path of the Flaming Sword,* the zig-zag in which the Sephiroth were sequentially emanated, has no path directly connecting to Binah and Chesed. The adept, aspiring to union with the Divine, must leap across it, fearlessly and unaided, creating for himself the transition of Daath.

4. Chesed: Mercy
The Four Fours

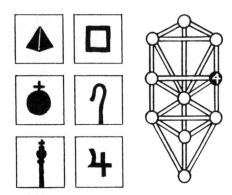

◆ The Builder
◆ The Framework of Manifestation
◆ The Loving Father who is
          King
◆ The Receptacle of All Powers
◆ The Kindly Shepherd

Symbols: The Pyramid, The Square, the Orb and Equal-armed Cross, the Crook, the Sceptre.
Planet: Jupiter
Color: Blue

> *In Chokmah is the Radix of blue and thence is there a blue color pure and primitive, and glistening with a spiritual Light which is reflected into* Chesed. *And the Sphere of its Operation is called* Tzedek *or Justice and it fashioneth the images of material things, bestowing peace and mercy; and it ruleth the sphere of the action of the planet Jupiter. And* Al *is the title of a God strong and mighty, ruling in Glory, Magnificence and Grace. And the Archangel of* Chesed *is* Tsadkiel, *the Prince of Mercy and Beneficence, and the Name of the Order of Angels is* Chasmalim, *Brilliant Ones, who are also called the Order of Dominions or Dominations. The Sephira* Chesed *is also called Gedulah or Magnificence and Glory.*

Chesed is the first Sephira below the Abyss, and the first of the six Sephiroth making up Microprosopus, the seventh Sephira, Malkuth, being the "Bride of Microprosopus."

Chesed is the *Demiurge* (the Lesser Creator) which is actually the power described in the Book of *Genesis.* The first part of that book describes not the origin of Kether out of the Unmanifest, but the origin of Microprosopus, from the *Elohim* of Binah, in Chesed. The formless and void darkness of the Supernal Triangle gives rise to manifestation, which is *form* and *light.* There is no light in

Binah, only a "thick darkness," nor is there form, only what we have called the "will to form."

In Chesed is found the beginning of manifestation, the externalization of the combined potencies of the Supernals. It is the initial urge toward material structure as we know it and, as such, is the administrator of the Laws first proposed by Binah. Chesed is Chokmah on a lower arc, from which emanated the pure form of Binah. As evolution proceeds toward Chesed, across the Abyss, and back to the Pillar of Mercy, the positive impetus of that Pillar acts on the energies of Binah (The Divine Energy of Kether is externally modified and transformed through the various stages of the Tree of Life). This may help to explain the attribution of male deities to the "female" side of the Tree of Life, and *vice versa.* To reiterate: as Chesed emanates, it must now deal with the form which was created by Binah, and it does so in terms of the positive qualities of the Pillar of Mercy. There is a good analogy in the *Emerald Tablet of Hermes Trismegistus,* which describes the action of various energies on what it calls the *One Thing.* God so arranges that the Father of this One Thing is the Sun, its Mother is the Moon; it is carried in the Belly of the Wind, and nursed by the Earth. The pattern of Sun (Fire), Moon (Water), Wind (Air) and Earth is clear. To truly understand the Tree of Life, we must constantly remember that we are dealing with multiplicity in unity.

The One Thing evolves from Sephira to Sephira across the Tree of Life. As the Tablet continues: "It ascends from the Earth up to Heaven, and descends again, newborn, on the Earth, and the Superior and the Inferior are increased in Power." What is described here is the constant renewing effect of the Ain Soph, which stimulates birth, death and rebirth on an increasingly higher and more powerful level.

As Binah is best understood in its relationship to Chokmah, so Chesed must be studied as the equal and opposite of Geburah. In the swing of energies back and forth on the Tree of Life, Chesed builds up (anabolism) on the principles proposed by Binah, while Geburah tears down (catabolism) reflecting the dynamism of Chokmah. The Tree works in cross-patterns.

Chesed is Mercy. Geburah is Strength. They are the two arms of the man, one which gives, and the other which takes away. Chesed, related to Jupiter, is a Mighty King. He is the kindly and benevolent ruler. Geburah, related to Mars, is also a king, but he sits in a chariot, armed for battle.

The text of the *Thirty-Two Paths of Wisdom* describes Chesed as containing all the Holy Powers meaning, again, that it is the first of a new sequence and is related to Kether by its primacy in another order. The image of a mighty and loving ruler conveys the idea that it is a potency which guides and controls the course of manifestation. It establishes the underlying framework on which matter is built. It is the realm of the *archetypes* described by Plato in the ninth book of his *Republic,* and the various symbols of Chesed make suggestions about the function and purpose of these archetypes.

The first is the *Pyramid,* a tetrahedron used as a building form by the society which gave us the first monumental stone architecture. It brings together four sides, each of which point upwards. Energy flows down from above, and is spread equally through each of the sides. Thus does Chesed contain all the Holy Powers. It is renewed manifestation of the *Four,* encountered first in the Primordial Elements of Kether, and establishes the archetypal pattern for matter fully expressed in the subdivided elements of Malkuth. Moreover, we recall the pentagram as the symbol of perfected mankind, having four lower elemental points and the upper point of Spirit which is a directing force, once the Elements are in balance. The principle of the pyramid is the same, and amplifies the text which describes Chesed as "measuring and cohesive," as well as "receptacular," meaning that it is a receptacle for the Higher Powers.

In line with the aspects of rulership, to Chesed are also assigned the *sceptre* an the *orb.* Both are found in various cards of the Tarot deck. The sceptre is phallic and relates to Chokmah, while the orb represents aspects of Binah. It also suggests the rulership of the Four Kerubim, first found in Kether, over the manifest kingdom of Microprosopus, formed by Chesed and the next five Sephiroth.

The final symbol of Chesed is less obvious than the others. This is the crook of a shepherd, or a bishop in his role as the pastoral shepherd. Another title for Chesed is *Love,* which in this case means the love of the ruler for his subjects, or the shepherd for his flock. The crook is also found in *The Hierophant,* the card of organized religion, which should be carefully studied in terms of this Chesed symbolism.

Those familiar with Dion Fortune's work will be aware that she related the "masters" to Chesed. Fortune, Bailey and others, have written of such masters as human beings evolved beyond the need for earthly incarnation, remaining by choice to assist the spiritual development of mankind.[78]

The Fours

Perfection, realization, completion, making a matter settled and fixed.

FOUR OF WANDS, Lord of Perfected Work (Venus in Aries).
Angels of the Decan: Nanael (ננאאל) and Nithal (ניתאל)

This is Chesed in Atziluth, the influence of Chesed in the World of Pure Spirit. Here Venus, the planet of love and luxury, is activated by the Mars energies of Aries. If this placement were to occur in an astrological reading it could mean a brief romance, or warm but fleeting feelings of some sort. But this is not the precise meaning of Venus in Aries on the *Four of Wands.* There are, in fact, a number of cards where the meaning of Planets in Signs differs from that commonly accepted, because the card combines Sephirothic and astrological symbolism.

It must be kept in mind that *the Zodiac is the Mundane Chakra of Chokmah; it appears in the lowest of the Four Worlds.* The cards represent the totality of that to which the Signs of the Zodiac refer. Venus in Aries is the outer attribute of the card. The greater meaning is the Chesed energy, the pure four in the world of Yod-Fire. It is, therefore, a perfection, a completion of the process initiated by the Supernals.

Crowley uses a very interesting device here, which is the crossing of four wands, each of which carries the head of the ram (Aries) and the dove (Venus). Waite's card is also a play on the wands, using them as the support for a garland-canopy. This illustrates the card's meaning of *perfected work, settlement and rest after labor.*

FOUR OF CUPS, Lord of Blended Pleasure *(Moon in Cancer).*
Angels of the Decan: Hayayel (הייאל) and Mevamayah (מומיה).

This is Chesed in Briah, the influence of Chesed in the unconscious mental realm. The moon naturally rules Cancer, and here its alternating flow is mitigated. It is a card of pleasure, but with reservations: in the Golden Dawn and Crowley cards all of the cups hold water, but the uppermost ones overflow, while those beneath do not, suggesting pleasure coming to an end. The energies of this card are very passive, almost indifferent as Waite's seated figure indicates. The meaning in divination is *blended pleasure and success, receiving pleasure but mixed with some slight discomfort and anxieties.*

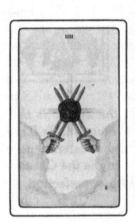   

FOUR OF SWORDS, Lord of Rest from Strife (Jupiter in Libra).
Angels of the Decan: Leviah (לאויה) and Kelial (כליאל).

This is Chesed in Yetzirah, the influence of Chesed in the Astral World. Swords are generally destructive, but here the love and munificence of Jupiter triumphs over the cutting qualities of Primal Air and the Golden Dawn rose (as in the Chokmah card, *Two of Swords*) is restored. Thus, *rest from strife is* the meaning of the card. The position of Jupiter in Libra is compassionate and sensitive, often having religious overtones as are seen in the Waite card. There a Christ figure is shown, in stained glass, above a resting knight.

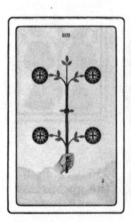 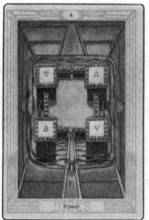  

FOUR OF PENTACLES, Lord of Earthly Power (Sun in Capricorn).
Angels of the Decan: Keveqiah (קוקיה) and Mendial (מנדאל).

This is Chesed in Assiah, the material world. It is the fullest expression, the grounding, of the Chesed energies. Thus Crowley says that this card is like a "fortress."[79] His card shows "Law and Order, maintained by constant authority and vigilance," each of the four Elements being held in balance.

The divinatory meaning comes from the position of the Sun in Capricorn which, with its light and warmth assures material success, but nothing beyond the moment. Waite illustrates this condition of *assured material gain,* and *earthly power completed but nothing beyond.*

5. Geburah: Strength
The Four Fives

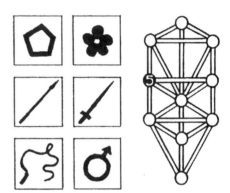

◈   The Destroyer
◈   The Warrior King
◈   The Power of Judgment
◈   The Clarifier
◈   The Eliminator of the
       Useless

> *Symbols:* The Pentagon, The
>   Tudor Rose of Five Petals,
>   the Sword, the Spear, The Scourge.
> *Planet:* Mars
> *Color:* Red

> *In Binah is the Radix of Red, and therein is there a red colour, pure and scintillating and flashing with flame which is reflected into* Geburah. *The Sphere of its operation is called* Madim *or violent rushing Force and it bringeth fortitude, and war and strength and slaughter, as it were, the flaming Sword of an avenging God. And it ruleth the Sphere of Action of the Planet Mars. And* Elohim Gibor *is the Elohim, Mighty and Terrible, judging and avenging evil, ruling in wrath and terror and storm, and at whose steps are lightning and flame. And its Archangel is* Kamael *the Prince of Strength and Courage, and the Name of the Order of Angels is* Seraphim *the Flaming Ones who are also called the Order of Powers. The Sephira Geburah is also called* Pachad, *Terror and Fear.*

Geburah is the perfect balance of Chesed. As Chesed builds up, Geburah tears down. As Chesed is loving and merciful, Geburah is terrible and demanding of due.

The fifth Sephira, called *Strength,* is often considered the most difficult Sephira to approach because its lessons may be so overwhelming and devastating. It offers a necessary corrective in our lives by tearing away all that is useless, undesirable or outdated. We see the action of Geburah in the fire sweeping a blighted and dried forest, in a war which tears down a diseased society, or in any situation in our lives where we are forced by circumstance to begin anew. Thus is Mars, the planet as well as the Roman God of War, attributed to Geburah.

Often the influence of Geburah is mistakenly considered evil, insofar as it brings destruction in one form or another. It is, however, a necessary and holy force in the Universe asserting, often painfully, a requisite balance. In the Tarot, for example, the *Fives* are all cards in some way connected with strife, the degree varying according to the World (Suit) in which they function. But strife and destruction on the mundane level always brings with it a learning experience. Who could say that they have experienced a truly difficult situation in which they have learned nothing?

Geburah is a strict discipline which is ultimately necessary and positive, and which serves well those who appreciate its virtue. It conveys the ability to judge clearly, as well as the willingness to be judged. This is described by the Hermetic axiom: "Watch the Watcher, Examine the Examiner, Judge the Judge." Without the warrior sentinel qualities of Geburah, the merciful Chesed qualities would overflow in an evil imbalance of force. And here we must reiterate that there is a constant interaction between the two Sephiroth, a flow and rhythm which is continual.

Dion Fortune points out that "The great weakness of Christianity lies in the fact that it ignores rhythm. It balances God with Devil instead of Vishnu with Siva. Its dualisms are antagonistic instead of equilibriating, and therefore can never issue in the functional third in which power is in equilibrium. Its God is the same yesterday, today, and forever, and does not evolve with an evolving creation, but indulges in one special creative act and rests on His Laurels."

In the Qabalistic system this rhythm is most dramatically seen in the pull between Chesed and Geburah, the left hand which giveth and the right hand which taketh away. The Golden Dawn required the initiation of Geburah, that of the *Adeptus Major* before that of Chesed. One must have learned perfect control before being trusted with the abundance of the Fourth Sephira. And here, the attribute deriving from the initiation of Geburah is *Power.*

In the sacred texts, Geburah is related to both Kether and Binah. It is like Kether (Unity) in that it is a source of great power flowing outward. It unites itself to Binah in that it tears down the hard structures first envisioned in Binah and then realized archetypally in Chesed. This is, in effect, an application of the death potential implicit in the birth through Binah. While the magical image, that of a bearded warrior in his chariot, is masculine, the primary qualities of Geburah are feminine. This idea is suggested by the attribution of the five-petaled rose to Geburah. The rose is the symbol of Venus, a Goddess closely associated with Mars. We shall see that the energies of the One are transmitted from Geburah through the Higher Self center of Tiphareth, into Netzach, to which Venus is assigned. Moreover, it should be noted that in *The Golden Dawn Tarot* the rose is represented on the two, three, four, five, seven and eight of Swords. The use of this rose, shown variously whole and hewn apart, is particularly brilliant symbolism on the part of MacGregor Mathers.

Any five-sided symbol may be related to Geburah, one of which is the *pentagon,* and another of which is the *pentagram.* The latter is used in invoking and banishing, and represents a potent regulation of force. It is only through the relentless self-discipline of Geburah that the Elemental points of the pentagram may be brought into perfect balance in the individual. This is a fitting symbol for that realm of the Tree directly above the (Tiphareth) experience of understanding the mutable nature of the Personality in incarnation. In Geburah is a certification that the true forces of the Individual are under control of the Spirit represented by the uppermost point of the pentagram, and an initiation into the actual nature of that Higher Self first encountered in Tiphareth. The experience has been described as a devastating immersion in the Fires of Truth, where all that is unworthy is burned away. It has also been described as a brutal silence of self-assessment.

The other symbols of Geburah are weapons. *The spear* represents a destruction which may be swift and complete, while the *scourge* and the *chain* suggest the continual application of great force. This is the difference between the compensating force which cuts away directly, and that which (as in meditation) is a slow acting and continuous discipline. The final symbol of Geburah is the *sword*, which bears special mention in that it is one of the "magical" instruments of the Order of the Golden Dawn. Beside the symbol of the four Elements (or Tarot suits), the Wand, Cup, Dagger and Pentacle, there are two additional weapons. These are the Lotus Wand and the Sword. While the Lotus Wand stands primarily for the Will, and relates to Kether, the Sword represents the great power exercised by the individual under perfect self-control. The strength of Geburah is his greatest weapon.

The Fives

> *Opposition, strife and struggle; war, obstacle to the thing in hand.*
> *Ultimate success or failure is otherwise shown.*

The fives bring serious problems into all areas symbolized by the Elements. To Wands (energy) the Fives bring quarrel and strife; to Cups (love, friendship) the Fives bring the destruction of relationships; to Swords (sickness and trouble) they bring certain defeat in a given matter and to Pentacles (business and money) they bring material hardship. Yet success or failure is shown by other cards in a divination. The Fives simply announce that a difficulty exists.

FIVE OF WANDS, Lord of Strife (Saturn in Leo).
Angels of the Decan: Vahaviah (והויה) and Yelayel (יליאל).
This is Geburah in Atziluth, the influence of Geburah in the World of Pure Spirit. Here the powerful effects of Saturn in Leo, a fire sign, are quarreling and strife. This card should be compared with the *Five of Swords*, the Lord of Defeat. The nature of Wands is a continually outpouring force, so the Saturn influence here is agitating and disturbing rather than signaling a contest completed. Crowley calls this a "volcanic energy."[80] His card shows the Golden Down wand of a Chief Adept crossed by the Phoenix Wand of the Adeptus Major of Geburah

and by the Lotus Wand of the Adeptus Minor of Tiphareth. This card symbolizes the nature of the energies rather than the condition of discord shown by Waite.

 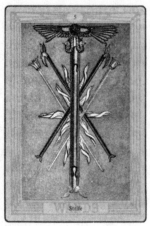  

FIVE OF CUPS, Lord of Loss in Pleasure (Mars in Scorpio).
Angels of the Decan: Livoyah (לוויה) and Pehilyah (פהליה) .

This is Geburah in Briah, the influence of Geburah in the Mental World. Mars in the water Sign Scorpio produces an extremely emotional effect. Loss of that which is loved is symbolized by the once-full cups on the Golden Dawn and Crowley cards, and by those overturned at the feet of Waite's solitary figure. The watery nature of this card is totally disconsonant with the fiery nature of Geburah, and means the loss of pleasure. This is also one of the cards which can mean death if the cards around it are supportive of this interpretation. It may mean the death of a loved one, not the querant himself.

One element of the Crowley card which may seem peculiar is the inverted pentagram, associated with the Devil and evil generally. It is used here to mean the triumph of matter over spirit.

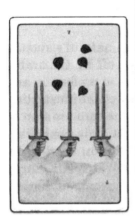   

FIVE OF SWORDS, Lord of Defeat (Venus in Aquarius).
Angels of the Decan: Aniel (אניאל) and Chaamiah (חעמיה).

   This is Geburah in Yetzirah, the influence of Geburah in the Astral
World. This card (with the *Nine* and *Ten of Swords*) is among the most
destructive in the deck. A relationship has already been noted between the
sword of Geburah and the rose of Venus which is also the rose of the Rose
Cross. They are closely related energies, Mars being the consort of Venus
in mythology. What we are shown in the Golden Dawn card is that when
the Sword of Geburah sweeps through the Air of Yetzirah, the growth energies of Venus are no match for it, and the petals of the rose are scattered, literally,
to the winds. Crowley's card shows this same dispersion of forces behind
the Swords in the shape of the inverted Pentagram. Waite illustrates the divinatory
meaning of the card: *defeat, loss, failure, contest finished and decided against
the person.*

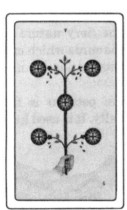 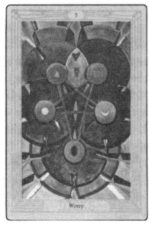  

FIVE OF PENTACLES, Lord of Material Trouble (Mercury in Taurus). *Angels of the Decan:* Mibahiah (מבהיה) and Pooyal (פיבאל).

This is Geburah in Assiah, the influence of Geburah in the Material World. Here a distinction should be understood between material trouble and the ruin of all things implied by the *Ten of Swords.* The natural structure brought into Taurus by the energies of Mercury is thrown off by Geburah's influence at a higher level. The result, in a divination, is loss of profession and monetary resources as is suggested by Waite's rather trite and cliché illustration of figures "out in the cold." The more subtle implications of the card are seen in the Golden Dawn version, where four roses are breaking apart. This symbolism is amplified by Crowley, whose once more inverted pentagram carries the symbols of the five *Tattvas,* geometric forms meaning Fire, Water, Air, Earth and Spirit. In the Hindu system, these are the underlying currents of matter, here shown to be totally unstable in their reversal.

6. Tiphareth: Beauty
The Four Sixes
The Four Princes

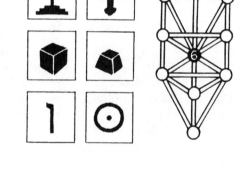

◈   God the Son
◈   The Sacrificed Gods
◈   Consciousness of the Higher
◈   Self and of the Greater Masters
◈   The Vision of the Harmony of
       Things
◈   Healing and Redemption
◈   The Elemental Kings

Symbols: The Calvary Cross,
    the Rose Cross, the Truncated
    Pyramid, the Cube, Vau.
Planet: The Sun
Color: Yellow

> *In Kether is the Radix of a Golden Glory and thence is there a pure, primitive and sparkling, gleaming golden yellow which is reflected into* Tiphareth. *This is the* first reflected Triad *completed. And the sphere of its operation is that of* Shemesh, *the Solar Light, and bestoweth Life, Light and Brilliancy in metallic matter, and it ruleth the sphere of action and of the Sun. And* YHVH Eloah va-Daath *is a God of Knowledge and Wisdom, ruling over the Light of the Universe; and its Archangel is* Raphael, *the Prince of Brightness, Beauty and Life. And the Name of the Order of Angels is* Melechim, *that is Kings or Angelic Kings, who are also called the Order of Virtues, Angels and Rulers.*

The initiation of Tiphareth is the first of the greater initiations into the meaning of the Self. Here the individual encounters his or her own Higher Self, and *sacrifices* the Personality, that which was hitherto believed to be the true self. And while this description may appear glib, the initiation of Tiphareth is literally a losing of what one has known to be life, a sacrifice of that life for a greater reality. This is the real meaning of the passage: "For whosoever shall save his life shall lose it; and whosoever will lose his life for my sake shall find it."[81]

A sacrifice, in these terms does not mean the relinquishment of something much desired, rather, it is the "translation of force from one form to another." This is a translation of force directed by the will.

Once more, nothing on the Tree of Life is static. God grows, unlike exoteric Christianity where, at its most primitive fundamentalist level, existence is viewed as a simple dichotomy between good and evil, the Qabalah describes a Universal Energy (The One) which goes through varying conditions. We, ourselves, through a natural process of evolution, become different Gods in turn, and sacrifice one principle to another.

Tiphareth is the center of the Tree of Life and, as such, is called the "Mediating Intelligence." The powers of all the other Sephiroth flow into it, where they stand balanced and sanctified. The vision of Tiphareth is of the Universal Harmony, a vision also linked to its nature as a healing center where all is brought into harmonious inter working. It is the center, also, of the planets. In the Hexagram, each of the six points represents a planet (and a planetary Sephira), with the Sun at the middle of the figure (Figure 16).

Tiphareth is the light of the soul, on which the life of the soul depends. In the same way, the physical manifestation of Tiphareth, the Sun, provides the light and life support for the earth.

Throughout all serious esoteric writings, the term *light* repeatedly appears, and it may seem that this is a metaphor about the spiritual condition. But reference to light is not metaphorical; it is descriptive. Those with even minimal experience of the inner worlds will attest to the fact that much of the inspired literature of the East and West, interpreted by theologians as merely symbol, is a strikingly accurate description of spiritual experience.

The search for direct experience of this Light is the "Great Work" of the Personality in incarnation, and devotion to the Great Work is the virtue assigned to Tiphareth. The principle involved is that when the individual person improves in some way, that improvement works to the benefit of the entire human race. Moreover, as it was put by the Egyptian astronomer Ptolemy, in his *Centiloquy:* "A sagacious mind improves the operation of the heavens as a skillful farmer, by cultivation, improves nature."[82] Ultimately, the Great Work is the work of return to the Godhead from which the Universe emanated.

To deal with the mysteries of Tiphareth, one must first have undergone the initiations of Earth, Air, Water and Fire (Malkuth, Yesod, Hod and Netzach, respectively). No matter how a religious or esoteric *cultus,* whether Christianity, Buddhism or Qabalism, may describe the various component parts of the

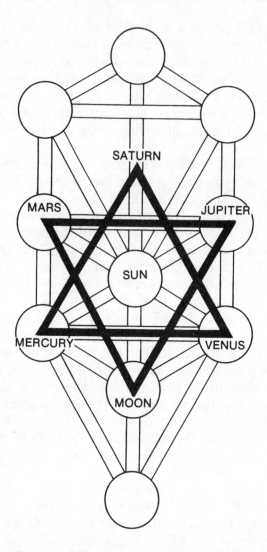

Figure 16. Attribution of Planets to the Hexagram. Planetary angles are
attributed according to the Tree of Life. The *Supernals* are represented
by Saturn, which is related to Binah.

Personality, or the initiation of the four lower Sephiroth, an integration must be
undergone before the descent of the Light which is God the Son. This integration is a personal "atonement" for the *Fall*. In Tiphareth is the *Redemption*.

As the Spirit in Tiphareth is King over the four Elemental aspects which
are the Personality, so the rulers of the actual Elemental Kingdoms of Earth, Air,
Water and Fire are found in Tiphareth. These are the *Malachim*, Elementals
who are Kings over the other Elements because they have gained immortality.
This occurs only through the intervention of human beings. Man is, in fact, the
initiator of the Elementals.

There is another very common biblical reference which takes on an extraordinary meaning when interpreted in Qabalistic terms: "Except ye be converted and become as little children, ye shall not enter into the kingdom of heaven."[83] Entering the Divine Light of Tiphareth is a renewal, a "conversion," or a "turning around," as the Greek word is often translated. The result of the experience is to become a child in a new world. So, *The Child* (which will, by definition grow into manhood within the new experience) is attributed to Tiphareth. Tiphareth is the Child who grows to adulthood and takes Malkuth (our material earth) as his bride. At the same time, Chokmah and Binah themselves were produced by the will of the Eternal Father in Kether. Thus Tiphareth, on the Middle Pillar, the Pillar of Equilibrium, is God the Son.

Readers who encountered this idea for the first time, as it related to the Court cards in *An Introduction to the Golden Dawn Tarot,* may have found it an appealing fairy tale: The King and Queen marry and give birth to a Prince, who marries the Princess, etc. But this is not mere fancy, it is an anthropomorphic symbolism explaining the operation of the יהוה wherever it appears. Tiphareth is the Prince, the Vau, of the formula.

But Tiphareth is also the realm of the Sacrificed Gods, Christ, Buddha, Osiris and others. So we understand that the Prince must die in order that the Universal Cycle be renewed.

There are a number of key symbols related to Tiphareth, of which the first is a figure based on *six.* This is the *cube,* a form taken twice-over in the double cube altar of Malkuth. Another six-sided figure, attributed to the Sephira, is the *pyramid which is truncated* or, in essence, has its top cut off. This pyramid represents Adam Kadmon, the six lower Sephiroth. It is the Archetypal Man, above whom are the Heavenly Supernals, Binah, Chokmah and Kether. The Supernals are the completion of the pyramid.

Another important Tiphareth symbol is the *Calvary Cross,* properly shown as black, surrounded by a circle, and mounted on three steps. This is the Cross of Wisdom through Sacrifice. *The Rose Cross* and *Rose Cross Lamen* are also powerful Tiphareth symbols.

The Sixes

Definite accomplishment and carrying out of a matter.

The underlying characteristic of all of the sixes is success which results from effort. In Atziluth, world of energy, this means victory. In Briah, world of pleasure, happiness is brought about after work to that end. In Yetzirah, world of quarreling and strife, success is earned by the strife itself. And in Assiah, world of business and commerce among mankind, this means material success.

SIX OF WANDS, Lord of Victory (Jupiter in Leo).
Angels of the Decan: Saitel (סיטאל) and Olmiah (עלמיה).

This is Tiphareth in Atziluth, the influence of Tiphareth in the World of Pure Spirit. The benevolence of Jupiter, in the fiery Sign Leo, brings success and possibly warm relationships. It is an aspect suggesting drama to some extent, and of victory which follows great effort. A perfect balance of powers is shown by the crossed wands which, in Crowley's card are those of the three adepts in Golden Dawn ritual. Waite emphasizes the idea of *victory after strife* with his mounted figure.

   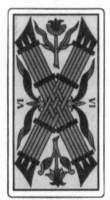

SIX OF CUPS, Lord of Pleasure (Sun in Scorpio).
Angels of the Decan: Nelokhiel (נלכאל) and Yeyayel (ייאל)

This is Tiphareth in Briah, the influence of Tiphareth in the Mental World. As Tiphareth in Atziluth means Victory after effort, so Tiphareth in the Watery world means the *beginning* of pleasure. Scorpio is a sign of hidden qualities, a sign of discrimination and magnetism. The scorpion may sting where the Will directs. So as the Sun activates the Scorpio energies, the gain or pleasure com-

   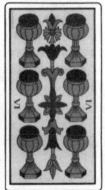

mences. There is the implication, though not the assurance, that it will build. The Golden Dawn and Crowley cards show partially-filled cups, while the Waite card suggests the beginning of pleasure by flowers emerging from the cups.

SIX OF SWORDS, Lord of Earned Success (Mercury in Aquarius).
Angels of the Decan: Rehaayal (רההעאל) and Yeyeziel (ייזאל).
This is Tiphareth in Yetzirah, the influence of Tiphareth in the Astral World. Saturn is the ruler of Aquarius, and here exerts its stabilizing power on the fleeting qualities of Mercury in that Air Sign. The success is the result of Saturn's work in this aspect. Thus the card is called the Lord of "Earned" Success. Here, again, the cutting qualities of swords are turned to positive advantage, and the Golden Dawn rose is resurrected after having been torn apart by the five warring swords of Geburah. In Golden Dawn symbolism, crossed swords are the positive power of Air. The swords which do not touch one another are the negative power of Air. And where the Swords come together and touch one another, or the rose, they may be positive or negative.

Crowley's card is particularly interesting in that the swords meet at the very center of a Rose Cross of six gold squares, which he explained, in grand nineteenth century terms, as meaning "the Rose Cross as the central secret of scientific truth."[84] Here again, the way of the Cross is that of suffering, which tends to underscore the meaning of this card as *success after anxiety and trouble.* The great difficulty with which reward is obtained is shown by Waite's boatman who carries souls across the River of Spirit.

SIX OF PENTACLES, Lord of Material Success (Moon in Taurus).
Angels of the Decan: Nemamiah (נממיה) and Yeyelal (יילאל)
This is Tiphareth in Assiah, the Material World. The changing qualities of the moon, its natural flow, its charm and subtleties, are merged with the hard work and deliberate earth qualities of Taurus. The result is sure success in business and other mundane areas.

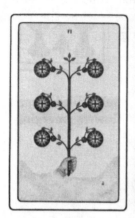

Only Crowley's card requires explanation. He has abstracted the hexagram around Tiphareth (refer again to Figure 16) with its planetary symbols, adding a central Rose-Cross of forty-nine (7 x 7) petals.

The Princes

> *These Princes are seated in chariots, and thus borne forward. They represent the* Vau *Forces of the Name in each suit; The Mighty Son of the King, and the Queen, who realizes the influences of both scales of Force; A prince, the son of a King and Queen, yet a Prince of Princes, and a King of Kings. An Emperor, whose effect is at once rapid (though not so swift as that of a King) and enduring (though not as steadfast as that of a Queen). It is therefore symbolized by a figure borne in a chariot, and clothed with armour. Yet is his power illusionary, unless set in motion by his Father and Mother.*

The Princes are very complex cards in that they are wholly activated by the King and Queen. As the text suggests, they have no motive power of their own, being pulled along in their chariots. But, from the standpoint of the enlightened Tarot, these cards are all-important. First, it will be seen that the lion, eagle, man (arch fairies here) and bull, are the Four Kerubim. These are very ancient symbols of the Elements, attached to many different religions. They appear among the Gods of the Assyrians; they are the four animals in the Old Testament vision of Ezekiel; they are the four symbols of the Christian Evangelists; they are the rulers of the Four Elements of the Qabalah. In Kether are the Primordial Elements, which become the united rulers of the Elements in Tiphareth, and which are individually expressed in Malkuth.

The Princes are the personified forces (Kings) of those elements brought into perfect balance in Tiphareth. If the cards are set out in a row—Wands,

Cups, Swords and Pentacles—the Golden Light of Spirit may be imagined as permeating the four, and directing the Kerubim to pull the chariots. These are the most refined aspects of the Personality; they are the Elemental Kings in ourselves. As such, the Princes may be taken in any direction by the Divine Will. The energy of the *Prince of Wands* may be applied with justice or with cruelty; the unconscious flow of the *Prince of Cups* may be subtle and artistic, or it may be very evil; the mental activities of the *Prince of Swords*, ideas, may be creative or destructive; the material qualities of the *Prince of Pentacles* may cause growth for good or evil.

The Princes may provide a point of entry for true understanding of the Tarot as a tool of enlightenment. And here the utility of the Princesses may also become clear, for they are the *grounding* of the lessons of the Princes on our material plane.

It will now be appreciated why the Princes, in a divination, often represent the coming and going of an event or person, and the Princesses often represent approval or disapproval of a matter.

PRINCE OF WANDS, Prince of the Chariot of Fire, Prince and Emperor of the Salamanders. (Last Decan of Cancer-first two Decans of Leo).

The Prince of Wands is Air of Fire, Specific Air of Primal Fire. In the Golden Dawn and Crowley cards, his chariot is drawn by the Lion of Leo, symbolizing enormous strength which may be turned in either direction, and which has the potential for violence if angered. In the Golden Dawn card the Prince holds the Elemental Fire Wand, while Crowley's Prince holds the Phoenix Wand associated with the fiery Sephira, Geburah.[85]

Generally, the Princes (Knights) in the Marseilles and Waite decks are unexceptional, and need not be discussed.

PRINCE OF CUPS, Prince of the Chariot of the Waters, Prince and Emperor of Nymphs and Undines (Last Decan of Libra—first two Decans of Scorpio).

The *Prince of Cups* is Air of Water, Specific Air of Primal Water. Here again, the Golden Dawn version is the inspiration for that of Crowley, both emphasizing the water lotus, and the serpent issuing from a cup. Wherever the serpent appears it is generally a reference to Chokmah, the Divine Wisdom, the Yod Force; here it has the fiery, menacing qualities of Scorpio. The cup, held by the Prince, is Heh, and encloses the Yod-Serpent. As Vau, the Prince carries out the activities of the Yod and Heh combined; here is Water. The chariot itself is pulled across the water by an eagle, water symbol among the four Kerubic emblems. At another level, the suggestion is that the calm appearance of water may hold violent and fiery energies, like sulfuric acid, which appears entirely benign until it has something upon which to act. Water symbolizes the personal, group, or universal Unconscious which bears dynamic energies.

PRINCE OF SWORDS, Prince of the Chariots of the Winds, Prince and Emperor of Sylphs and Sylphides (Last Decan of Capricorn -first two Decans of Aquarius).

The *Prince of Swords* is Air of Air, Specific Air of Primal Air. There is significant Yesod-moon symbolism here in that this is a card of mind. The dual fairies of the Golden Dawn card, and the three winged children of Crowley's card suggest that (like the mind itself) the chariot may be pulled capriciously in any direction. In the right hand of the Prince is the sword which invokes and creates, but in his left is the sickle which immediately destroys that which is created. In the Golden Dawn card the repeated pentagrams are a reference to the Sword of Geburah. But as the Prince's crest is a child's head with a pentagram on its forehead, we are told here that this Prince wields the sword with childlike innocence. This is an extension of the same symbolism found in the *Queen of Swords.*

PRINCE OF PENTACLES, Prince of the Chariot of Earth, Prince and Emperor of the Gnomes (Last Decan of Aries—first two Decan of Taurus).

The *Prince of Pentacles* is Air of Earth, Specific Air of Primal Earth. In the Golden Dawn card he holds a wand of earthly dominion in his right hand, and an inverted orb (material force grossly applied) in his left. The chariot is pulled by the powerful bull of Taurus. Crowley explained his version of this card in considerable depth, emphasizing the meditative qualities of the Prince. "He is," Crowley said, "the element of earth become intelligible."[86]

7. Netzach: Victory
The Four Sevens

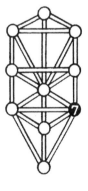

◈ Love
◈ Feelings and Instincts
◈ The Group Mind
◈ Nature
◈ The Arts

Symbols: The Girdle, The Rose, the Lamp.

Planet: Venus
Color: Green

> The beams of Chesed and Geburah meet in Netzach and thence in
> Netzach arises a green, pure, brilliant, liquid and gleaming like
> an emerald. And the Sphere of its operations is that of Nogah or
> External Splendour, producing zeal, love, harmony, and it ruleth
> the Sphere of Action of the Planet Venus and the nature of the
> Vegetable World. And Jehovah Tzabaoth is a God of Hosts and of
> Armies, of Triumph and of Victory, ruling the Universe in Justice
> and Eternity. And its Archangel Haniel is the Prince of Love and
> Harmony, and the Name of the Order of Angels is Elohim, or Gods
> who are also called the Order of Principalities.

Each of the Sephiroth on the Pillar of Mercy begins a sequence. Chokmah
is the primary force toward manifestation in the *Supernal Triangle.* Chesed is
the organizing idea behind the first form, and the first Sephira of the *Ethical
Triangle,* Netzach begins the *Astral Triangle,* and is the first of the Sephiroth
making up the Personality.

The Personality is viewed as being composed of four Elements, each of
which is represented by one of the lower Sephiroth. In this is a reflection of the
familiar יהוה formula, and of the familiar sequence of Fire, Water, Air and Earth.
These are the *Astral Elements.* Netzach is Fire, a lower form of the Yod-Fire
of Chokmah, reflected from Geburah through Tiphareth. Hod is Water, a lower form of the Heh-Water of Binah, reflected from Chesed through Tiphareth.
Yesod is Air and Malkuth is Earth. It will be noted that the final Heh of the
Divine Name is attributed to Malkuth in every instance, for this final Heh is the
result of the "Fall."

The attribution of the four Elements to these lower Sephiroth may appear to add one more frustrating complication to the Qabalistic system. But, in
fact, we have now reached the point on the Tree of Life where normal waking
consciousness may apply. It is with the Astral Triangle and the component parts
of the Personality, that any serious student may deal. The Order of the Golden
Dawn introduced its members to the Inner Planes through a system of *Tattva*
exercises, a sort of controlled "day dream" intended to bring the individual into
direct contact with the subtle Elemental realms immediately underlying the
material sphere of sensation. This method was considered preparatory to the
more advanced techniques of skrying with the Tarot cards, and to the most advanced and dangerous techniques of skrying with the squares of the Enochian
Tablets. Suffice it to say here that the astral realm, begun with Netzach, is the
realm of illusion *(maya).*

Netzach cannot be considered without Hod, its balance and opposite. For
as Netzach represents the instincts and emotions, Hod represents the intellect.
Feelings unchecked by reason, and reason unchecked by feelings, can be very
destructive. It is through the proper balance of feeling and reason that one is
able to rise, on the Middle Pillar, to the higher consciousness of Tiphareth.

Netzach is a particularly difficult Sephira to understand. This is partly because it represents the first undifferentiated projections of Tiphareth, and partly because it must be approached from the standpoints of both the Macrocosm and the Microcosm. When we deal with the Tree of Life, we are dealing both with the patterns of the human race, and with the patterns of the individual. But one of the lessons of the Mysteries is the extent to which this dichotomy is, in itself, an illusion.

On the one hand, Netzach is the undifferentiated Soul of Mankind, often described as the "Group Mind." The *spark* of the individual mind (appreciating again that this is described as a *fiery* Sephira) is a part of that group which, as it becomes self-comprehending, also comprehends the whole. For example, Netzach is the area on the Tree of Life to which the arts, music, painting, poetry, etc., are attributed. Every artist uses the qualities of Netzach, drawing his creative imagination from it (although to produce a serious work, that feeling must be tempered by the discipline of Hod-Reason). As the artist increasingly develops the ability to "create," and to understand the nature of the creative act, there also develops an understanding of the nature of the arts in general. The same may be said for a scientist, who functions through Hod, the Sephira where the general becomes specific.

The balance of Netzach and Hod may be shown in a simple diagram:

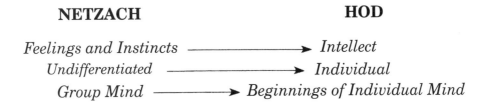

NETZACH		**HOD**
Feelings and Instincts	⟶	*Intellect*
Undifferentiated	⟶	*Individual*
Group Mind	⟶	*Beginnings of Individual Mind*

In view of this balance, it will be easily appreciated that Netzach is the Sephira to which the forces of nature are attributed, its angels being the *Elohim*. They are also called *Gods* in that they are so for the Personality in incarnation and for mankind as a race. They are the Gods of the lower sequence of the Tetragrammaton. Netzach is also the sphere of Venus-Aphrodite, the Goddess of Love. And as the title of the Sephira is *Victory*, it is to be understood that the Victory is in love.

What is called "love," particularly as it relates to Gods and religious systems, is often misunderstood. The misunderstanding has to do with the very nature of the Gods themselves. It has been said that "The Gods are the Creations of the Created...the Gods are emanations of the group mind of races; they are not emanations of Eheieh, the One and Eternal." The reference to the Group Mind states, in essence, that the Gods are of Netzach. This idea is graphically summed up in the diagram of the symbol of Venus, which encompasses the entire Tree of Life (Figure 17). It may also be recalled that the Order of the Golden Dawn declared itself to be under the rulership of Venus.

Figure 17. Venus on The Symbol of
the Tree of Life. This encompasses
all of the ten Sephiroth

The point here is that there are no Gods, save those potent forces
which we have formed in our own image, to serve our needs.
There is nothing but us. We are the above and the below of the
Emerald Tablet. We are at once, the many and the One. We are all
that is, though we draw our strength from the Divine Unmanifest
which is not. Thus, the manner in which we behave toward one another is of far
greater import than is generally appreciated. The love of one's fellow man, the
love of God, any sexual relationship which is a psychic balance and, in fact, any
balanced exchange of energy between individuals assists the race in the "Great
Work" of returning to the primal state from which it evolved. It is for this reason
that Netzach is described as a Sephira of polarities.

In Netzach we are considering a Sephira on the masculine pillar with
a female Goddess attached to it. However, the attribution of specific sexual
characteristics labeled "male" and "female" is appropriate only to our own sphere
of sensation. What is found in Netzach is the interplay of Mars and Venus. As
was previously discussed, Geburah has certain Venus qualities, symbolized by
the rose; Netzach has certain Mars qualities, indicated by the attribution of Fire.
Moreover, YHVH Tzabaoth, צבאות יהוה, is the God of Hosts and of Armies.

The relationship between Netzach and Geburah, and that of Hod and
Chesed may be slightly confusing when considered in terms of the emanation
of the Sephiroth on the Path of the Flaming Sword. That Path is important
in that it indicates both the sequence in which the Universe evolved, and the
course by which the seeker (save those who choose the devotional Path of the
Middle Pillar) may return. However, this does not represent the balance and
inter-relationships of energies on the completed Tree of Life.

There are three key symbols related to Netzach. These are the rose, the
girdle and the lamp. The rose is the most perfect of flowers, an attribute of Venus
often associated with love. The girdle, also, is a traditional Venus attribute. To
learn the secret of the knot in her girdle, means to direct the Venus forces of
nature, to tie them up, or to release them at will. The final symbol is the lamp,
the bearer of Fire, relating Netzach to Geburah and the powerful, warring,
forces of Mars. At another level, it is the ever-burning light of the Temple of the
Lower Self.

The Sevens

*Generally shows a force, transcending the material plane, and
is like unto a crown which is indeed powerful but requireth one
capable of wearing it. The sevens then show a positive result which
is dependant on the action then taken. They depend much on the
symbols that accompany them.*

 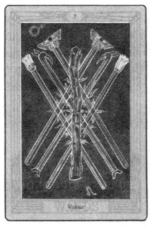  

SEVEN OF WANDS, Lord of Valor (Mars in Leo).
Angels of the Decan: Mahashiah (מהשיה) and Lelahel (ללהאל) .

This is Netzach in Atziluth, the influence of Netzach in the World of Pure Spirit. The position of Mars in Leo is one of courage and strength, but with threatening overtones: a fiery clash is certain, but victory in the fray is not.

It will be noted that the basic pattern was established with the Marseilles card which uses six crossed Wands and one central one. In adapting this design Crowley again uses the wands of the three Golden Dawn adepts, but crosses them with a very crude club to suggest that the battle in this card may be a disordered and disorganized one of uncertain results. Waite illustrates the idea of *opposition* and *possible victory, depending upon the amount of courage exercised.*

SEVEN OF CUPS, Lord of Illusory Success (Venus in Scorpio).
Angels of the Decan: Melchel (מלהאל) and Chahaviah (חהויה)

This is Netzach in Briah, the influence of Netzach in the Mental World. Venus in Scorpio is extremely intense and emotional, often involving deceit. Sometimes this is dissipation, a wallowing in emotions, or a self-deception. It can certainly be a card of egocentricity and selfishness. And, although the Golden Dawn card shows the cups to be completely empty, one might believe them to be full as Waite shows. Crowley, on the other hand, implies that there is a great warning in this card. His lotuses have become ugly and slimy, a perversion of the sacrament of his cup in *Six*, possibly brought about by the inflation of ego. Thus, the divinatory meaning of the card *is error, illusion and illusionary success.*

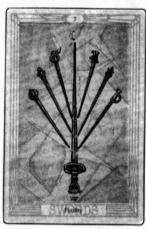

SEVEN OF SWORDS, Lord of Unstable Effort (Moon in Aquarius).
Angels of the Decan: Michael (מיכאל) and Hahihel (הההאל).
	This is Netzach in Yetzirah, the influence of Netzach in the Astral World. In the Golden Dawn card the Rose is restored, for it is a symbol primary to Venus, who rules Netzach. But the swords are precariously balanced against it, one against the other, an idea also expressed by Crowley's six planetary swords aimed against the larger one of the Sun. It is not entirely clear what is going on, particularly in the Waite card, which is genuinely enigmatic. And that is the point, for in divination this card means *unstable effort, vacillation* and *untrustworthy character.*
	The Moon in Aquarius indicates sociability, often religious inclination; the moon is less fluid and changeable here than in other positions. However, the balances which it establishes are precarious and easily upset.

SEVEN OF PENTACLES, Lord of Success unfulfilled (Saturn in Taurus). *Angels of the Decan:* Herochiel (הרחאל) and Mitzrael (מצראל).
	This is Netzach in Assiah, the influence of Netzach in the material world. As with the rest of the Sevens, there is very little good to be gained. Saturn in Taurus brings disappointment, and a great deal of work for little reward.

8. Hod: Splendor
The Four Eights

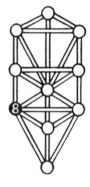

❖ Reason
❖ The Individual Mind
❖ Systems: Magic, Science
❖ Contact point of the Masters
❖ Language and Visual Images

Symbols: Names and Versicles, Apron.
Planet: Mercury
Color: Orange

> *The beams of* Geburah *and* Tiphareth *meet in* Hod *and thence arises in* Hod *a brilliant pure and flashing orange tawny. And the Sphere of its Operation is that of* Kokab, *the stellar light, bestowing elegance, swiftness, scientific knowledge and art, and constancy of speech, and it ruleth the sphere of the action of the planet Mercury. And* Elohim Tzabaoth *is also a God of Hosts and of Armies, of Mercy and Agreement, of Praise and Honour,, ruling the Universe in Wisdom and Harmony. And its Archangel is* Michael, *the Prince of Splendour and of Wisdom, and the Name of its order of Angels is* Beni Elohim, *or Sons of the Gods, who are also called the Order of Archangels.*

Hod is the concrete mind. It is the sphere of Mercury, and to it are attributed all that is intellectually systematized, such as the magical arts, literature, science and commerce.

It is at the base of the Pillar of Form beneath Binah, as Netzach is at the base of the Pillar of Force beneath Chokmah. And in these two lower Sephiroth is seen the same balance of form and force found in the Supernals. The difference is that this pattern is expressible in terms which can be conceptualized and understood by our minds. While in Chokmah and Binah it was necessary to speak in the most abstract and symbolic terms, such as the "idea of outpouring force," or "the idea of form which restricts force," we are now dealing with concepts which can be immediately understood in terms of the make-up of the individual Personality. The symbolism is closer to home. In the human Personality the Fire of Netzach is the animal intuition, while the Water of Hod is the concrete, rational, mind.

The Tarot, what Lévi romantically called the "*Book of Thoth*," is referred to Hod. Thoth (Egyptian), Hermes (Greek) and Mercury (Roman) are different names of the same God. Each is a messenger, patron of learning and teacher of the Mysteries. All language (a carrier of messages) relates to Hod.

In the Golden Dawn version of the tenth card of the Tarot, *The Wheel of Fortune*, the dog-headed ape at the bottom is *Cynocephalus,* companion of Thoth. It was also the Egyptian hieroglyphic symbol for writing. Cynocephalus related to the moon, as Thoth related to mercury. And in ancient astronomy the moon was believed to follow mercury like a faithful dog (note the dogs in all versions of *The Moon*, Key 18). By extension of this idea we understand that language is the faithful companion of the student of the Mysteries. Words of power are the greatest of human instruments.

This is the reason that *Names and Versicles* relate to Hod. It is not easy to persuade natural doubters that a word, properly vibrated, can have a powerful effect on the inner planes. Yet the effect of words on our own plane is obvious. Who can be indifferent to words such as "I love you," or "I hate you." But to be effective, words must have feeling behind them. In the same way that "I love you," or "I hate you" sound strange and empty unless expressed with emotion, the Words of Power of Hod are only effective when they are projected with the intense feelings of Netzach. In other words, the dynamic energy of Netzach is brought to bear through the vehicle of the words. This is the reason that so many fail in their attempts at ritual. Words alone will not suffice; the form of Hod is useless without the force of Netzach. And the reverse is also true.

Those who approach esoteric studies with great vitality and enthusiasm but lack the discipline of Hod are wasting their time. And those who fail to bring the intuition of Netzach to bear on the many words written about the inner sciences will quickly decide that the "Hermetic Mysteries" are pedantic and lifeless.

It is said that whosoever learns to pronounce the name of God, יהוה, will be master of the Universe. And when we see that the Qabalistic fourfold division encompasses many names (attributes of the *One),* each of which requires a different learning experience to "pronounce," the statement makes special sense. The names of the system are of Hod, but the beginning of the ability to properly use them is in Netzach, whose Gods encompass the whole Tree.

Form is limitation. It is restriction. There can be no form without a force which is in some way restricted. So found in Hod are the dynamic qualities of the Netzach force, which are limited in order that they can be dealt with through our normal process of thought. This limitation takes the *form* of both language and visual image, which are a far more interchangeable currency than some might believe. They are both sets of comprehensible symbols agreed upon by societies for the transmission of messages. We know that language is artificial and has no intrinsic qualities of its own. The same is true for visual images, such as the Sign of the Cross, the Tarot cards, or even what we perceive to be a tree on this earth. These are carriers of idea, which are neutral in themselves. For this reason, the *Hermaphrodite is* the magical image of Hod.

It is in Hod that the carriers of idea are separated out. In evolution, Hod completes the Pillar of Form. It is a stabilizing balance to the completion of Force, a balance which is modified in Yesod and emanates our material world in Malkuth. Hod and Netzach (like Geburah and Chesed) are effective only when their energies are actively merged in a third Sephira. In this case, we see the merger of Mercury (Hod) and Venus (Netzach) giving rise to the moon (Yesod).

The second major symbol of Hod, *the apron,* also refers to the moon, as does Thoth himself in one aspect. This apron is a traditional Masonic symbol. It is the symbol of the builder who is the craftsman of the Mysteries, and one which, when worn, covers the sexual organs attributed to Yesod. And, as we move to consider Yesod, we shall see the extent to which the manipulation of sexual energies is the basis of all practical work.

So, in the great scheme of return toward the Godhead from our material condition, Hod is a primary point, a point of conceptual transfer. Here the masters first contact their chosen disciples, clothing themselves in forms comprehensible to the human mind. Here are presented to the student the formal tools of the *Hermetic Path* (as opposed to the *Orphic Path* of Netzach, or the *Devotional Path* of the Middle Pillar).

All of this is a great deal less mysterious than it may seem. It may appear that to deal with Hod (or any other Sephira) means only the projection of oneself into this sphere, by ritual or meditative techniques. These are, of course, important. But we use the forces of Hod whenever we immerse ourselves in the documents of the Mysteries, or whenever we approach anything intellectually. The Sephiroth are integral parts of ourselves, in a state of constant activity. The principle of the practical Qabalah is that we turn our conscious attention toward a particular aspect of ourselves, and thereby gain access to the corresponding part of the greater Universe. As there are four hundred Trees of Life, we function consciously at the highest level which our spiritual development will allow.

One final point which must be made is that while Mercury is the teacher of the Mysteries he is also the God of deceit and trickery. One writer recently suggested that this aspect partly represents the "adaptability" required for esoteric work, and conferred by the Hod energies. But, as has been said, *the whole Astral realm seeks to deceive.* When we deal with the astral images, we do so with all of the perceptual vulnerability of our human minds. We are particularly susceptible to this in the alternately bright and murky sphere of Yesod. And it is in Hod that we begin to understand the mechanisms of our perceptions.

The Eights

Generally show solitary success; i.e., success in the matter for the time being, but not leading to much result apart from the thing itself.

  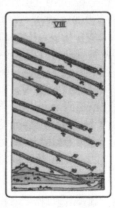 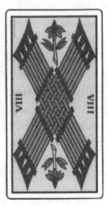

EIGHT OF WANDS, Lord of Swiftness (Mercury in Sagittarius).
Angels of the Decan: Nithahiah (נתהיה) and Haayah (האיה).
    This is Hod in Atziluth, the influence of Hod in the World of Pure Spirit. Mercury is not well placed here; it is in its detriment in Sagittarius. Its energies are mitigated and quickly expended in the Sign of the Archer, a phenomenon which Crowley has likened to electricity in his card. The divinatory meaning is *swiftness* or *rapidity*.

EIGHT OF CUPS, Lord of Abandoned Success (Saturn in Pisces).
Angels of the Decan: Vavaliah (וליה) and Yelahiah (ילהיה).
    This is Hod in Briah, the influence of Hod in the Mental World. Saturn in

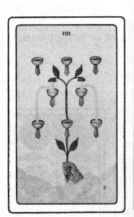 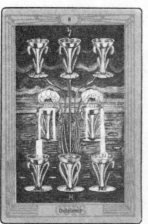  

the Water Sign Pisces brings about subtle problems, and a certain introspection which manifests as a sense of disinterest with the material condition. The effect of Water on Saturn is to produce discontent, the *abandoned success,* or *decline of interest in anything* which this card means. That idea is shown by Waite's figure which walks away from the cups.

 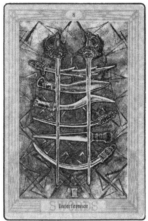  

EIGHT OF SWORDS, Lord of Shortened Force (Jupiter in Gemini).
Angels of *the Decan:* Vemibael (ומבאל) and Yehohel (יההאל).

This is Hod in Yetzirah, the influence of Hod in the Astral World. The weakness of Jupiter (expansiveness), here in its detriment, allows the natural dualities of Gemini to affect its positive energies. They are cut back or shortened, by desire to go first in one direction and then another. The application of Jupiter force in this sign may be erratic and unstable, or it may be intense and positive, though brief in duration. Crowley attempts to show this by making all eight swords different. Waite, on the other hand, illustrated the effect of this condition of energies: *shortened force, narrowness or restriction, a prison.*

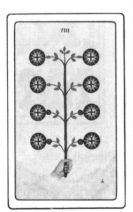   

EIGHT OF PENTACLES, Lord of Prudence (Sun in Virgo)
Angels of the Decan: Akaiah (אכאיה) and Kehethel (כהתאל) .

This is Hod in Assiah, the influence of Hod in the material World. The planetary aspect here is a very practical one which tends to cause concern with small details. Like the rest of the eights, any gain which may appear is limited, and "Prudence" is no great virtue. Waite's craftsman illustrates the meaning of the card in divination: *skill, prudence,* and *overcarefulness about small things, at the expense of the great.*

9. Yesod: The Foundation
The Four Nines

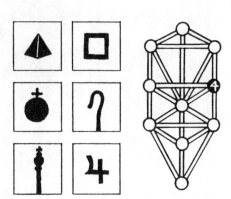

❖ The Astral Light
❖ The Storehouse of Images
❖ The Cyclic Energies underlying
          Matter

Symbols: The Perfume and Sandals
Planet: The Moon
Color: Violet

> *The beams of Chesed and Geburah meet in* Yesod, *and thence ariseth in* Yesod *a brilliant deep violet purple or puce, and thus is the third Triad completed. And the sphere of its operation is that of* Levanah, *the Lunar beam, bestowing change, increase and decrease upon created things and it ruleth the Sphere of Action of the Moon and the nature of mankind. And* Shaddai *is a God who sheddeth benefits, Omnipotent and Satisfying, and* Al Chai *is the God of Life, the Living One. Its Archangel is* Gabriel, *the Prince of Change and Alteration. And the name of the Order of Angels is* Kerubim *or Kerubic Ones who are also called the Order of Angels.*

As we approach the ninth Sephira what has previously been considered theoretically may become very practical. In Yesod are those energies, directly underlying the material world, which are manipulated in various forms of meditation and in what is called "magic." These currents are known as the *Astral Light* or *Akashic Fluid.* In the mid-nineteenth century Von Reichenbach, one of the first to attempt scientific investigation of psychic phenomenon, described this as the *odic force,*[87] a term still occasionally employed. Whatever this energy is called, it is an energy which each person has the capacity to experience and to profoundly develop. Everyone feels the presence of the Astral Light, though most dismiss it as a generalized neurological stimulation, attributable to some vague physical cause. It may be felt as an overall tingling sensation, or as a pervasive warmth often resulting from prayer or sexual stimulation. A few discover that this feeling can be intensified, and the energy made to move around the body at will.

This force is sexual, and it is seen that in Microprosopus Yesod covers the generative organs. Those who excite this force through meditation, prayer, sexual stimulation or ritual methods, do so using precisely the same mental mechanisms. It has been said that "God is sex," and the records of ecstatic union made by those such as Saint Theresa are highly erotic. When the Astral Light of Yesod, the sexual forces, are directed consciously, and circulated throughout the body as in the Qabalistic *Exercise of the Middle Pillar,* the effect can be overwhelming.

The Astral Light has often been described as an electrical, or magnetic current. Indeed, as one "brings down the Light," the effect is of one's body being highly charged. Yet this is an energy which is *plastic.* It is mentally malleable. Not only can it be circulated throughout the body, or projected in certain spiritual operations, but it is the raw material from which visual images are built on the Astral Plane.

Each individual has an *Etheric Body* (which leaves the physical body naturally in sleep, or is consciously projected by the adept), formed of the Astral Light. Thus, Yesod is termed the *Foundation.* It is that which activates the Four Elements of Malkuth, repeating a pattern seen throughout the entire Tree, beginning at Kether: four elements which are rooted in a fifth.

The energy of the Astral Light is, in the East, called *Kundalini* (the Serpent) and it is declared by Qabalists that "Kundalini is coiled in Yesod." It is not a difficult stretch of mind to the correct esoteric interpretation of the Serpent in the Garden of Eden, or to the meaning of the Serpent shown on the Tree of Life touching each and every Path. This is the same Serpent of Wisdom which holds its tail in its mouth.

One particularly appropriate aspect of the symbolism of the Serpent here is that the reptile moves by *undulations.* In the same way, the Astral Light weaves back and forth. It follows distinct cycles which underlie and activate the cycles of our physical existence. The phases of Yesod cause a continual motion of charge and discharge on the physical plane, expressed as light and dark, waking and sleeping, etc. Thus, it is truly said that one cannot deal with Malkuth without first understanding Yesod. And of course, by extension of this idea, one cannot deal with Yesod without first understanding Hod.

Parenthetically, it is to Yesod that parapsychological research is directed, since it is possible to use some of the current tools of science to quantify its effect on the sensory plane. Those who work in this area of research have found it necessary to at least postulate the existence of some force like the Astral Light, as an explanation of the ways in which wonders such as *psychokinesis* (the ability to move objects mentally) are accomplished.

The moon is the "Planet" (so described by ancient astronomy) attributed to Yesod. As it waxes and wanes, it is said to control the motion of the tides. And the supposed disorienting effect of the full moon on some is reflected in our very term *lunatic.* Yet we conceptualize the moon as belonging not only to the insane, but to lovers. The psychologist may find a common root in both conditions (which is the point), but one is ugly and the other beautiful. Such is the typical dichotomy of the symbols attached to the moon. It is both the Witch Goddess Hecate, in its darkness, and the moon Goddess Diana in its brightness. It is on the latter aspect that the esotericist concentrates, for with the increase of the moon there is a concomitant increase in the Astral Light underlying our plane, which may be turned to practical use.

A relationship between Yesod and Binah is suggested by the moon's control of the *waters.* Yesod is actually *Air,* which moves the water. Binah is the Great Sea, and is Isis. This is the Universal Unconscious from which all form ultimately develops. As Binah is the will to form, so Yesod is the storehouse of formal images directly behind our conscious experience.

As the lowest level of the Astral World, Yesod is the realm of images cast off by mankind, bright and dark. It contains the *Akashic Record,* which is both the history of races and of each individual mental act of man. Blavatsky claimed that much of her extraordinarily detailed writing was gleaned psychically from this record, a flamboyant claim at least.

The images of Yesod are fabulous in their beauty and seductiveness; they can also be hideous and frightening. These are the dreams and fears of humanity, built up since the beginning of time (note, again, the relationship with Binah). It is, in fact, a great ocean, into which every pebble of thought is thrown, producing a wave which continues eternally. However, these Yesod forms are illusive. They are not real in the sense that the term would be applied to the experience of Tiphareth. Recall that the moon has no light of its own; Yesod can only reflect the light of the Christ-Osiris-Buddha center of Tiphareth. Yet this reflection is of the greatest importance for the developing individual, since one cannot look directly into the Sun, and must learn about that force by considering its image reflected in the waters of the moon.

The lower Astral is also called *maya* or *illusion.* The powers of the Astral plane are pleased to let us believe whatever amuses us. They will provide visions to corroborate the most absurd of notions while at the same time inflating our egos, a very dangerous and common result of work at this level. This is a maze for the unsuspecting which can be effectively negotiated only by those whose sights are unfaltering set on Tiphareth. The vision of Yesod, that of the "Machinery of the Universe," may be hard won by those tightly locked into the framework of their personalities.

It should be clear, by this point, that an understanding of the cosmic tides of Yesod's Astral Light, and its use, confers power. And, contrary to popular belief, and to the numerous systems of enlightenment preaching firm moral values, understanding of, and ability to manipulate, the Astral Light has nothing whatsoever to do with virtue. It is explored purely and simply by meditative discipline. There are some exceedingly unpleasant people walking the earth today who may rightly lay claim to real understanding of the workings of our Universe.

The symbols of Yesod are the *sandals* and the *perfumes,* both relating to practical magic. The consecrated sandals worn within the mystic circle, affirm that one stands on sacred ground and (in their neutrality) allow for the transfer of energies between the Earth below and the Sun above. Yesod is the intermediary between Malkuth and Tiphareth (a two sided-mirror). Perfumes suggest its fluid and etheric qualities: Incense floats through a church or temple, subtly affecting the minds of the participants. Its qualities are suggestive, yet fleeting and illusory, which is the nature of Yesod.

The Nines

> *Generally they show very great fundamental force. Executive power, because they rest on a firm base, powerful for good or evil.*

 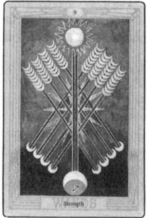  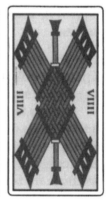

NINE OF WANDS Lord of Great Strength (Moon in Sagittarius).
Angels of the Decan: Yirthiel (ירתאל) and Sahiah (שאהיה).
This is Yesod in Atziluth, the influence of Yesod in the World of Pure Spirit. The lunar powers acquire great strength in Sagittarius, although wherever Yesod and the moon are concerned, there is always another side to the coin. Successes are accompanied by strife and apprehension. The good health which this aspect conveys is certain, but with doubt about the course it may later take. In divination the card means *great strength, power, recovery from sickness.*

NINE OF CUPS, Lord of Material Happiness (Jupiter in Pisces).
Angels of the Decan: Saliah (סליאה) and Aariel (עריאל) .
This is Yesod in Briah, the influence of Yesod in the Mental World. Here the benevolence of Jupiter, functioning through the water of Pisces, effects happiness and satisfaction in Malkuth. This is a card of pleasure and sensuality

which should be compared with the *Ten of Cups*, the success of which is more lasting.

Both the Crowley and Golden Dawn cards show nine cups overflowing and arranged in a square intended to suggest Chesed-Jupiter and the perfection of water force here. Waite, on the other hand, illustrates the more mundane aspects of the card in its meaning of *complete success* and the *fulfillment of wishes*.

NINE OF SWORDS, Lord of Despair and Cruelty (Mars in Gemini).
Angels of the Decan: Aaneval (עֲנוֹאֵל) and Mochayel (מֹחִיאֵל) .

This is Yesod in Yetzirah, the influence of Yetzirah in the Astral World. It takes little familiarity with astrology to recognize that the fiery Mars energy could do no good in the sign of dualities. In the Golden Dawn card the rose has been completely destroyed, while Crowley's version shows "poison and blood" dripping from the nine jagged and rusty swords. Waite's card stresses the card's despair, and the other divinatory meanings of *illness, suffering* and *cruelty*.

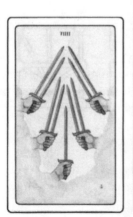
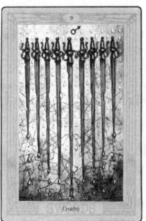

NINE OF PENTACLES, Lord of Material Gain (Venus in Virgo). *Angels of the Decan:* Hazayel (הזיאל) and Aldiah (אלדיה)

This is Yesod in Assiah, the influence of Yesod in the Material World. Venus in Virgo brings great efficiency, but with a relative lack of overt feelings. The aspect tends also to favor the amassing of things; it is thus a card of material gain. This is suggested by the Golden Dawn Pentacles, each of which has a fully-developed rose bud beside it, the central one having two buds to indicate continuing growth and acquisition on the physical plane.

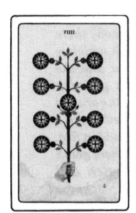   

Crowley's card is particularly interesting, being far more complicated than it might first appear. He says of it: "The disks are arranged as an equilateral triangle of three, apex upwards, close together; and surrounded at some distance by a ring, six larger disks in the form of a hexagram. This signifies the multiplication of the original established Word by the mingling of 'good luck and management.' "[88]

In divination the card means *inheritance* or *material gain*.

10. Malkuth: The Kingdom
The Four Tens
The Four Princesses

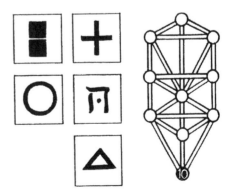

◆ The Earth on which we walk
◆ Kether below
◆ The Completion
◆ The Inferior Mother
◆ The Bride of Microprosopus

Symbols: The Altar of the Double
  Cube, The Equal Armed Cross,
  The Mystic Circle, The Triangle of Art,
  Heh Final .
Colors: Citrine, Olive, Russet, Black

> *And from the rays of this Triad* [Netzach, Hod, Yesod] *there appear three colours in* Malkuth *together with a fourth which is their synthesis. Thus from the orange tawny of Hod and the green nature of Netzach there goeth forth a certain greenish 'citrine' color, yet pure and translucent withal. From the orange tawny of Hod mingled with the puce of Yesod there goeth forth a certain red russet brown, 'russet' yet gleaming with a hidden fire. And from the green of Netzach and the puce of Yesod there goeth forth a certain other darkening green 'Olive' yet rich and glowing withal. And the synthesis of all these is a blackness which bordereth upon the Qlippoth.Thus are the colours of the Sephiroth completed in their feminine or Rainbow scale.*
>
> *Moreover, though the Tree of Life operates through all the Ten Sephiroth, yet it is referred in a special manner to Tiphareth. Also, though the branches of the Tree of Knowledge of Good and Evil stretch into the seven lower Sephiroth and downwards into the Kingdom of Shells, yet it is referred especially unto Malkuth. Similarly with Netzach and Hod, the right and left columns of the Sephiroth are referred respectively thereto.*
>
> *In Malkuth* Adonai ha-Aretz *is God, the Lord and King, ruling over the Kingdom and Empire which is the Visible Universe.*
>
> *And* Cholem Yesodoth, *the Breaker of Foundations (or* Olam Yesodoth, *The World of the Elements) is the Name of the Sphere of the Operation of Malkuth which is called the Sphere of Elements from which all things are formed, and its Archangels are three:* Metatron, *the Prince of Countenance reflected from Kether, and* Sandalphon, *the Prince of Prayer (feminine) and* Nephesch ha Messiah, *the Soul of the Reconciler for Earth. And the Order of Angels is* Ashim *or Flames of Fire, as it is written 'Who maketh his Angels Spirits and his Ministers as a flaming Fire' and these are also called the Order of Blessed Souls or the Souls of the Just made Perfect.*

Malkuth is the most complicated of the Sephiroth; Kether is the most simple. And yet, applying the principle of "As above, so below," we appreciate that Kether is in Malkuth and Malkuth is in Kether. Ultimately, God is in everything we know, from the flower in the field to the dirt on which we walk. No matter what is on the earth, it is infused with the Divine Nature. The separation between creator and created is artificial. God is Man. Man is God. We are God collectively, and we are God individually. We are parts, and we are the whole. The perceived separation is the result of "The Fall," and the Great Work of returning to the Godhead begins with the recognition (or, perhaps, the suspicion) that our perceptions have been inaccurate. Thus, to Malkuth is assigned the virtue of discrimination. Its spiritual experience is the "Vision of the Holy Guardian Angel," an aspect of the Higher Self. It is in Malkuth that its existence is demonstrated, whereas to Tiphareth is ascribed the conscious union of the Personality with this Higher Genius.

The idea of unity in all, and of the Divine Power indwelling in every aspect of our material world may seem obvious to those with a natural inclination toward the Mysteries. But, over the centuries, many religious sects have taught that the material world is inherently evil, a point of view which is ultimately counterproductive and escapist. The same may be said for certain fundamentalist Christian attitudes which suggest that man should "give himself up to the will of God" to the extent that it is a virtual abrogation of individual responsibility.

The Qabalah teaches that the body is the Temple of the Holy Spirit, and that unless we learn the lessons of Malkuth there can be no lasting progress beyond. The fact is that our first spiritual lessons come from those around us. And if we cannot function effectively on the material level, learning from the day to day patterns which we have chosen for our incarnation, it is unlikely that we will be able to function effectively on a more refined spiritual plane. The ability to sense the importance of the ordinary is a special form of discrimination.

All meditation, all Tarot divination and meditation, begins and ends with an affirmation of the strength and stability of the Earth. One must first be grounded before invoking the Divine Light. And, particularly, at the close of a projective exercise, it is necessary to potently affirm a return to normal consciousness. Otherwise a dissociation or pathological confusion of planes may result.

The lesson of Malkuth, the balance of the four aspects of the Personality, through a process which might be described as one of *compensation,* is all important as one learns to "Rise on the Planes." The Personality must be totally readjusted and rebalanced after each new spiritual experience, a process which takes place in Malkuth. The waking consciousness is reintegrated as self-perspective changes.

We learn not in a consistent flow, but rather through a natural process of activity and passivity, stop and go. First we acquire information, or a new set of values, and then we stop to integrate that material into our system. This must happen before the lessons can be applied, which is the reason that one cannot truly use the knowledge of any Sephira without having been initiated into the Sephira above it.

Repeatedly throughout the Tree, there has been reference to the Four Elements in the pattern of the יהוה. Malkuth is the sphere where the elements are ultimately based. They intermingle to produce the stability which we know as matter. These are not the same as the fire, water, air and earth which we see and touch, although they are the motive force behind those elements. In the simplest of terms (although it may sound totally fanciful), when one lights a match one does so only through the Fire Force of the *Salamanders,* Elemental Fire.

The Elementals, which, in the *Tattva Exercises* are encountered in more or less agreed-upon anthropomorphic shapes, are the forces behind the forms of the *Mundane Chakra,* the material world.

The Mundane Chakra of each category of existence is in Assiah, the lowest of the Four Worlds. Here we may again consider the idea that each Sephira contains an entire Tree. The Malkuth of Malkuth in Assiah is the ground on which we walk; the Tiphareth of Malkuth in Assiah is the Sun in our sky; Netzach is Venus; Hod is Mercury; and Yesod is the moon. Yet that which we perceive is only the surface of the material world. *Matter* (the whole of Assiah) is composed of particles invisible to the eye. We see them only through enormous electronic magnification in the same way that the forces which activate these particles can only be seen with the inner vision.

The exercise of the Tattvas are of Assiah (although they may easily be deepened into the Yetziratic World). When we meditate with the Gnomes, we are tapping the forces of stability directly beneath our sphere of sensation, forces which are an amalgam of aspects of three Elements within the fourth. Malkuth is a quadripartite unity. To deal with the Sylphs means to handle the motive force or Air, directly beneath Yesod's mundane Chakra, the moon. The Undines are in Hod-Mercury, and the Salamanders of Netzach-Venus.

A great deal will be gained by meditation on the position of Malkuth at the base of the Tree of Life on the Middle Pillar. It is a receptacle for all of the energies of the Tree. They feed into Malkuth, and are grounded in its stability. The word *inertia* has been applied to this Sephira, meaning a state of rest (stasis) rather than inactivity, as continual motion is the law of nature. The difference between Malkuth and other Sephiroth is that it is self-contained in the same way as is Kether.

Malkuth is called the *Bride of Microprosopus,* a title which relates beautifully to the Tarot Princesses. The Prince is Tiphareth, who rules over the personality it projects for each incarnation. But for the personality to perform its task, it must function within a given structure. The Princess, taken as a Bride by the Prince (who is actually a King) is the very structure (Kingdom) through which the Prince rules. For example, we repeatedly have noted that in Christian iconography the Virgin Mary (Binah-Isis) is *The Church.* She is the building, she is the rituals, she is the supportive structure without which the religion would not function.

Considered at a less symbolic level, the choice of the Prince to take the Princess as his Bride is our own personal choice to enter a new incarnation, with a new personality. The Higher Self of Tiphareth builds the personality using the sequential energies of Netzach, Hod and Yesod. That personality is expressed through the vehicle of matter in Malkuth, the Sephira also referred to as the *Gateway.* Two principles unite, giving rise to a third, which is expressed in a fourth: יהוה.

Insofar as Malkuth is the Earth, it is active and productive, and is called the *Inferior Mother.* On the lower arc, she is an expression of the energies of

Binah, the *Supernal Mother*. And here we realize that the union of the Vau and Heh Final, like that of the Yod and Heh, must produce something further. What is produced is a renewed activity at the point of Kether, which re-activates the outgoing force of Chokmah, which sustains the formalizing energies of Binah, and so on. It is a continuous cycle symbolized by the egg, or by the serpent which holds its tail in its mouth. But this cycle becomes ever tighter, pulling closer to Kether with each downward and then upward swing. There must eventually come a point in the evolution of the Spirit of Humanity, where the Tree of Life no longer describes our Universe.

The primary symbols of Malkuth are the *Altar of the Double Cube,* and the *Equal-Armed Cross*. The Altar of the Western Mysteries is black, and is formed of two cubes, on top of the other. The reference here is to the "As above, so below." Moreover, the six sides relate to Tiphareth. The Equal-armed Cross is the balanced Elements.

The other two symbols are the *mystic circle,* which defines and encloses sacred ground, and the *triangle of art* in which evocation takes place. *Evocation is* very different from *invocation*. To evoke is to bring something from another plane into physical manifestation, generally using heavy incense as an etheric vehicle. To invoke is to call upon a specific form of the Divine, Presence, which is in the nature of prayer, though a great deal more practical.

The Tens

> *Generally show fixed, culminated, completed Force, whether good or evil. The matter thoroughly and definitely determined. Similar to the force of the Nines, but ultimating it, and carrying it out.*

TEN OF WANDS, Lord of Oppression (Saturn in Sagittarius).
Angels of the Decan: Reyayel (רייאל) and Avamel (אומאל) .

This is Malkuth in Atziluth, the influence of Malkuth in the World of Pure Spirit. The destructive powers of Saturn are amplified by the swiftness of Sagittarius, leading to material force selfishly applied, usually with cruelty. Crowley shows the nature of this force by using wands which are no longer elegant but which, rather, are crude clubs. Waite's card uses a heavy burden to suggest *cruelty and malice, overbearing force and energy, injustice.*

TEN OF CUPS, Lord of Perfected Success (Mars in Pisces). *Angels of the Decan:* Aasliah (עשליה) and Mihal (מיהאל).

This is Malkuth in Briah, the influence of Malkuth in the unconscious Mental World. Here is a situation where the generally understood astrological meaning of an aspect does not apply. In an astrological reading, Mars in Pisces, a watery sign, would signify a dispersal of energy and a degree of frustration. But the meaning here is that the fire of Mars causes the waters of the final sign of the Zodiac to rush furiously in Briah, bringing great success on the material plane. As all of the card images suggest, the happiness is "inspired from above." On the other hand, it should be remembered that the Tarot, when used for divination, is best applied to mundane matters, and the meaning of this aspect may be considered different if applied to a more spiritual plane. In ordinary divination, the meaning is *matters definitely arranged and settled as wished, permanent and lasting success.*

TEN OF SWORDS, Lord of Ruin (Sun in Gemini).
Angels of the Decan: Dambayah (דמביה) and Menqal (מיקאל).

This is Malkuth in Yetzirah, the influence of Malkuth in the Astral World. From the standpoint of material things, this is the most destructive card in the deck, and no one likes to see it appear in a spread. But those who use the Tarot as an instrument of spiritual development learn not to take life's experiences at face value. And insofar as the Tarot is used to predict future events, the statement can be made about it that can be made about astrology, "The stars impel,

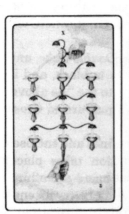   

they do not compel." We are not slaves to our destiny, but have the capacity, through inner processes, to considerably improve our earthly lot. To do so is no less ethical than resigning a position when it is clear that some work-related disaster is on the horizon, or walking on the sidewalk when "the cards tell you" that if you walk in the street you will probably be struck by an oncoming automobile. We should use the capacities we have been given.

The Golden Dawn divinatory meaning of this card is *ruin, death, failure, disaster.* This is more of a death card than is *Death,* which generally means a situational death, a transformation.

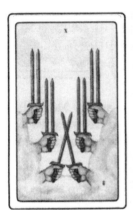   

TEN OF PENTACLES, Lord of Wealth (Mercury in Virgo).
Angels of the Decan: Hahaayah (ההעיה) and Laviah (לאויה).

This is Malkuth in Assiah, the influence of Malkuth in the material, World. Mercury, God of commerce, rules the earthly sign Virgo. Its placement here assures material gain so vast that it may lose its importance, a situation described as an *embarras de richesses.*

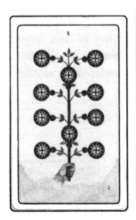   

The Golden Dawn version follows the same pattern as the Marseilles deck showing gain by the roses in full bloom. Both Waite and Crowley use the whole Tree of Life to suggest completion; following the planetary attribution, Crowley's Tree shows various symbols for Mercury.

The Princesses

> *They represent the forces of the* Heh *Final of the Name in each suit, completing the influences of the other scales. The mighty and potent daughter of a King and Queen: a Princess powerful and terrible. A Queen of Queens, an Empress, whose effect combines those of the King, Queen and Prince...Yet her power existeth not save by reason of the others, and then indeed it is mighty and terrible materially, and is the Throne of the Forces of the Spirit. Woe unto whosoever shall make war upon her when thus established!*

PRINCESS OF WANDS, Princess of the Shining Flame, The Rose of the Palace of Fire, Princess and Empress of the Salamanders, Throne of the Ace of Wands.

The Princess of Wands is Earth of Fire, the personification of Specific Earth of Primal Fire. In the Golden Dawn card her hand rests upon a golden altar decorated with Rams' heads (Aries) reminding us that in the system of Decans it is Aries which both begins and ends the series. The Fire being "sacrificed" on the altar of Malkuth, the Fire of the Wand (now so imposing as to be considered a dangerous club), and the Fire beneath her feet shoot upwards. This card is a dynamic and unpredictable as the *tiger* which is the crest of the Princess.

In this card, as in all of his Court cards, Crowley attempts to represent the activity of the force in question. His swirling, dancing figure, inseparable from the tiger, is the mundane aspect of Fire. Here, especially, Crowley's dependence on the Golden Dawn designs is clear.

One must, finally, comment on the Waite "Pages," and the "Knaves" of the Marseilles deck, both of which are exoteric. Insofar as these cards symbolize the "Bride of Microprosopus," they are understood to be female because the Heh final is the *Inferior Mother*. Waite knew this, and in representing a young man was perhaps avoiding an idea which he considered to be an esoteric secret.

PRINCESS OF CUPS, Princess of the Water and Lotus of the Palace of the Floods, Princess and Empress of Nymphs and Undines, Throne of the Ace of Cups.

The *Princess of Cups* is Earth of Water, the personification of Specific Earth in Primal Water. In the Golden Dawn card there are three important symbols: the *turtle,* the *swan* and the *dolphin,* the latter having been discussed in regard to the *Two of Cups.* The turtle is a symbol of wisdom (because it withdraws into its own shell); it is also related to long life in some systems.[89] But the swan in the key symbol for this Princess, who wears a cloak of soft feathers. The swan is related to Orpheus (who chose to be reborn in that form), and thus to the lyre and all musical forms. The tradition among seaman is that the swan brings good fortune.[90] As in his *Princess of Wands,* Crowley abstracts the three symbols of the Golden Dawn card, although he describes the form issuing from the cup as the *tortoise* which in Hinduism has on its back the elephant which supports the Universe. This is, therefore, a card of emergent life from the sea, and of matter crystallizing within water.

PRINCESS OF SWORDS, Princess of the Rushing Winds, Lotus of the Palace of Air, Princess and Empress of the Sylphs and Sylphides, Throne of the Ace of Swords.

The *Princess of Swords* is Earth of Air, personification of Specific Earth in Primal Air. The Golden Dawn Princess stands at a silver altar which bears no fire, only smoke which may be blown in any direction by the Air of Yetzirah. She is intended to represent a mixture of Minerva (Goddess of Wisdom) and Diana (Goddess of the moon and of the hunt). The crest describing her personality, is a head of Medusa. Medusa was at one time a most beautiful woman who, because she offended Athena, was transformed into a hideous creature with hair of serpents. The very sight of her would turn men to stone.[91] Thus, the indication here is that the personality of the Princess is not entirely pleasant. It should also be noted that it is *Perseus* who severs the head of Medusa. He is also represented on the Golden Dawn version of *The Lovers* rescuing Andromeda from her earthly shackles. Mathers, a great symbolist, unquestionably intended that we make this connection.

PRINCESS OF PENTACLES, Princess of Echoing Hills, Rose of the Palace of Earth, *Princess and Empress* of the Gnomes, Throne of the Ace of Pentacles.

The Princess of Pentacles is Earth of Earth, the personification of Specific Earth in the World of Primal Earth. Her Golden Dawn attribute is a winged Ram's head (made a helmet by Crowley) suggesting that she is a completion of that found in the *Princess of Wands*. The Princesses are less dependant of one another than are the other Court cards, insofar as the Elements are blended in Malkuth.

THE MAJOR ARCANA ON THE TREE OF LIFE

Applications of the Sepher Yetzirah

As has been indicated, the modern Tarot is usually related to the *Sepher Yetzirah* or *Book of Formation*. This brief, but major, document of esoteric cosmology purports to demonstrate the rational framework and course of creation of our Universe. Yet, as with all truly enlightened works, it is not intended to be read; it must, rather, be used as a stimulus to meditation.

The *Sepher Yetzirah* uses the symbolism of highly abstract words to describe those energies which the Tarot represents in pictures, the corresponding links being the twenty-two letters of the Hebrew alphabet. Thus, any comment on a Hebrew letter may also be taken to be a comment on the Tarot card to which that particular letter is attributed.

To approach the Tarot from the standpoint of the *Sepher Yetzirah* adds a fascinating dimension to the study of the cards. Moreover, the ancient document is so short that this is not a difficult task.

Let us begin by applying selected passages of this work to the Tarot Trumps as they are traditionally placed on the Tree of Life (Figures 18 and 19).

The Maternals: Air, Water, Fire

From the Spirit he produced Air, and formed in it twenty-two sounds, the letters. Three are mothers, seven are double, and twelve are simple, but the Spirit is first and above these.[92]

א *The Fool* is Air. All of the other Tarot cards are implicit in this Transitional Air; they all arise from Air.

From the Air He formed the Waters and from the formless and void made mire and clay, and designed surfaces upon them, and hewed recesses in them,

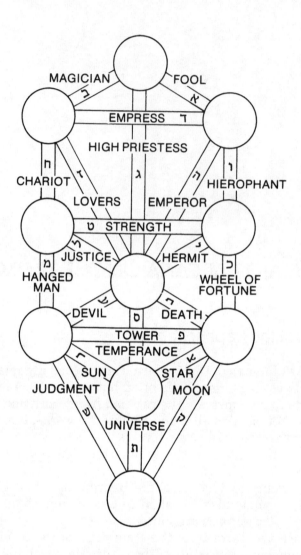

Figure 18. Attribution of the Major Arcana to the Tree of Life

and formed the strong material foundation.

מ *The Hanged Man* is Water. It is the basis of matter, and is a part of Microprosopus on the Tree of Life, at the side of the Pillar of Severity. Alchemists call Water the "root of all minerals."

From the Water he formed Fire and made for himself a Throne of Glory with Auphanim, Seraphim and Kerubim, as his ministering angels; and with those three he completed his dwelling...

ש *Judgment* is Fire. The final maternal connects Microprosopus with its bride, Malkuth, again on the side of the Pillar of Severity.

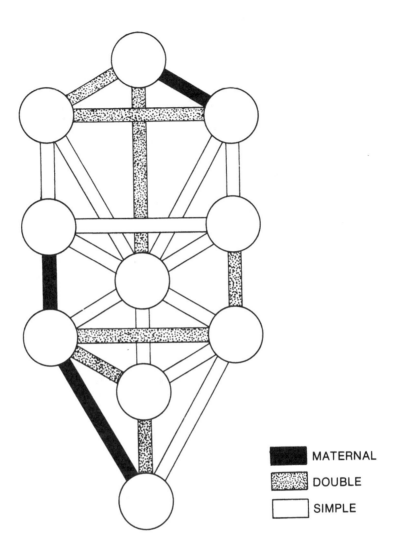

Figure 19. Attribution of Maternal, Double and Simple Letters to the Tree of Life

As the Path of the Flaming Sword (Figure 20) which is the Path of emanation of the Sephiroth, crosses the Abyss from Binah to Chesed where no Path
exists, so there is the possibility of passage across the Abyss from Chokmah to
Geburah (although this is not a viable possibility for the developing spirit). Were
this done, it would be possible to move up and down the Tree of Life using only
three Paths, those of the Maternals. From Kether the Path of *The Fool* leads
to Chokmah. From Chokmah it is a leap across the terrible abyss to Geburah.
From Geburah is the Path of *The Hanged Man* into Hod. Finally, the Path of
Judgment leads into the material completion of Malkuth.

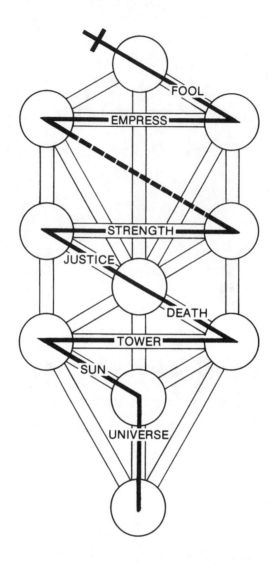

Figure 20. The Cards on the "Path of the Flaming Sword"

There is a quality of "mind game" to working with the *Sepher Yetzirah* in this way, but the method is essential to understanding the ways in which the Tarot may be used as a vehicle for high Qabalistic principle.

The Double Letters: Planets, Localities, Days, Gateways, Contrasts

The initial commentary on the double letters states that they are so called *"because each letter represents a contrast or permutation."* In fact, each of these seven letters has two pronunciations, one hard and one soft.

The letters refer, in order, to life and death, peace and war, wisdom and folly, riches and poverty, grace and indignation, fertility and solitude, power and servitude. These are the pairs of opposites which we can apply to the designated Tarot Trumps.

These Seven Double Letters point out seven localities; Above, Below, East, West, North, South, and the Palace of Holiness in the midst of them sustaining all things.

This describes the hexagram, related to the central Sephira on the Tree of Life (Figure 16 on page 90).

These Seven Double Letters He designed, produced and combined and formed with them the Planets (stars) of the Universe, the Days of the Week, and the Gates of the soul (the orifices of perception) in Man.

At the onset it is important to appreciate that as the planets are attributed to Paths (Figure 21), they are not the same as planets attributed to Sephiroth, which are, at one level, the bodily *Chakras* or *Metals* of the Alchemists. To *The Magician*, for example, Mercury is applied, but this differs from the Mercury which is the mundane chakra of the Sephira Hod. It is what Mathers called the "Philosophic Mercury."

The Paths involving planets must be considered *transitional*, as are those Paths to which Elements are attributed: they always represent the action of one energy on another because they link together two Sephiroth. The same may be said for the Paths of the Zodiac, where the action of one planet on another occurs through the intermediary of the Sign of the Zodiac. It would be pleasant to be able to suggest that this is not actually as difficult as it appears, but such is not the case. To understand these concepts may require a herculean effort on the part of one who approaches them purely intellectually. The corrective comes for those who project themselves by meditation into the Tarot cards. The actual experience of these energies is the only way to make real sense from principles, of necessity, expressed coldly.

    ב *The Magician* is Mercury, Life-Death.
    ד *The Empress* is Venus, Peace-War.
    ג *The High Priestess* is the Moon, Wisdom-Folly.
    כ *The Wheel of Fortune* is Jupiter, Riches-Poverty.
    פ *The Tower* is Mars, Grace-Indignation.
    ר *The Sun* is the Sun, Fertility-Barrenness
    ת *The Universe* is Saturn, Power-Servitude.

These are the primary attributions of the planets to the Tarot cards, though, as is indicated in the illustrations, each Sign of the Zodiac is ruled by a planet. There are only three Paths on the Tree of Life without some planetary reference; these are the Paths of the Maternals. A most important principle is imbedded in this fact, and in the specific placement of the Maternals on the Tree of Life.

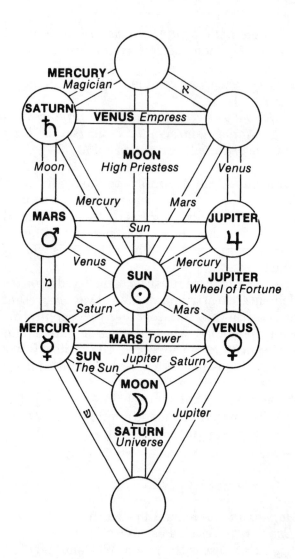

Figure 21. Planetary attributions to the Tree of Life. The Planets attached to Sephiroth are indicated in heavy type. Also in heavy type are those planets directly attributed to Paths; associated Tarot Trumps are given beneath. The seven planetary Paths are the seven double letters of the *Sepher Yetzirah*. Planets in light type are Paths attributed to signs of the Zodiac ruled by those planets. Note that the only Paths which do not in some way relate to planets are those of the Hebrew letters called *Maternals:* א (Air), מ (Water) and ש (Fire).

The Simple Letters of the Zodiac

The twelve simple letters...are the foundation of these twelve properties: Sight, Hearing, Smell, Speech, Taste, Sexual Love, Work, Movement, Anger, Mirth, Imagination and Sleep.

...These Twelve Simple Letters he designated, and combined, and formed with them the Twelve celestial constellations of the Zodiac.

(Figure 22 shows the Signs of the Zodiac on the Tree with the corresponding Tarot Keys. This should be studied with Figure 23, which considers the attribution of Elements to the same Sign on each Path).

ה   THE EMPEROR is Aries, Sight.
ו   THE HIEROPHANT is Taurus, Hearing.
ז   THE LOVERS is Gemini, Smell.
ח   THE CHARIOT is Cancer, Speech.
ט   STRENGTH is Leo, Taste.
י   THE HERMIT is Virgo, Sexual Love.
ל   JUSTICE is Libra, Work.
נ   DEATH is Scorpio, Movement.
ס   TEMPERANCE is Sagittarius, Anger.
ע   THE DEVIL is Capricorn, Mirth.
צ   THE STAR is Aquarius, Imagination.
ק   THE MOON is Pisces, Sleep.

Thus, the totality of the human condition is represented in the twenty two cards of the Major Arcana, the Maternal cards are the primary spiritual forces; the double letter cards are the opposing conditions affecting the individual in incarnation; the single letter cards are the activities in which the individual engages.

In terms of the Microcosm and Macrocosm, the Maternal Letters are the *roots* of any given form of consciousness, the double letters are the *gateways* or orifices of the body, and the simple letters are the *organs*. Some very profound insights will result from meditation on the incarnation of the various aspects of the letters.

The Cube of Space

A slight feeling of despair may be a common reaction to one's first encounter with this diagram (Figure 24), which may appear to add the last straw to what is an already unbearably heavy weight of symbolism. But in actuality, anyone who can follow a subway map of New York City will have no problem with the Cube of Space. It is a sort of internal map of the Universe, given in the *Sepher Yetzirah,* where a direction is assigned to each letter of the Hebrew alphabet.

Many of the symbols discussed in this book are a great deal more accessible than they might at first appear. The Cube of Space is a good example, and

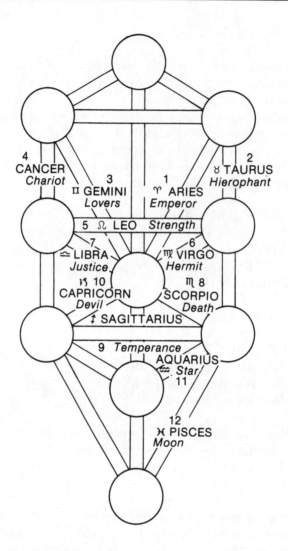

Figure 22. Signs of the Zodiac on the Tree of Life. The Twelve Zodiacal
Paths are the twelve simple letters of the *Sepher Yetzirah*.

one which may serve to demonstrate the extent to which Qabalistic symbols are
meant to be used in our internal learning process.

If we sit quietly, we may conceptualize our thoughts, feelings and spiritual
being as controlled from a central point within our heads. Perhaps this could be
called the "I" point. Once we have focused on this internal point, we can begin to
consider how it relates to principles of an inner Universe. These principles are
the corners and directions of the cube. So what we do is to imagine that our consciousness is inside a cube, giving our intelligence something concrete, though
artificial, with which to begin inner exploration.

The Cube of Space is simple enough, though it is a very different pattern
of symbolism than is found on the Tree of Life. And, while the *Sepher Yetzirah*

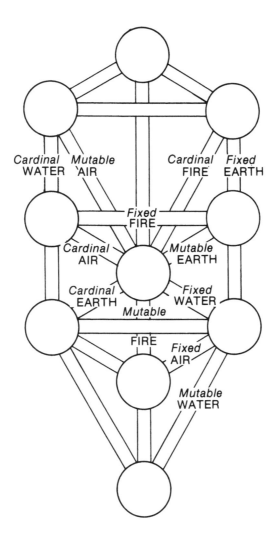

Figure 23. The Signs of the Zodiac on the Tree of Life
as *Cardinal, Fixed* and *Mutable* Elements.

describes this Cube of Space very precisely, it is not so easily related to the Tree! The problem arises in that the document does not specifically ascribe letters to Paths between Sephiroth as is understood today. And, as we have seen, some versions of the Tree do not show a complete twenty-two Paths.

One possible explanation, espoused by a large number of scholars, is that the book represents a purposeful attempt to fuse two different methods of approach to the inner worlds, using a type of logic similar to that of the Neopythagoreans, popular in the second and third centuries C.E. [93] The least that can be said is that (like the *Bahir)* there are aspects of the *Sepher Yetzirah* which are not easily accommodated into our modern symbolic structure.

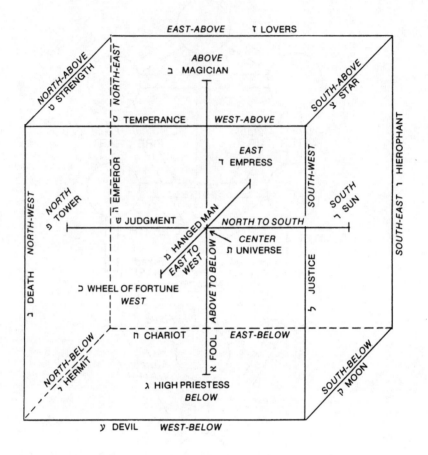

Figure 24. The Cube of Space

On the other hand, the Cube of Space demonstrates certain relationships not at all obvious on the Tree of Life. One primary example is the symbolic crossing of the three Maternals at the point of *The Universe* (Tau). It is
also more consistent with the directions of traditional ritual: East, West, North
and South. Gareth Knight describes this as the "Upper Room,"[94] a method of
relating our mundane spatial perspectives to an inner experience, as a matter of
orientation.

It must, however, be stressed that none of the external systems truly indicate the quality of the inner experience of the Paths. The reason that they all
appear so complex and disjointed is that they attempt to suggest experiences

which our language is inadequate to describe. No matter how dogmatic one may be about the intellectual intermesh of symbols, the most intricate commentary on these matters is often like the medieval clerics who postulated the number of angels that would fit on the head of a pin. Yet some statements which appear to be symbolic turn out to be very precise descriptions of a universal experience. It is up to the discrimination of the student to decide which is which. Only the inner experience of these Paths makes clear what the various systems of symbols are trying to explain. And until such time as we directly encounter the energies underlying our existence, we strive to form concepts about those energies through such artificial devices as the Tree of Life, and through such methods as the Qabalistic manipulation of numbers.

Numerology

Qabalistic numerology is called *Gematria*. This involves nothing more than taking the numerical value of each Hebrew letter in a word, and adding those values together. Theoretically, words of the same total value bear some conceptual relationship, although the principle can be taken to absurd extremes. Gematria can be a petty trap.

The interrelationship of numbers and letters often, however, points to some profound ideas. For example, we have considered the interaction of Chokmah and Binah, whose union gives rise to Tiphareth: the Yod and Heh produce the Vau. As a number, Yod is 10 and Heh is 5. Added together they are 15, which reduces to 6, the numerical value of Vau. Even the most sceptical may agree that for the relationship of the numerical values to be precisely that relationship assigned to the letters as philosophical values is interesting. These patterns occur with such frequency and consistency that they seem clearly intended to teach.

Westcott's fine explanation of Gematria is reprinted by Aleister Crowley in his *Equinox*.[95] We repeat here one of his examples which uses the God Name רוח אלהים (Ruach Elohim), meaning the Spirit of Elohim. The numerical value of this phrase is easily derived, as is shown below. Having found the letters to have a total value of 300, we discover a parallel in that the letter *Shin* also has a value of 300. Shin is the maternal letter of spiritual Fire.

If the 300 is reduced, it becomes 3, the number of Binah, implying a relationship of both the Ruach Elohim and the potencies symbolized by Shin, to the first formative Sephira. The system of numbers is an extraordinary way to derive "secret" teachings. But a gentle warning should be issued here. Many serious students become so immersed in deriving numbers from Hebrew words, that they become lost in small details, failing to see the forest for the trees. The complexity of Qabalistic study, especially following some of the most ancient Hebrew methodologies, can be a trap. A person can become so absorbed, so mired in details, that the primary aim of self-development may be lost.

ר = 200
ו = 6
ח = 8

א = 1
ל = 30
ה = 5
י = 10
ם = 40

Total 300

LETTER (Final)		NAME	EQUIVALENT	VALUE	MEANING
א		ALEPH	A	1	Ox
ב		BETH	B, V	2	House
ג		GIMEL	G, Gh	3	Camel
ד		DALETH	D, Dh	4	Door
ה		HE	H	5	Window
ו		VAU	O, U, V	6	Nail or Hook
ז		ZAYIN	Z	7	Sword or Armor
ח		HETH	Ch	8	Fence, Enclosure
ט		TETH	T	9	Snake
י		YOD	I, Y	10	Hand
כ	(ך)	KAPH	K, Kh	20,500	Fist
ל		LAMED	L	30	Ox Goad
מ	(ם)	MEM	M	40,600	Water
נ	(ן)	NUN	N	50,700	Fish
ס		SAMEKH	S	60	Prop
ע		AYIN	Aa, Ngh	70	Eye
פ	(ף)	PE	P, Ph	80,800	Mouth
צ	(ץ)	TZADDI	Tz	90,900	Fish hook
ק		QOPH	Q	100	Ear, back of head
ר		RESH	R	200	Head
ש		SHIN	S, Sh	300	Tooth
ת		TAU	T, Th	400	Cross

The Hebrew Alphabet

Through Gematria a "total" energy is considered as the sum of its parts. The same approach can be taken graphically, by using the Tarot to spell God Names. *Ruach Elohim,* for example, is composed of the energies symbolized by the following:

ר *The Sun*
ו *The Hierophant*
ח *The Chariot*
א *The Fool*
ל *Justice*
ה *The Emperor*
י *The Hermit*
מ *The Hanged Man*

Sets of Paths

Another way to consider the Keys is in terms of *equilibrium and opposites* (Figure 25). Here *The Fool* is viewed as the opposite of *The Magician*, or *The Chariot* the opposite of *The Hierophant* on the basis of their position on the Tree of Life. It is important to note that position is the consideration here, since some authorities establish card opposites in other ways.

Beyond Gematria as a means for examining the Tree's internal workings, one begins to look for Paths that are related in special ways. In this regard, we have already suggested that certain sets of (three) Paths define aspects of the Self, *i.e.*, the Supreme Spiritual Self, the Higher Self and the Personality. Other sets of Paths are more obvious, such as those of the *Flaming Sword* (Figure 20), where each card is important to the process of emanation of the Universe.

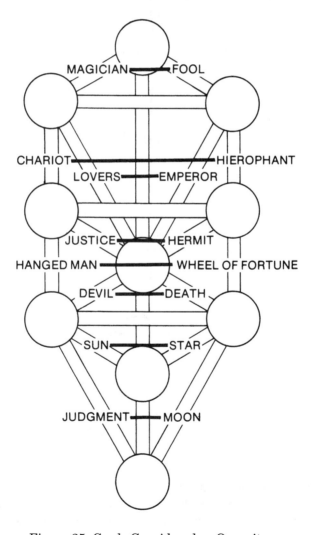

Figure 25. Cards Considered as Opposites

One of the most potent sets of Paths is that of the Middle Pillar and involving *The High Priestess, Temperance* and *The Universe* (Figure 26). What this diagram says, in essence, is that through the experience of three separate types of energy, we may attain knowledge of the Ultimate Godhead.

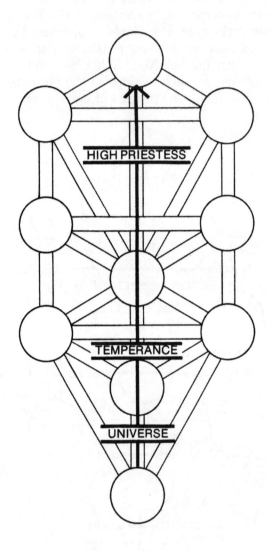

Figure 26. The Cards on the Middle Pillar. There are only three cards which are actually on the Middle Pillar, but to travel these Paths means also to "cross through" the potent energies symbolized by three other cards. Note also that the Path of the *High Priestess* extends through the Abyss.

If we apply the definitions of the *Thirty-Two Paths of Wisdom* (Figure 27) in the same way, we find these three major Paths described, in order of their progress toward the Godhead, as: *The Administrative Intelligence* (*The Universe*), the organizing structure behind our material environment; *The Intelligence of Probation* (*Temperance*), perhaps the most difficult Path on the entire Tree of Life, one of Spiritual Alchemy and of the dreadful "Dark Night of the Soul," leading to knowing immersion of the Personality into the consciousness of the Higher Self; *The Uniting Intelligence* (*The High Priestess*), the Path by which all that has appeared to be separated from the Godhead is re-united.

The point here is the extent to which the ancient Qabalistic documents amplify our appreciation of the Tarot and *vice-versa*.

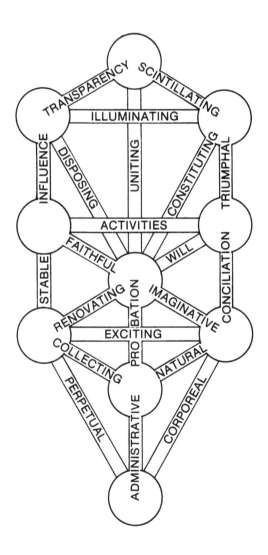

Figure 27. The Paths from *The Thirty-Two Paths of Wisdom*

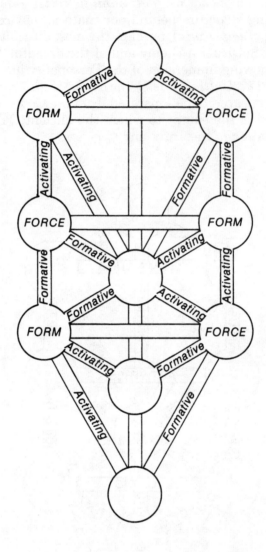

Figure 28. Patterns of Form and Force on the Tree of Life. The *Activating Paths* are the י, the *Formative Paths* are the ה; the crossing Paths and those of the Middle Pillar are the ו. Note that the word "formative" is used here rather than "passive," chosen by some authorities. There is no inertia on the Tree of Life; it is in a state of constant activity, the formative process being a response to the activation. This is not neutral in the sense that the word passive would imply. Here one might usefully consider the fact that *The Emperor* is a Formative Path, rather than an activating one, and the fact that Binah (like the Path of *The Emperor*) is bright red in Atziluth.

The Initiatory Scheme of the Tarot

As we have seen, the Tree of Life is based on one very simple principle, that of a positive and a negative which, between them, produce a third and balanced energy. These are the Yod, Heh and Vau of the Divine Name. A variety of terms describe this pattern, such as: Male, Female, Neuter, or Father, Mother, Son. Figure 28 labels the Sephiroth centers of *Form* and *Force,* whereas the Paths are called *Activating* and *Formative.* This slight distinction is made to point out that the Sephiroth are centers of energy, while the Paths are the subjective experiences between those centers.

Before proceeding further, it seems important to point out that the complex discussion which follows is presented not so much for its content as for its *method* of analyzing the Tree.

The Tree of Life is a system of triangles made up of Paths which are Activating, Formative and Balancing. This is an absolute Qabalistic given, a universal pattern. In light of this pattern, let us return to the idea that each of the key triangles on the Tree refers to one part of the soul: The Supernal Triangle is the Supreme Spiritual Self, the Ethical Triangle is the Higher Self, and the Astral Triangle is the Personality in incarnation. This idea, which was particularly developed by Dion Fortune,[96] places special importance on nine Tarot cards:

THE SPIRITUAL SELF

SUPERNAL TRIANGLE

The Fool *(Activating)*
The Magician *(Formative)*
The Empress *(Balancing)*

THE HIGHER SELF

ETHICAL TRIANGLE

STRENGTH *(Balancing)*
HERMIT *(Activating)*
JUSTICE *(Formative)*

THE PERSONALITY

ASTRAL TRIANGLE

TOWER *(Balancing)*
STAR *Formative)*
SUN *(Activating)*

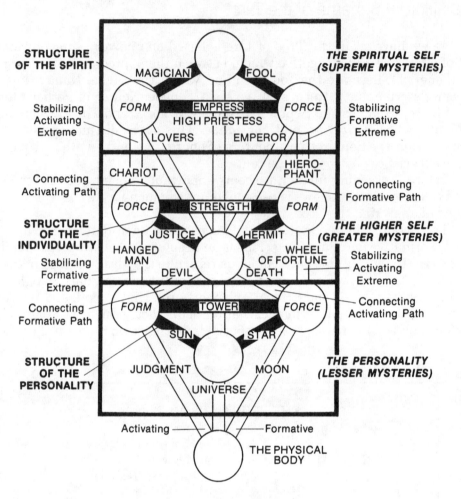

Parts of the Soul

Figure 29. This very complicated chart is based on the idea that each of the Triangles on the Tree represents a given part of the soul, *The Spiritual Self, The Higher Self* and *The Personality*. If we accept this idea we are accepting that nine of the Paths (shown in black) are givens, each being the positive, negative or balance *of* one aspect *of* the soul. The question must then be asked: How do the other thirteen Paths relate to the given nine?

The core structure of each part of the Self is composed of three aspects, an *Activating* (Yod-Fire), *a Formative* (Heh-Water) and an energy which is *Balancing* (Vau-Air), as is shown in Figure 29. One important clue to the symbolism is that Heh-Water, wherever it appears means *consciousness*. In some Tarot cards this is a Universal Consciousness, while in others it is the personal consciousness. Yod-Fire is the motive principle (what Fabre d'Olivet called the "intellectual volative principle"). It is that on which consciousness acts. Vau-Air is the balance between these two, which sustains their interaction. What is important to appreciate is that the pattern is implicit at all levels. And, having seen the activities of the Yod, Heh and Vau within the core structures of the Self, we look for the same pattern in the Path energies around these core structures.

The nine cards of the Self are clearly defined. What is then required is an appreciation of the relationship of the other cards to these givens. We know, first of all, that each Path represents a specific lesson about the Self, a lesson required to fully understand the core aspect (triangle) of the Self to which it relates. Here it will be seen that the subsidiary Paths operate in the same pattern of zig-zag energies across the Tree as do the Sephiroth. Considering only the outermost Paths:

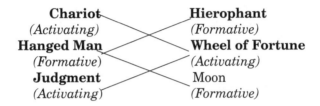

Chariot   **Hierophant**
(Activating)   *(Formative)*
Hanged Man   **Wheel of Fortune**
(Formative)   *(Activating)*
Judgment   Moon
(Activating)   *(Formative)*

The four upper Paths are the extremes of energy which maintain the opposite Pillars and which may thus be called Paths of *Stabilizing Extreme* energy which is either *Activating* or *Formative*. We then discover that at each level, the two Paths on either side of the balanced Middle Pillar share the qualities of the cards beside them, an even more complicated and interesting scheme appears, one which reveals card relationships obvious in no other way:

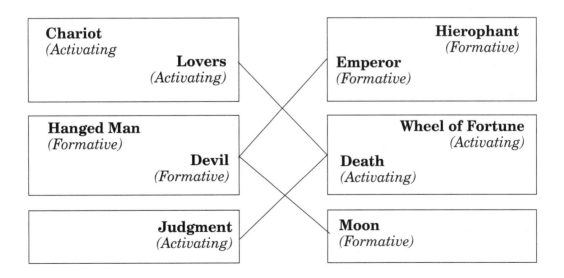

Chariot
(Activating

            Lovers
            (Activating)

                       Hierophant
                       (Formative)
Emperor
(Formative)

Hanged Man
(Formative)

            Devil
            (Formative)

                       Wheel of Fortune
                       (Activating)
Death
(Activating)

            Judgment
            (Activating)

Moon
(Formative)

Each Stabilizing Extreme Path is related to an inner *Connecting Path* (i.e., *The Lovers, The Emperor, Devil, Death*). These inner Paths connect the levels of the Self, rather than being a part of either Pillar; they may also be considered the lesser extremes of Activating and Formative energies. These, and the Paths of the Middle Pillar can be called *probationary Paths*.

To some extent, these definitions are arbitrary, yet it is essential that we make an attempt to place what we know into an overall intellectual perspective. From there we begin to internalize and personalize concepts so that we view our own lives differently than before. This process can be frustrating and painful.

Everyone who works seriously with the Tree of Life reaches a point where they are no longer able to take the symbols at face value, where the symbols seem somehow shallow and empty. It is then that one begins to ask: How do each of the Paths and Tarot Keys relate to me personally? The question may grow from an internal observation of one's own thinking process, what the Hermetic Mysteries would call "watching the watcher." We are all aware, of our own consciousness, although it is something on which very few people ever stop to focus. And as we observe our own process of attention to ourselves, we may well ask how the consciousness, as well as the observation of it fits on the Tree of Life.

To answer this question, let us consider our own bodies. The Qabalah neatly fits our physical vehicles into Malkuth (using the one Tree system) or Assiah (on the four Tree system). Moreover, while the body is a totality, working as a unity in whatever physical operation we may perform, we conceptualize its components as separate for the sake of understanding their individual contribution to the whole. The head is not the hand, although one does not function without the other. And it is not difficult to apply the various parts of the Tree of Life to the body. No great intellectual effort is required.

But when we become aware of our own consciousness, the Personality "I" that functions in our heads, we may experience difficulty in relating what we observe to the Tree of Life. Our self-awareness (which is in actuality limited to the Personality for most) does not fit anywhere on the Tree of Life *in toto*. The package of thoughts and feelings which we observe does not seem specifically applicable to any Sephira or Path. It can be said that Hod is intellect, that Netzach is intuition and feelings, or even that Yesod is our faculty of imagination. But when we think about something we are not functioning exclusively in Hod, anymore than when we use our imagination we are functioning exclusively in Yesod.

These qualities are not specific, they are fluid and interwoven. In fact, we are, of necessity, functioning on all Paths at once. Our Personality consciousness is the combined effect of what happens on these lower Paths. We cannot separate our thinking capacity from our feeling capacity, but we can focus on either (the alchemical process of *"dissolution"*). To do so is to begin the conscious travelling of a Path, where we encounter the trail left by many others who have pursued the same process. The Paths are partly the artificial separation out of twenty-two discrete aspects of consciousness; they are also the encounter of the same specific qualities in the universal consciousness of humanity. Using the formula

"As Above, so Below," we begin by studying our own personal intellectual and intuitive functions. As we begin to understand these, we also begin to recognize their patterns in all created human beings.

It may, thus, be appreciated why it is only possible to express these qualities in terms of symbols. The separation of the Body, the Personality, the Higher Self and The Spirit is only conceptual, the symbols providing a focus for study of any specific aspect of the inherently indivisible whole.

32. THE PATH OF TAU

The Universe
The Twenty-first Key

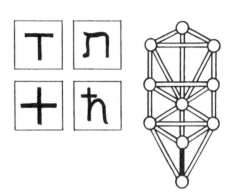

- ◈ PATH COLOR: Indigo
- ◈ RELATED SOUND: A Natural
- ◈ PLANET: Saturn
- ◈ MEANING: Tau Cross, Equal
      Armed Cross
- ◈ DOUBLE LETTER: Power-Servitude
- ◈ ESOTERIC TITLE: The Great One
      of the Night of Time

THIRTY-TWO PATHS OF WISDOM: *The Thirty-Second Path is the Administrative Intelligence, and it is so called because it directs and associates in all their operations the seven planets, even all of them in their own due course.*

Study of the Paths begins not with the first card, *The Fool*, but with the last, *The Universe* .[97] This is because we ascend the Tree of Life, working from our material perspective ("below") to the realms of Pure Spirit ("above"). Our understanding of the more refined universal patterns is based on what we learn on this earth. It is with the earth that serious esoteric work begins and ends, as long as our Divine Consciousness is functioning through a physical vehicle.

The Path of Tau, *The Universe*, joins Malkuth (The Earth) with Yesod (the Foundation). It is the first Path out of the material condition and leads toward an understanding of the Personality forged by the Higher Self of Tiphareth for each incarnation. The *Thirty Two Paths of Wisdom* calls this the "Administrative Intelligence," and says that it "directs and associates in all their operations the seven planets." Symbolically, this Path connects the earth with the balanced powers of Microprosopus represented by the *Hexagram* (seven Planets on the Tree of Life.)

Tau is the last letter of the Hebrew alphabet. Between Aleph and Tau is the entire Universe, referred to in Christian Greek terms as the *Alpha and Omega,* the beginning and the end. Tau means *cross,* a T-Cross as well as one which is equal-armed, which is appropriate to its position on the Cube of Space as described in the *Sepher Yetzirah.*

That book refers to Tau as the "Palace of Holiness, sustaining all things." It is both "Power and Servitude." And, when considered on the Cube of Space, it is found to be at the exact central point of the three Maternal Letters, Aleph, Mem and Shin, the symbolic forms of energy from which manifestation was created. The Path of *The Universe* is the key to all of this because it falls at the point where they all cross (refer again to Figure 24). This crossing point, where these primary energies are balanced, is the *sanctum sanctorum* of the devotional Mysteries. Some writers have even described this Path as "Heaven," or "Nirvana," meaning that here one experiences the consciousness of the Greater Universe, an ultimate reality by comparison with our sensory condition. And by the formula of "As above, so below," we understand that our experience of the completed universal pattern below tells us something about the Creator above.

One symbol which can be applied to both *The Fool* and *The Universe*, the beginning and the end, is the *swastica* or *gammadion*. In Kether its arms spin so rapidly that they merge and are perceived as a unified point. Such is the lesson of *The Fool*. On the Path of *The Universe*, however, it could be said that the swastica has slowed its spin so that each of the arms is completely perceptible and are seen to be perfectly balanced around the central point. This is the complete expression of The One in matter.

In discussing *The Universe* we are really discussing the world of matter. Most people have a dualist conception of themselves: they are body and mind, and when they dream or meditate, the images which come to them are considered to be divorced from the physical. Yet the Mysteries have stated for generations that the Cosmos is all mind, and that the distinction between mind and body is one of perception, not of actuality. In fact, when we close our eyes and see pictures, what we are first seeing is the most refined form of matter, the images and energy forms which are closest to the physical condition. The concept which must be grasped (an admittedly difficult one) is that most of the physical world is unseen. It is for this reason that on the scheme of the Four Worlds, the Malkuth of Assiah alone is described as our sphere of sensation. The idea is symbolized in the card by the seven pointed star representative of the *Seven Palaces of Assiah*. To experience the Path of *The Universe* is to be taken to the gateway of these seven palaces.

The Universe symbolizes a Path where the components of the Universal Plan become apparent, without necessarily being understood. One may enter the Holy of Holies, and encounter these forces in such a way as to be "in them, but not of them." What is important is that, as opposed to other Paths, the energies are all present in their full expression, and are self-balanced. This, as well as the idea that Tau is the central point of the Aleph, Mem and Shin Paths, is what is meant by the equal-armed cross.

From the standpoint of practical mysticism, *The Universe* may be considered the most important card in the deck, for it is the point at which we begin the process of inner exploration. It is the point where we step abruptly into a reality that may be at once frightening and reassuring because so much of what we encounter on this Path is of our own making. It is on this Path that we encounter our own individual personality consciousness, all that is inside our heads, divorced from the security of physical reality. It is the initiation of the Personality into its own structure, which is a Microcosmic Universe. At the same time, we encounter symbols and ideas which are of a greater consciousness than our own, and begin to see the ways in which our being relates to a total universal picture.

This is a Path which can only be successfully traveled by those who have begun to bring their Personalities into a self-understanding balance; those who have not will find themselves tormented by phantoms of their own making, and the gates closed to them. On the other hand, those who have truly come to grips with the life experience will find inner help and encouragement at every step. It is on the Path of *The Universe* that one discovers the extent to which the process of inner exploration is guided and, particularly, the very real protection and assistance given mankind by the Archangels. Until one begins these exercises, the Archangels are merely an abstraction, something in which one can vaguely believe or disbelieve.

A word of caution might be in order here. Insofar as *The Universe* is a Path of entry to the Astral, it must be reiterated that the Astral "seeks to deceive." A great many people believe themselves to be on one Path or another when they are, in actuality, entertaining themselves with an extended fantasy. We must be extremely cautious in accepting any of the images which appear to us as a "reality" of any sort, until we have applied every test of reason and feeling. There comes a time when we know that what we are experiencing could not possibly be of our own making because we are actually *learning*. We are acquiring new information which can often be verified or corroborated by research. One way or the other, a considerable amount of the gross must be sorted out before we come to the subtle. This is one of the most important lessons of *The Universe*, a Path which must be approached with the virtue of Malkuth, that of *discrimination*. It is only through discrimination that we can place ourselves in the "Administrative" balance symbolized by the dancing woman draped with the Caph-shaped scarf (reference to the *Wheel of Fortune*) and surrounded by the animal symbols of the Four Elements.

In Qabalistic terms, what is represented is, again, the principle of the four united by a fifth which is Spirit. Here we may recall that the earliest Qabalists (as in the *Sepher Yetzirah)* discussed only three Elements: Air, Water, and Fire, with Earth and Spirit being a later addition to the philosophy. And, as we have seen, the Tree of Life has changed form over the centuries to accommodate such conceptual changes. One such important change has related to the Thirty-Second Path which in some schemes is the only Path connecting the sphere of sensation to the rest of the Tree. The addition of the Paths of Shin (*Judgment*) and Qoph (*The Moon*) while primarily bringing the number of Paths in line with the Hebrew Alphabet, secondarily declared a direct connection between Malkuth and the two side pillars.

One very interesting illustration from the Sixteenth Century shows a man holding the entire Tree by the Path of *The Universe.*[98] So we see that for four hundred years, at least, the essential interpretation of this Path as an experiential foundation for consciously travelling all of the other Paths has not changed, though the concept has been slightly mitigated by the addition of the two Paths.

The principle that we grasp the entire Tree through what is taught on the Path of the Universe is very profound, and brings us back to the idea of the "as above, so below." We have discussed the "will to form," of Binah, the Great Mother, which is the origin of life consciousness, and which is Saturn in the exalted Supernal Realm. This is the same energy, now completely expressed, found on the Thirty-Second Path. The female figure at the center of the card is the fullest expression of the Great Mother who is *The Empress.* She is Isis, the *Aima Elohim;* she is Binah; she is Saturn; she is all the principles behind what we perceive as matter, the Cosmic Dancer who administers and activates the Elements. She is also a doorway to and from Malkuth, Saturn who both gives life and destroys it, the great tester who rules both birth and death. When we die, leaving behind our "animal skin," it is on this Path that we rise like the dancer symbolically surrounded by a ring of stars.

All of the key Tarot decks are agreed that the female figure should be surrounded by an oval shape of some sort. In Crowley's deck this is a ring of stars. In the Marseilles and Waite decks this is a wreath. In the Golden Dawn deck the oval is formed by twelve spheres (the twelve Signs of the Zodiac) bound together by seventy-two pearls (the *Shemhamaphoresch,* or Seventy-Two Names of God). What is symbolized is both the womb of the human female, through which the child passes in birth, and the Great Womb into which the soul passes in death.

The profound symbolism of the Great Mother through which one passes as a doorway to and from life is, unfortunately, minimized by some writers (including Case) who state that "tradition" claims the female figure to be hermaphroditic. That idea is unreasonable, but may be an honest attempt on the part of some Qabalistic theoreticians to reconcile the femininity of the Path with the Magical Image of Yesod into which it leads, a "Beautiful Naked Man."[99] The latter represents the eternal outpouring of the Christ-Spirit from Tiphareth, personified within Yesod before it passes down to Malkuth. The Christian mystery is not simply an event of two thousand years ago to be recalled with reverence; it is a secret key to a natural pattern. The Christ (Buddha or Osiris or Krishna) force continues to be born into our world, be sacrificed for the benefit of mankind, resurrected and assumed. This is, like the Yod Heh Vau Heh, continual to the end of *time,* which will be the end of the race's need for sensory experience. Time is, of course, one of Saturn's primary restrictions.

As long as we are functioning within the framework of time an event, including the down pouring and uprising of Tiphareth force, must have a beginning, a middle and an end. Life processes run in waves, or spirals which come back upon themselves. This is the natural course of the akashic fluid of Yesod. Thus, again, is the woman shown dancing. She swirls and revolves as opposed to her most abstract form of energy, *The Empress,* where she is placed solidly on a Supernal Throne. This spiral Force of nature is directed by the wands which she carries: they represent active and passive energy, each of which has two poles.

Crowley's card shows these natural forces as the serpent Kundalini, described as "Coiled in Yesod." This is a reference to the primary sexual forces of nature to be encountered with *The Universe.* These are the forces which we learn to direct in ourselves and onto which we impose the strictures of Binah, the Great Mother, the Great Sea.

Water is very important to this Path which is the Great Sea of consciousness in its most dense and difficult expression. The Thirty-Second Path might be considered a dark cave, filled with treacherous caverns and tunnels, some of which lead to the Light, but others of which lead to the Qlippoth.

31. THE PATH OF SHIN
Judgment
The Twentieth Key

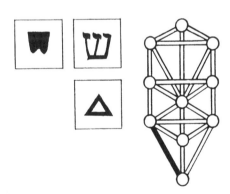

- ❖ PATH COLOR: Glowing Orange Scarlet
- ❖ RELATED SOUND: C Natural
- ❖ MEANING: Tooth
- ❖ MATERNAL LETTER: Fire
- ❖ ESOTERIC TITLE: The Spirit of the Primal Fire

THIRTY-TWO PATHS OF WISDOM: The Path of Shin, Judgment, *joins Malkuth (the Earth) with Hod (Splendour), the base Sephira and completion of the Pillar of Severity. The Earth is thus connected with that which is the ultimate expression of Binah, the Will to Form. It is an activating Path of intellect, while its opposite, The Moon is a formative Path of emotion.*

What is shown here as "judgment" is a process undergone by the Personality as it strives to become conscious of its own inner working. But the judgment is not momentary or limited. It is, as the *Thirty Two Paths of Wisdom* describes, *perpetual*. It is the continuous monitoring of the progress of the Personality toward universal consciousness. That which is deemed unworthy by the angelic powers, invoked by the desire of the student travelling the Paths, is slowly burned away by the redeeming fire, a process which is actually physical.

The Golden Dawn text calls this Path the "Splendour of the Material World," pointing out the relationship of the Path to the physical body. What is shown here is a resurrection, a rebirth. This resurrection is based on the developments of the opposite card to this Path, *The Moon*, and relates to actual physiological changes which occur in the student as the result of the disciplined quest for a greater reality. In other words, the resurrected body is physiologically rebuilt, a process stimulated by the energies of Qoph, *The Moon*. This is what Paul Foster Case describes as the process of building a master's body.

This is also a Path where the components of the Personality first encountered in *The Universe*, are critically analyzed and evaluated (judged). It is the bright and fiery probationary path of the intellect, as *The Moon* is the dark, cold and watery probationary Path of the emotions. These are Paths introductory to the true nature of the Self in incarnation and can thus be extremely difficult. In fact all of the Elemental Paths (*The Fool, The Hanged Man, Judgment*) are difficult to understand. The problem arises partly in that on each of these Paths all of the Elements are present, in either expressed or unexpressed form. We shall return to this concept.

First, let us consider the pattern of the Maternals. The *Sepher Yetzirah* states that Air produces Water which produces Fire. *The Fool* is pure Air, *The Hanged Man* is Air acted upon by Water, *Judgment* is Air and Water acted upon by Fire within the vehicle of Earth (the *crucible* which, in Spiritual Alchemy, is our own body).

The Golden Dawn and Waite cards picture Air above, with Water between two sections of Earth. It is understood that the Air, Water and Earth are being heated and activated by Fire. There are no flames here, for the action is a slow and steady (perpetual) one brought about by the Archangel. This effect is on the component dualities of the individual, which are symbolized by Fire and Water: Mind-consciousness (Water) is activated by the Dynamic Principle (Fire) in the presence of the equilibriating energy (Air) within the physical vehicle (Earth). The Path of *Judgment* is, therefore, aimed at producing a balance within the individual, necessary for a total understanding of the Personality structure and its relationship to the greater Universe.

But to say that "balance" is produced on this Path raises a question. One might well ask how it is possible for there to be balance in any Path which is not on the Middle Pillar. The answer is found in the idea that *every symbol is a duality, containing its own opposite.* As with the flashing colors, a symbol is only functional insofar as it is a self-contained balance of two extremes. To extend this principle to the Paths, we see that each Path must contain the essential components of its opposite Path. Here we may return to the example of Hod and Netzach, which relate to *Judgment* and *The Moon* respectively. Intellect applied without feeling is as pathological as feeling applied without intellect. When we travel the Path of *Judgment* we learn the lessons of *The Moon*. And, taken to the most refined aspect of the Tree of Life, when we travel the Path of *The Magician* we learn the lessons of *The Fool*. Such cards are different, but mutually explanatory. It is not possible to deal with any card without its opposite energy being present. And since the cards represent types of consciousness, it can be said that everything which we experience, every idea, every activity, co-exists in us with its opposite.

Such lessons on the Paths are extremely practical, although this cannot be obvious as one begins to juggle the slippery concepts related to the four symbolic Elements. On the other hand, the pictures on the cards bear a strong relationship to the visual experience of the Paths, and a great deal can be learned by meditation on them. Path images are archetypal representations of actual inner roads built through centuries of mind work by the most advanced men and women of all ages. These images are largely constructs built to assist us by those who have gone before. It is in this that many falter, believing the construct (the concretized symbol on the astral plane) to have a reality of its own. It is only beyond the lower astral that one touches upon the realities which activate the symbols.

We may step onto the *Judgment* Path and experience initially what is shown in the Tarot card. Yet beyond these visual constructs, we come to understand that the Path is the enervating, activating effect of the cosmic motive principle on the individual consciousness: the Fiery Spirit permeates the Personality consciousness in the descent of energy into matter. In the purposeful ascent of the Path of Shin the last illusions of the separateness of the Personality are burned away.

To reiterate the Qabalistic symbolism: Shin contains all four Elements: Fire, Water, Air and Earth. This concept may be explained developmentally:

The evolution of the Cosmos is from the most simple to the most complex. It goes from nothing to something. This is (applying the principle of "As Above, so, Below") a process not dissimilar to that of the *zygote*, which begins as a single cell, is fertilized and grows into a living human organism. The cells of the zygote multiply over and over again until they are a body which is the receptacle of the Holy Spirit on this Earth. At any stage of development, from the single fertilized cell, to the finished product, the whole is implicit in the developing parts. Thus does the *One* grow to the ten or ten thousand or ten billions of uncountable mind cells which form the corpus of the Universe. The ultimate simplicity is *The Fool*, and the ultimate complexity is *The Universe*. But *The Universe* and all the other cards are implicit, unexpressed, in *The Fool*. Thus, with the cards in between, we find different stages of that which is expressed and unexpressed. Given any specific card on the Tree, the energy of all the cards above it are expressed while the energies of those cards below it are present but unexpressed. Each defines a stage of development. And, using this logic, it may be appreciated that in *The Fool* Air is expressed, while Water and Fire are implicit. In *The Hanged Man* Air and Water are expressed and Fire is implicit. When we come to *Judgment* we again find Air and Water expressed, now set in motion by the full expression of Fire.

Here it must be repeated that these patterns will be utterly meaningless until a real understanding of that which is symbolized by the various "Elements" emerges. Every Qabalistic symbol relates to some specific part of the self, the Tarot Keys being very precise definitions of parts of the human whole.

The Paths of *Judgment, The Universe* and *The Moon* are aspects of the normal waking consciousness of the Personality. They also represent stages of self understanding. *Judgment* is the card where the divine forces meet the aspirant for the Mysteries, where the Personality is lifted from the tomb of matter and evaluated on the extent to which it has balanced the four Elements of Malkuth. It is for this reason that people have such varying experiences on this Path; each Personality must face what it is and has been, very squarely, answering the call of the angel whose presence has been invoked by the fire of desire. In all accounts it is Gabriel who blows the trumpet of the *Last Judgment*, and most will assume that it is Gabriel who is represented here. But this is not a Last Judgment at all, and the Archangel is *Michael*, Angelic Ruler of Hod.

Further information about this card is conveyed by the meaning of the Hebrew Letter, insofar as the name of each letter is a word. Yet, as such words are attributed to the Tarot Keys there is wide latitude for interpretation within the confines of the qualities described by the given word. Shin, in this case, means *tooth*, suggesting hardness, sharpness and biting. It can be interpreted as the teeth which chew prior to the ingestion of energy into the system, i.e., as that which causes a release of energy (the *kundalini* force). Tooth can also be taken to mean that which kills, here meaning the final blow to the perception of the Personality as separate.

Such descriptive words amplify the symbolism of numbers, so important to the Hermetic Qabalah. As has been demonstrated, the number 300 assigned to Shin reduces to 3, the number of the Sephira Binah; the number of the card, 20, reduces to 2, that of *The High Priestess*. The principle here is that numbers of the Hebrew letters are reduced and manipulated relative to the ten Sephiroth, while the numbers of the cards (0-21) relate to other cards. Of course, the connection with other cards is made on more than numerical grounds. For example, the fact that Shin is Fire suggests that it relates to two other important cards, *The Tower* (Mars) and *The Sun*

This connection with *The Sun* is underscored in the Golden Dawn *"Book T,"* which describes the angel in this card as Michael, Ruler of Solar Fire. It is he who blows the trumpet calling down the influence of Binah. Another reference to the Supernals is the red cross banner, which stands for the Four Rivers of Paradise, as well as the four letters of the Divine Name.

The rainbow in the Order's card, containing serpents representing the fiery Seraphim, is undoubtedly that which surrounds the fiery Throne of God described in *Revelation*.[100] This rainbow encloses the Archangel who seems to emerge from the fire triangle itself.

At the base of the card, rising from the tomb facing the angelic presence, is *Arel,* Ruler of Latent Heat. He is also the candidate for the Mysteries who follows this Path of Fire. The male figure at the left is Samael, Ruler of Volcanic Fire. Opposite him is Anael, Ruler of the Astral Light, represented in duplicate in that she is Demeter-Persephone and Isis-Nephthys.

Crowley's card, called *"The Aeon,"* departs completely from tradition, and is important in that his personal philosophy is more imbedded in this imagery than in that of most other cards of the *Thoth Tarot*. Overall, the Crowley deck is illustrative of the *Book of the Law,* a document which he stated was revealed to him and which is the core of his teaching. *The Aeon* also relates to what he called the *Stele of Revealing*.[101]

This card, he explained, supersedes all earlier concepts of the Key, and shows the harmonious and spiritual state of human existence which will be on the earth in the mid twenty-second century. That condition is symbolized by the Sky Goddess Nuith, and her consort Hadit (represented as a golden orb of light). They produce Horus, here shown seated and standing, his active and passive forms. Crowley also points out that another name for Horus is *Heru,* which is synonymous with *Hru,* called "The Great Angel set over the Tarot."

What Crowley proposes here is highly consistent with Qabalistic doctrine, *i.e.*, that the system evolves to meet the needs of spiritual evolution of the race. Assuming that *Judgment* represents a stage in the development of the race and of the individual Personality consciousness, he is suggesting that there will come a time in the not so far distant future when the spiritual make-up of humanity will have so advanced that *Judgment*, as previously known, will no longer describe the experience of this Path. He further asserts that we are now passing into a five hundred year period of extreme darkness and trial, preparatory to a new Aeon of Light.[102]

30. THE PATH OF RESH
The Sun
The Nineteenth Key

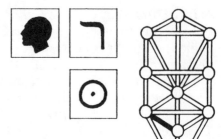

◆ PATH COLOR: Orange
◆ RELATED SOUND: D Natural
◆ PLANET: Sun
◆ MEANING: Head
◆ DOUBLE LETTER: Fertility-
　　Barrenness
◆ ESOTERIC TITLE: The Lord of
　　the Fire of the World

THIRTY-TWO PATHS OF WISDOM: *The Thirtieth Path is the Collecting Intelligence and is so-called because Astrologers deduce from it the judgment of the Stars, and of the celestial signs, and the perfection of their science, according to the rules of their resolutions.*

The Path of Resh connects Hod (Splendor) with Yesod (the Foundation), and is the first of the Paths of the Personality triad to be encountered in rising on the Tree. It is an active Path on the intellectual-formative side; it is the activating force of the Personality which, like the Higher Self and the Spiritual Self, is composed of a "masculine" (intuitive-dynamic, Yod) and a "feminine" (intellectual-formative, Heh) and a set of energies which are the result of the opposing interaction of the two (equilibriating, Vau).

The Sun (Resh) is described as the "Collecting Intelligence," meaning that it exercises control over a number of given components, in this case the Signs of the Zodiac which are symbolized by the twelve rays emanating from *The Sun*. These Signs are the twelve guideposts of Personality and receptacles of planetary influences, one of which governs the birth and life course of each incarnation.

Thus *The Sun* is central not only to the incarnation at hand, but acts as a link between the Personalities which have been experienced in other incarnations. It is also "collecting" in that all of the component parts of the Personality, discovered on these lower Paths, are here infused with the dual action of the sun, light and warmth. It may appear curious, but these are considered intellectual qualities.

The activity of this Path is intellectual. In fact, the Path of *The Sun* is the highest level of the human intellect, as *The Star* is the highest level of the emotions. They are balanced by *The Tower*, although looking at that card may hardly inspire confidence that a balance is taking place. Yet this represents the effect of the combined energies of *The Sun* and *The Star*. More will be said of this in a later section.

Resh means *head,* which is consistent with the idea that this is the highest Path of human intellect, and that this is the "Collecting Intelligence." In this regard there is an interesting illustration from an alchemical manuscript of 1606, showing a figure with an orb-shaped body which is headless, but holds the Sun above. Beside this figure is written: "The World."[103] The head is the Sun itself, held above the material body; without the Sun-head, there could be no world. Mathers corroborates this idea by calling *The Sun* the "Splendour of the Material World." So the card basically represents the intellect acting upon the dualities of the human condition, consciousness and its earthly vehicle. This is the point of connection of the human intellect with the higher intellect, the Greater Life. The Sun is also the Son who carries on the work of the Father.

The Thirtieth Path is a composite one: The Four Elements, the Signs of the Zodiac and the planets are all involved, under the rulership of the sun, as is symbolized by the Hexagram. That figure means the perfect integration of Personality and Higher Self. On the Tree of life this is shown as the interaction of the Astral and Ethical Triangles, God the Son of Tiphareth being primary to both. However the energies may be symbolized, the Path of *The Sun* is a very important initiatory one.

The experience of *The Sun* is very profound, for it is an introduction to the inner sun which is the light of the Personality as the physical sun is the light of the material world. On this Path one experiences the warmth and light but, as on the plane of sensation, it is a sun at which one cannot look directly without suffering damage. The opposites attributed to Resh by the *Sepher Yetzirah,* fertility and barrenness, remind us that the same sun which illuminates and causes growth can destroy utterly. The blessing of the farmer is the curse of the solitary traveler in the desert, and it is on this Path that one discovers the great potentials of this power. This is the initiation of the Personality to the great source of Inner Light, an initiation which takes place within the physical vehicle (walled garden) and affects the dual components of the Lower Self (Personality).

An important point must be repeated here, one all too often neglected by those who discuss the Paths: Work on the Paths brings about definite physiochemical changes in the human body. In his study course, *The Thirty-Two Paths of Wisdom,* Paul Case emphasizes the extent to which this is the case. In describing the Path of Resh, he says of the person who has achieved adepthood:

> ...marked inner differences from the average person are due to
> psychological contrasts to the mental states of ordinary human
> beings, but they are also the outer signs of organic changes inside
> the skin of the new creature. He is chemically and structurally
> unlike *genus homo*. There are different constituents in his blood
> stream. Through his nervous system pass currents of force not
> present in most human bodies because in his organism channels
> are open which are closed in the physical vehicles of most per-
> sons. Centers in the nervous system and in the brain, and glands
> related to them, function differently in the body of an adept from
> the way they do in the bodies of the greater number of his contem-
> poraries.[104]

It must also be borne in mind that the Personality, the component parts
of which are symbolized by these lower Paths, functions through the body as an
experience-collecting vehicle for the Spirit. One of the most serious mistakes
which can be made is to conceptually divorce the physical body from the powers
which created it and which function through it. This is the crucible of the alchemists, and the sun is an important symbol in the alchemical process of "turning
lead into Gold."

The Paths of the Personality lead directly into the physical vehicle, *i.e.*,
that consciousness which we know as "self" is directly connected to our bodies. The Higher Self functions through the Personality if its influence is to be
brought to the physical plane, as Pure Spirit must function through the Higher
Self. Of course, there is no actual separation between these three: *The Tree of
Life describes a racial perception of a pattern of separation. But since perception
varies widely from organism to organism, each individual must literally create
his or her own Qabalah.* The experience of the Path of Resh is critical to the development of this individual Qabalah. It is, moreover, the Path where one may
receive the acceptance and imprint of those beings who direct the inner learning
experience of the student. It is the point at which the student may be admitted
to candidacy for the greater initiation of Tiphareth.

A considerable number of discoveries are made on this Path leading into
Hod, a realm described by some as the point where the inner teachers exert
their influence on the material world. This is a Path where the nature of the
relationship between mind and body may become clear and where one begins
to understand the control and limitations of the intellect. It is also a Path of
awakening to the use of the tremendous sexual power of Yesod. It is the point at
which sexuality is understood to be the great "secret" force manipulated by the
initiate of the Mysteries.

Yesod is the Moon, sexuality, the ebbing and flowing Astral Light beneath
our material existence. Hod is Mercury, the first differentiation of the specific
Personality. It is hermaphroditic, both male and female, as these qualities have
yet to be separated out when considering the Sephira on a downward course

toward manifestation. The Path of *The Sun*, thus considered developmentally, is the point of childhood of the emerging Personality as it builds toward a new incarnation. When we travel this Path upwards, we return to this point of new innocence. It is, quite literally, a growing younger, a process of birth backwards until we reach a stage where there is some recollection of the source from which we emerged.

This youthfulness, the childhood of the sun, is represented in Waite's card. Here, following an iconography developed by Lévi, a child is shown riding a white horse, symbol of Apollo, the Sun God. The implication is that on this Path we become the child Apollo.

The Golden Dawn card, basically following the Marseilles version, shows two naked children in a garden enclosed by a wall. One is standing on Earth, the other is standing on Water. These are the purest expression of the positive (male) and negative (female) principles in incarnation, interwoven as in the Chinese *Yin* and *Yang*. The active male principle operates through the solid Earth, while the passive female principle operates through the fluid consciousness of Water. They hold hands to indicate that their activities are reciprocal. This is also a reference to Gemini, the sign which links Taurus (Earth) and Cancer (Water). Gemini was also the sign referred by the Greeks and Romans to Apollo and to the Sun.

The relationship of the sun to the Zodiac is of some importance, as is indicated by the twelve rays in both the Golden Dawn and Crowley cards (Waite used 22 and the Marseilles deck 16). The Zodiac relates to Chokmah, from which the energy of this Path ultimately derives. The patterns of this energy are, moreover, shown by the salient and wavy rays, the alternating male and female currents. The seven falling *Yods* (Chokmah, again, being the ultimate source of the Yod) refer to the energies of the planets, under solar rulership, descending into matter.

Crowley's card is related to *Judgment*, which he called *The Aeon*. It shows *Heru-Ra-Ha*, the Lord of Light who is the ruler of the new aeon to come, the next stage of human development. Appreciating this emphasis, it is curiously amusing to realize that Crowley has based the card on his own family crest, "the sun charged with a rose on a mont vert."[105]

According to his explanation, the rose surrounded by the signs of the Zodiac shows the development of solar influence. The green mound of earth beneath the rose-sun means fertility, and is so shaped as to suggest aspiration toward the higher. As in the other versions, there is a walled enclosure, but here the children are outside of it, meaning that humanity is no longer bound by the "prejudices of the people that date morally from about 25,000 B.C.E."[106] Most interesting, perhaps, is Crowley's point that the cross, from the formula of the Rose-Cross, will expand into the sun and twelve rays. It will no longer be limited by four arms, but will radiate outward freely.

One especially significant idea connected with this Path is, as the Golden Dawn ritual of the Twenty-Ninth Path states, that the "Sun embraces the whole of creation in its rays."[107] This idea is conveyed in a variety of ways, such as by the four sunflowers and twenty-two rays in Waite's card, meaning the Four

Worlds and Twenty-Two Paths. The Golden Dawn card shows ten flowers, to represent the totality of the Tree of Life. And Crowley's card, as has been noted, attempts to show the expansion of the rose and cross in relationship to the central sun of manifestation. Thus, it too refers to the totality of creation made warm and bright by the rays of the sun. Of course it is necessary, once more, to observe the distinction between the two sides of the *Abyss*. Creation and light mean all of Microprosopus to which Tiphareth is central. Potential, yet darkness, refers to Macroprosopus, *i.e.*, the Supernal Triangle.

29. THE PATH OF QOPH
The Moon
The Eighteenth Key

   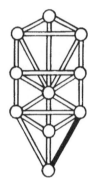

◈   PATH COLOR: Crimson (Ultra violet)
◈   RELATED SOUND: B Natural
◈   SIGN: Pisces (Mutable Water)
◈   MEANING: Back of Head, Ear
◈   SIMPLE LETTER: Sleep
◈   ESOTERIC TITLE: The Ruler of Flux and Reflux. The Child of the Sons of the Mighty.

THIRTY-TWO PATHS OF WISDOM: *The Twenty-ninth Path is the Corporeal Intelligence, so-called because it forms every body which is formed beneath the whole set of worlds and the increment of them.*

The Path of Qoph connects Netzach (Victory) with Malkuth (The King-dom), and is described not only as the "Victory of the Material World," but as the "deceptive effect of the apparent power of Material Forces." Crowley calls this Path the "Gateway of Resurrection...the threshold of life...or spiritual re-birth, which may be considered at two levels: First, in the course of incarna-tion, it is the stage of the soul's organization of the physical body which it will inhabit. It is a "sleep" (as attributed to Qoph by the *Sepher Yetzirah)* preceding the waking mortal consciousness, a form of pre-consciousness differentiating into matter from the collective unconscious of Netzach. Second, in terms of the spiritually-developing individual, it is a conquest of the phantoms reflected from the material world, what the Golden Dawn described as "The Child of the Sons of the Mighty," meaning the "creations of the created." This is a watery Path of probation, where the student must face and conquer the phantoms of the dark-est recesses of the individual mind, as well as those of the race. In that sense it can be a terrible and frightening Path, involving real dangers to the emotional stability of those who are not strong enough to handle this experience; such in-ner disturbance may actually result in serious physical problems. On the other hand, tradition states that the successful treading of this Path confers the pow-ers of "bewitchments and casting illusions." When we slay the dragons of the deep recesses of our sleep-consciousness, and understand their mechanisms, we gain the capacity to manipulate those qualities in ourselves as well as in oth-ers.

The meaning of Qoph is the *back of the head.* It is behind the head itself, which is Resh (*The Sun*). Thus, what is symbolized by *The Moon* is anterior to the bright intellectual awareness of *The Sun.* At this level of the Tree the moon only reflects the light of the sun; the Path at the center of the card is going from the dark side of the moon, toward the light side on which the Sun shines directly. Here is should be noted that Crowley disagreed pointedly with the Golden Dawn and Waite interpretation which say that the Moon is in its increase.[108] The ratio-nale given is that the crayfish is the symbol of Cancer, meaning that when the Sun is in Pisces, the Moon will be increasing in Cancer. So the Crayfish emerg-ing from the Water, at one level, was intended to mean: "the sun below the hori-zon as he ever is when the moon is increasing above."[109]

Another important idea expressed in the Golden Dawn manuscripts is that of the crayfish imagery developed from the scarab or dung-beetle.[110] Crowley de-veloped this idea, making the dung-bettle central to his card and emphasizing the darker aspects of the Path. He called this "The Waning moon of witchcraft, and abominable deeds...the poisoned darkness which is the condition of the rebirth of Light.[111] The rebirth of the Light out of a hideous and abominable darkness is his primary concern, one admirably symbolized by the beetle, a reference to Khephera, Father of the Gods, and the great God of creation and resurrection.[112] The beetle, or scarabaeus, (called khephera by the Egyptians) was the God's key symbol. As a species, this is a beetle which lays its eggs in a ball of dung, which it pushes along, and from which the eggs eventually hatch as they are subjected to the warmth of the sun. The dung-ball was considered to be like the sun itself, for it contained all that was necessary for growth and nourishment.

In some respects the form emerging from the waters is both the highest and the lowest. It is the very originator of life as it is Khephera, the God who is said to have emerged as a beetle "from the watery mass of Nu." It is the highest creative force, beginning its material self-expression as the lowest organic form. The crayfish means the organic evolution of the human race; it also refers to the cellular development of the physical vehicle from the inner roots of nature. And, as an originator of form, Pisces (ruled by Jupiter) relates to Chesed. The very earliest Golden Dawn papers, the so-called *Ancient Cypher Manuscripts* say of Pisces "by it the waters of Chesed flow down,"[113] meaning that it is a primary formative consciousness at the lowest level of the Tree.

Of course, the most important Tarot reference to the moon is with *The High Priestess,* the Path of Gimel leading directly from God the Father to God the Son. *The High Priestess* is the source of the crystal clear waters of consciousness emerging from the Godhead. The same waters are seen here in *The Moon*, but they are polluted! This is not to imply that there is anything intrinsically evil on this Path. Rather, its phantoms relate to the density of the physical body, that compound organism affected by all three Paths leading into Malkuth: *Judgment, The Moon* and *The Universe*. As has been described, the process of travelling the Paths has a definite effect on the body. The physical vehicle is subtly modified as the light descends into it, and as the Personality becomes increasingly aware of the presence and activities of the Higher Self.

Relative to the human body, the Path of *The Moon* is an organizing (formative) one. It is described in the *Thirty-Two Paths of Wisdom* as the "Corporeal Intelligence," which Case tells us means "body consciousness." He notes also that the root of the word "corporeal" in Hebrew means "to rain upon."[114] In each of the three cards Yods are shown "raining" down upon the Path. Or, as Pausanius described, these might be the tears of the Moon Goddess, which caused the Nile to rise and fall.[115] There is, in any event, a general agreement that something descends from the Moon to the Earth on this Path as is symbolized by the falling Yods.

In Waite's card there are fifteen Yods, a possible reference to the bondage of matter symbolized by the fifteenth Key, *The Devil*. The Golden Dawn card shows four yods, one for the powers of each of the Four Worlds, while Crowley uses nine as a reference to Yesod. He describes these as "drops of impure blood"[116] meaning the cycle of menstruation. He describes the Path as a stream of serum tinged with blood.

Indeed, the activity of menstruation and its dark blood is intimately connected to this Path, the Path of childbirth presided over by the Greek Goddess Artemis."[117] As the sister of Apollo, the Sun, Artemis was the Moon. Like her Roman counterpart, Diana, she was a Goddess of the hunt, travelling through brutal and mountainous woods with her pack of hounds. Thus is childbirth linked with the most savage aspects of nature. The Goddess, like the Path, can be vicious and unforgiving, her legend being filled with qualities at once dark and vindictive. Any breech of her regulations was immediately and ferociously punished. So, from the standpoint of Greek legend, the dogs of *The Moon* may be considered to be those of Artemis, ready to attack and destroy those who displease her. The very idea is barbaric and uncivilized, as is the Path of Qoph. This is a primitive Path, one of raw animal nature. It is a Path of animal instincts (the law of the jungle), passions and energies uncontrolled by intellectual, moral or ethical considerations. This can be a very cruel Path, showing us aspects of ourselves which society forces us to repress, but which are an integral and undeniable part of our human make-up. Yet we approach the images and lessons of this Path with our whole being, applying reason to that which we encounter, as we apply feeling to that which is encountered on the Path of *Judgment*.

The Moon is one of the cards for which tradition has provided a very definite structure, both the Golden Dawn and Waite cards being wholly dependant on the design shown in the Marseilles version: Two dogs (in Waite's deck they are a dog and a wolf) stand threateningly beneath a personified moon, between two desolate towers. A crayfish is in the water below. Here it is at least interesting to observe that in the Marseilles version no Path is shown, and it is only by inference that one realizes that the crayfish will eventually pass between the two very ferocious dogs.

Mathers and Crowley were in agreement that these should actually be considered the jackals of Anubis, the scavengers of the dead. Anubis was the jackal God, and the great God of the Underworld, charged with both the judgment and the embalming of the deceased. In the Tarot this means the natural deterioration of the physical body in death, the return of its energy into the unseen, as well as a suggestion of correspondence with the Path of Shin, *Judgment*. The implication is that the activity of natural forces on the body in death is concurrent with the "weighing of the soul" on that Path.

Anubis is a very complex God of lunar opposites, as is suggested by Crowley's dual figures. Anubis is a God of light and of darkness, of death and of resurrection, whose cult was a fascination to those ancient societies in the shadow of Egypt. Describing the subtleties of this deity's cult to the Romans, Plutarch wrote:

> By Anubis they understand the horizontal circle, which divides the invisible part of the world, which they call Nephthys, from the visible, to which they give the name Isis; and as this circle equally touches upon the confines of both light and darkness, it may be looked upon as common to them both—and from this circumstance arose that resemblance which they imagine between Anubis and the dog, it being observed of this animal that he is equally watchful by day and by night. In short, the Egyptian Anubis seems to be much of the same power and nature as the Greek Hecate, a deity common both to the celestial and infernal regions.

Pursuant to the idea of Anubis and resurrection, there is a definite relationship to the Christ legend. It can be said, however whimsically, that in an obscure medieval symbolism the lobster is a symbol of the risen Christ.[119] And, one must be exceedingly cautious in dismissing such symbolism out of hand, because of the Tarot's very elusive, but unquestionably medieval, origins. In the fourteenth century every symbol, however occult, was related to Christ.

One way or the other, birth, death and resurrection are pivotal concepts on the Path of *The Moon*. These are not symbolic processes; they are biological, and occur in the darkness and the light of our sense perception. The energy process, a cyclic wave motion, is shown by Crowley as a pattern of both above and below, linked by the Beetle of the Sun.

To reiterate the meaning of this murky Path in the most simple of terms: this is the natural energy from which our physical bodies develop in the womb. It is a process that is continual throughout our lives, as cells die and are replaced. The work of this Path is ended with the dissolution of energy back to its source, which is Netzach.

To understand this Path is to understand the relationship of our Personality consciousness to the physical vehicle built for each incarnation, a very difficult undertaking for most people, who perceive themselves as having existence only through their bodies. Here the meaning of the simple letter Qoph, sleep, gives an important clue. During the cyclic phase of withdrawal of consciousness from the physical, most people continue to act on information and fantasies closely related to their bodily existence. Their dreams are filled with the shades of matter which, once consciously transcended, is the conquest of the Path of *The Moon*.

28. THE PATH OF TZADDI
The Star
The Seventeenth Key

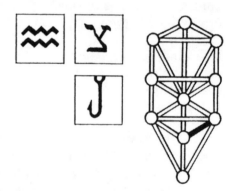

◈   PATH COLOR: Violet
◈   RELATED SOUND: A-Sharp
◈   SIGN: Aquarius (Fixed Air)
◈   MEANING: Fish Hook
◈   SIMPLE LETTER: Imagination
◈   ESOTERIC TITLE: The Daughter of the Firmament: the Dweller between the Waters.

THIRTY-TWO PATHS OF WISDOM: *The Twenty-eighth Path is called the Natural Intelligence, and it is so-called because through it is consummated and perfected the Nature of every existing thing beneath the Sun.*

The Path of Tzaddi, *The Star*, connects Netzach (Victory) with Yesod (The Foundation). It is a very powerful Path which points out the way in which the Divine Energy inherent in each individual is properly approached. The letter Tzaddi means *fish hook,* implying meditation, a process closely linked with the

use of imagination. In these terms meditation is described not as taking out of something, but as a putting in (merging) of two streams of individual consciousness with the greater consciousness. And while this is a Path of primal intuition, the vessels represent a separation and then reintegration of the Chokmah force (feelings and intuition, at this level) and Binah force (intellect). The symbolism of the fish hook in meditation is easily extended to the Tree of Life: The hook (Tzaddi, *The Star*) is put into the waters of Mem (*The Hanged Man*) to catch the fish (Nun, *Death*). Water is, again, a symbol of consciousness. As we experiment with meditation and imaginative visualization, casting ourselves into the Universal Sea, we seek an understanding of the very processes of life and death.

The *Thirty-Two Paths of Wisdom* describes this Path as the *Natural Intelligence,* suggesting the raw forces of nature attributed to Netzach; the *Elohim* (Gods of Netzach) are synonymous with nature itself. Moreover, this Natural Intelligence is related to the energies symbolized in another card, *Strength*. The number of *The Star*, 17, reduces to the number of *Strength*, 8. That card represents the conscious control of Kundalini energy, variously described as *solar* and as *sexual*. We recall that the serpent Kundalini (the same which tempts Eve on the Tree of Knowledge of Good and Evil) is said to be "coiled in Yesod," although when it is shown on the Tree of Life it touches each and every Path. As we encounter the Kundalini force, the sexual energies in ourselves, we approach the Greater Mysteries of Tiphareth, the Solar Logos which is the central star of our existence. The process of approach is a kind of yoga, involving the enervation of centers of energy. It is this energy which we use in the meditation process; it is both the means and the goal of enlightenment, for, as the text states of Tzaddi: "Through it is consummated and perfected the Nature of every existing thing beneath the Sun." *The Star* is the means of perfection; it is the method.

As Case states of this method: "Meditation is really a function of the ego, which raises to the conscious level the powers of the automatic consciousness of Yesod...however much it may seem to us at first that meditation is a personal activity, when we really succeed in meditation we discover that what happens is not that we meditate, but rather that *we are meditated.*"[120] The idea is that the

Higher Self (what Case is calling the Ego) brings the Personality into meditation. The "fish hook" is partially the search of the Personality consciousness for reality in the context of meditation, but it is also the angling of the Higher Self to pull the Personality up from its depths of self-enclosure. The figure on this card is the most pure manifestation of the Great Mother at the level of the Personality, and prior to its enclosure in matter. For this reason it is completely unveiled: it is the *perfection* of the physical form of nature, *i.e.*, of "every existing thing under the sun,*"* meaning below the level of Tiphareth. This is the same figure first found in *The Empress*, robed and crowned; it is the same figure as *The High Priestess*: it is the same figure found in *The Universe*.

In the Golden Dawn card the woman is shown pouring the contents of both urns (Chokmah and Binah) onto the earth so that they "unite and form a river at her feet."[121] In the Waite card the urns are pouring their substance onto earth and water. Crowley's symbolism is far more complicated. He represents two breast-like cups, one gold and one silver: "From the golden cup she pours this ethereal water, which is also milk and oil and blood, upon her own head, indicating the eternal renewal of the categories, the inexhaustible possibilities of existence. The left hand, lowered, holds a silver cup, from which also she pours the immortal liquor of her life...She pours it upon the junction of land and water. This water is the water of the Great Sea of Binah; in the manifestation of Nuith on a lower plane she is the Great Mother."[122] Crowley describes the repeated spirals on this card as a reference to the shape of the Universe as calculated by Einstein and his followers. He points out that only in the lower cup are there rectangular forms and says that "In this may be discovered the doctrine which asserts that the blindness of humanity to all the beauty and wonder of the Universe is due to this illusion of straightness."[123]

The Golden Dawn representation of *The Star* carries more specific information about this Path than the others, although it is hidden in the intricacies of number. On this card the seven primary rays of the star, and the fourteen secondary rays add up to 21. This is the number of *Eheieh,* the God name of Kether, telling us that the relationship of this Path to the Godhead is far more direct than is obvious on the surface. Moreover, the Golden Dawn imagery carries with it an explanation of why *The Star*, transposed with *The Emperor* by Crowley, belongs firmly planted on the Twenty-Eighth Path where tradition has placed it.

The Key to all of this is the two trees on either side of the female figure. These are the *Tree of Life* on the right, and the *Tree of Knowledge of Good and Evil* on the left. Biblical scholars will immediately recognize the symbolic trees described in *Genesis;* Adam and Eve were forbidden the fruit of the latter tree, though not of the former.

The Bird of Hermes above the *Tree of Knowledge of Good and Evil* (the Ibis) amplifies the meaning of the Tree in this card. It is a reference to *The Magician*, the card of Hermes-Thoth-Mercury. In Hebrew the word *kokab* means star, but more specifically it means *Mercury*. Thus we understand that it is necessary to apply the willpower of the Magician, the directing force in meditation, if we are to learn the lessons of this Path.

The *Zohar,* speaking of the *Tree of Knowledge of Good and Evil* explains that "if a man lives uprightly, it is a Tree of Good, but if he lives unjustly, it is a Tree of Evil."[124] This does not imply the acceptance of any social doctrine or law, or any rule of social conduct. It means simply functioning in accordance with the Universal Will. And here in the card, we see that the lower branches of this Tree are a reversal of the principles symbolized by the branches above. Each branch represents one of the seven Planets (six around the Sun), with Saturn representing all three Supernals (Figure 30).

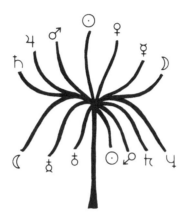

Figure 30. The Tree of Knowledge of Good and Evil

So we understand that this Tree, related to the expulsion of Adam and Eve from the condition of "heavenly bliss" symbolizes the dualities of good and evil, pain and pleasure, harmony and disunities of the human condition. The bird above, while a reference to *The Magician* and the will, points out that wisdom emerges from a right understanding and control of the daily aspects of our lives. The Hermetic Mysteries serve to explain all that is called good or evil in our lives, and to help us to transcend the limitations which are imposed by these qualities. It will also be seen that the *Tree of Knowledge of Good and Evil* is toward the side of the Pillar of Severity. Its opposite, *The Tree of Life is* on the side of the Pillar of Mercy, for it is a gift of God balancing the severely polar lessons of the other Tree. The very practical point implied here is that we must continually refer the lessons of the inner worlds, the results of meditation, to our daily lives, and *vice versa.*

What is shown in this Key is the Garden of Eden, a state of beginnings. But a complicated question arises as to why that garden should be represented in a card so low on the Tree of Life and, indeed, why it should form one of the primary Paths of the Personality. This is explained by a reference of this Path to a higher Path, that of *The Emperor.*

The correct Hebrew title of this card is הכוכבים *(ha-kokabim),* meaning *the Stars,* rather than *the Star.* Case made this point, noting that some early French and Italian decks use the plural *Les Étoiles* and *Le Stelle* for this reason.[125] And while Case did not expand the idea, admirers of Crowley will immediately recall the statement from his *Book of the Law*, causing him to reverse *The Emperor* and *The Star*, that "Tzaddi is not the Star." Indeed it is not a single star, nor is it *The Emperor*. Yet there are many Qabalistic ways in which *The Emperor* (Heh) and *The Star* (Tzaddi) correspond. One such link, again demonstrated by the master of Gematria, Paul Case, has to do with the fact that the Hebrew *ha-kokabim* has the same numerical value as אבן האדם (*ehben ha-Adam*), *The Stone of Adam*.[126] This is a symbolic reference to the union of the Supernal Father, Chokmah, with the Sun, Tiphareth i.e., the Path of *The Emperor*. Netzach is the Chokmah energy at its lowest arc, on the base of the Pillar of Mercy. Its *Elohim* are the lower expression of the *YHVH Elohim* of Binah, which the book of *Genesis* tells us created the Garden and the two Trees. The Path of *The Star* is, thus, the lower Eden, the Eden of the Personality. The Path of *The Emperor* is, as will later be considered, the fiery aspect of an upper Eden, the Eden from which the Higher Self emerges.

The Star shows Eden "restored" by Adam, a reference to Tiphareth, to which Adam is attributed. This lower Eden is a state to which the Personality can directly relate. Here, too, we recall that the creation of a person, the formation of the individual consciousness from the collective unconscious, begins from the point of Netzach. It is also the highest level of the Personality's intuition, as opposed to the Path of *The Sun*, which is the highest level to be reached by intellect.

The airy sign Aquarius, associated with peace, love and inspiration, is given to this Path. In the ancient world, Saturn was said to govern Aquarius, which refers us again to Binah and, in fact, to *The Universe*. Here it should be clear that *The Star* relates to a great many more Paths than most other Keys and, as such, is of special importance. Crowley stated the reason for this better than other commentators. He said that "here the Universe is resolved into its ultimate elements."[127]

This resolution is implicit in the very figure of the central star itself, which is a merging of many lights. It is a shining forth from a central exalted point which has been related to *Lucifer*. That angel is seen not as an underworld figure, but as the Light-Bearer, the "Morning and Evening Star," usually considered to be the Planet Venus, the mundane Chakra of Netzach.

27. THE PATH OF PEH
The Tower
The Sixteenth Key

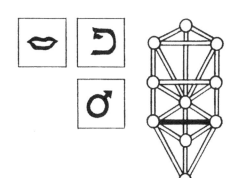

- ◈ PATH COLOR: Scarlet
- ◈ RELATED SOUND: C Natural
- ◈ PLANET: Mars
- ◈ MEANING: Mouth
- ◈ DOUBLE LETTER: Grace, Indignation
- ◈ ESOTERIC TITLE: The Lord of the Hosts of the Mighty

THIRTY-TWO PATHS OF WISDOM: The Twenty-seventh Path is the Active or Exciting Intelligence and it is so called because through it every existent being receives its spirit and motion.

The Path of Peh, *The Tower*, connects the center of the reasoning process (Hod) with the center of the intuition-desire nature (Netzach). It is the equilibriating Path of the Personality, related to Mars, and to the North, the quarter known traditionally in the Mysteries as "the place of greatest darkness," because it is said that the sun never shone in the North of Solomon's Temple. Yet we are instructed that light comes from darkness, that "gold cometh from the North," and that "Enlightenment has its origin in the hidden sources of power which terrify the minds of the ignorant."[128]

Peh is a double letter, meaning that it is one of the "gateways of the soul," with two possible directions of passage. As a word, Peh means *mouth,* an orifice related both the taking of nourishment into the system and to speech. In the first case we understand that it is through the function of this devastating

Path that the higher energies are brought in to enervate the Personality. And while spiritual nourishment passes into the system via this symbolic mouth, speech passes out of it.

Anyone who has done some practical esoteric work is aware of the singular importance of words and of the sounds of which these words are composed. The *vibration* of a God Name (its utterance in such a way that it can actually be felt in the body) has a definite effect on the physical vehicle as well as a concomitant effect on the psychic vehicles. This is a fact easily tested by the student, although the effect on the psyche may not be completely perceived by the waking consciousness.

"Words of Power," properly vibrated with martian force, help to bring about the destruction of our personal towers, false concepts and institutions which we believe to be reality. But it should be understood that to tear something down is to make room for something new. Mars may be a God of war and destruction, but it is also the God which rules over the fertility of crops.[129] And, relative to speech, we know that the *Logos* is also the *Word*.

Most versions of this key picture a tower, set in a desolate landscape, being struck by lightning. Figures fall from it as the crown is struck off. In the most simple of terms, this symbolizes the sudden destruction of our perception of what constitutes reality. The tower is the concept of what most people call "I," the Personality awareness being shattered by an influx of force revealing something of the nature of the Higher Self. The tower also symbolizes all man-made institutions, whether that means government, religion, or any accepted values.

Yet this is not to be construed as the striking down of evil. In fact one title of the card is *The House of God*. The spiritual learning process involves the continual building up and striking down of concepts formed only as useful stepping stones into the inner worlds. For example, on the Paths we first encounter the Archangels in anthropomorphic guise. This appears to be their reality, particularly if we may not have believed that Archangels exist in the first place. What we encounter are contact pictures which have been established through centuries of meditative practice. These are a useful creation of man, rather than being the true and pure consciousness of the Archangelic beings. To encounter the Archangels as formless consciousness means to destroy another tower which we have created. Yet these towers are necessary and sacred. They are, like the densest expression of ourselves, our bodies, temples of the Holy Spirit. Appreciating this, we learn to apply the underlying principles of each Path without being bound by their necessarily artificial outward manifestation. We know that any Path we follow is, by definition, artificial, whether that be Qabalah, Hinduism, Catholicism, Judaism or Buddhism, and that each carefully laid brick of these structures will ultimately be destroyed.

One key symbol of *The Tower* is its very isolation. It stands on a desolate mountain top. Most individuals perceive themselves in this way, as totally separate units of consciousness. So the destruction of the tower means to experience the True Ego, which is not ours alone. The lightning flash on the tower is a sudden realization, or flash of perception, of our real identities. That lightning is in the shape of the circle and spear of Mars to indicate the power which initiates the experience.

On the Golden Dawn and Waite cards the lightning strikes the crown at the top of the tower, an obvious reference to the Crown of Kether. But what is symbolized here is the false crowns of our existence, those man-made values which we believe to control us. And one of the meanings of the crown here is the *will,* the Primal Will of Kether which is the only true reality. Our conscious attempt to align ourselves with this Primal Will brings about the destruction of our belief that we actually have a personal will.

The reference to Mars on the 27th Path points to the Path's correspondence with Geburah, the fifth Sephira. Here the activity of Geburah in tearing away obsolete values takes place. Of course, it must be reiterated that the Sephiroth are the centers of objective energy, while the Paths are our subjective use of those energies. In varying degree, the energies of all of the Sephiroth are on all of the Paths, in this case that of Geburah being predominant. We also recall that Netzach and Geburah, Venus and Mars, are integrally linked, and that the Gods associated with both Hod and Netzach are called the *Gods of Armies.* It is for good reason that Crowley subtitled his card *War.* Throughout esoteric literature spiritual self-development is often described in martial terms. The *Bhagavad Gita,* for instance, describes a symbolic battle of the component parts of the Self: Krishna is the Higher Genius, guiding Arjuna onto his inner, and personal, field of battle. Far too many people make the mistake of assuming the process of spiritual development to be one of "sweetness and light," a misconception fostered primarily by Christianity. *The Tower* points out that inner growth must be a painful and overwhelming process. Nature is not always kind to us. Once we invoke the inner forces we soon discover that what we get is what we need, and that is not always what we want. Most of all, it is often not what we expect. The branches of the Tree of Life are, as this card suggests, filled with surprises.

The surprise and suddenness of insight is symbolized both in the Golden Dawn and in the Waite card by the lightning flash. Crowley's version represents the same principle, but attempts to demonstrate some of the more subtle shades of meaning of the Path. He tells us also that his card represents the "preface" to the coming of a new era shown in the 20th Key, *Judgment* His version of *The Tower* represents the destruction of the old order.

As in *The Star*, Crowley uses straight, geometric lines to mean that which is made by man. He points out that since perfection is *Nothing* (meaning the *Ain Soph* and literally *no thing):* "all manifestations, however glorious, however delightful, are stains." [130]

In his card the all-seeing Cosmic Eye observes and directs the disruptive process of the tower's destruction, while Dis, a Roman God of the dead, belches flames from the structure's base. On either side are the serpent and the dove, representing "the two forms of desire...the will to live and the will to die..." He says that they are also the "masculine and feminine impulses." [131]

In both the Golden Dawn and Waite cards two figures are shown falling from the tower. Case explained them as the dual modes of the lower personal consciousness (consciousness and subconsciousness) while Mathers called these the Kings of Edom. Waite presumably agreed with Mathers insofar as his two figures both wear crowns.

Reference to the Kings of Edom leads us to some very subtle meanings of this card. The fall of the Kings of Edom refers to the conquest of that nation by the Jews, led by Judas Maccabeus. There is, however, a much deeper meaning imbedded in that fall, a meaning which is discussed at some length in the *Zohar.* That book states that prior to the creation of our Universe there were other Universes, or forms of existence, with which the Divine Creator was displeased, and which he thus reduced to a state of chaos or nothingness.[132] *The Tower*, furthermore, has other biblical implications. It is the Tower of Babel, a parable wherein the relationship of speech-tower is clearly shown: After the flood the descendants are said to have settled in Babylonia (Babel) where they built a city of brick. They built a tower in a supposed attempt to reach up to, and conquer, the heavens. Seeing these men as coarse and ambitious, God sought to punish them. Where previously "the whole earth was of one language and of one speech," and men could work in unison, God imposed diverse languages, forcing a dispersion across the land. In symbolic terms, the building of a tower of false notions results in confusion; it is acceptance of the limitations of "language," meaning the strictures of any particular culture. In this sense, then, the tower also represents the structure of individual religious systems. Those who are locked into the bricks and mortar of any system are unable to see beyond that system to the Divine Unity and purpose which is the light of all true religions.

The extent to which the implications of this card go far above even the level of the Higher Self center of Tiphareth is shown by the three windows in both the Golden Dawn and the Waite cards. The number three is a reference to the Supernal Triangle, meaning that the activity of *The Tower* somehow involves our cosmic selves. Crowley uses the symbol of the Cosmic Eye (the third eye of inner vision) but the meaning is precisely the same. Here is the involvement of God the Father. What happens is that the Path of *The Tower* may be considered the affirmation of the Primal Will that It alone is the True Crown, thus bringing into balance in the Self the pure positive (Chokmah) and the pure negative (Binah) which stand at the top of each pillar in our individual, internal Trees of Life.

In fact, the whole Tree of Life is involved in this Path. Waite suggests this by placing the Tower between two sets of falling Yods (the descending Spirit), adding up to twenty-two, the number of the Hebrew letters and of the Paths. Here it will be recalled that the Lightning Flash is the very means of creation of all ten Sephiroth.

In the Golden Dawn card an even more profound suggestion is made concerning our human value systems. On the right hand is seen the Tree of Life, while on the left is another tree which is the Qlippoth. As the Tower is struck down, the opposites of "good" and "evil" are suddenly viewed differently, and one knows that all that *is* in the Universe is a part of the One Creator. And again, as has been repeatedly stated: every created thing contains the seeds of its opposite.

To this point we have considered the psychological implications of the Path, ideas which may easily be derived from meditation on the card. But *The Tower* involves some symbolism rarely found in print. This symbolism is purely sexual.

In the past the meaning of certain symbols was only broadly suggested because many in polite society might find them shocking. One such symbol is the Tower itself, which is a phallus. Moreover the *mouth* (Peh) may be interpreted at one level to mean the opening of the male reproductive organ, that from which the Yod, seed of life, issues. Crowley's card more than hints at this by the form of the mouth breathing fire on the lower right. And in his diary of 1923 he is very explicit as he speaks of "the blasted tower which is really a phallus shooting forth lightnings of seed."[133] The fire is the destroyer and the renewer, for it forces the transmutation of energy from one form to another. It is, thus, the initial activator which will ultimately lead to fruition. This becomes clear as one asks the question: What happens to the tower, here seen in the process of being consumed? The answer is that what happens is exactly the same as in our physical world when something burns. Energy is released to be restructured and to manifest in another way.

This is an extremely important lesson about the nature of transmutation of energies in the Universe imbedded in this card. The transmutation is so all-pervasive that it is found at every level of the Tree of Life. Knowing that the Mars energy is the universal sexual force of Microprosopus, and that the image of the tower is in some (though not all) ways the phallus, points to one important meaning of the card. It is the higher sexual energy destroying the perception of the Personality about the nature of the sexual function; it is destruction of the perception of the sex organ itself in orgasm. And, as earlier noted, one of the precepts of the Mysteries accurately states that "God is sex." Needless to say, this precept was not much bantered about in the Victorian era.

There is still another complex mystery to be encountered here. This is the mystery of *circumcision,* an idea implied by the striking of the "Crown" from the top of the Tower. This is unquestionably one of the most secret meanings of the card, and one which is supported by Gematria. The letter Peh has a value of 85, which we discover to be the same value as the Hebrew word for circumcision. It might also be added that when they conquered the Edomites, the Jews forced them to be circumcised, which allowed the Edomites to be absorbed into the Jewish society.

The rite of circumcision is of very obscure origin, but it is a practice known to have been spread by the Egyptians.[134] Biblical texts show that a number of ideas were involved: 1) It was related to preparation for marriage. In the case of the Mysteries, this may be taken to mean what is called by alchemists the "Chemical Wedding." 2) It was a rite of initiation into a social group. 3) It was a "redemption offering," as is described in Leviticus.[135] 4) Most important, it was a token of the *covenant* between Abraham and God. In ancient terms this meant an agreement between two parties, not as a contract in the modern sense of the word, but as a bilateral pledge of loyalty.[136]

Thus it may be interpreted that the fall from the tower, the sacrifice of one's perception of the sexual function (a symbolic circumcision) is required continually of mankind to maintain the covenant between Abraham and God, *i.e.*, to maintain the given Path by which one may return to the Source of All. But this is also initiatory; it is a preparation for the "Knowledge and Conversation of the Holy Guardian Angel" of Tiphareth.

Interestingly enough, the biblical text calls for circumcision of all male children on the eighth day of their lives. The correspondence with the eighth Sephira, Hod, connected to Netzach by the Path of *The Tower* can certainly be suggested.

The Tower is the phallus. But this symbolism does not mean in any way that the Path is exclusive to those functioning in male incarnations. The Path of Peh exists prior to the point of differentiation of the sexes for incarnation, and is thus amalgam of both masculine and feminine energies. On this Path one must focus on the male component of the sexual force, as on other Paths one must deal with its female components. A male or female body does, however, make some differences in the way one approaches the lower Paths beneath Tiphareth. Energies are polarized differently in the experience of a Path, according to the sexuality of the physical vehicle. This makes no practical difference in individual working; only in group working are such polarities of necessity considered.

26. The Path of Ayin
The Devil
The Fifteenth Key

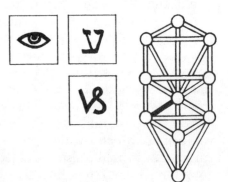

◈ PATH COLOR: Indigo
◈ RELATED SOUND: A Natural
◈ SIGN: Capricorn (Cardinal
    Earth)
◈ MEANING: Eye
◈ SIMPLE LETTER: Mirth
◈ ESOTERIC TITLE: The Lord of
    the Gates of Matter; the Child of
    the Forces of Time

THIRTY-TWO PATHS OF WISDOM: *The Twenty-sixth Path is called the Renovating Intelligence, because the Holy God renews by it all the changing things which are renewed by the creation of the world.*

 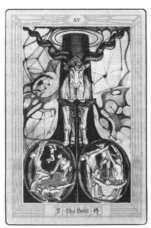  

The Path of Ayin, *The Devil*, connects Tiphareth, the center of the sun consciousness, with Hod, sphere of Mercury and of the intellect. The twenty-sixth Path is formative and, in terms of the structure of the Self, is an intellectual bridge between the Personality and the Individuality.

Of all the Paths, this may be the most difficult for those rooted in Western cultures to understand, for its interpretation flies in the face of the meaning which most people have come to attach to the Devil. In Qabalistic terms, the Devil is not viewed as an evil entity having its own separate existence. Rather, it represents a special mystery which must be penetrated before one can directly know the Higher Principle of the Self. The Devil, which is the adversary, is the Master of manifest form which we must face and conquer.

Paul Foster Case, in his study course, went farther than any other writer in pointing to the profound implications of this card. He said: "Of all the keys of the Tarot, Key 15 is one of the most important. It is the symbolic veil for the greatest practical secret of occultism. It both conceals and reveals the secret of the powers ascribed by tradition to Moses, David and Solomon. This is the same great secret Pythagoras learned in Egyptian temple schools. It is the great Arcanum of Alchemy and magic. To know it is to be able to make the Philosopher's Stone and the Elixir of Life. Yet those who know it *cannot tell*. For the essential point is beyond the power of words to express."[137] Here we understand that we are dealing with a Path on the Tree of Life which is a transition between the intellect of normal waking consciousness and true spiritual consciousness.

There are three Paths leading directly into Tiphareth: *The Devil, Temperance* and *Death*. Each of these Paths represents a special trial. But it must be reiterated that the student is not required to travel all three Paths. Those who choose the devotional Path of the Middle Pillar need deal only with *Temperance*, leading from Yesod to Tiphareth. Yet the choice of following each and every Path means the acquisition of control over the energies which each Path symbolizes; every Path confers a unique power. On the other hand, to travel the Middle Pillar means to understand and balance, within the Self, the energies of all twenty-two Paths. The difference here is that one can understand these (conceptual) aspects of consciousness, without necessarily developing the ability to manipulate these same energies. It might be said that what differentiates the student magician from the Catholic monk is a greater level of curiosity. Some, of course, come to occult studies through a desire for raw power, but quickly learn that if such power is acquired and misused there is a devastating price to pay. There is no question that the devotional-meditational Path is a much safer one than the magical Path.

That which is symbolized by *The Devil* is, in fact, raw power. It is the force which brings about the transmutation of *The Tower*, a fact underscored by the relationship of this card to Mars: *The Devil* is the sign Capricorn in which Mars is exalted. This is a weighty, even blind, sign of Earth, one which symbolizes both the highest and the lowest. Yet it is considered a sign of initiation, or release from the limitations of matter. It is limitation that is suggested by the rulership of Capricorn by Saturn, the planet of Binah, the Great Mother. Capricorn governs the limitations of form, whether that means the enclosure of matter or of time, the artificial system by which we meter and enclose all activities.

The Devil represents the average person's misperception of reality, the belief that our material condition is "real" in the true sense of the word. This misperception is symbolized here in two ways: First, the Devil is intended to be seen as a humorous figure, the bogey-man of our collective childhood. Our belief in the *illusion* of matter created by the energies symbolized in this card is actually laughable, and it is here more than implied that laughter and good humor about our lives is a tool which will help us to transcend the illusion. We must learn not to take our perceptions of the material world seriously. Mirth is the first great corrective.

Second, our misperception of the real nature of things is suggested by the inverted Pentagram on the Devil's head. The sacred symbol of mankind, turned upside down, means that most people's vision of the world and its relationship to a spiritual reality is itself upside down. And the meaning of the letter Ayin, *eye,* means that the lesson of this Path is a reorganization of perspective, a new vision of things. *Eye* symbolizes both our acceptance of what we see in the sensory world as real, and the greater vision which comes through the use of the inner eye. To accept what our physical eye tells us is to be subject to illusion and bondage, a state symbolized in the Golden Dawn and Waite cards by the chained figures. The figures are horned to show that they are, however unwittingly, the servants of this comical creature.

One primary statement of this Path is that the Devil does not exist as he is postulated by the ignorant. As is written in the *Emerald Tablet:* "all things were from One, by the meditation of One," meaning that there is nothing in the Universe not of God, including the so-called Devil. The card contains one of the greatest mysteries of the Qabalah, which is that the Devil is the necessary means of reaching the Christ-Buddha consciousness of Tiphareth. Described variously as the "source of the forms and appearance of relative existence," and as the "Lord of the Gates of Matter and Child of the Forces of Time," the Devil is both the tempter and the redeemer. He is also described as the "Prince of the

Powers of Air," indicating that this energy is mediating in the flow of Astral currents. Air is to be understood here as the whole of Yetzirah, the Astral Plane which controls the ebb and flow of matter.

This Path confers the ability to bring right-side-up the Devil's Pentagram and to lift his torch upward. In practical terms, this means the ability to reverse the currents of Astral Light. Intellect and disciplined meditation are the means by which this may be accomplished, and by which the Philosophers Stone and Elixir of Life may be produced. The process begins with the intellect of Hod, and leads into the intuition of Tiphareth. This is the meaning of the text of the *Thirty-Two Paths of Wisdom,* which describes Ayin as the *Renewing Intelligence.* We understand that it is only through the forces of the Devil, and our right understanding of them, that we may come directly to the Light of God the Son. The scriptures state that even Christ, Himself, passed through the temptation of the Devil. In this the way is pointed out for us more clearly than fundamentalist Christians could ever begin to suspect.

Eliphas Lévi called this Path "The first physical manifestation of the Divine Breath." And here we recall that "Saturn eats its children," meaning that while the creation of the illusion of form is essential to manifestation on the earthly plane (and is what manifestation actually means) the "dissolution of these forms is essential to the Path of Return." For the alchemists, *dissolution* means *analysis,* which is precisely what we apply when we intellectually separate the component energies of ourselves and our Universe into twenty-two Paths on the Tree of Life. First we must conceptually (as well as practically) separate out these component parts, then we must *reintegrate* them through our understanding of their operation. To extend an analogy made earlier: it is only by focusing on each part of our body system, considering each organ separately that we come to an understanding of how the organs work together to maintain our physical being. The reintegration, in this sense, is our overall view of the interaction of the organs. Having come to this overall view, we can then begin to actively apply the new knowledge. This is a positive phase of using what we know. It is the step which follows the dissolution and re-integration. But as we function within an earthly incarnation, everything must be related back to our mundane condition. Each lesson must be grounded.

This is the psychological meaning of a process which has been described in symbolic terms over the centuries. Our psychology has given us words for relationships of energies which the ancients could only symbolize. Words such as "subconscious" and "unconscious" have become such an integral part of our vocabulary that they are taken for granted. We are thus, more prepared than any other age to deal with the concepts of the Mysteries, including what has been variously termed the Akashic Fluid, the Odic Force or the Astral Light. This force is manipulated, for whatever end one may choose, through an understanding of *The Devil.* Here Lévi (who used the term "Great Magical Agent") describes the process of manipulation as, *to dissolve, to consolidate, to quicken, to moderate.*[138] This is dissolution, re-integration, activity and grounding. The same qualities can be described as Fire, Water, Air and Earth.

The requisite interaction of the Four "Elements" is also suggested in the Golden Dawn and Waite cards: The inverted torch is Fire, the eagle's claws are Water, the wings are Air, and the grotesque body of the Devil is Earth. One interesting, though even less obvious symbolism is in the Devil being represented with the ears of an ass, a mythological reference pointing toward a sexual interpretation of the card. *Priapus* was the Roman God of the phallus, to whom the ass was traditionally sacrificed.[139] (Readers will note that it is virtually impossible to make this statement without seeming to intend a bad pun).

The symbolism of the Golden Dawn and Waite cards is essentially the same, with one exception. In the Golden Dawn card the Devil holds a single horn in his right hand. This is intended to be the horn of a ram, the beast of Aries, the Path of *The Emperor* ruled by Mars. In this, Mathers pointed to the most profound meaning of the card, for this is also the Jewish *shofah,* the ram's horn which sounds the call to prayer at Yom Kippur. Thus does the Devil hold up the very means of release from bondage. In him is both that which enslaves and that which confers freedom. Moreover, we are led to understand that what is symbolized by the Path of *The Emperor* is the pure energy (recalling Aries to be the first Sign of the Zodiac, and initiator of Spring) which causes the fall of *The Tower*, and the testing of *Judgment.* All bear a relationship to Binah, which is a fiery red in Atziluth.

Crowley's card is far more complex than the others and is, again, explicitly sexual. He describes the Key as representing "creative energy in its most material form," and as "Pan Pangenetor, the All-Begetter." His goat is Pan standing on the highest mountain-top on earth, against "a background of the exquisitely tenuous, complex, and fantastic forms of madness."[140] Between the legs of the goat is the wand of the Golden Dawn Chief Adept. It takes little observation to realize that what Crowley has represented in his card is a penis with two testicles, appropriate in that he considered this card to mean the most male of all male energies. He makes a further statement by having the tip of the male organ outside the card, symbolically in the greater heavens, while the testicles contain the bound-up forms of physical manifestation.

Undoubtedly there are many who will be made uncomfortable by the recurrence of pointedly sexual symbolism in the cards. This symbolism has been understood by initiates of the Mysteries for centuries, but it is only recently that our society has reached a stage of maturity where such ideas may be discussed openly and in proper perspective. Certainly, any adult will agree that orgasm is the most powerful natural force to affect the human body, yet it is merely an indicator of a power of God so overwhelming that our minds cannot begin to conceive of it.[141]

26. THE PATH OF SAMEKH
Temperance
The Fourteenth Key

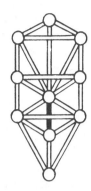

◆ PATH COLOR: Blue
◆ RELATED SOUND: G Sharp
◆ SIGN: Sagittarius (Mutable
   Fire)
◆ MEANING: Prop
◆ SIMPLE LETTER: Anger
◆ ESOTERIC TITLE: The Daughter
   of the Reconcilers, the Bringer
   Forth of Life

THIRTY-TWO PATHS OF WISDOM: *The Twenty-fifth Path is the Intelligence of Probation, or is Tentative, and is so called because it is the primary temptation, by which the Creator trieth all righteous persons.*

The Path of Samekh, *Temperance,* leads from Yesod to Tiphareth, from the Moon to the Sun, from the Personality to the Higher Self. It is among the most important and difficult Paths of the entire Tree, and one on which the very enormity of the Great Work may be experienced. It has been called a Path which leads eventually to the "Dark Night of the Soul,"[142] a Path on which one enters a deep tunnel in the belief that the Light is to be found at the end of it. This is a Path of trial and temptation, called the *Intelligence of Probation.* It is also known as the "Daughter of the Reconcilers, the Bringer Forth of Life." In his *777* Crowley made this comment on the letter Samekh: It is "The womb preserving life. Self-control and self-sacrifice govern the wheel."[143] All of these phrases direct us to the idea that behind this card, ultimately, is the Great Mother, the יהוה אלהים *(YHVH Elohim)* of Binah. For this reason the central figure of both the Golden Dawn and Crowley cards are female. Moreover the Twenty-Fifth Path is that of *Sagittarius,* the Archer who is also Diana the Huntress, Goddess of the moon. This repeats the principle that all of the figures of the Tarot (except *The Fool*) are Mother-Binah and Father-Chokmah under different guises.

In her function as Diana she governs the tides of earth, and the fluctuations of the Astral Current. She is the natural framework and support for the waxing and waning of the energies of existence. She is the *prop,* the very meaning of the word Samekh. The Great Mother is, thus, the "Womb preserving Life." She is restriction and control over natural energies; all of the energies of the manifest Universe are controlled and manipulated within specific bounds and restrictions.

In their *Voice of Isis,* Hariette and Homer Curtis describe the Universal Mother as the "power of bringing forth in humanity the Divine Child or the Christ."[144] It is that which in every individual brings about the contact of the Personality with the inner Divine Light. This is, in Qabalistic terms, the Knowledge and Conversation of the Holy Guardian Angel. Rising on the Path of *Temperance* leads to our bearing of the Child, which is ourselves reborn. Key 14 is the beginning of an awareness of the Higher Self of Tiphareth. The card demonstrates not the experience itself, but how the experience is brought about, i.e., through an exchange and balance of opposites which can only be symbolically described. The use of symbols here has nothing whatsoever to do with secrecy, but is merely reflective of the inadequacy of language to describe the process.

Crowley's card is the most specific, showing the process in alchemical terms, where Fire becomes Water and Water becomes Fire. And, as we appreciate that the primary Alchemy takes place within the body of the alchemist we can also appreciate that this card is describing an actual physical effect. It is not nearly so symbolic as some might believe.

The willful interchange of Fire and Water is the merging or tempering of energy opposites within the body, here symbolized by a stream poured back and forth from one vase to another. This is the *Living Water,* consciousness vivified by being merged with the Fiery Spirit. The process is one of bringing the Spirit into the body so that it *tempers* the consciousness, and is itself tempered by the consciousness, thus forming something new, something which is "more than the sum of its parts." This is the personal application of the Yod (Fire) and Heh (Water) uniting in the individual to produce Vau (Air) within the body which is Heh-final and Earth.

The process involves an inner manipulation of sexual energies. Indeed, the symbolism of the arrow released upward is one of spiritual orgasm. Such an interpretation may appear extreme, but is actually well-accepted in Christian iconography. The ecstasy of Theresa, the sixteenth century mystic and Saint, is described as an angel thrusting a flaming arrow into her heart. This symbolism of the piercing arrow which brings ecstasy and enlightenment appears to be a universally applicable (indeed *archetypal)* description of a real process.

What happens is the establishment of a rhythmic masturbatory motion of inner energy. The mental control of this energy, its conscious manipulation, is symbolized by the interchange of Fire and Water, or by the interchange of fluid between vases. The key to this actually simple process is the infinity symbol, the figure eight which Waite uses above the figure of his magician It is an ebb, and flow which is confined, i.e., is used within very specific perimeters (thus the womb symbolism) but which is taken in either direction at will. As one changes the rate of vibration of this inner energy, one raises or lowers the level of consciousness, i.e., moves from Chakra to Chakra or from Path to Path.

To explain all of this in a more simple way: At the lowest level, Water (which we have previously described as *consciousness)* being acted upon by Fire (the sexual, Kundalini energy) produces the images of the Astral, the pictures which form in our minds. These are the Air (Vau) quality, as our minds are the grounding Earth. The principle is one of producing a consciously-controlled vision (what Jung called "active imagination") which is limited by the will. The important point to understand is that most of the word symbols of Alchemy, Hermeticism, Qabalah, etc., describe processes to which anyone can relate. They are neither remote nor complicated, especially at the level of Assiah. And, in some respects, this whole symbolic language has been totally superseded by the language of psychology as established by Carl Jung and others.

It should be added that the *metals* described in alchemical literature are the same as the Seven Chakras of the Hindus, the Seven Planets and the Sephiroth of Microprosopus. These words have been used as codes over the centuries, meaning seven distinct levels of objective consciousness. Thus, when one speaks of a Planet ruling a sign of the Zodiac, what is meant is the relationship of a Sign to a given center of energy both in the Greater Universe and in the Human body.

Sagittarius is the sign of the Zodiac related to *Temperance.* Its Planetary ruler is Jupiter, meaning Chesed, but also to some extent the *Wheel of Fortune,* tenth key of the Tarot.

Chesed is suggested by the blue colored robe worn by the Golden Dawn angel, the color of the Twenty-Fifth Path in Atziluth. On the figure's breast is a golden square, a further reference to Chesed, to the number *four* and to matter. In the Waite card the square is covered by a triangle, meaning that all of the manifest Universe is governed by the Supernals. Here we recall that Chesed is the architect of all manifestation, working with the pure "potential to form" of Binah.

To reiterate the important meanings of *Temperance*: 1) It refers to an actual physical process, one which has been the secret of mystics for centuries. 2) This process involves an interchange of opposite energies directed by the will. 3) The process is set in motion at the level of the Higher Self. It is instituted in Chesed, the most refined level of Microprosopus to which the Higher Self is central, and the Sephira where the will to form of the Great Mother is enacted. 4) Until this process is accomplished, the Higher Self cannot be known to the Personality.

The whole experience is one of preparation of the Personality, and the body in which it is operating, to deal with an influx of Light which would be devastating to a system unready to handle such energy. Most important here is the monitoring of progress, the continual testing from above. It is the angel here which is at once the Higher Self and the initiatory forces of nature, which pours the elixir from vase to vase. This is an ongoing process of testing, measuring to see how much the physical vehicle can bear. When it can handle the stress of the energy interchange here symbolized, the arrow is released. On the other hand, the angel makes certain that no individual is allowed more than it can handle. The result of taking on too much at once is an admonishing jolt, from this angel, not soon to be forgotten. The angels, described as sentinels at each inner gate, are there for our own protection.

Some special insights may be derived by considering the description of the letter Samekh in the *Sepher Yetzirah,* although the terms in this document lend themselves to an extraordinary range of interpretation. The word *anger* (רוגז) is referred to Samekh. However, Case states that this is a "blind," and that the original meaning of the Hebrew word was *quivering* or *vibration.*[145] Such an interpretation is entirely consistent with the alchemical symbolism, for the interchange of Fire and Water is a control of inner vibrations. But there are two other meanings of "anger" which might be appropriate to this Path. First is the idea of anger in the sense of *divine rage,* a passion so overwhelming that its force draws the bow and releases the arrow of Sagittarius on the upward Middle Pillar. Second, is an aspect of the Mysteries only rarely discussed, and certainly germane to the Twenty-Fifth Path: this is the very real hostility often felt by the student toward the Path itself, as he or she works day after day and seems to be getting nowhere. Such hostility and frustration is in itself a major test; it is part and parcel of the work prior to the emergence of inner proofs. The anger, if it may be called that, is dispelled along this Path, as the Spirit begins to fill the vessel in which the elements have been purified to receive it.

The relationship of this Path to three others provides one of the best interlocks of Qabalistic symbolism, for the combined letters of the three lowest Paths, ק, ש, and ת, spell the Hebrew word for *bow.* The same word also means *rainbow,* a recurring symbol in the Tarot. These three Paths are the forces which, when combined, send the arrow skyward toward Tiphareth. These are the three minor tests prior to the major testing of *Temperance.* To even approach the twenty-fifth Path one must have begun to temper the "Water" of *The Moon* (ק) with the "Fire" of *Judgment* (ש) and ground the interchange on the Path of *The Universe* (ת). This work is suggested in *The Universe* by the bi-polar rods carried by the central figure.

The Golden Dawn and Waite cards are very similar in their symbolism, both following tradition very closely. The Golden Dawn vases are red and blue to symbolize an interchange between opposite energies (Chokmah and Binah in their Atziluth colors). The vases on the Waite card are gold to show that all of this is an operation of the Sun. That Planet is also represented by the sign on the angel's forehead, and by the sphere above the Golden Dawn angel's head. In both cases, also, the angel has one foot on solid water and the other on land meaning solid matter and fluid consciousness. The Water is somewhat representative of Yesod, the lower source of this Path, the *Foundation* which is the source of the dualities of our sensory condition and which controls their ebb and flow. These are the opposites which we seek to manipulate through the conscious use of the Solar Fire shown in the background as a flaming volcano.

Crowley's symbolism is at once more complicated and more explicit, although the meaning of the card which he calls *Art is* precisely the same as the others. And, of those cards in which Crowley deviated radically from traditional design this is one of the most successful. It graphically demonstrates complex and subtle principles only vaguely suggested by the Waite and Golden Dawn cards.

Crowley points out in his *Book of Thoth* that this card is the complement and fulfillment of Key six, Gemini, *The Lovers*. It is "the Consummation of the Royal Marriage which took place in Atu VI...It is the same formula, but in a more advanced stage. The original duality has been completely compensated; but after birth comes growth; after growth puberty; and after puberty, purification."[146] There is a perfect interchange. The alchemical Red Lion has become white, and the White Lion has become red. Water is poured onto Fire, Fire is merged with Water, all within a golden cauldron which is understood to be the purified physical vehicle.

It will be seen that a tiny arrow rises toward the breasts of the figure, which are arranged in the form of the six planets of Microprosopus around the sun. Moreover, the method of successfully treading this Path is cryptically given in the Latin inscription around the figure: *Visita Interiora Terrae Rectificando Invenies Occultum Lapidem* which means, "Visit the interior parts of the Earth; by rectification thou shalt find the hidden stone." The stone, sometimes referred to as the *Philosopher's Stone* is the ultimate goal of Alchemy.

Obviously, it would be impossible to expand here on the system of Alchemy and the Great Work, to which Crowley refers. It must, however, be added that Crowley's use of alchemical symbolism has some private meanings specific to his system. As in *The Tower*, he mentions that there is a special secret here, known to IX° initiates of his O.T.O., and one which readers will not be surprised to discover is again blatantly sexual.

In his book *Sexuality, Magic and Perversion* Francis King explains a "code" in which the sexual techniques of the O.T.O. were described: "This code was drawn from the traditional technical terminology of Alchemy. The penis was referred to as the *athanor*, the semen as the *serpent* or occasionally the *blood of the red lion*, while the vagina was called the *curcurbite* or *the retort*. The secretions that lubricate the vagina were called the *menstrum of the Gluten*, sometimes abbreviated to the *menstruum*, and the mixture of semen with vaginal lubricant was termed the *First Matter*, or when supposedly transmuted by the magical powers of the participants in the rite, the *Amrita* or *Elixir*.

"The initiates of the IX° claimed that success in almost any magical operation, from the invocation of a God to 'procuring a great treasure' could be achieved by the application of the appropriate sexual technique."[147]

24. THE PATH OF NUN
Death
The Thirteenth Key

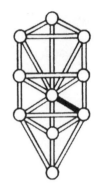

◈ PATH COLOR: Green-blue
◈ RELATED SOUND: G Natural
◈ SIGN: Scorpio (Fixed Water)
◈ MEANING: Fish
◈ SIMPLE LETTER: Movement
◈ ESOTERIC TITLE: The Child
   of the Great Transformers; The
   Lord of the Gate of Death

THIRTY-TWO PATHS OF WISDOM: *The Twenty-fourth Path is the Imaginative Intelligence, and it is so called because it gives a likeness to all the similitudes which are created in like manner similar to its harmonious elegancies.*

The Path of Nun, *Death*, is one of the three Paths leading from the Personality to the Higher Self. As a preface to its study one may usefully consider comments by Case and Crowley. Says Case provocatively: "Key 13 tells the Secret of Secrets... he who knows the secret has in his hands a power which might be used to overturn the world. Yet no person learns it until he is truly prepared, and more than anything else, this means such *ethical* preparation that no temptation to misuse this power could ever be sufficient to turn the knower from the path of strictly constructive and beneficent application of the force he is able to control."[148] One may also recall Case's statement about *The Devil* that "It is the symbolic veil for the greatest practical secret of occultism." As we shall see, the similarity of description for these two cards is no coincidence.

Crowley comments on the far-reaching implications of this particular card. In discussing the *fish,* meaning of Nun, he says: "This symbol resumes the *whole* Secret Doctrine."[149]

The great importance of this Path is pointed out by its very position on the Tree of Life. It is on the Path of the Flaming Sword between Tiphareth and Netzach, meaning that it is the Path of emanation of the Lower Creator's Energy into matter; it is the Path on which the energy of God the Son is transformed into the first sphere, or pattern of energy underlying the material world. In terms of the individual man, this is the Path on which the Higher Self directs the Personality "downward" into incarnation. Considered on an upward course of personal evolution, it is the Path on which the Personality energy, projected by the Higher Self, is absorbed in physical death or reconceptualized in initiation. The Great Work involves much which could be called psychological reorientation; there is a perceptual change about the nature of reality and about what constitutes the Self. This is one aspect of the "transformation" on this Path.

The transformation involves leaving the *desire nature* of Netzach and being absorbed into Tiphareth. This desire nature is the very essence of the Personality which functions entirely in terms of the satisfaction of its needs and wishes. The very will to live, meaning the desire of the Personality to continue to function in the sensory condition, is abrogated on the Path of *Death* Here the temporary and illusory nature of the Personality is correctly self-perceived. The Personality undergoes a willful "death," surrendering everything that it believes itself to be. Most difficult is that this total surrender of life, this initiatory sacrifice, must precede the experience of cosmic awareness. One is required to give up the totality of one's being, one's very life, in relative darkness yet in the faith that there will be a resurrection into the Light. As Jung puts it: "By descending into the unconscious, the conscious mind puts itself in a perilous condition, for it is apparently extinguishing itself."[150] It is, as Gareth Knight described, a "Dark Night of the Soul," much as on the Path of *Temperance*, another of the three Paths leading from the Personality to the Higher Self. One may proceed to the experience of the Higher Self on any of these Paths, but the lessons of all three Paths must be mastered. *The Devil, Temperance* and *Death* are different perspectives and aspects of the same thing, *Temperance* being the Path of meditation between Ayin and Nun. This might more easily be understood by considering the idea that the figure of *The Devil*, the angel of *Temperance* and the skeleton of *Death* are all aspects of the Higher Self.

Encountering such a tightly defined trinity of Tarot Keys, one may wonder how the universally applicable principle of the יהוה may relate. In this case *Death* is Yod-Fire, *The Devil* is Heh-Water and *Temperance* is Vau-Air, the result of the interaction of the other two. The *Sepher Yetzirah,* of course, speaks of only the Yod, Heh and Vau. As applied to these three cards, the Yod Heh and Vau are forces interacting in our own physical vehicle, the Heh final.

It will be seen that while the Tree of Life has a Path called *Death*, there is no opposite Path of birth. This can be explained in two ways. The first is that *The Devil*, which enchains in matter, is in some ways the card of birth. But, more important is the fact that both birth and death are essentially the same transition. As one is born into this world, he dies to an inner world; as one dies to this world, he is born back into the same inner world of origin. So this card represents the symbolic passing through a gateway which is at once the utter destruction of one phase of energy, and the transformation of that energy into something else. But the transformation is directed from above. Thus is the Tarot Key called *The Child of the Great Transformers*. It is also the *Lord of the Gates of Death*. Nun is not the Great Transformers themselves, he is their *Child*. Nun is not Death, rather he is the keeper of its Gates. Herein lies an important principle for the real understanding of this card.

Another symbolism which may be very helpful is an alchemical one. To this Path is attributed *putrefaction,* the decaying black mass in the crucible which eventually turns into gold. It is the emergence of new life from death. Of the four cards shown, only Crowley's suggests this idea. The Crowley, Golden Dawn and Marseilles versions all show the skeleton of Death wielding a scythe, a tool of the harvest which is also a symbol of *time,* and thus of Saturn-Binah, giver and destroyer of Life. Only in Crowley's card does the destructive sweep of the scythe also produce bubbles in which new forms of life are seen to be developing. This is the resurrection which follows the transformation of death. In fact, both Crowley and Mathers attribute the skeleton to Osiris, a God slain and resurrected.

Of course, in all cases, the skeleton represents that which remains after the maggots of Earth have consumed the flesh. The skeleton is the framework of the organ system, and is thus central to growth and fruition. Interestingly enough, as the word Nun is a verb it means *to sprout* or *to grow.* In this we can view the skeleton as a symbolic and perpetual *seed.* The plant dies in the winter, but not before producing seeds which will regenerate its image in the spring. The image which carries over is a kind of spiritual skeleton, a pattern unaffected by the transformation of the plant: The plant becomes the seed, which again becomes the plant. This is what is meant by the words of the *Thirty-Two Paths of Wisdom:* "...*it* gives a likeness to all the similitudes which are created in like manner similar to its harmonious elegancies." Meditation on this idea will reveal the ultimate message of the *Death* card, which is rather a distillation of the entire Great Work or, as Crowley said of the fish symbol, "resumes the whole Secret Doctrine."

Nun means *fish;* Tzaddi means *fish-hook.* And while the *Sepher Yetzirah* relates *imagination* to Tzaddi, the later *Thirty-Two Paths of Wisdom* calls Nun the *Imaginative Intelligence.* To make this symbolism less mysterious, the documents imply that on the Path of Tzaddi we begin to develop the tools of creative imagination which are required to tread the difficult Path of Nun, i.e., to make the transition between Personality and Higher Self. Again, everything is summed up by the fish symbolism.

The fish is a traditional symbol of what the alchemists call *First Matter,* an almost impossible subject to describe, but which is the mind-substance of everything that is. Gareth Knight says that the best modern definition is offered by Coleridge and is the "Primary Imagination."[151] The fish has also, since perhaps the second century C.E., been a key symbol of Christianity. In the earliest Church the Eucharist was not specifically represented, but was implied in a number of innocuous meal scenes. The most common of such scenes was the

Agape or *Friend's Meal* (from the Jewish *Berakah*, meal of blessing). Iconographers describe such scenes as a *fractio panes,* meaning that bread is broken symbolically. In the earliest Agape scenes, several figures are shown around a table with a fish at the center. This fish, always shown alive, and often in dual form, represents Christ who offers himself as the symbolic meal.

Christ came to be associated with the fish, primarily through the imagery of the "miracle of loaves and fishes," another convenient way for the early Christians to secretly represent the Eucharist. It is also related to a title of Christ: *Jesus Christ Son of God Savior.* When the first Greek letters of this title are combined, they spell *Ichthos,* the word for fish.[152]

The environment of fish, that from which it comes, is water, and in Christian terms, this means Christ coming from Mother Mary, Binah, who is often called *Stella Maris* and the Great Sea.

The astrological sign attributed to Nun, Scorpio, is symbolized in three ways. It is the *Scorpion,* the *Serpent* or the *Eagle.* This is the transition on the Path of *Death* from the dangerous creature which poisons and crawls upon the earth, to the Serpent which *weaves* its way (a reference to the Astral Light) upward, to become the Eagle which soars above all heads.

Crowley uses all three of these symbols. His skeleton has the Scorpion and Serpent at the feet and an Eagle behind the head. Most suggestive is that the Serpent wraps around the Fish. This is a circular, swirling activity, a movement which the *Sepher Yetzirah* describes as the attribute of Nun. In this context, movement means change, continual transformation which is the skeletal pattern of the Universe, that on which all else is predicated.

Movement is the primary activity of the Mars force ruling Scorpio. And as Mars is involved, so are *Death, The Tower* and the fifth Sephira, Geburah. Moreover, *The Emperor* is this Mars energy during the daylight, while *Death* is the same energy in the dark of night. This is, again, the darkness of unknowing, the "Dark Night of the Soul" described by Saint John of the Cross. What he says of this condition applies to *The Devil, Temperance* and *Death*: "...although this happy night brings darkness to the spirit, it does so only to give it light in everything; and that, although it humbles it and makes it miserable, it does so only to exalt it and to raise it up; and although it impoverishes it and empties it of all natural affection and attachment, it does so only that it may enable it to stretch forward, divinely, and thus to have fruition and experience all things, both above and below..."[153] His reference to the loss of natural affection and attachment is a comment on the diminishing of the desire nature of the Personality. There develops, in fact, a dreadful emptiness, almost a complete disinterest in everything, even concerning whether one lives or dies. Life's processes cease to hold value. Yet with this feeling, one pushes ahead, almost mechanically, but with great faith. The soul moves forward inch by inch, in an indescribable blackness (the "dark night," the "putrefaction") in the belief, and not always so sure, that the light will eventually appear to lead the way.

All that is involved relates to the sexual energies. Scorpio rules the sexual organs as Mars rules Scorpio. It is the reproductive energy which is consciously directed in practical exercises such as that of the *Middle Pillar.*[154] Crowley's version of *Death* best indicates this activity.

The Golden Dawn card is quite traditional, with two exceptions. First, the eagle of Scorpio is in the upper right, changing from the form of the fiery serpent. Opposite this is the darkened Spiritual Sun which is intended to represent the process of putrefaction, from which spiritual gold will eventually emerge. It is also the Christian "Darkness at Noon."

Waite's departure from tradition, showing Death as a mounted skeleton in armor represents another aspect of the Path, which is its warrior quality. Here Waite has drawn on medieval representations of Death, depicting him as the Black Knight. Behind him is the fallen King of matter; before him a Bishop in fish-head mitre, supposedly intended to indicate the passing of the Piscean Age. The rising Sun behind the dual towers, first seen on the Path of *The Moon*, is also a reference to resurrection, the conquest of death. Finally, and most interesting in this version, is the banner with the white rose of ten petals, five inner and five outer. Insofar as the rose is based on five, it is a reference to the martian force of Geburah. But the totality of the ten petals means the involvement of the entire Universe under Kether, because of its white color. This also means *The Fool*, and Uranus, to which the white rose is related.

23. THE PATH OF MEM
The Hanged Man
The Twelfth Key

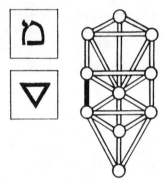

◈   PATH COLOR: Deep Blue
◈   RELATED SOUND: G Sharp
◈   MEANING: Water
◈   MATERNAL LETTER: Water
◈   ESOTERIC TITLE: The Spirit
     of the Mighty Waters

> **THIRTY-TWO PATHS OF WISDOM:** *The Twenty-third Path is called the Stable of Intelligence, and it is so called because it has the virtue of consistency among all numeration.*

The Hanged Man, the Path of Mem, connects Hod and Geburah on the Pillar of Severity. It is also a connecting channel between the Personality and the Higher Self, although its initiatory implications are very different from those three Paths leading directly into Tiphareth. This Path, and the symbolism of the card, is a complete departure from anything previously encountered.

This is a curious imagery, and most people react to it by turning the figure right side up. The eighteenth century writer Court de Gebelin even thought

the hanging figure to be a mistake, claiming that the man was originally a symbol of Prudence, standing on one foot while deciding where to put the other.[155] And though such an interpretation may seem comical today, it is actually only in the past few decades that the true and complex meaning of this Tarot Key has been publicly revealed. Arthur Edward Waite avoided the issue as well as any other knowing writer of his day. He said: "It is a card of profound significance, but all the significance is veiled...I will say very simply on my own part that it expresses the relation, in one of its aspects, between the Divine and the Universe."[156] Perhaps the best clue offered by Waite is that the figure is intended to represent a Fylfot Cross (Swastica), and is thus related to Kether in some very essential way.

Most important is that this is the Path of Water, the letter Mem being one of the three Maternals. And, in some respects, this is a Path of *baptism* into Maternal Water. In fact, it could be stated that the experience of each Maternal Path is a baptism: Shin is the baptism of Fire (*Judgment*), Mem is the baptism of Water (*The Hanged Man*) and Aleph is the baptism of Air (*The Fool*). The Water baptism is the central, and pivotal experience of the entire Tree of Life.

Water means Consciousness, the First Principle of the alchemists, the non-wet substance of which everything is produced. This substance, sometimes called the *Thinking Principle*, is symbolized by water because it has some of the qualities of physical water, particularly in its wave movement. In its lowest expression it is the Astral Fluid first discovered on the Path of the *Universe* drawn down from Yesod, the Foundation. This helps to explain the particularly cryptic description of Mem from the *Thirty-Two Paths of Wisdom:* "The Twenty Third Path is called the Stable Intelligence, and it is so-called because it has the virtue of consistency among all numerations." That is to say that the Intelligence operates in every sphere (Sephiroth and Paths, i.e., "numerations") and in the same way. The Astral Fluid, the Water, underlies everything that is. One can describe the qualities and activities of this Water, but it is not until the Twenty-Third Path that one is actually absorbed into it, i.e., is "drowned" in these waters and perceives himself or herself as an intrinsic and inseparable part of the One Consciousness.

We are, today, living in a period when much of the complicated and remote symbolism of the past is being expressed in very comprehensible psychological terms. In discussing an experience of the Collective Unconscious, Carl Jung quite literally describes the experience of *The Hanged Man*. He speaks of

> ...a boundless expanse full of unprecedented uncertainty, with apparently no inside and no outside, no above and no below, no here and no there, no mine and no thine, no good and no bad. It is the world of water, where all life floats in suspension; where the realm of the sympathetic system, the soul of everything living begins; where I am individually this *and* that; where I experience the other in myself and the other-than-myself experiences me...the collective unconscious is anything but an encapsulated personal system; it is sheer objectivity, as wide as the world and open to all the world. There I am the object of every subject, *in complete reversal of my ordinary consciousness* [author's italics] where I am always the subject that has an object .[157]

Almost four hundred years earlier, in his *Dark Night of the Soul*, St. John of the Cross recorded his own experience of what is shown as *The Hanged Man*, though in Christian terms: "With his gentle hand he wounded my neck and caused all my senses to be *suspended* [author's italics] ...I remained lost in oblivion. My face I inclined on the Beloved. All ceased and I abandoned myself, leaving my cares forgotten among the lilies."[158] This may be compared with another of Jung's statements: "There I am utterly one with the world, so much a part of it that I forget all too easily who I really am. 'Lost in oneself' is a good way of describing this state...the unconscious no sooner touches us than we *are* it— we become unconscious of ourselves."[159]

Hindu mystics describe this state as *Samadhi,* referring to a condition where the physical processes are literally suspended in trance, while the consciousness affects a union with the Divine. This was a state with which Crowley was obsessed. He wrote: "I was absolutely convinced of the supreme importance of devoting my life to obtaining Samadhi."[160] In fact, when he came to believe that the so-called Secret Chiefs of the Order of the Golden Dawn had chosen him to succeed Mathers, he wrote: "I made it a condition that I should attain Samadhi; that is, that I should receive a degree of illumination, in default of which it would be presumptuous of me to put myself forward."[161]

Crowley also makes it clear that Samadhi, which he defines with unusual simplicity as "Union with the Lord," is a general term for a number of states, involving different degrees of trance. In his *Confessions* he describes a devastating experience of the highest form of Samadhi, on the Path of *The Fool*.[162]

From the standpoint of Tarot what is important is that the Path of *The Hanged Man* is only the first entry into a sequence of states of union. While this experience may be one which we spend our lives seeking, it is only one step along the Great Way. In this regard, Crowley again offers excellent instruction. Writing of Alan Bennett's increasing desire to become a Buddhist monk, he says: "The phenomena of Dhyana and Samadhi had ceased to exercise their first fascination. It seemed to him that they were insidious obstacles to true spiritual progress; that their occurrence, in reality, broke up the control of the mind which he was trying to establish and prevented him from reaching the ultimate truth which he sought. He had the strength of mind to resist the appeal of even these intense spiritual joys. Like physical love, they persuade their dupe to put up with the essential evil of existence."[163]

The idea is that we must move constantly upward on the Tree of Life. It is not until one has experienced a next higher Sephira that the qualities of the Sephira beneath it is completely understood, and can be directed. Here we see that the Path of Mem leads directly to Geburah, above Tiphareth. Geburah is the active part of the Higher Self. It is the fiery energy on the Pillar of Water below Binah. It is that on which the feet of *The Hanged Man* rest.

The key symbol here is the cross above the triangle, which is also the emblem of the Hermetic Order of the Golden Dawn, indicating that the principles of *The Hanged Man* represent the essence of that order's teaching. Moreover, this card represents a summation of the teaching of the entire Tarot, as in the *Book T* alledgedly found in the hands of Christian Rosencreutz when his tomb was opened, and supposedly containing the most secret of the ages.

It is not uncommon, as in the Waite card, for the figure to be hanged from a *Tau Cross*. In fact, the symbolic relationship between Tau and Mem is profound. Tau is at the very center of the Cube of Space, and is crossed by the lines of *The Fool* (Aleph), *Judgment* (Shin) and *The Hanged Man* (Mem). But Mem final, the completely closed form of this letter used when it occurs at the end of a word, is also attributed to this exact center point. The symbolism says, in essence, that *the completion of Mem is Tau*. Both Mem and Tau are suspended at the center of the Cube of Space.

The reversed figure on the card represents the suspension of personal consciousness, where a greater reality imposes a complete reversal of perspective. This has been described as the "human spirit suspended by a single thread." Yet this is a willing suspension, a sacrifice which is a baptism, but which is also a crucifixion. This, then, is a card of the Dying God.

One might well ask why this crucifixion should be on one side of the Tree. The reason is that this is an essentially intellectual experience, as is implied by the position of the legs of *The Hanged Man*. The cross above the triangle is the four above the three, the imaginative qualities of *The Empress* (3) subordinate to the rational qualities of *The Emperor* (4). This is the ultimate sacrifice of desire to a rational principle.

A balance to this experience is to be found in the *Wheel of Fortune*, directly opposite *The Hanged Man* on the Tree of Life. *The Hanged Man* is rest; the *Wheel of Fortune* is activity. Expressed in another way, *The Hanged Man* is what happens when the wheel stops turning: the suspension or *Crucifixion in Space is* the willful arrest of the *Wheel of Fortune* On the other hand, the *Wheel of Fortune* is the activation of that which is inactive on the Path of *The Hanged*

Man. As is written on the *Emerald Tablet,* this is multiplicity in unity, the activity and passivity of the One Thing.

It has, hopefully, been demonstrated that the Path of *The Hanged Man* must be approached very differently from the lower Paths. There is a reversal of conceptual framework which is at once a willful suspension and a refinement of observation. The meditator becomes the object of his own meditation. He becomes the "other" which had been the object of pursuit; the "other" becomes him.

One of the primary qualities of this Path is that it is a Path of eternally unresolved possibilities. It is openness without beginning or end, the exact opposite of the *Wheel of Fortune,* which encloses in eternal motion. When the Mem is closed, it becomes Tau. Tau is Mem reversed. 12 (*The Hanged Man*) is 21 (*The Universe* reversed. This is the Tarot secret of the Dying God on the Path of Water.

This mythology of the Dying God is very universal; every culture seems to have some form of it, whether that be Christ, Osiris or a local deity. *The Hanged Man* is one rather peculiar aspect of this cross-cultural myth. In Norse mythology the God Odin sacrificially hanged himself from the branches of the World Tree.[164] In Greece, the Goddess Artemis was annually hanged in effigy, and at her sacred grove in the Arcadian Hills was known as the "Hanged One."[165] Any number of such ritual hangings could be cited, none of which is a final death. These are merely reversals where the feet of the God are planted in the *Anima Mundi* and not on the earth.

The death and resurrection of any God relates to this Path, and is described as *a Kabiric Death.* In the myth of the Kabiri, one brother is slain by the three others. His dismembered body is discovered, and is, with great joy, resurrected for the good of humanity.[166] The parallel with the Osiris legend is clear. In that story the body parts of Osiris are scattered about the land, collected and resurrected.

The death of the God is a natural, continuing, event, and is symbolized by the ritual formula IAO, meaning Isis, Apophis, Osiris, symbolizing fruition, death and then resurrection. This formula also relates to that of the Yod Heh Vau.

As usual, Crowley's version of the card is more complicated than that of either Mathers or Waite. His figure, which emphasizes the Cross and Triangle, is suspended from the Egyptian *Ankh,* a form of Tau. Behind it are the Elemental Tablets,[167] summing up all of nature. His left foot hangs from a coiled serpent which is the "creator and destroyer who operates all change." The lower serpent represents the effect of the work of God: "Through his Work a Child is begotten, as shown by the serpent stirring in the Darkness of the Abyss below him.'"[166]

22. THE PATH OF LAMED
Justice
The Eleventh Key

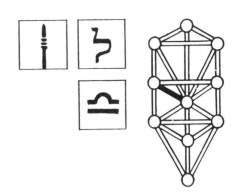

- ◆ PATH COLOR: Emerald Green
- ◆ RELATED SOUND: F Sharp
- ◆ SIGN: Libra (Cardinal Air)
- ◆ MEANING: Ox Goad
- ◆ SIMPLE LETTER: Work
- ◆ ESOTERIC TITLE: The Daughter
    of the Lords of Truth; The
    Ruler of the Balance.

THIRTY-TWO PATHS OF WISDOM: *The Twenty-second Path is the Faithful Intelligence, and is so called because by it spiritual virtues are increased, and all dwellers on earth are nearly under its shadow.*

The Path of Lamed, *Justice* is between Tiphareth and Geburah. Lamed means *ox-goad*, the spear-like prod which keeps the ox moving down the road. This attribution points to the letter's special relationship with Aleph (ox) on the Path of *The Fool*. Their interaction is exceptionally complex, although the essential principles can be simply stated: *Justice* maintains the balance of the Tree, so that the outpouring energy of *The Fool* (this has sometimes been called the "Holy Ghost") will operate within the confines of a natural pattern. *Justice* is the administrator of the laws of Binah, written by *The Hierophant* It is the "Ruler of the Balance."

It is called the *Faithful Intelligence* "because its spiritual values are increased, and all dwellers on earth are nearly under its shadow." This should not be interpreted to mean the Intelligence *of faith*. Rather it is the Intelligence which *is faithful* to that symbolized by *The Fool*. Without Lamed, Aleph could not function as it does. Moreover, the entire Tree of Life is related to the Twenty-Second Path, the number of which is the totality of all the Paths. *Justice* is not one solitary figure or force, it is an amalgam of all the Paths which are self-focused. The alignment of forces has been described as being within the essential life force symbolized by *The Fool*.

The activity of *Justice* is at work continuously in the above and below, in the Greater Universe and in the individual soul. Taken to the most mundane, as we drive a vehicle down the road, *Justice* is our correcting of the wheel back and forth in either direction to keep the vehicle centered. Such a purposeful equilibriating function occurs in our bodies, where nourishment must be balanced and continual to keep them operating as proper repositories for the Spirit. And an equilibriating function occurs in our personalities, where no constant extreme of behavior can be tolerated if we are to operate effectively in our environments. Justice works both through reason and through natural force. We may decide to bring something of ourselves into balance, but if we do not make that decision, it will be made for us. If we deprive our bodies of sleep, we find ourselves forced to rest. We may simply collapse. The same process occurs at all levels of *Justice* (i.e., through the Four Worlds). We may make a conscious decision, or it may be made for us. In any event, this Intelligence is "Faithful;" it guides and protects us.

Crowley's title, *Adjustment,* is appropriate. This is a Path where whatever is necessary is done to bring the organism into equilibrium, a process which, as the symbol of the sword suggests, is not always pleasant. This is the sword of Geburah which cuts away all that which is unnecessary, the extraneous dead wood of nature. It is a severe experience, though no punishment is implicit. There is no question of good, bad, right or wrong. As Gareth Knight expresses it: "The point to remember in all this is that all the God Forms are aspects of the soul itself and not external agencies. Thus the process may be considered psychologically as a condition of self-assessment."[169] The soul weighs itself on the scales in the left hand and then makes necessary adjustments wielding the sword in the right. One will observe that when the Sephiroth are placed in the human body, Geburah is at the right hand and Chesed at the left.[170]

The sword of *Justice*, the weapon of *Elohim Gibor* (God of Geburah) is fearsome. It can be swift and devastating in its cutting away of what is no longer needed. It can make war; it can enforce peace. But the sword has two edges, one of which destroys and the other of which consecrates as in the conferring of knighthood. The cutting away of the negative aspects of body and soul is a return to purity, a consecration. This idea of renewed purity is reinforced by the attribution of Libra and the kidneys, which cleanse waste from the body system. Another parallel, suggested by some writers, is that this Path relates to *Purgatory,* a condition of consciousness after death where the self-assessing soul is cleansed of the dross of its earthly incarnation.

Pursuant to the idea of incarnation and reincarnation, this card is said to represent *Karma,* a principle generally understood as the reaping by a newborn soul of what it has sown in past lives. Paul Case, however, insisting that the term has been often misunderstood, states that what Karma really means is *action.* This is active and continuous adjustment between many incarnations.

He also describes this key as related to *education,* insofar as Lamed means *to teach.*[171] This is an especially interesting observation, not found elsewhere. The conscious maintenance of balance is definitely a learning process. We learn, often slowly and painfully, how to analyze and re-balance ourselves as necessary for different situations. The more we learn of the inner worlds, the more subtle and difficult this becomes. Perfect balance is a formula so precise that the Egyptians symbolized its delicacy as the human soul weighed against a feather.

These ancients had a concept of "right, truth, law and rectitude" expressed by the single word *maat.* This originally meant "that which is straight," but came to mean also a rule, a measure of some kind, or a law.[172] *Maat* was symbolized by the feather, against which either the heart of the deceased or his whole body was weighed. In illustrations, we find this weighing administered by Anubis, and the results recorded by Thoth. Crowley relates both of these Gods to the Nineteenth Path, *Strength,* which is the balance between Geburah and Chesed. The implication is that the adjustment which takes place on the Twenty-Second Path is administered and recorded through the processes of the Nineteenth Path.

As a Goddess, *Maat* represented moral law and truth. She was, in essence, the personification of the concept of *maat.* It is this Goddess who is shown on the Crowley card, crowned with her attribute, the ostrich feather. The weighing of souls is, of course, also implied in the Golden Dawn, Waite and Marseilles versions, the latter two being medieval in tone.

In the Golden Dawn card the figure of a woman rests her feet on a jackal, the animal attributed to Anubis who supervises the weighing of souls. She holds scales which, as in the Crowley card, are black as a reference both to Binah and to Saturn. This means not only assessment, but *restriction,* which is also *time,* an important aspect of the administration of the law. By contrast, the Waite version, as well as that produced by the BOTA, shows golden scales, meaning that the individual soul is measured as it stands within the pure golden Light of Tiphareth. It is only under this Light that the sword of Geburah does its work, as is suggested by the *Maat* legend. *Maat* relates to the Sun God, *Ra.* She is, in fact known as the "Daughter of Ra," as she is Qabalistically named the "Daughter of the Lords of Truth." The Egyptians also called her "Queen of Heaven."

Most important is that Maat is the regulator of the path of the sun. The Egyptian texts suggest that it is through Maat that the sun subsists, for Ra is said to "rest upon Maat," and to "live by Maat."[173] In our terms this means that the principles of The Path of *Justice* maintain Tiphareth. But insofar as Ra is the source of all light, he is also *The Fool.* Thus one can paraphrase, and say that *Aleph rests upon Lamed,* and that *Lamed is the regulator of the Path of the Divine Life Force.*

The relationship between Aleph and Lamed conceals a great secret of the Tarot, one which is, as Crowley said "beyond all planetary and zodiacal considerations," meaning Kether. In his *Book of the Law,* אל is said to be the key to the entire Universe, revealing a mystery of unspeakable profundity. On the Tree of Life, אל is also the God Name of Chesed, the Demiurge (Lesser Creator) from which Microprosopus is formed.

A great many planets are involved in this card. First is Venus, which rules Libra, to which this Path is directly attributed. Mars is related because this is an exercise of the purging energies of Geburah. The Sun is involved not only because the Path runs from the Sun to Mars, but because Justice must take place in the clear bright sunlight of Truth. Saturn has already been mentioned, and is exalted in Libra. Finally there is Jupiter, Planet of Chesed, and of אל.

To state that Libra is ruled by Venus is also to state that behind *Justice* stands *The Empress*, the primary Path of Venus which is the perfect balance between the energies of Chokmah and Binah. The reference is also to the nature forces of Netzach.

Having noted that Lamed in some way refers to all of the Twenty-Two Paths and Hebrew letters, it is interesting to recall that Venus refers to all of the Sephiroth. Venus is the only planet whose symbol encompasses every single Sephira on the Tree of Life (see Figure 14), the implication being that love is the ultimate power of the Universe. Thus, to say that Venus rules Libra-Lamed is to say: *that which encompasses all of the Sephiroth rules that which encompasses all of the Paths*. This may be understood by again considering the idea that the Sephiroth are objective, while the Paths are subjective. Objectivity and subjectivity are complementary conditions. One cannot exist without the other, any more than the color red can exist without the possibility of green, or the energies of Mars can exist without those of Venus. Even the floor of the Golden Dawn card, on which lies the jackal of Anubis, refers to complementary conditions, those of Greater and Lesser Creators: The *white* (which actually represents pure brilliance) is Kether, while *purple* is the color of Chesed in Atziluth. All of the symbolism here points to the idea that this figure is keeping opposites in balance. It is a regulator of energy.

Perhaps surprisingly, Waite emphasizes the Mars aspect of *Justice* over its Venus aspect by having the figure clothed primarily in red. And if his card is considered on the pattern of the Tree of Life (when the card is placed on the Path of Lamed) it will be seen that the raised sword points to Geburah while the scales are lowered in the direction of Tiphareth. The same purple as in the Golden Dawn tile floor appears on the *cloth of honor* behind the figure. The background itself is yellow, meaning Tiphareth.

The differences in the colors of the three versions of *Justice* point out the differing concepts of the designers. The Golden Dawn emphasizes green, flashing against a red throne with a pale blue background. Crowley's card relies on the blues and greens of the Twenty-Second Path in the Four Worlds. The blues are especially vibrant as a reference to the effect of Jupiter on the Path.

Crowley's *Adjustment is* among the most abstract of his Keys. He calls the figure not only the Goddess Maat, but also *Harlequin,* "the partner and fulfillment of *The Fool*." The figure stands within a diamond-shape which is the *Vesica Piscis*. Behind her is a throne of spheres and pyramids, in groups of four, meaning "Law and limitation." This is another reference to Chesed. As Maat she wears ostrich feathers, with the Uraeus serpent, Lord of Life and Death, on her forehead. She holds the sword (a male symbol in this context) in such a way as to suggest sexual union, and the "completion" of the female. This is what is described in *777* as "The Woman justified. By equilibrium and Self-sacrifice is the Gate."[173] A scale, springing from a point above her head, weighs all that *is* in creation, the Alpha and the Omega. She is total equilibrium, yet in constant motion: "She is the ultimate illusion which is manifestation; she is the dance, many-coloured, many-wiled, of Life itself. Constantly whirling, all possibilities are enjoyed, under the phantom show of Space and Time; all things are real, the soul is the surface, precisely because they are instantly compensated by this adjustment. All things are harmony and beauty; all things are truth: because they cancel out."[174]

21. THE PATH OF CAPH
The Wheel of Fortune
The Tenth Key

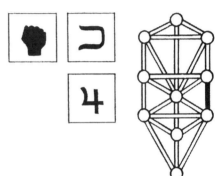

- ◈ PATH COLOR: Violet
- ◈ RELATED SOUND: A Sharp
- ◈ PLANET: Jupiter
- ◈ MEANING: Fist
- ◈ DOUBLE LETTER: Riches, Poverty
- ◈ ESOTERIC TITLE: The Lord of the Forces of Life

THIRTY-TWO PATHS OF WISDOM: *The Twenty-first Path is the Intelligence of Conciliation, and is so called because it receives the divine influence which flows into it from its benediction upon all and each existence.*

The Path of Caph, the *Wheel of Fortune*, runs from Chesed to Netzach. It is the connecting Path between the Personality and the Higher Self on the Pillar of Mercy under Chokmah. The *Thirty-Two Paths of Wisdom* calls it the *Intelligence of Conciliation,* implying that it has a mediating function. And, in view of what has been considered about the regulation of energy on the Path of *Justice,* it is not surprising to learn that Jupiter is assigned to this Path, or that Jupiter is said to govern the circulation of the blood.

Caph is a double letter, one of the "gateways of the soul." To it are attributed the opposites of *riches and poverty* which could be considered the natural fluctuation of the Jupiter forces on this Path. Of course, the riches and poverty are not of this earth, they are of the Soul itself.

Figure 31. Lévi's Interpretation
of the Wheel of Ezekiel (Redrawn
from his *Sanctum Regnum*)

As a word Caph means *fist.* It is the closed hand which symbolizes grasping comprehension, as well as the completion of an activity or the closing of a circle. It is closed, and yet it is in a state continuous motion, a cycle always in many stages at the same time. In this regard Caph is the scarf covering the dancer in the *Universe* card. Moreover it will be found that as Caph is the closed hand, the card preceding it, *The Hermit* (Yod) is an open one.

The wheel, so important to this Path, is a very ancient symbol of life itself, the very turning of which, in some systems, is a prayer. It is the wheel of birth, death and rebirth. It is the wheel of karma. But it is emphatically *not a* wheel of chance or accidents. There are no accidents in the Universe, which is one of the key lessons of this card. We are solely responsible for our own destinies. Fortune provides us what we earn, which is not always pleasant.

The key to the *Wheel of Fortune* is duality and the interchange of energies between opposites which make the wheel spin. The wheel is the activity of all manifestation, as is symbolized in the Golden Dawn version by the twelve spokes. These are the Signs of the Zodiac, each in its correct Atziluth-Path color. The Crowley deck uses ten spokes to symbolize the totality of the Sephiroth, while Waite uses a system of eight spokes based on twice four: the letters T A R O and the יהוה. The pattern of Waite's wheel is based on the *Wheel of Ezekiel* illustrated by Lévi in his *Magical Ritual of the Sanctum Regnum,*[175] and described by the older occultist in very complex terms:

The Wheel of Ezekiel contains the solution of the problem of the quadrature of the circle, and demonstrates the correspondences between words and figures, letters and emblems; it exhibits the tetragram of characters analogous to that of the elements and elemental forms. It is a glyph of perpetual motion. The triple ternary is shown; the central point is the first Unity; three circles are added, each with four attributions, and the dodekad is thus seen. The state of universal equilibrium is suggested by the counterpoised emblems, and the pairs of symbols. The flying Eagle balances the man; the roaring Lion counterpoises the laborious Bull.

Kether, the Crown, Tiphareth, Beauty; and Yesod, Foundation, form a central axis, while Wisdom, Chokmah, equilibrium with Understanding, Binah; and the Severity of Justice, Geburah, makes a counterpoise with the Mercy of Justice, Chesed.[176]

Insofar as dualities in active manifestation are implied here, it might be suggested that two wheels would better describe what is intended than one: that is, one wheel interlocked in another like a gyroscope, each turning in different directions. This really illustrates what is meant by the *Intelligence of Conciliation*. It is the mediation of activity between rotating opposites. Rotation, in this sense, means a sequence, something which begins and ends and then begins again. This means periodicity, rhythms of activity as well as cause and effect, what the Golden Dawn text calls the "counterchanging influence of Light and Darkness." Waite describes this activity as "the perpetual motion of a fluidic Universe...the flux of human life. The Sphinx is the equilibrium therein."

The Sphinx is considered to be a stablizing element in the midst of change. Thus in both the Crowley and the Waite cards it sits at the very top of the Wheel. In the Golden Dawn card, however, it is removed from the Wheel entirely. While Crowley and Waite emphasize the Sphinx as a balancing phase of cyclic energy, the Golden Dawn card emphasizes its role as the guardian of the gateway of the mysteries, holding the secret of life and death.

This interpretation is a later (largely Greek) one, colored to some extent by eighteenth century romanticism. In Egypt the Sphinx was originally a portrait of the Pharoah, symbolizing his great power (the lion's body) over adversaries. This view is corroborated by numerous reliefs in which the Sphinx-Pharoah is shown vanquishing his enemies.

The best known Sphinx is that presumed to be Cheops, who built the Great Pyramid about 2500 B.C.E. When the Greeks saw this monumental sculpture, more than 1500 years later, they took it to mean all that was mysterious and magical, a sense reflected in the tale of Oedipus on the road to Thebes. The Sphinx barred the road and asked each traveler the question: "What walks on four legs in the morning, two legs at noon, and three legs in the afternoon?" Those who failed to answer the question were destroyed. Oedipus, however, knew that the answer was man, himself, who crawls in childhood, walks on two legs in adulthood, and uses a cane in old age. The response of the Sphinx to

Oedipus' correct answer was to throw itself into the sea, an action replete with meaning for the student of the Qabalah.

The Greeks brought one important modification to the Sphinx image. What was originally the portrait of a pharoah on a lion's body became a woman on the body of a male lion. Thus, the Sphinx came to represent not only man with the raw power of the animal kingdom, but also a balance of male and female in the same form.[177]

The special importance of the Sphinx to the Golden Dawn is discussed in the order's papers on the Enochian Mysteries:

> Now learn a mystery of the Wisdom of Egypt. When the Sphinx and the Pyramid are united, thou hast the formulae of the Magic of Nature. These are the keys of the wisdom of all Time; and its beginning who knoweth it? In their keeping are the sacred mysteries and the knowledge of Magic and all the Gods. In the ritual of the 32nd Path leading into the Theoricus Grade, it is thus written. The Sphinx of Egypt spake and said: 'I am the synthesis of the Elemental Forces. I am also the symbol of Man. I am Life. I am Death. I am the Child of the Night of Time.'[178]

Most original here is the concept that the Sphinx is the synthesis of the Elemental Forces. As the root of all Elements, it is also the upper fifth point of the Pentagram—Spirit above the four Elements. It stands above the four lower points of Fire, Water, Air and Earth and represents the spirit which activates them. In this regard, ancient documents refer to the Sphinx in four forms: Bull, Eagle, Man and Lion.[179]

It is not entirely clear why Waite has shown these animal symbols holding books, although we must assume this to be a standard reference to the Four Gospels. The Lion, Eagle, Man, and Bull, found in the vision of *Ezekiel*,[180] and possibly of Assyrian origin, were taken by Christianity to represent the Four Evangelists, Matthew, Mark, Luke and John. And when the Kerubiim are shown holding books, it means the different aspects of Christ about which each Evangelist wrote.[181] Here Waite may be extending an assertion by Lévi that the Wheel is comparable to the Greek monogram of Christ. What is important, at any event, is the amalgam of four Elements on this Path. The Sphinx is the Kerubiim all in one. Moreover, the Pyramid which, when united with the Sphinx supposedly provides a magical formula, is four-sided and refers to Chesed.

The Sphinx is, thus, a cardinal symbol of manifestation. It is both that through which one passes in birth or death, and that which controls the passage. It is the directing aspect of the Higher Self in Tiphareth; it is protective, and a Keeper of the Gates which keeps the Personality from absorbing more than its system can handle. To be able to correctly answer the question of the Sphinx (that answer being an extension of the Greek axiom: *Man, know thyself*) means that one is prepared to pass through the gates of inner consciousness. To pursue the Oedipus legend: When the question was correctly answered, the Sphinx threw itself into the sea. This means that, being no longer needed, the "gate" now being open, the Gate Keeper was absorbed back into the Great Sea of consciousness. More accurately, it was absorbed back into the Individual Higher consciousness which created it. On the other hand, the Sphinx "slays" those who are unready to pass consciously beyond the restrictions of time and space, concepts valid only in terms of matter. The destruction by the Sphinx of those travelers who cannot answer its question, is the protection of the Personality by the Higher Self. But it may also be considered the real death process. Those who know the nature of the Sphinx (All of Fire, Water, Air and Earth) may pass consciously from one state to the next, while others fall into a deep sleep, a "destruction" of awareness from which the soul gradually awakens into a new condition. Beside the wheel itself, the Sphinx is the only element common to the three modern versions of the Key shown here. The Golden Dawn card has only two figures, that of the Sphinx and the *Cynocephalus*. The Waite card shows the Sphinx, *Hermanubis* and *Typhon,* as does Crowley's version.

The figures in the Marseilles key represent a transitional period in the Wheel of Life iconography. The wheel, which seems to have originated during the Romanesque period (11th-12th centuries), was a popular device for representing humanity at the mercy of changing fortune.[182] In the earliest versions human figures were shown on the wheel, with one above that is ruling. Animal figures were probably introduced toward the end of the fifteenth century to underscore mankind's animal nature and the mutability of life. Thus, the Marseilles card shows very generalized figures of good and evil, with a ruler above who balances these aspects on the wheel. The imagery serves to remind us, by comparison with the other cards, of the extent to which the symbolic explanation of the Tarot has been embellished over the past two hundred years. From the mid-nineteenth century on, each of the card's figures has borne a very specific mythological reference.

Beginning with the Golden Dawn card: What is called the *Plutonian Cynocephalus* is a dog-faced ape sitting beneath the wheel. This animal, symbolizing *time* and *eternity,* is the traditional companion of Thoth (Hermes-Mercury), and is the hieroglyphic symbol for *writing.*[183] Thoth is the inventor of writing and the scribe of the Gods, who waits, especially, upon Osiris. It is he, called the *Lord of Holy Words,* who records the results of the weighing of souls on the Path of *Justice.* Thoth is also said to have measured time, dividing it into years, months and seasons. Thus time and eternity is attributed to his companion, the Cynocephalus, which the ancients referred to the Moon, the "planet" believed to follow Mercury.

The implication of the Golden Dawn illustration is that the Sphinx and the Cynocephalus are two different (above and below) aspects of the stable force which monitors and regulates life's seasons. The Sphinx is the quadripartite Elemental Being guided by the Higher Consciousness (the human head). The Cynocephalus (body of the faithful ape linked with the head of a form almost human) means the "words" which we use. These words are the vibratory patterns of existence which turn the wheel. And, as the Gospel of St. John begins: "In the beginning was the Word, and the Word was with God, and the Word was God."[184] This passage has to do with the Lesser Divine Creator, the Demiurge which we have identified as Chesed, origin of the Path of the *Wheel of Fortune* In general the card means that when the Higher Self brings the Four Elements under control, the "words," vibratory patterns, become our faithful companion, and we are no longer bound to the wheel.

The Waite and Crowley cards, both more traditional than that of the Golden Dawn, must be interpreted in terms of the interaction of Sphinx, Hermanubis and Typhon. Hermanubis is a dual God, which Case mistakenly called a combination of Hermes and Anubis, but actually combining Horus and Anubis. He is *Heru-em-Anpu,* meaning Horus *as* Anubis. This God form, a later Egyptian development, is described by Wallis Budge as possessed of "two distinct and opposite aspects; as the guide of heaven and the leader of souls to Osiris, he was a beneficent God, but as the personification of death and decay he was a being who inspired terror."[185]

The myth of Typhon or *Typhoeus* is of Greek origin. Typhon was involved in the wars of supremacy of the Gods. He was a monster so horrible that even the Gods fled at the sight of him. But, as the legend goes, he was eventually subdued by Zeus, who set him afire and buried him under Mt. Aetna. So Typhon became known as the fire-breathing monster who personified volcanoes and typhoons. He was also called the *Father of the Sphinx.*

As his mythology developed, Typhon was associated with the Egyptian God, Set, brother and murderer of Osiris. Set was the symbolic dark side of Osiris (recalling the Golden Dawn text stating that this card involves the "counterchanging influence of Light and Darkness"). Typhon is also associated with the Dragon Aphophis, who is the *accuser* in the *Book of the Dead.* Insofar as Typhon is shown as a snake, as in the Waite card, he is one of the forms of Set.[186] All of this is linked together by the idea that Anubis, who is also Horus, is often represented (like St. George) slaying the Serpent.

Thus in Typhon and Hermanubis we have phases of energy which supersede ("slay") one another, three types of energy which underlie manifestation. These appear at the center of Waite's Wheel as the symbols of Salt ⊕, Sulphur ⚱ and Mercury ☿. The fourth figure, the same as the sign of Aquarius ♒, is the alchemical symbol for *dissolution.*

In the Hindu system, what the West calls the "Three alchemical Principles," are called *Gunas.* The Gunas are *Sattva, Rajas* and *Tamas.* Sattva is the philosophic Mercury, superconsciousness. Rajas is Sulphur, activity, passion and desire. Gunas is Salt; it is ignorance and inertia, subconsciousness. The idea that the *The Wheel of Fortune* symbolizes the revolution of natural phases is generally accepted, though there is some confusion about which of the Gunas is applied to which figure. Crowley states that the Sphinx is Sulphur, Hermanubis is Mercury and Typhon is Salt.[187]

The Golden Dawn version, on the other hand, would allow the Sphinx to be considered nothing less than the Superconsciousness, Sattva, the Philosophic Mercury. And we see that in Waite's card the Sphinx sits above the Mercury sign on the Wheel.

In the Golden Dawn papers it is stated that Mercury is attributed to Kether, Salt is attributed to Chokmah and Sulphur is attributed to Binah. The "Three Principles of Nature" are also related to the three Maternal letters of the *Sepher Yetzirah.*

20. THE PATH OF YOD
The Hermit
The Ninth Key

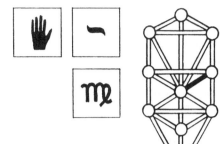

- ◈ PATH COLOR: Green-yellowish
- ◈ RELATED SOUND: F Natural
- ◈ SIGN: Virgo (Mutable Earth)
- ◈ MEANING: Hand
- ◈ SIMPLE LETTER: Sexual Love
- ◈ ESOTERIC TITLE: The Prophet
  of the Eternal, the Magus
  of the Voice of Power

THIRTY-TWO PATHS OF WISDOM: *The Twentieth Path is the Intelligence of Will, and is so called because it is the means of preparation of all and each created being, and by this intelligence the existence of the Primordial Wisdom becomes known.*

The Path of Yod, connects Tiphareth (the Christ-Buddha center) and Chesed (the Architect of Manifestaton). In brief, it represents the self-sustained, primal beginnings of manifestation. It is the very point of origin of our manifest Universe, in direct contact with the Divine Source of All. It is the Path from the Demiurge out of darkness. It is the coming of the Light of manifestation through Microprosopus.

Insofar as the sign *Virgo* is attributed to the twentieth Path, we understand the Hermit to be ever-virgin, pure, and totally innocent. And insofar as it represents a gateway to the bridge between Macroprosopus and Microprosopus, it involves certain qualities of Daath. These Daath qualities are represented by the very isolation of the figure: There is something naturally mysterious and compelling about this figure standing alone in the desert holding its own source of light. One immediately thinks of Diogenes in search of an honest man, or Moses (whose head supposedly emanated rays of light) or Christ as the "Light of the World." One may also consider, in studying this solitary figure, that monasticism first began in the Egyptian desert in the third and fourth centuries after the death of Christ. Extreme asceticism and withdrawal from society were considered a means of perfection. In fact, the very word *hermit* comes from a Greek word meaning *desert,* the place where some of the earliest monks lived in walled-up rooms of one window.

The higher the card on the Tree of Life, the more important it is that we let the card suggest such images as they will. The image of a desert, for example, is a very potent one. Conceptually, it is an expanse of earth as indefinably vast as the ocean. And as we consider Binah in the image of deep, dark, endless waters, we may envision the desert as a crystallization or precipitation out of Binah's vast sea of consciousness.

The Hermit is an expression of the same energy as *The Fool.* It is at once the wise old age of the Child (of the Golden Dawn *Fool* card) and the virgin beginning of a new sequence. It is the purity and innocence of *The Fool* as it is transformed in the projection of Microprosopus through Binah. The idea that *The Fool* (child) is at the same time *The Hermit* (old man) may best be understood by meditating on the snake which holds its tail in its mouth, the traditional symbol of wisdom.

It has been stated that *Justice,* the Path opposite *The Hermit,* administers the energies in manifestation of *The Fool.* Thus, we appreciate that *Justice* and *The Hermit* must also work together in some basic way. One clue to this mystery is, again, in the ל + א, *Justice + The Fool,* which is also the God Name of Chesed, point of origin of the Path of *The Hermit.*

Most important is that *The Hermit* represents communication between the Higher Self of Tiphareth (the *Ruach)* and the Spiritual Self of Kether (the *Yechidah).* For this reason the Golden Dawn text calls *The Hermit* the first of three great initiatory cards, the others being *Strength* and *The Chariot.* In this regard it should be pointed out that the experiences of all these Paths may be gained on the Path of *The High Priestess.* That Path not only encompasses all Paths above Tiphareth, but crosses the Abyss with its devastating experience of *Divine reconciliation through isolation.*

However *The Hermit* may be described, it is pre-eminently one of union. It represents the first point of awareness by the Higher Self of the Supreme Spiritual Self, explicable only in the most erotic of imagery. This idea is supported by the *Sepher Yetzirah,* which attributes *sexual love* to the simple letter Yod. But this is not the sexuality of coition, for the card is the essence of isolation and singularity. The "sexuality" is self-contained and self-sustaining, a quality cryptically described in the Golden Dawn documents as "Prudence."

Yod is related to Kether not only insofar as it is isolated and self-contained, but also in that it forms the graphic root for all of the other letters of the Hebrew alphabet. Moreover, the Yod is phallic. It is the Male-Fire which rushes out toward the Female-Water. In the Golden Dawn version this is symbolized by the sign on the front of the Hermit's hood. The Yod within a fire triangle means that the Yod is the very essence of Spiritual Fire within Microprosopus. It is, thus, an aspect of the Chokmah Force. It is the All-Father in manifestation below the Abyss, which is related to the *Logos*.

The concept of Logos, while not at all difficult, is often misunderstood. Logos is a Greek term usually considered to mean *word,* which came to represent a principle of both Greek and Hebrew metaphysics. In the simplest possible terms: The Logos is a link, an intermediary between God and Man. The same is true for any sacrificed God, including Christ, Osiris, or Buddha.

On the Tree of Life Tiphareth is the objective Logos, the objective center of energy produced by the Demiurge (Chesed) as a direct link of the Lower with the Higher. But, in terms of the Paths, which are subjective, the link is on the Path of Yod. This is to say that while objectively Tiphareth is the Logos center; subjectively, in order to understand this transitional energy, we must rise above Tiphareth toward Chesed, through *The Hermit.*

Qabalistic attitudes toward what is called the Logos relate largely to Philo, a Jewish philosopher living at the time of Christ. He was a synthesizer of Greek and Hebrew thought. To the Hebrews the "word" (vibration) was Power. To the Greeks, the Logos was "spermatic," meaning that it was the source of All. Heraclitis described it as a Divine Fire which stimulated and maintained order. The Stoics saw the Logos as an all-pervading force in the world. Later the neoplatonic doctrine of the Logos in emanations influenced the writer of the *Sepher Yetzirah.*

What Philo did, no mean trick, was to combine the Jewish concept of Word, with the Platonic concept (related especially to the *Timaeus)* of manifestation evolving from a point of transition between the Godhead and Man. *The Hermit* may be considered a "Word" (Vibration) uttered into a vast space. The Word is that which continually stimulates the development of manifestation, which energizes the principles of form which it has produced.

While the Hermit is often considered a Christ figure, he is better related to *Moses* who led his people across the same Egyptian desert in which monasticism developed centuries later. Moses was first related to the Logos by an early Gnostic sect taking its name from the Simon Magus described in the *Acts of the Apostles.* These "Simonian Gnostics" of about the second century C.E. believed that the Book of *Exodus* was an allegory of the soul being led by the Logos (Moses) through the desert of life into the spiritual promised land.[188]

In other terms, Moses is the *Thaumaturge,* the arch-magician. His staff is a wand of enormous power which strikes water from rock, and turns into a serpent at his bidding. This latter act refers to the use of the Kundalini (Yod) force by the Adept-Magician. That force is the Sacred Fire which is the essence of the Logos transmitted by the phallic wand.

One other correspondence between Moses and the Logos is found in the interaction between the prophet and God as the burning bush. The word of God is not issued directly, but comes through Moses as intermediary, the function of the Logos. More than this, Moses may be considered a *tool* of the Supreme

Father, carrying out His Will. In this regard, the *hand,* man's ultimate creative tool, is attributed to Yod. *The Hermit* is the very hand *of* God.

The hand of *The Hermit* is open as opposed to that of *The Wheel of Fortune.* The open hand is a sign of ultimate power, found especially in Byzantine representations of the *Pantocrator,* Christ as the Ruler of the Universe. But the open hand is also a sign of innocence; it may give and take freely without the impediments of thought or moral restrictions. The open hand represents *The Hermit* as prophet, the completed adept.

Insofar as *The Hermit* is the Adept-Magician, he is the agent of the Supreme Will and, as such, the *Thirty-Two Paths of Wisdom* calls the Twentieth Path the *Intelligence of Will.* There is a strong link between *The Hermit* and the Path of *The Magician* (the *Intelligence of Transparency)* since Virgo is ruled by Mercury. This means that the Philosophic Mercury ultimately directs the course of the Yod-Fire on the Paths.

The fact that Virgo is an Earth sign may be somewhat confusing in that any discussion of *The Hermit* invariably centers on the idea of fire. Hopefully it has been understood that the fire in question here is not the same as either Elemental Fire or Maternal Fire. *The Hermit* could be called the "First Earth" within which a Sacred Fire operates. The Yod force, again, ennervates to keep the world in order, a stimulus which could be described as a fertilization. The concept is an extremely difficult one which has to do with multi-faceted potentiality. Approached from another direction, it could be said that the most ordered existence is earth, here represented as wholly barren, but with the potential for all life. In the Golden Dawn card, the importance of Binah in this process is suggested by the red band around the Hermit's waist. The Venusian green of earth is bound up by the Atziluth-red Binah cord.

The Golden Dawn emphasizes the earthy, monastic qualities of the figure. And while it may be stretching the symbolism to make the suggeston, the dual robes recall the titles of Binah and Chokmah: *The Outer Robe of Concealment* (Binah) and *The Inner Robe of Concealment* (Chokmah). The staff is, of course, referred to Chokmah. It is held here in such a way as to suggest that it is to be planted, and will grow leaves and flowers.

Of the four versions, only Crowley's suggests the *motion* and activity which is essential to the Yod. And, as usual, his card requires more explanation than the others. He emphasizes, for example, the idea that *The Hermit* is rooted in Binah, by cloaking him entirely in red.

Before the red figure is the *Orphic Egg* with a serpent wrapped around it. In the ancient Orphic Mysteries this signified the Cosmos encircled by the Fiery Spirit, which is Yod. Behind the figure is Cerberus, the three-headed dog who guards the gates of Hell, and who has been tamed by the Hermit. The spermatazoon is symbolic of the Yod energies in the material world, while the staff which transmits the sexual force, is completely hidden. As Crowley states: "In this Trump is shewn the entire mystery of Life in its most secret workings. Yod=Phallus=Spermatazoon=Hand=Logos=Virgin."[189]

Yod has been called *The Crown,* meaning that it is the highest point of the Logos, the primary energy from which manifestation derives. And, of course, any reference to Crown points to Kether, the Crown above All.

The last symbol to be considered is the lamp which, in all versions refers to Tiphareth, and makes a statement about the very nature of light. In the Golden Dawn rituals this principle was expressed in three languages: *Khabs am Pekht* (Coptic); *Konx om Pax* (Greek); *Light in Extension.* This means that light is the principle of manifestation, that on which all of creation is built. So the Hermit may be said to represent a glyph on the nature of primal manifestation beneath the Abyss, and of the relationship between light and the Sacred Fire symbolized by Yod.

One would expect that the placement of the letters Yod, Heh and Vau on the Tree of Life would have profound meaning. Thus it is particularly intriguing to realize that these letters work together as a trinity from Chesed to Tiphareth to Chokmah, and back to Chesed. Yod is *The Hermit*, Heh is *The Emperor* and Vau is *The Hierophant*, all functioning to the side of the Pillar of Mercy on the Tree of Life. The intention here is not to offer an explanation, but to suggest a very valuable subject for meditation.

19. THE PATH OF TETH
Strength
The Eighth Key

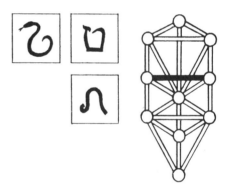

❖ PATH COLOR: Yellow-
        Greenish
❖ RELATED SOUND: E Natural
❖ SIGN: Leo (Fixed Fire)
❖ MEANING: Snake
❖ SIMPLE LETTER: Taste
❖ ESOTERIC TITLE: The Daughter
    of the Flaming Sword

> THIRTY-TWO PATHS OF WISDOM: *The Nineteenth Path is the Intelligence of all the activities and spiritual beings, and is so called because of the affluence diffused by it from the most high blessing and most exalted sublime glory.*

In our upward progress on the Tree of Life the Path of *Strength* leads to the edge of the Abyss, as did *The Hermit.* And as we come closer and closer to the source of All, the Ultimate Simplicity, it is perhaps paradoxical that the symbolism becomes increasingly complex. In the lower cards, energies and experiences can be accurately described in words. But at this level on the Tree, and above, we learn primarily by meditation on the interrelationship of symbols, in which great profundities are secretly imbedded. Few, for example, might even suspect

that this picture of a woman with a lion could have such vast meaning.

In terms of evolution, the nineteenth Path is the first Path of Microprosopus, the Lesser Countenance. It is the outpouring of energy from Chesed to Geburah in the process of manifestation; it is the primary Path of the Higher Self, linking the great opposites below the Abyss. *It is the Path on which Fire becomes Light,* for manifestation is Light, whereas the Supernals are a darkness which is fiery. Thus, in his *Book of Tokens* Case speaks of "the radiant Darkness of the Limitless Light."[190]

To the Path of *Strength* are assigned both the Hebrew letter Teth and the most powerful sign of the Zodiac, Leo. Leo is the *lion,* while Teth means *snake,* and the interchangeability of the lion and snake symbolism is a key to the meaning of the card. As the symbols interchange, we understand that the realities which they represent can also be interchanged. The One Spirit takes any form It wills, which is an important lesson of this Path. The idea is clearly expressed in the *Zohar:* "The three principle elements of nature are Fire, Air and Water. Really they are one in use and substance, and are able to change the one into the other. It is the same with Thought and Speech and Logos, they are one and the same in themselves."[191]

As the serpent holds its tail in its mouth it represents *wisdom* and the *Universe* (noting here that *taste is* attributed to Teth in the *Sepher Yetzirah),* whereas the same serpent is described in *Genesis* as the *tempter.* Moreover, insofar as it is the fiery, vital Life Force, it is also the *redeemer.* This is the same, apparently contradictory idea encountered with the primary card of matter, *The Devil*, which is also both tempter and redeemer. And, interestingly enough, the lion is occasionally related to Saturn, the supposed "place of dwelling" of the Devil. Fortunately, the Qabalah allows us to put these symbols into very clear perspective, as Binah-Saturn is the ultimate source of the Devil's imprisoning matter.

It must be admitted that the lion has been used in so many different cultures and symbolic pantheons, that it may be claimed to have mutually exclusive meanings. But, generally, references to the lion have to do with its physical strength (This is not a card of intellect in any way). The greatest strength of which one can conceive is the light of the Sun, the ruler of Leo. And, as we shall consider, it is the lion which is permitted to open the Sacred Scroll of the Apocalypse. This means that the solar power, represented by this card, can open the higher levels of consciousness beyond the Sun (Tipahreth) itself. In symbolism, this is shown most graphically by representations of the Sun God Mithra, whose body is human, but whose head is that of a lion.

The lion symbolism always implies a brute force which may be used constructively or destructively. This is the very Path on which the Sword of Geburah is formed, indicating that the possibility of the philosopher being overwhelmed by the power which he or she invokes is always present. Such danger is stressed, for example, in the story of Daniel in the lion's den, one closely related to the symbolism of this card. Daniel is, like Moses, a Magician (Thaumaturge) holding back the destructive power of the lions through sheer force of will.

Daniel, the three Hebrews in the fiery furnace, Noah, and other such figures were chosen by the earliest Christians as Biblical representatives of salvation. On the wall of a catacomb, a depiction of Daniel means, in essence: "let him who is buried here be saved as Daniel was saved from the lions." Thus, a simplistic faith in divine protection came to overshadow a symbolism of far greater consequence, that of the enlightened individual controlling the "animal potency" underlying all existence.

In the symbolism of Alchemy, the lion takes three separate forms. First, there is the *Green Lion,* the energy of nature before it is purified and subjected to the will. Next is the *Red Lion,* represented on the card of *Strength.* This is the force of nature under perfect control, what the Alchemists would describe as the Sulphur (solar energy) combined with Mercury (will). Waite underscores this meaning by showing the infinity sign of *The Magician* above the woman's head; this is the directing willpower of the twelfth Path, what Mathers calls the *Philosophic Mercury.* Finally, there is the *Old Lion,* meaning the completely purified consciousness, the linking of all components of the soul with the Highest Spiritual Self which is "older than time itself."

The lion figures in ancient legends and in Christian legends, such as the story of Saint Jerome, where the saint removes a thorn from the lion's paw and the grateful animal becomes his servant.[192] The consistent thread running through such tales has to do with the wise person who subjugates the wild animal through the force of his humanity. It is the highest quality of mankind controlling the highest quality of beast (of which the lion is "king"), an idea sufficiently common in history that it may be considered an extension of Jung's *Wise Old Man* archetype. In this regard, we appreciate that each and every one of the Tarot trumps has come to represent a body of teaching, legend, or tradition, deeply rooted in the group soul of mankind and expressed in different ways throughout history.

Pursuant to the relationship of the symbolic lion with the sun, there is some possibility of confusion. At one level the lion is the *Kerub of Fire,* symbol of one of the Four Elements. But this is not the same as the lion of the sun's Spiritual Fire, or Kundalini, which is also the serpent.

The fiery lion-serpent is one aspect of the Life Force which, in manifestation, is a duality of activity and passivity. Kundalini, the Sacred Fire, is the active phase of this energy, purposely unleashed and directed by the will. This is suggested by the double ends of the rods in the hands of the figure in *The Universe*, a card related to *Strength* in several ways.

It will, for example, be noted that the scarf on the figure in the Golden Dawn card is similar to that worn by the figure in *The Universe*. Both are *veils*. Both are concealing of principles, though at different ends of manifestation. *Strength* is the beginning of Microprosopus, while *The Universe* is the completion of the process. The woman who has tamed the energy of the lion, and the woman who dances in space surrounded by the Four Kerubiim, are both expressions of that which is, at the highest level, called *The Empress*.

This is a very powerful Path, one on which it is not possible for a sensitive person to meditate without profound effects on the psyche. The card may come to be appreciated as a statement of methodology, whereby the will power controls the vital life energy. Case's *Book of Tokens* suggests that the secret of this methodology lies in number, although as used in that text the word means the germ of separation into what can be counted as divided from the One: "Number veileth the power of the Elohim, for Number is that thick darkness whereof it is written, 'And Moses drew near unto the thick darkness Where God was;' and again, 'Tetragrammaton said that he would dwell in the thick darkness.' " And, it continues: 'Of that darkness the Serpent is a sign, the Great Serpent, the royal snake of Egypt. This is the Serpent of temptation, Yet from it cometh redemption. For the Serpent is the first appearance of the Anointed One.' "[193]

Strength represents a very important initiatory formula dealing with the serpent power. It is this power which is used to stimulate the various *chakras*, or centers of energy in the body. The principles imbedded in number (as defined above) teach us how to use this power, which is not to suggest that the process is cold and distant. On the contrary, Crowley's title, *Lust,* is quite appropriate. What is involved is the development of a "divine frenzy," as is meant by the frequently-repeated instruction: "Inflame Thyself with Prayer!" Or, as the Alchemists express it, "The heat of the furnace makes the Stone." The heat is a great passion within the confines of an exercise such as that of the Middle Pillar.[194]

The method is a recurring theme in the correspondence courses of Paul Case. In one lesson, he says of inner exercises: "By prolonged practice...pursued sometimes for months and years without apparent result, those who follow the Way of Liberation effect changes in their subconsciousness. These changes are symbolized by Key 8 and produce at the same time the result shown in Key 16."[195] Repeatedly he states that the whole point of meditational exercises is an actual and subtle change in the structure of the body cells. And those who are familiar with Dion Fortune's definition of the Qabalah as the "Yoga of the West," will appreciate that Case directly said things at which she only hinted.

When we have the important keys *all* mystical literature suddenly opens up and seems genuinely simple. Such may be the case with the *Book of Revelation (The Apocalypse),* which generally confounds most biblical scholars, and is the source of some extraordinary scholarly nonsense. *Revelation,* like the *Book of Genesis,* has been speculated to be "one of the great Qabalistic documents," and one may not be surprised to find that Tarot interpreters often relate the card of *Strength* (or Crowley's *Lust*) to that work by St. John.

In *Revelation* it is stated that the lion, representative of the Tribe of Judah (the descendants of David), had "won the right to open the scroll and break its seven seals."[196] But as the seals are to be broken we discover that the lamb has taken the place of the lion. *The lion has, in fact, become the lamb of "Seven Eyes."* These are the seven Chakras which are activated by the Lion-Serpent Power. This is the taming of the lion by the woman in *Strength.* In Qabalistic terms this means that to bring the energies symbolized by the lion under perfect control, is to open the seals on the Book of Reality above the Abyss. The symbolism refers to the method by which one may know that from which manifestation emerges, the Supernal Triangle of the Tree of Life. It should be noted here that the Path of Teth is the highest on the Tree with no direct connections into the Supernals. It is, thus, an important Path of transition. It is, like *The Hermit,* a gateway to the experiences of Daath.

In the Golden Dawn version of both cards, Daath is suggested by the desert. As we cross the desert, going upwards, we are led out of bondage by the Logos itself (Moses as the Light). Even Crowley's card may be interpreted in this way, though he has placed his card on the eleventh Path, traditionally given to *Justice.* His symbolism is perfectly consistent with the meaning of the Golden Dawn or Waite cards, relative to Daath, of which he commented in the *Equinox:* "In Daath is said to be the Head of the Great Serpent Nechesh or Leviathon, called evil to conceal its Holiness."[197] This reasoning is interesting in terms of his card *Lust,* where he represented the seven-headed beast of the Apocalypse, with which he personally identified. One may suggest that Crowley related himself to the beast under the same philosophical twist as he described for the serpent, i.e., an evil which is only apparent, and actually concealing of the greatest good. One can argue theologically that God creates only good, and that what appears to be the greatest evil must actually conceal good.

At any event, some may find it very uncomfortable, even pathological, that Crowley has so woven the trappings of his own personality into the cards, although it requires some study to understand the extent to which this is the case. Others may find his choice of imagery curious, wondering that he should illustrate a card of such spiritual potency as *Strength* with the Scarlet Woman of the Apocalypse, riding the Beast. Crowley made the connection through Gematria on the number 666, to which he related his own name, the sun, his so-called "Stele of Revealing," and the Beast of Revelation.

Although the image is somewhat enigmatic in this context, Crowley has used the Whore of Babylon to represent the epitome of virginity, that which is symbolized in the Golden Dawn card by the four flowers (Chesed) and by the wreath in Waite's card. The principle is, again, that of the greatest evil concealing the greatest good.

    The woman is of the same innocence as the hermit. She is *virgo intacto* and it is only as such that she can, with complete safety, deal with the lion. She might also be considered one of the Vestal Virgins keeping the Sacred Fire.

18. THE PATH OF CHETH
The Chariot
The Seventh Key

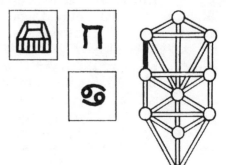

- ◈   PATH COLOR: Red-Orange
- ◈   RELATED SOUND: C Sharp
- ◈   SIGN: Cancer (Cardinal Water)
- ◈   SIMPLE LETTER: Speech
- ◈   ESOTERIC TITLE: The Child
      of the Powers of the Waters; the
      Lord of The Triumph of Light

    THIRTY-TWO PATHS OF WISDOM: *The Eighteenth Path is called the House of Influence (by the greatness of whose abundance the influx of good things upon created beings is increased), and from the midst of the investigation the arcana and hidden senses are drawn forth, which dwell in its shade and which cling to it from the cause of all causes.*

The Path of *The Chariot* runs between Geburah (*Strength*) and Binah, the Great Mother on the Tree of Life. It is the highest and, thus, the most profound Path on the Pillar of Severity. It is also the third initiation in the series of *Hermit*, *Strength* and *Chariot* meaning that it is an introductory experience to the Supreme Spiritual Self. It is an initiation across the Abyss, appreciating that once one crosses the Abyss, all of its crossing Paths are understood. The four Paths beside *The High Priestess* are *in toto*, the experience of the "Garden of Eden," as will be understood by considering the Element attached to each Path: *The Chariot* is watery (Cancer), *The Lovers* is airy (Gemini), *The Emperor* is fiery (Aries) and *The Hierophant* is earthy (Taurus). These are also the Four Rivers of Paradise, which flow together into Tiphareth from the Path of *The High Priestess*

The Chariot represents a completion which Waite called a "conquest on all planes,"[198] meaning that *The Chariot* carries the influence of the higher to all of the lower planes. *The Thirty-Two Paths of Wisdom* describes this as the "House of Influence (by the greatness of whose abundance the influx of good things upon created things is increased)..." Here the ancient text implies that through this Path one may discover the secrets of the hidden senses "which dwell in its shade," meaning the Supreme Darkness above the Abyss.

This card also represents the vision of Ezekiel,[199] wherein the prophet described the appearance of "four living creatures." Each had four faces, that of a man, a lion, an ox and an eagle. Beside each of the creatures was a wheel, "like a wheel within a wheel," and as the creatures moved, so the wheels moved. Above the heads of these apparitions was "a vault glittering like a sheet of ice." Above the vault was a throne, and on the throne was a radiant figure. The implication is that the creatures (Elemental energies of the manifest Universe) are the chariot.

Students of Jewish mysticism may be naturally curious about the roots of this card, since it is suggestive of one of the most important trends in early Jewish thought, that of the *Merkabah*. The Merkabah is the chariot which carries the Throne.[200]

Of this trend, Gershom Scholem says: "The earliest Jewish mysticism is throne-mysticism. Its essence is not absorbed contemplation of God's true nature, but perception of his appearance on the throne as described by Ezekiel."[201] He further states that while in the earliest days, writers spoke of the "ascent to the Merkabah," the later writers discussed enlightenment as the "descent to the Merkabah,"[202] presumably meaning a journey into the depths of Self. One way or the other, there is the implication that the chariot is stationary, as it is shown in the Waite, Crowley and Marseilles cards, an imagery supported by Case, who says that the number of the card, seven, is traditionally related to *rest*. This is a mystery, for while the chariot moves continuously through the planes, it is at rest.

Of course, the fact that this card is a clear reference to Ezekiel does not mean that it is indisputably related to Merkabah thought. Ezekiel was a very popular figure in the West during the apparent period of the invention of Tarot, as the art attests. Yet if we are to suppose that the originators of the

Tarot had even the slightest knowledge of Qabalah and Jewish metaphysics, we must assume that they were familiar with its oldest expression, Merkabah, and would not have used an image of a chariot casually. The intention here is not to attempt to answer this question, only to acknowledge that it exists and that it is one which may cut to the very core in defining what is modern and what is ancient in the system of Tarot.

Eliphas Lévi, who is something of a bridge between ancient and modern esotericism, made an interesting contribution in his design for *The Chariot* card. This was never a part of a Lévi deck, although Oswald Wirth incorporated most of Lévi's ideas into his Tarot of 1889.

In *Ritual of Transcendental Magic,* Lévi wrote of *The Chariot:*

> *A cubic chariot*, with four pillars and an azure and starry drapery. In this chariot, between the four pillars, a victor crowned with a circle adorned with three radiant golden pentagrams. Upon his breast are three superimposed squares, on his shoulders the *Urin* and *Thummim* of the sovereign sacrificer, represented by two crescents of the moon in Gedulah [Chesed] and Geburah; in his hand is a sceptre surmounted by a globe, square and triangle: his attitude is proud and tranquil. A double sphinx or two sphinxes joined at the haunches are harnessed to the chariot; they are pulling in opposite directions, but are looking the same way. They are respectively black and white. On the square which forms the fore part of the chariot is the Indian *lingham* surrounded by the flying sphere of the Egyptians.[203]

Waite followed Lévi closely, his only iconographic contribution being the addition of a river behind the chariot (reference to the waters flowing from *The High Priestess* and to the water sign, Cancer). He has also added a city which we may interpret to mean the "Heavenly Jerusalem," or the "City of God" above the Abyss. Thus *The Chariot* is shown as intermediary. It is both the *above* and the *below;* it is perfect control on more than one plane of existence, while at the same time it protects the sanctity of the "Throne" by maintaining the necessary separation of those planes which it affects.

The relationship of Chariot to Throne is amplified by our knowledge that the angels of Binah are called אראלים *(Aralim),* Thrones, while those of Chokmah are called אופנים *(Auphanim),* Wheels. This is consistent with the idea of Binah as representative of all three Supernals, Binah, Chokmah and Kether and is important insofar as the Throne is actually Kether (it is not of Kether, it is Kether).

There is no way in which these relationships can become comprehensible except through meditation, and the student should not feel discouraged if the words seem difficult. The really important point here is the relationship of the Divine Spirit to that which in some way contains It. The meaning of the Hebrew letter Cheth, attributed to the eighteenth Path, is *fence* or *enclosure.* *The Chariot* is a wheeled enclosure which holds the Spirit in its "movement" through all planes. Two principles can be derived here: 1) First is the very idea that an enclosure is necessary, something external to the Self which carries that Self through various levels of the manifest Universe. 2) The idea that the vehicle serves a protective function, as Case's *Book of Tokens* says of Cheth:

> I am the hedge of protection
> Enclosing the field of existence.
> In this field thou dwellest.
> And I am thy defense
> Against the darkness which is without.
> Yet is this hedge of safety
> Also a wall of limitation,
> And the darkness against which it defendeth thee
> is the radiant Darkness of the Limitless Light,
> too brilliant for thine eyes.[204]

In interpreting this passage, Case refers to the *Ain Soph* "which is to us a darkness, because it transcends our earthly vision." He also relates this to the idea that "Osiris is a black God,"[205] meaning that Osiris (a sacrificed God) was resurrected and then arose above the Light to a Darkness which is at the very pinnacle of the Supreme Spiritual Self in Kether. This experience of the Spiritual Self, pictured in *The Chariot*, has also been described as the "exaltation" of Alchemy, where the alchemist becomes the Philosopher's Stone.

Of the four versions of the card, Crowley's most strongly emphasizes the relationship of *The Chariot* to the text of Ezekiel, with its "living creatures." His card expands on the dual sphinxes proposed by Lévi, whereas the Golden Dawn follows the earlier design of the Marseilles deck in which the chariot is drawn by two horses.

Crowley states that he was much influenced by Lévi's card design, and since he also claimed to be Lévi's reincarnation, he may have wanted to emphasize the development of "his" earlier work. He has, thus, taken Lévi's dual sphinxes and turned them into the four Kerubiim, each of which has four sub-elements, as in the *Tattvas*. This is consistent with the biblical text which describes each of the four creatures as having four faces. Moreover, we have previously made the connection of the sphinx with the pentagram, which represents the Four Elements crowned by Spirit. The pentagram, as a five pointed figure, is appropriate to Geburah, the lower end of this Path. Geburah is also symbolized in Crowley's card by the red wheels, meaning that its energy is the motive power of the chariot. The complement of Geburah, Chesed, is implicit here in the various uses of the *four*. Chesed-Jupiter is important on this Path because it is the beginning of manifestation, in Microprosopus, of the Four Elements which are the symbolic "support" for the Heavens. In the cards of both Crowley and Waite, the Binah-canopy is supported by four pillars which are the Elements, and which are the יהוה. These are also the four columns of the *Tree of Life in a Solid Sphere* (cover illustration).

Above the golden armored figure in Crowley's card is a crab, symbol of the sign Cancer. Almost imperceptibly woven into the canopy, in a fine gold line, is the word "ABRACADABRA," an apparent pun on "ABRAHADABRA," a word which Crowley called "one of the most important Key numbers of the *Liber Al...* the word of the Aeon...the cypher of the Great Work." The value of this word corresponds to that of Cheth (חית) ; ח =8, י =10, ת =400, adding to 418.[206]

One significant idea found in the Crowley and Golden Dawn cards is the implication of something martial, not unlike the *Bhagavad Gita,* where the pursuit of enlightenment is symbolized by warring factions which we understand to be within each seeker. Here, on the highest Path of the Pillar of Severity, the soul warrior of Geburah has reached a pinnacle. Crowley shows him with ten stars on his armor (representing Assiah-Matter) and seated in a position of sublime meditation. In his hands he holds the *Holy Graal,* a cup into which we look directly.

For their card, the Golden Dawn chose to represent Odin, God of war, usually shown riding through the sky. The attribute of Odin is appropriate insofar as he was also a God of spiritual development who, like *The Chariot,* has been related to both the above and the below.[207]

The primary emphasis of the Golden Dawn card is on the control of the dualities in manifestation by the Supreme Spiritual Self. Here the black and white horses are commensurate with Lévi's black and white sphinxes, as well as with the black and white columns of the Mysteries called *Joachim* and *Boaz* in the "Temple of Solomon." Between the two horses is an eagle's head, the kerubic symbol for Water. The chariot itself is blue to suggest Chesed. The orange of the warrior's robe refers to *Hod,* the intellect. Thus, we are pointed toward *The Magician*, the Path to which Mercury is attributed. Waite also referred to Hod by using an eight-pointed star on the crown of the charioteer, personification of the Spiritual Self.

As was mentioned, the movement of *The Chariot* conceals a mystery of great significance. In the Golden Dawn card it clearly descends from the sky, symbolizing the descent of the Holy Spirit into manifest creation ("the influx of good things upon created beings"). This is a much more simple iconography than is found in the cards of Crowley or Waite, and is reminiscent of the Chariot of the Sun. In Greek Mythology the Chariot of Helios, the sun, moved daily across the sky pulled by four horses. The relationship of the sun to *The Chariot* card is of critical importance because the chariot moves between the Light, centered in Tiphareth and the Supreme Darkness at the hidden side of Kether. In Waite's card this Chariot is a stone cube referring to the physical Universe, as well as to the *Cube of Space,* which Gareth Knight has called a construct within Tiphareth. This idea is amplified by Case's suggestion that while the Throne is Kether, the place of the Throne is Tiphareth.[208]

But another complexity must be introduced. Despite the fact that *The Chariot* is related to the sun, it is guided by the moon. And, from the standpoint of the Tree of Life, and of the earliest Greek mythology, *the sun is subordinate to the moon. The Chariot* follows this order, for it is the sign Cancer, ruled by the moon (and in which Jupiter is exalted). On the Tree of Life the Path leading from Tiphareth to Kether is the cardinal Path of the moon and of Water, *The High Priestess*. What takes precedence here is the Water (pure consciousness) that the moon represents. It may also be mentioned that in the symbolic pantheon of metals, silver at one time also took precedence over gold.

It was not until the period of Greek history when the Apollo myth began to take over from that of Helios as the sun God, even coming to be represented as driving the Chariot of the Sun across the sky each day, that the sun began to be considered of greater importance than the moon.[209]

All of these symbols are, of course, deeply involved with the history of religions and with anthropology, which assigns occasionally contradictory meanings to a given symbol. The corrective is that the Tarot cards, as archetypal images, represent truths which remain immutable despite the limitations of the attempts to describe them.

17. THE PATH OF ZAIN
The Lovers
The Sixth Key

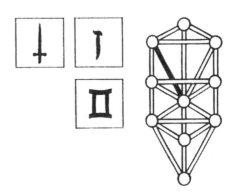

◈ PATH COLOR: Orange
◈ RELATED SOUND: D-Natural
◈ SIGN: Gemini (Mutable Air)
◈ MEANING: Sword or Armor
◈ SIMPLE LETTER: Smell
◈ ESOTERIC TITLE: The Children of the Voice; The Oracle of the Mighty Gods

THIRTY-TWO PATHS OF WISDOM: *The Seventeenth Path is the Disposing Intelligence, which provides Faith to the Righteous, and they are clothed with the Holy Spirit by it, and it is called the Foundation of Excellence in the state of higher things.*

The Path of Zain, *The Lovers*, between Binah and Tiphareth, connects the pure consciousness from which form emerged with the central point of all manifestation, a complexity which can barely be suggested by the image on a Tarot card. It is perhaps for this reason that the design of the card has changed over the centuries. In most of the earliest versions, such as the Marseilles Tarot, it was called *The Lover* (singular) and showed a man between two women, above whom was a cupid with a poised arrow. Presumably this single lover made no sense to later Tarot artists, and in the eighteenth century the card began to appear with two "lovers" and a uniting figure of some sort.

Yet the early concept of "the lover" is very profound, for this card does not represent the mundane love of two persons. It is, rather, the dualities of a

single individual, wilfully united in pursuit of Divine Love. Crowley's point that the card should really be called "The Brothers" is well taken. In fact, the Key's true meaning is imbedded in its sign of the Zodiac, *Gemini, The Twins.* The dual energies which the Lover proposes to unite are equal and opposite, i.e., "twins." The uniting of these twins is a major step upwards, toward the Godhead on the Tree of Life.

The principle is that as Divine Energy surged across the Abyss into manifestation, stable dualities were formed. The Great Work is a "marriage" of these dualities of manifestation, a return to a primeval state. Thus, this Path may be considered the aspect of the *Garden of Eden* from which mankind was expelled, but to which it may earn re-entry by consciously dealing with what has been called the inner *Sun* and *Moon.* The whole key to the Great Work is the uniting of the Sun and the Moon under Mercury (the planet ruling Gemini).

In relating this symbolism to the Path of *The Lovers,* Case performed a fascinating exercise in Gematria. He took the Hebrew title of the Path from the *Thirty-Two Paths of Wisdom,* and broke it down into its component parts. The Path of Zain, is called the *Disposing Intelligence,* הרגש (ha-regesh), from which the following is derived: (ה means *the*), ר *is* the Sun, ג is the Moon, and ש is Fire. So הרגש[210] means the Sun + Moon + Fire. On the Tarot card, the Sun is the man, the Moon is the woman, and the Divine Fire above the Abyss is represented by the angel or Cupid.

In explanation of this, Case states that the Sun is self-consciousness, while the Moon is subconsciousness. These are both aspects of the one Life-Breath, each working through half of the body. And "When the Solar and Lunar currents of the Life-Power are rightly perceived, rightly discriminated, and when their operation is kept in proper order, the personality of the man engaged in this practice becomes a free, unobstructed channel for the outpouring of the cosmic life force."[211]

Case was discussing not the Waite deck, but his own BOTA version, a "correction" of the earlier deck which changed the symbolism little, but improved the drawing quality and eliminated the personified minor cards. Thus, one would expect explanations of the cards by Waite and Case to be similar, even despite Waite's apparent caution about what he put into print. Such similarities, however, are few and where Case considered this card one of dualities unified by the Spiritual Self, Waite merely emphasized its relationship to the Garden of Eden. He referred to Adam and Eve and to the Tree of Knowledge of Good and Evil, but made no mention of Spiritual Alchemy in this card which he called "love before it is contaminated by gross material desire," adding that "in a very high sense, the card is a mystery of the Covenant and the Sabbath."[212] One might well suggest that such comments, drawn from his *Pictorial Key to the Tarot* are so cryptic as to be almost useless to the serious student. The intention here is not to deprecate Waite, who must be respected for maintaining his oaths of secrecy, but to point out the extent to which there are two explanations to every card, an exoteric one and an esoteric one.

In all versions of this Key, no matter how it may be described or how different the design, the esoteric meaning is the same. They all mean the union of manifest opposites under the Divine Love of the Supernals through Binah. It is, as Waite stresses, the Garden of Eden, but it is the Garden from which the soul itself is expelled in manifestation and to which it may return. The same message is in Crowley's card, which shows the theme of union as an alchemical "Marriage" of the component parts of the seeker. The Golden Dawn also represents this spiritual union, but with an important difference. The seeker works actively for this to come about: the Higher Self descends to release the Personality from bondage, recalling the idea, encountered with *The Hanged Man* that while the Personality believes itself to be the pursuer, it is actually the pursued.

The legend of Perseus and Andromeda, used to make this point, contains some fascinating implications for the interpretation of the card. In the myth, Andromeda was the daughter of the king of the Ethiopians and Cassiopeia, who boasted that she was more beautiful than the Nereids (daughters of the sea God, Nereus). In anger the Nereids complained to Poseidon, who flooded the land and then sent a terrible monster to inhabit it. The only way that this monster could be vanquished was for the king's daughter, Andromeda, to be sacrificed to it, and she was thus tied to a rock on the shore.

Perseus, however, who had just successfully taken the head of Medusa, saw Andromeda and fell in love. He wanted to marry her, which the father insisted was only possible if the monster were slain. So Perseus killed the monster, but Andromeda's uncle, nevertheless, tried to prevent the marriage by sending attackers against the hero. Perseus, in turn, displayed the frightful head of Medusa, and turned his adversaries to stone after which he and Andromeda lived more or less happily ever after.

However, in one ancient interpretation of the story, Perseus, Andromeda, her father, mother and the monster were brought into the sky where they became constellations of the same names.[213] In Qabalistic terms, this could be taken to mean that the actions of Perseus (the Spiritual Self) resulted in the return of all participants to the sky, i.e., the Godhead. And while that explanation may seem a bit strained, such mythologies were part of the general culture at the time of the Hermetic Order of the Golden Dawn and were often interpreted in esoteric terms.

The stress of the Golden Dawn card is on the extent to which the process of this Path is a very active one, for the self-control and will (Mercury) which directs the movement and integration of the opposites is not passive as the other cards tend to suggest Perseus here has the same fiery, dynamic and inspirational qualities ascribed to the serpent.

Another indicator of activity on this Path is the attribution of the *sword* to Zain. This is an instrument of active division and separation; it is a sword of perception which cuts to the core of things, and defines clearly. And insofar as such perception is attributed to Zain, to it is also attached the sense of *smell,* thus implying not only the most direct, but also the most subtle of awareness and response.

While the sword is rarely found in this Tarot Key, it is very common in alchemical representations of the same theme as, for example in the "Eleventh Key" of Basilius Valentinus, the seventeenth century alchemist. In his illustration are two female twins, each mounted on a lion and holding a figure of the sun and of the moon. Behind them is a man in *armor* (another meaning of Zain) and holding a sword. The caption reads: "The twins Sun and Moon are united by the conjunction which seems to be death."[214] So we understand that the consummation of this marriage requires a "death." Indeed, to successfully pursue this Path across the Abyss means the death even of one's own Higher Self. It is a willful and total self-destruction and immersion into the Divine. The separation and re-integration of the dual components of the manifest Self demands subordination of the Ego to the One Divine Principle. The sword destroys utterly those who will travel across the Abyss. Thus is the Path called the *Disposing Intelligence;* it is an experience which is the completion of the process begun on the Path of Samekh, *Temperance.* Taken together, *Temperance* and *The Lovers* are the alchemical formula of *"solve et coagula."* The Sword separates out (dissolves), an activity which we have previously shown to mean *analysis.* This is followed by a *synthesis,* or reintegration in a new way. Therefore, *solve et coagula.*

It can actually be quite intriguing to see how all of the complicated symbols of Alchemy—lions, eagles, glutens, suns, moons, etc., reduce to some very basic psychological concepts. But here, again, we appreciate that such descriptive terms did not exist until the present day, and we are forced to interpret the codes of the early Qabalists, of Mathers, of Waite, and even of Crowley. And in *The Lovers,* this requisite decipherment of language is especially difficult.

Crowley, in fact, stated that *The Lovers* and *Temperance* were the most difficult cards of the Tarot, which is certainly true. The Path of *Temperance* requires a complete integration of the Personality in its subordination to the Ego in Tiphareth. The Path of *The Lovers* requires a complete integration of the totality of the Self manifest in Microprosopus, for the return of the soul to the aspect of the "Garden" from which it emerged. In more basic terms, *Temperance* is the balance of the Lower Self; *The Lovers* is the balance of the Higher.

By comparison with the Waite and Golden Dawn cards, Crowley's *Lovers* is intellectually superior. Certainly no version of *The Lovers* has ever been more daringly explicit in revealing the secret of the Path.

What is shown here is the "Royal Marriage," of opposites, presided over by the hooded figure who is at once the Hermit and the personification of Mercury. Above are the figures of Eve and Lilith, with Cupid aiming an arrow symbolizing the *will*. The marriage takes place between the Black King and the White Queen. He wears a gold crown, bears a lance, and is attended by the Red Lion. His black child, interchanged with the White Queen's child, holds the base of the King's lance in one hand and a club in the other. She is attended by the White Eagle and her white child, who carries flowers in one hand and supports the base of the Grail in the other. In the lower section of the card is the Winged Orphic Egg, the very essence of life itself, which is the product of this union.

Perhaps the most curious assertion made by Crowley about this card (for which he gives no basis whatsoever) is that in some original form it presented the story of creation. He claims that at the center of the card was Cain, shown having just slain Abel. This is described at some length in *The Equinox*.[216]

Although a reference to bloodshed may seem out of place in a card of marriage, we are told that the shedding of the blood of the brother is the very key to *The Lovers* "The shedding of blood is necessary, for God did not hear the children of Eden until the blood was shed."[217] Crowley elaborates on this idea in a footnote, wherein he explains that the bloody sacrifice is not necessarily black magic. He says: "One should assume into one's own being, ceremonially, the whole karma of the creature slain."[218] But the process is not to be viewed as a unique and singular experience, for Crowley tells us that the "integration of the card can only be regained by repeated marriages, identifications and some form of Hermaphroditism."[219]

So the process is one which is both reciprocal and repeated over and over again. First one "brother" dies and is absorbed into the other. Then there is a return to a balance of opposites after which the second brother is killed and absorbed into the first. The process is defined by the infinity sign of Mercury/Magician, since *the Sun and Moon unite under Mercury.*

Insofar as the marriage occurs repeatedly, the use of the number twelve in both the Waite and Golden Dawn cards is highly significant. In Waite's card the Tree of Life behind the male figure holds twelve flames; in the Golden Dawn card there are twelve points on the star of Perseus' shield. The twelve in both cases refer to the Zodiac and the perfection of each of the types of incarnation. Theoretically, return to the Godhead requires that we incarnate repeatedly and perfect each of these types in turn.

As a marriage of the King and Queen under a floating Cupid, *The Lovers* relates to the *Chemical Wedding of Christian Rosencreutz,* written at the beginning of the seventeenth century.[220] This is a work which, like the *Fama Fraternitas* is one of the key documents of Hermetic-Qabalism. And, unlike so many alchemical texts, the *Chemical Wedding* is immensely readable, having the charming qualities of a fairy tale. Yet is remains one of the most profound pieces of esoteric symbolism ever written. Those who read the text, and meditate on it, will gain exceptional insights into both *The Lovers* and *Temperance*. One such insight relates to the suggestion that blood is spilled on this Path. There are, in fact, a number of "events" at the *Chemical Wedding* which reinforce this idea.

16. THE PATH OF VAU
The Hierophant
The Fifth Key

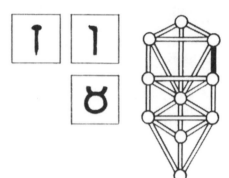

- ◈ PATH COLOR: Red-Orange
- ◈ RELATED SOUND: C Sharp
- ◈ SIGN: Taurus (Fixed Earth)
- ◈ MEANING: Nail or Hook
- ◈ SIMPLE LETTER: Hearing
- ◈ ESOTERIC TITLE: The Magus of the Eternal.

> THIRTY-TWO PATHS OF WISDOM: *The Sixteenth Path is the Triumphal or Eternal Intelligence, so called because it is the pleasure of the Glory, beyond which is no other Glory like to it, and it is called also the Paradise prepared for the Righteous.*

The Path of *The Hierophant,* Vau, leads from Chesed to Chokmah and is the uppermost Path on the Pillar of Mercy. It is described in the Golden Dawn documents as "The Zodiac acting through Taurus upon Jupiter," which may sound simplistic, but which is very accurate. This is the action of Chokmah, as the spermatic potential of the manifest Universe, upon the first manifestation.

Chokmah is the Supernal Father as Chesed is the Father in manifestation. Chokmah is the Yod of Macroprosopus; Chesed is the Yod of Microprosopus.

Thus is the Path of Vau a powerfully masculine one to which Taurus, the bull, is applied. It is *Fixed Earth* in the Zodiac, meaning that it is a stable foundation. And here, our earlier definition of this Path as a "stabilizing extreme" is particularly useful.

The Hierophant is the opposite Path of *The Chariot*, the vehicle (stabilizing active extreme/Cardinal Water) by which the soul is carried across the Abyss. *The Hierophant* is the celestial road on which *The Chariot* rides; it is the absolute foundation of the process of revelation; it is a rock-solid base of experience between the Supreme Spiritual Self and the Ego of Tiphareth, of which *memory* is one aspect.

The idea that *The Hierophant* relates to memory may be considered in light of the meaning of the word Vau, which means *nail* or *hook*. A nail binds together, it unifies, suggesting that a primary function of *The Hierophant* is to link Microprosopus with Macroprosopus, i.e., the Great Universe with manifestation. It is the *Triumphal* or *Eternal Intelligence* by which all that we are is forever tied to the Divine Spirit. This binding consciousness is described in a variety of symbolic ways, such as: it links the Sun and the Moon, or it ties together the Above and the Below. It is also related to *teaching*, that which introduces higher ideas into the lower organism. Expressing it another way, it can be said that the intelligent energy which binds the pure Inner Spirit to the outer aspects of manifestation is also the source for our understanding of that Inner Spirit. It is the *only* source. *The Hierophant* is the only teacher. He is, as the esoteric title of the card states, "The Magus of the Eternal."

In many versions of this Key, the seated figure is shown as the Pope. The imagery was explained by A.E. Waite with the suggestion that this is "a particular application of the more general office that he symbolizes. He is the ruling power of external religion, as the High Priestess is the prevailing genius of the esoteric, withdrawn power."[221] Paul Case emphatically disagreed with this, saying that "On the contrary, he is the *Pontifex*, the 'bridge-maker' who provides a connecting link between outer experience and interior illumination."[222]

But, as we shall presently consider, Waite touches on some very important concepts in this card, which he called the *"summa totius theologiae,* when it passed into the utmost rigidity of expression."[223]

Relative to the traditional use of the Catholic pontiff in Tarot, it should be appreciated that until very recently western esotericism was inextricably bound to Christianity. At the period when the cards emerged, metaphysics was merely a way of looking at the given faith, which was above question as a system. There were no viable alternatives. Thus, the great esotericists were either Catholic priests, or those who sought the approbation of the Catholic hierarchy for their research. By example, one can cite the correspondence of Henry Cornelius Agrippa with the great humanist abbot, John Trithemius. The abbot, himself an avid student of these matters and a Hebrew scholar,[224] warmly responded to receipt of Agrippa's *Of Occult Philosophy:* "With how much pleasure I receive it no mortal tongue can express nor the pen of any write."[225] Neither the prelate nor the younger occult philosopher were condemned for their work, because it was actually carried out within the confines of accepted Catholic doctrine.[226]

Thus, for the originators of the cards to have used the image of their Pope to represent the Mysteries of the energies of the Path of Vau, the Supreme Teacher, was reasonable. This image is problematical only to those attempting to separate the Hermetic Qabalah from the Renaissance Christianity in which it was unquestionably nurtured.

To the fifteenth century metaphysician this was not only the Pope as administrator of the inner pathways, but it was the Pope as the teacher speaking *ex cathedra* (from the Throne). In Catholic doctrine, when the Pope speaks *ex cathedra,* his word is infallible. And when the leader of the faith speaks infallibly, all must listen. Thus to Vau the *Sepher Yetzirah* attributes *hearing.* The act of listening is shown in the Waite card by the two figures kneeling before the Pope. We should take them to mean the opposite aspects of ourselves in the human condition, united in their listening attention to the Universal Teacher. These two figures are the Sun and Moon currents of the body, reason and intuition, consciousness and subconsciousness, etc. These qualities are anthropomorphized as priests, i.e., participants at the altar rather than spectators. The implication is that both are an integral and inseparable part of the process of enlightenment, and that their obedience has been pledged to the principle represented by *The Hierophant.*

Waite's hierophant blesses from his position between the two columns of the Mysteries. At his feet are the crossed keys of Heaven (gold, sun) and Hell (silver, moon). This latter is so attributed because one of the moon Goddesses rules the underworld. In his hand is the papal cross, what has been called the "triple cross of the Western peoples."[227]

Not surprisingly, the Golden Dawn and Crowley cards have both moved away from the figure as Pope. The Golden Dawn figure retains the three-tiered papal crown, but as a symbol of the Supernals. The emphasis is placed on the role of the hierophant as shepherd and teacher of the Law. Crowley, whose early training left him with intensely anti-Christian feelings has produced a hierophant reminiscent of one of the *titans,* the primeval deities of the Greeks. His main stress was on what we have called the "grounding" of the Key, for his Kerubiim at the corners of the card are the tentative expression of the primordial Elements of Kether which pass down to Chokmah as the Sphere of the Zodiac. And while we think of the Zodiac as twelve, it is in reality four triplicities. Each Element is broken down into three signs, Qabalistically related to the Yod, Heh and Vau.

The Hierophant is the administrator of the duality which emerges with Chokmah, is structured by Binah, and which begins as manifestation below the Abyss in Chesed. It is thus related to Tiphareth, the central point of manifestation. Tiphareth is suggested in two ways here. The first is by the Vau itself, the third letter of the Tetragrammaton, and the Son. The second is the number attributed to Vau, six, which is also that of Tiphareth.

A more obtuse reference to Tiphareth is Crowley's use of the five pointed star on the breast of the Hierophant. As the primordial Elements evolve downward, they do so under the control of the fifth Element, Spirit. The principle of the pentagram holds even in Kether, where the Primordial Elements are held in perfect unexpressed unity by a fifth which, at that exalted level, is the Ain Soph. This perfect unity is expressed by the swastica in motion, the central point of which is commensurate with the uppermost point of the pentagram.

What Crowley has done in placing the pentagram so prominently here is to affirm the uniting of the Above and the Below, a process in which the symbolic moon always plays a key part. For the moon is found both above and below the sun on the Tree of Life. It is Yesod, and it is *The High Priestess*. Here both are implied, for the moon is exalted in Taurus.

The fact that Taurus is ruled by Venus refers us to *The Empress*, the Path of Daleth which is the mean between Chokmah and Binah, just as Vau is the product of the Yod and Heh. *The Empress* is "Mother Nature," the fertilized Universal Consciousness which is at the root of *The Hierophant*'s teaching. In this regard it should be observed that *The Hierophant* is on the "feeling" (Venus-Netzach) side of the Tree of Life. We learn its lessons through intuition, as we learn the lessons of its opposite, *The Chariot*, through intellect. On this Path intuition is applied to concepts collected by reason and built up by memory.

Pursuant to the idea of Venus-*Empress* behind Earth-*Hierophant* there is a very interesting interplay of symbols: ♁, the sign meaning Earth becomes ♀, the sign of Venus, when it is reversed. Also the sign of Taurus itself, is a uniting of the symbols of sun (☉) and moon (☽). ☉ + ☽ = ♉. And, as we have seen in the other cards, the uniting of the sun and the moon always refers to the Garden of Eden. Vau is what the *Thirty-Two Paths of Wisdom* calls the "Paradise Prepared for the Righteous." *The Hierophant* is the earthy aspect of the Garden as *The Chariot* is watery, *The Lovers* is airy and *The Emperor* fiery. What we have explained as the grounding or the earthiness of the Garden is the "Law" expounded by the Hierophant. The Golden Dawn card shows this as a scroll (the same scroll of the Law which is held by *The High Priestess* in the Waite deck).

The scroll holds the "Word" which one hears through *The Hierophant*, and which is also the Logos. For the Word is creation, and to understand the created Universe is to hear the Word. This is the essential meaning of the Golden Dawn and Waite cards.

Crowley's card, which is considered one of the most important of the Tarot, contains many traditional elements, but adds some symbolism which is entirely personal to Crowley's philosophy. He explains the image of a child within the pentagram within a larger hexagram: "This symbolizes the law of the new Aeon of the Child Horus, which has supplanted that Aeon of the 'Dying God' which governed the world for two thousand years." And elsewhere he adds "...for the rhythm of the Hierophant is such that he moves at intervals of 2,000 years."[228]

The hierophant sits on a bull between two elephants, holding a wand with three interlocking rings. These rings symbolize the Aeons of Isis, Osiris and Horus (The child in the pentagram is Horus). Beneath is the "Scarlet Woman." Above is what Crowley called an "oriel," meaning a *window* (referring to

Heh, *The Emperor*) built out from a wall on brackets, in this case nine nails (Vaus). The symbolism means the linking of the Above and the Below: The window is the passageway for Light (manifest Spirit) between Macroprosopus and Microprosopus.

In the Golden Dawn card the figure holds a crook, one of the symbols of Chesed suggestive of Jupiterian benevolence. But Crowley warns that the card is not necessarily benevolent, affirming an idea in the *Book of Tokens* that Vau (the Fifth Key) is the severe root of Geburah [229] Crowley takes this one step farther: "Though the face of the Hierophant appears benignant and smiling, and the child himself seems glad with wanton innocence, it is hard to deny that the expression of the initiator is something mysterious, even sinister. He seems to be enjoying a secret joke at somebody's expense. There is a distinctly sadistic aspect to this card..."[230] Crowley insists that this is quite natural as the Key relates to the original bull legend, that of Pasiphae. In that Greek myth Pasiphae falls in love with a sacred white bull, the union of which produces the *Minotaur.* This is, however, a very questionable interpretation. On the other hand, it is agreed by most authorities that there are some very unpleasant aspects to this Key, having to do with its position intermediate between the Above and the Below. This issue and its implications are very cleverly related to Gnosticism by Richard Cavendish in his work, *The Tarot.*

Taken in descending order, the trumps from the Juggler to the Pope recall the Gnostic accounts of the creation of the Universe. It was believed that in the beginning the One became Two by thinking, so that there was a mind and a thought. The Juggler can be equated with the Divine Mind, the Female Pope with the thought in its original purity, and the Empress as the thought after it has become impregnated by the mind to become the Mother of all the lower powers. Among those lower powers was the Demiurge or cosmocrator, the maker of the visible world. . .Gnostics frequently identified the Demiurge with the God of the Old Testament. He was regarded as an evil power, the maker and ruler of matter and flesh in which the divine spark of spirit is held prisoner...The Pope also has some sinister undertones. Gnostics maintained that the evil Demiurge invented conventional religion and morality to keep men enslaved to him by inducing them to worship him and obey his laws.[231]

The Demiurge, the Lesser Creator who rules over manifestation, was the great deceiver. Thus the initiate of the Valentinian Gnostic Mysteries was taught to ignore the authority of this creator,[232] whom Mead described as "hanging from Spirit at the very boundary of the phenomenal Universe."[233] It appears, in any event, that Cavandish is quite correct in his assertion that the negative qualities ascribed by tradition to this card have their roots in Gnosticism.

The implications of Gnostic thought are, in regard to Tarot, both complex and exciting. One who has studied the Qabalah at some length may be surprised to find the same concepts expressed in the language of early Christianity. As one authority expressed the question: "Is Gnosticism Christian Qabalism? Except for the name of Jesus we are in a completely Jewish world. These are the Mysteries of the *Zohar* and of the Hasidim."[234]

15. THE PATH OF HEH
The Emperor
The Fourth Key

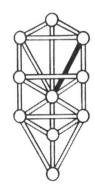

- ◈ PATH COLOR: Scarlet
- ◈ RELATED SOUND: C Natural
- ◈ SIGN: Aries (Cardinal Fire)
- ◈ MEANING: Window
- ◈ SIMPLE LETTER: Sight
- ◈ ESOTERIC TITLE: Sun of the Morning, Chief Among the Mighty.

THIRTY-TWO PATHS OF WISDOM: *The Fifteenth Path is the Constituting Intelligence, so called because it constitutes the substance of creation in pure darkness, and men have spoken of these contemplations; it is that darkness spoken of in Scripture, Job xxxviii.9. "and thick darkness a swaddling band for it."*

The higher we rise on the Tree of Life, the more obvious it becomes that the Tarot trumps only point the way toward concepts which the mind cannot otherwise grasp. Until the present day this was a great deal more difficult because the language of psychology did not exist. Our terms such as "conscious," "subconscious" and "unconscious" are extremely useful tools because they conceptualize something inordinately fluid. Thus, in our present state of development, we easily deal with shades of consciousness within ourselves. We are coming closer and closer to an ability to deal with formlessness, pure consciousness. This is the promise of the so-called Age of Aquarius, although it is rarely stated in such terms. The student who begins to understand the next five Tarot Trumps (*The Emperor, The Empress, The High Priestess, The Magician* and *The Fool*) will have taken a long step into that new age.

To this end it must be emphatically restated that the entire Tarot deck reflects the Universe which is made up of permutations of *The One*. From the One emerges opposites which are activating and formative, male and female. It is accurate to say that all male and female figures in the Tarot are Chokmah (יה) and Binah (יהוה אלהים) wearing the robes of different planes, actually levels of vibratory rate, of the Universe.

The Fool is the One God energy. *The Magician* and *The High Priestess* are the first differentiation into masculine and feminine within the Macrocosm and the Microcosm. These are the personal, subjective energies of the Macrocosm and the Microcosm. These are the personal, subjective energies of the Paths, as opposed to the objective, Universal energies of the Sephiroth.

The Qabalistic principle is that *The Magician* is the consort of *The High Priestess*. Considered psychologically, we know that *The Magician* stands for the will, while *The High Priestess*, the "Root of Water," is the pure unconscious. So to describe *The Magician* as the mate of *The High Priestess* refers to the activity of the directing will of the One on the Great Ocean of undifferentiated consciousness *which it has itself projected*. In the Qabalah we are always dealing with reflexive qualities; God creates thought, then creates mind to hold that thought. Everything has to do with the perception and activity of The Divine Spirit on Itself, a process which various systems of symbols attempt to suggest. As was described in considering the *Wheel of Fortune*, the Alchemists spoke of the Divine Self-interaction in terms of *Sulphur, Salt* and *Mercury*. These same terms may also be applied to the upper level cards of the Tarot. *The Magician* is Mercury, *The Empress* is Salt and *The Emperor* is Sulphur. Crowley has gone so far as to position his Emperor so that the body forms a triangle and cross, symbol of the alchemical Sulphur. ♀

The Magician (Philosophic Mercury) acts upon *The High Priestess* (pure consciousness) and they are, by their union, transformed into *The Emperor* and *The Empress*, Sulphur and Salt. Of course, all of this may seem little more than an obscure abstraction, a bending of words almost for their own sake. But when we consider these principles as aspects of our own consciousness, they are quite basic.

When we close our eyes and allow free-form images to float by us, taking whatever direction they will, we are tapping into the life energy "ruled" by *The Empress*. When we begin to think about what is happening before our eyes, classifying the images according to color, subject, or any other criterion, we are calling *The Emperor* into play. We are acting upon form.

This is another of those cards where Paul Case brought exceptional insight to bear, as he explained why *The Emperor* is on the Path below *The Empress*. He says: "Because she is the manifesting power which brings forms into being he has something to rule...*The Magician*, who appears now as *The Emperor*, would have nothing to control or transform did not subconsciousness send up from its depths a stream of images to be classified by the exercise of reason."[235]

It should be obvious that there is a certain crossover of the Yod and Heh energies. *The Empress* is the balance between Chokmah and Binah. She is the growth which comes from the interaction of the male and female, as in the fertilized cell. She is pure fruition. *The Emperor*, on the other hand, while a potent masculine energy, is Heh on the Paths, meaning that its function is determined by Binah. This is a formative Path, its activities are rational and classifying, as is underscored by its bright red color, that of Binah in the World of Pure Spirit, Atziluth. The lower we descend on the Tree of Life, the more the male and female energies are interwoven. And, by this reasoning, one might assume that the only "pure" male and female in the Universe are at the level of Chokmah and Binah, which is unfortunately not the case.

Having come to the level of the Supernal Paths, it is necessary to introduce an idea which may be perceived as destructive to the entire tower of male and female principles so neatly established to this point. Let us state the problem abruptly: Chokmah (חכמה, Wisdom), meaning the primary quality of maleness, is a female noun. And, if we are willing to accept the assertions of Gematria, the idea that sages of the past have buried truths in the interaction of numbers applied to each letter, or that each letter is itself a holy symbol, can we believe that the very gender of the title is insignificant here? Obviously not. However, the gender of the Hebrew noun for wisdom is not often mentioned by writers on the Qabalah, because it appears to be an irreconcilable problem of language.

But let us here take the point of view that whatever "gives birth" is exercising a primary female quality *at the moment of birth*. Adam is the first (symbolic) male, but insofar as his rib became the first female, he conceived and gave birth, thus performing a female function. The female was inherent in the male. What we are describing is not exactly androgyny, or even bi-sexuality, since it is a real transformation of the function of a given energy. Within all that is male there is female, and within all that is female there is male. In Jungian terms, the male harbors the perfect female image in his unconscious, as the female harbors the perfect male image in her unconscious. These are images of the Self as opposite gender, the "contrasexual component." This is what Jung called *anima* (female) in males and *animus* (male) in females. These idealized qualities are personified as the *Magna Mater,* the Great Mother who is Binah and as the *Wise Old Man,* a personification of spiritual principle who is Chokmah.[236] On the Paths, *The Empress* is anima and *The Emperor* is animus. In Latin *anima* means soul, while *animus* means spirit; the very concept of soul represents the enclosure, or definition of boundaries of spirit, the Heh creating boundaries around the spiritual Yod. Thus the perfectly developed male type on the Paths is *The Emperor*, and the perfectly developed female type is *The Empress*. These are archetypal images which we meet in "rising on the planes" and with which we actually converse on the Paths.

Whatever terms may be used to describe *The Emperor*, he remains the bridge between The Father (Chokmah) and The Son (Tiphareth). And the very fact that the Sun of Tiphareth is exalted in the sign of this Path, Aries, indicates that *The Emperor* exercises some control of the solar energy of the Higher Self. Thus the Path of Heh is called the *Constituting Intelligence,* meaning that it assists in the building up of the Light of Tiphareth from the utter darkness of the Supernal Triangle, as rational genetic structure directs the rising of the plant from the intense darkness of the earth.

The importance of Tiphareth to *The Emperor* is indicated by Crowley in his use of a sun behind the Emperor's head, and in the overall two color scheme. The card has been painted in martian reds and sun-yellows, warm colors suggesting a furious rush of activity which may be short-lived. There are also martial overtones, although it is only in Waite's card, with its armored figure, that this is emphasized, which is somewhat surprising considering the Golden Dawn text: "the General...the Conqueror, hot passionate, impetuous." The Golden Dawn card itself shows a ruler who, while he has absolute dominion, as is symbolized by the orb and cross in his left hand, is not a warrior. He is precise and firm, applying a mathematically measured reason to all things, but he does not wield a sword. The sword is carried not on this Path of the fiery aspect of the Garden of Eden, but on its airy counterpart, *The Lovers*. And while the driver of *The Chariot* of the water aspect is Odin, God of War, he is not shown at battle. In fact, the greatest sub-surface belligerence is with the earthy part of the Garden, *The Hierophant*.

It may now be suggested that these four cards, when considered in terms of a fifth, *The High Priestess*, constitute a practical formula for the crossing of the Abyss. They are the means of attaining the Garden of Eden, which is the amalgam of multiple states of energy.

Pursuant to the garden theme, it must again be noted that Crowley proposes an interchange of *The Emperor* with *The Star*,[237] which we believe to be a mistake. In dealing with *The Star*, we describe *The Emperor* as the "fiery aspect of the Garden of Eden," to which the Higher Self relates, while *The Star* is the Eden of the Personality. In both cases these are states where the general has just become specific, a pristine point where the consciousness can look both forward and backward. Thus is *sight* attributed to Heh. This is the self-observation of the One. It is the first Path to which a sensory function is attributed in the *Sepher Yetzirah,* suggesting that sight is the first of the senses as Aries is the first in the sequence of the Zodiac. And as the first sign, *The Emperor*, Aries, emerges directly from Chokmah *The Sphere of the Zodiac.* That *The Emperor* is based in the Chokmah energy is symbolized by the grey stone throne on which he sits in the Golden Dawn and Waite cards.

The *Constituting Intelligence* is understood as the first phase of a natural cycle. It stimulates the development of natural structures, as "Aries brings forth the Spring." The Golden Dawn card symbolizes this by the Aries/Ram wand, the wielding of the Aries energy by *The Emperor*, and by the ram beneath his feet.

In this one would expect the Emperor to be represented as a dynamic and masculine figure at the very peak of his abilities. Both the Golden Dawn and Crowley cards have taken this approach. Waite, on the other hand, followed by Case in the BOTA version, represents the Emperor as the traditional "Ancient of Days," the One who is older than time itself, the Supernal Father. Here there is disagreement as to whether the figure should be shown full-face or in profile, the profile tradition having been accepted by the Marseilles deck which shows the Emperor seated facing the viewer's left. Crowley adopted the same symbolism apparently agreeing that it is impossible for one to know the totality of the Emperor while in this earthly existence. On the other hand, the "Ancient Bearded King seen in profile" is symbolic of Kether and its relationship to the Ain Soph, not Chokmah. Presumably this explains the decision of Mathers and Waite to show the Emperor's full-face.

Most of the symbols on these cards are traditional: The *Veil of the Abyss* behind the Golden Dawn Emperor, Waite's *ankh cross* or the one symbol on which all four cards agree, the *"orb of dominion."* Crowley, however, has made some obscure symbolic references. *The bee* and the *fleur de lys,* for example, are described by him as related to the generalization of the paternal power.[238] Another obscure symbol is the eagle on the Emperor's shield. The Marseilles card also uses an eagle, though it is merely a reference to imperial power. But Crowley's eagle is two-headed, with a crimson disk behind. He explains that this is the alchemist's red tincture related to the sun and to gold. A similar white eagle on his *Empress* card refers to the moon and to silver.

One final aspect of Crowley's card is symbolically problematical. At least his explanation of it seems unsatisfactory. We refer to the lamb at the lower right of the card, of which he says: "At his feet, couchant, is the Lamb and Flag, to confirm this attribution on a lower plane; for the ram, by nature, is a wild and courageous animal, lonely in lonely places, whereas when tamed and made to lie down in green pastures, nothing is left but the docile, cowardly, gregarious and succulent beast. This is the theory of government."[239] One may be delighted by Crowley's wit, but somewhat puzzled by his use of an accepted symbol of the meek and mild Christ to mean something "docile, cowardly, gregarious" and even "succulent." It is difficult to avoid the conclusion that this is another of Crowley's attacks on traditional Christianity, although the image is certainly inspired by the Golden Dawn ram.

14. THE PATH OF DALETH
The Empress
The Third Key

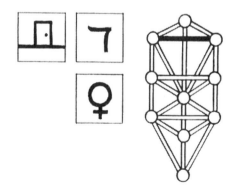

◈ PATH COLOR: Emerald Green
◈ RELATED SOUND: F-Sharp
◈ PLANET: Venus
◈ MEANING: Door
◈ DOUBLE LETTER: Wisdom, Folly
◈ ESOTERIC TITLE: The Daughter
    of the Mighty Ones.

THIRTY-TWO PATHS OF WISDOM: *The Fourteenth Path is the Illuminating Intelligence, and is so called because it is that Brilliant One which is the founder of the concealed and fundamental ideas of holiness and of their stages of preparation.*

The Path of *The Empress* connects Binah and Chokmah. As such, it is the mediating Path of the Supreme Spiritual Self. It is the Path of unity of the Father and Mother, the Path on which their interaction occurs. In this regard, *The Empress* called the "Daughter of the Mighty Ones."

As Chokmah has the potential to emanate the pure "female," so Binah has the potential for the creation of all life forms. Thus the Waite deck and others show the Empress pregnant, in a state of incubation and passivity which is the result of the merging of the energies of Chokmah and Binah. *The Empress* is the universal womb in which all manifestation is gestated. It is a transitional state of energy between the Above and Below which has been called the "Gate of Heaven."

Daleth means *door*. It is a door which effects a transition from the One into many. In fact, the key to this card is multiplicity. While the robe of the High Priestess is ideally represented as simple and diaphanous, that of the Empress is appropriately covered with all the jewels of creation.

Of course, in this and in the three cards remaining, words are strictly metaphorical. In fact, at the level of the Supernal Triangle, the Tarot pictures themselves unconsciously communicate a great deal more about the forces involved than could any words. Yet even there we may be painfully aware of the inadequacies of our anthropomorphic symbolism in attempting to present a concept of pure fruition. *To* this end one might offer an analogy having to do with Netzach, the most dense level of the Venus energy. As an exercise, the student should try to conceive of *pure emotion,* that is feeling which has no subject and no object, which is neither love nor hate, but which is the raw material of both. That may convey something of *The Empress* who is the Great Mother of ideas,

Mother Nature.

Almost every culture has some form of Earth Mother, or Mother of the Gods. And in almost every case, this maternal Goddess gives birth to an intermediate deity which directly rules the earth, such as Christ. Not infrequently, also, God the Son appears through a "virgin birth," although as Frazer observes, the idea of a miraculous birth probably comes down from a period when man had not yet recognized that children are the result of sexual activity.[240] Thus, the Virgin Mary, the Christian version of God the Mother, may be related to the Empress after she is pregnant or has given birth to Christ. Before this, she is the High Priestess.

It is important to bear in mind that the Great Mother is inextricably linked with the earth, for in incarnation we function primarily from the perspective of earth. All that is natural to the formation of life on earth is the province of *The Empress* . She builds life forms around the spirit of life, establishing laws of the Universe, having to do with formalization and restriction.

But beyond the idea of law, or formalization, which we have repeatedly stressed in terms of the Supernal female energy, there is another idea which must be stressed: that of *love. The Empress* who establishes the laws of Macroprosopus, and gives birth to Microprosopus, is also Venus-Aphrodite, Goddess of Love.

In the *Thirty-Two Paths of Wisdom* Daleth is called the *Luminous Intelligence,* as the Path of Chokmah is called the *Illuminating Intelligence.* The implication is that the brilliance of Chokmah illuminates all things as it passes through the doorway which is *The Empress.* "Luminous" has the meaning of being filled with light, as well as emitting light. Yet in this context it will be appreciated that light, per se, is referred to manifestation below the Abyss. The illuminating qualities of Chokmah are the potential for the light which is emanated by Binah, and which is Microprosopus, the Lesser Countenance *The Empress* may aptly be called the *Mother of Light. To* pass through her on the Path of return is to enter the Supreme Darkness. One may pass through a door in either direction, which is one of the points to the card.

The dualities of the Empress-doorway relate particularly to the Roman God *Janus,* always shown with two faces going in opposite directions.

Janus was the God of doorways (*janua* means door) who presided over communications (the passage of ideas) and who controlled the affairs of men. He was considered the God of Gods, *Janus Pater* who, like the Empress, oversaw creation. Ovid described him as *chaos,* within which life was latent.[241] Originally, Janus was also a solar deity, another parallel with the Empress, who is the Mother of the Sun. In fact, almost everything that can be said about Janus can be said about the Empress, despite the fact that the primary God form related to this Path is Venus-Aphrodite.

In Greek mythology Aphrodite rose naked from the foam of the sea, riding a scallop shell. Wherever she stepped onto the land, flowers grew .[242] Thus, *The Empress* can be described in terms of luxurious proliferation, each facet of nature being so compelling, so beautiful, if not hypnotic, that it is possible to lose sight of the overview of the Path. As Crowley warns: "...the student who is dazzled by any given manifestation may be led astray. In no other card is it so necessary to disregard the parts and to concentrate upon the whole. "[243]

While Aphrodite is usually called "Goddess of Love," she is also known as the "Goddess of Desire,"[244] a title with special implications for students of the Mysteries. Netzach is often called the center of desire, for to feel is to desire. But there is also a practical lesson in that desire is born with the most abstract principle of form. It is often stated in eastern literature that to lose all desire, i.e., to want nothing is to become truly one with the Universe. The coming to, or leaving of, desire, is one aspect of the doorway which is Daleth.

The symbol of Venus encompasses all of the Sephiroth on the Tree of Life (see Figure 17), another indication that the idea of love is the formative energy of the Universe. Here one should also consider the fact that the lower appearance of Venus is in a Sephira, and is thus *objective*. Netzach is a part of the Astral Triangle of Personality. But when the Venus energy appears in the highest realm of the Tree of Life, is it on a Path, i.e., it is *subjective*.

Three planetary forces find their objective expression as Sephiroth low on the Tree of Life, while their subjective expression, as Paths, are found at the opposite extreme. These are Hod-Mercury, *The Magician*; Yesod-Moon, *The High Priestess*; and Netzach-Venus, *The Empress*. Thus, the entire Astral Triangle of Sephiroth is expressed subjectively in relationship to the Supernal Triangle. There is a very profound mystery imbedded here.

Turning to the card images, we find that the Golden Dawn *Empress* stresses ruling qualities more than do the Waite and Crowley designs. This is somewhat better symbolism than Waite's luxurious treatment in that it allows for the fact that the Empress can destroy as well as create. In the Mathers' card the outer robe is the green of Netzach-Venus, but inside is the dynamic and fiery red of Binah in Atziluth. For *The Empress,* growth and destruction are concurrent activities. In ourselves, for example, cells are constantly being born as old cells die. This is the process of growth, destruction and renewal. Thus does *The Empress* function in us, the Microcosm. To know the energies of this Path of Daleth, the door, is to understand and be able to manipulate the three-fold process. This is a process which reconciles opposites, as is shown by the ankh cross, a symbol of life combining male and female, held suggestively at the womb of the Empress. In the other hand she holds an orb of the sun, meaning that she dominates the Heavens (the orb and cross of the Marseilles Tarot means domination of the Earth).

Like the Emperor, the Golden Dawn Empress sits before a veil, meaning that to pass beyond her is to cross into a completely new level of consciousness where her laws no longer apply. The veil points to a dramatic separation.

No such separation is indicated in the Waite card which emphasizes the flow of life, *The Empress* in her phase of munificent fruition. She is Mother Earth and Mother Venus, carrying the planetary sign on her dress and on her shield. The heart shape of the latter is a rather trite way of showing that she is the Goddess of Love. Her pearls and the Cypress trees in the background are also sacred to Venus, while the foreground wheat refers to the figure as Isis. On her head is a crown of twelve stars, the same Zodiac found on *The Fool*. It is the crown of the *Illuminating Intelligence* (Chokmah/Sphere of the Zodiac). She is also intended to be understood as the woman of Revelation who is "clothed with the sun."

The real key to this card is the stream of crystalline pure water flowing downward at the right. This is the water from which Aphrodite is born, what is "activated," i.e., churned into foam, by the "will" of *The Magician*. This is a continuous process whereby the pristine consciousness of *The High Priestess* gives rise to the unconscious thought patterns of *The Empress*. In the microcosm this means creative imagination, our own ability to create mental forms, to structure concepts. In the Macrocosm this means the same structuring, but of the "pictures," which are general to the human race, rather than specific to the individual. In *The Empress* are thought forms which become more dense as they are expressed into manifestation, and are administered by the Sun-center of Tiphareth.

There is an important practical parallel here. God creates the Universe (continuously) by thought. We do the same thing. We create a reality by imagining it, by thinking it into being. All that we create in our minds *becomes*. This is one of the basic precepts of the Mysteries which is all too often misunderstood or approached with ridicule. At any event, as one grows in spiritual power, the implications of responsibility for what one thinks, are very profound.

In his card Crowley shows *The Empress* as representative of alchemical Salt, the inactive principle which is energized by alchemical Sulphur to "maintain the whirling equilibrium of the Universe."[245] Here the figure is designed in the shape of the alchemical symbol, a circle with a line bisecting it horizontally. The twisted blue shapes represent flames, and her birth from water. She holds a chalice-like lotus, a living form of the Holy Grail. At her waist is the Zodiac; above her head are the birds of Venus, sparrow and dove; at her feet are the pelican who feeds her young with her own flesh (a common Christian symbolism of some interest in that the Great Mother gives birth to God the Son, who is self-sacrificed) and a shield with the alchemical white eagle corresponding to the red eagle of *The Emperor*.

To reiterate Crowley's alchemical references: *The Magician* is *Mercury*, *The Empress is Salt* and *The Emperor is Sulphur*. These attributions should be considered in terms of the attribution of the same symbols in the Golden Dawn documents: Kether is Mercury, Chokmah is Salt, and Binah is Sulphur.[246]

13. THE PATH OF GIMEL
The High Priestess
The Second Key

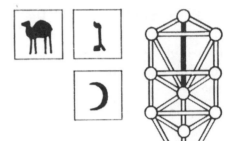

◆ PATH COLOR: Blue
◆ RELATED SOUND: G Sharp
◆ PLANET: Moon
◆ MEANING: Camel
◆ DOUBLE LETTER: Peace-War
◆ ESOTERIC TITLE: The Princess of the Silver Star.

THIRTY-TWO PATHS OF WISDOM: *The Thirteenth Path is named the Uniting Intelligence, and is so called because it is itself the Essence of Glory. It is the Consummation of the Truth of individual spiritual things.*

Having just considered the Path of *The Empress*, one of warm enclosure (a literal return to the cosmic womb) and of maternal protection, the Path of *The High Priestess* may be somewhat disconcerting. It is as if the Supreme Mother has removed her smiling mask, to reveal her true face, which is cold and expressionless, though beautiful. All of the material help of *The Empress* has vanished. There are no more illusions. We must face the crystalline reality of our own absolute free will, the most difficult task of the Mysteries related to the crossing of the Abyss.

The Paths of Gimel (*The High Priestess*), Samekh (*Temperance*) and Tau (*The Universe*) may be considered aspects of the same energy which together make up the devotional Middle Pillar. This is suggested by the Path colors in Atziluth, which are indigo (deepest blue) and blue which is the color of water and of the moon. These three Paths all relate to the moon.

Gareth Knight describes the Path of Tau as the "Gateway to the inner planes," and those of Samekh and Gimel as "Dark Nights of the Soul."[247] The term "Dark Night," coined by the sixteenth century monk, St. John of the Cross, means the desolation and terror that is felt as one is in the middle of the Path towards truth, but has not reached the end. This is particularly applicable to the Path of *The High Priestess*, which traverses the frightening desert-Abyss.

But there is the implication that we may be borne across this desert by the forces of the Path itself, for Gimel means *camel*. It is a beast which may carry us on the Path which is at once the longest and the most important on the Tree of Life.[248] The Path is the first to come from the Supernal Triangle (potential) to the Ethical Triangle (the "actual"). Moreover, its very position on the Tree, between God the Father in Kether and God the Son in Tiphareth, shows it to confer the very highest initiation.

This initiation is through that virgin essence which has been called the "lower Chokmah." There are correspondences between the Path and the Sephira, which can be established by Gematria: The names *Gimel (*גמל*)* and *Chokmah* (חכמה) both add to 73. But, more important, is the idea that *wisdom* is alternately expressed as masculine or feminine. The word is feminine in most languages, though applied in Chokmah to the quality of primary maleness. To say that *The High Priestess* is the lower Chokmah is to say that as the One expands outward, the seed of expansion contains the means of its own limitation. Then, as Crowley put it: "This first and most spiritual manifestation of the feminine takes to itself a masculine correlative, by formulating in itself any geometrical point from which to contemplate possibility."[249] The concept is an impossibly difficult one, and here, more than in other cards, we are faced with the fact that the terms most descriptive of these principles may seem totally nonsensical. The common description of the key is more approachable, that being *The High Priestess* as the most pure essence of consciousness, symbolized in the Tarot as the very source of all Water.

The source of Water is the idea behind the idea behind form. Case amplified this concept in saying that. "...no matter how many forms develop from it, the virgin substance is itself unchanged. Like water, which holds matter in suspension or solution, this substance remains over itself. Here is one key to the alchemical mystery of the First Matter. Here, too, one may find a clue to the inner significance of the virgin myths of all religions."[250]

Almost every writer on Tarot has found such keys to keys in *The High Priestess*. She is often, in fact, described as the "Inner Mysteries" or esotericism as opposed to *The Hierophant* who is sometimes identified with exoteric religion. But *The High Priestess* must be studied in terms of *The Magician*, in that she carries out what he initiates. This interaction can be discussed in a number of terms. She can be called the *Root Matter* and he the *First Matter (Prima Materia)*, or she can be considered the result of his self-consciousness. However it may be symbolized, *The Magician* symbolizes a condition prior to unconscious "thought." This condition acts upon *The High Priestess* in such a way that the Gimel Path becomes the "mind" capable of carrying the thought forms of which the Universe will eventually be composed. She is he source of the vibratory patterns of the Universe which underlie everything. Thus, the Crowley card shows a figure composed of waves of energy, under which are the mental forms affected by those waves. Moreover, nothing can grow in the garden of *The Empress* without this underlying structure of energies.

The Wisdom of *The High Priestess* is in regulation. Her fluctuating rates of vibration establish the direction (sets the pattern) for the First Matter *(Prima Materia=Philosophic Mercury=Magician)* as it "descends" toward a condition of greater density. It is for this reason that the moon is attributed to this Path. The vibratory pattern, the waxing and waning, and all of its other attributes, are here found at the most pure source. The moon represents fluctuations, dualities, tides. It is the moon which controls the tides of the waters of consciousness.

The moon is cold, harboring neither good nor bad. Its potent currents, as the meaning of the double letter Gimel, *war/peace,* suggests, may be problem-solving or causing. But no matter what the result of the activity of *The High Priestess*, she herself remains unchanged, incorruptible, ever virgin. She is moreover, the vessel for all the operations of the Supernal Triangle; it is within her that the activity of Mercury, Sulphur and Salt takes place. She is the *Uniting Intelligence,* an activity which is also related to the Four Elements.

We have shown how four Paths rising into the Supernal Triangle each represent a different Element, and have suggested that each is an aspect of the "Garden of Eden." *The High Priestess*, again, is the Uniting Spirit, that fifth Element which is symbolized by the uppermost section of the pentagram. To reiterate: *Hierophant*=Earth, *Lovers*=Air, *Chariot*=Water, *Emperor*=Fire and *The High Priestess*=Spirit. She is at once the source and uniting regulator over the four other Paths. She is also the source of the Four Rivers of Paradise: *The Pison* (River of Fire), *The Gihon* (River of Water), *The Hiddikel* (River of Air) and *The Phrath* (River of Earth).

The idea of *The High Priestess* as pure vessel is commensurate with the retentive qualities of the camel, an animal which stores water for a long desert voyage. This suggests another type of retention, *memory*. Within *The High Priestess* are, in fact, concealed the memories of the race as well as those of the Cosmos. Her veil suggests this concealment. In the Golden Dawn card it is draped around her, covering her eyes so that it is impossible to look directly into her face. The Waite card uses a hanging cloth behind the figure, which has the same meaning. But the Crowley *High Priestess* seems veiled with light itself. He calls her the "soul of light" in the sense that it is light which conceals the True Spirit. This is the spirit which we have called a "Fiery Darkness," and which is the substance of the Supernal Potential. This is *The High Priestess*, in any version of the card, understood to be clothed in light. This is the light before the Abyss above Tiphareth. It is a light so brilliant that none may look upon it who have not become of the same nature.

What is required here is a rethinking of the essence of light. All religions stressing light are based on a Tiphareth Sun-God. These include Christ, Buddha, Apollo, Osiris, Ahura Mazda, etc. What is important is that, unlike organized religion, the Mysteries teach that *light does not reveal; it conceals by its very brilliance.*

The Path of *The High Priestesss*, like the moon itself, goes from the most brilliant light to the most intense darkness. Thus, the principles of the moon and its deities, Diana-Artemis and Hecate, apply. Of course, one can choose from numerous variations on the same theme, appreciating that mythology grew out of social needs to a large extent. Thus, we find that Hecate, as described by Hesiod, was the original triple-Goddess ruling Heaven and earth. Later periods concentrated on her more unpleasant aspects as Goddess of the underworld, and the darker aspects of magic. She remained, nonetheless, associated with the moon as Hecate-Selene, the "far shooting moon," an aspect of Artemis.[251]

Artemis, in one legend the sister of Apollo and daughter of Zeus, was the bringer of light and the eternal virgin.[252] And as we find that *The High Priestess* is called the "Princess of the Silver Star," we are also told that Artemis was known as the "Maiden of the Silver Bow." This suggests *Temperance*, the lower extension of *The High Priestess*, which is Sagittarius, the Archer. Its arrow may fly heavenward, or deeply into the earth.

Artemis was also the triple Moon Goddess. First she was the maiden, then the (orgiastic) nymph, then the old crone [253] She was all the phases of woman at once. These aspects of the moon are symbolized by the crown of the High Priestess in Waite's card: the full moon is shown at the center, with the waxing and waning moon represented at either side.

One might well wonder how it is possible for Artemis to be at once eternal virgin and orgiastic nymph, but that is the whole mystery of *The High Priestess*. It is rather like the play *Camino Real*, by Tennessee Williams. Every month, by the light of a full moon, an old gypsy woman turns her prostitute daughter back into a virgin, which is, as she says, "quite a trick."

The idea of *The High Priestess* as the *Uniting Intelligence*, the reconciler of opposites, is represented by Waite as the two pillars, black and white, from the supposed Temple of Solomon. They symbolize the union of all polarities on this Path, of which the card number is 2. This is the number of reflection and duplication. And as we called upon the infinity symbol of Waite's *Magician* in discussing the Path of Samekh (*Temperance*), that figure also applies here on the upper extension of Samekh, the Path of Gimel. To restate our thesis: *The High Priestess* acts on the *First Matter* of *The Magician* and causes it to function in the pattern of the figure eight on its side. One cycle is opposed and duplicated, though the flow of energy is totally unified. The energy of *The Magician* is held in a reciprocal, alternating, pattern by that which is called *The High Priestess*. This holding, enclosing and duplicating function is the first female quality on the Tree.

In more contemporary terms, *The High Priestess* is what Jung called the *"virgin anima,"*[254] related to the "virgin's milk," which he called the "Life giving power *of* the unconscious." The alchemically symbolic virgin's milk fed to the "Stone" as mother's milk is fed to a baby, is synonymous with the water *of The High Priestess*.

The Golden Dawn and Waite cards both suggest the dispersal of this water from *The High Priestess*. In the Golden Dawn version, the figure stands upon a moon above waves ; in the Waite version, the robe *of The High Priestess* seems to turn into water at its base. Crowley's card is more technical than the others in that it represents a very complicated set *of* wave forms. More than the others, his design captures the quality of the Path. Crowley states, in fact, that his card is "very peculiarly a glyph of the work of the A.A."[255] In his BOTA course, *Tarot Fundamentals,* Case also attaches broad meaning to the card, which he explains as a summation of the seven Hermetic Principles of the *Kybalion* (discussed in our introduction).[256]

Case's BOTA card, a modification of Waite's *High Priestess*, is less evocative than that of the Golden Dawn or Crowley. On the other hand, Waite's symbolism is extremely precise. *The High Priestess* is shown as the unifying agent between the two columns of the Temple; unification and balance being also represented by the cross on her breast, which Waite called a solar cross .[257] Behind her is the veil of the Temple, covered with palms and pomegranates. Waite was not very explicit about the reason for this choice of plant forms, although Case says (rather unconvincingly) that the palms are male, while the pomegranates are female .[258] Waite's comments, however incomplete, suggest another explanation. He says of *The High Priestess*: "...she is really the Secret Church, the house which is of God and man."[259] This implies that she represents all the inner tenets of religion. One might, therefore, suggest that the palm is a traditional Christian symbol representing the "triumph" of Christ on his entry into Jerusalem. The pomegranate, on the other hand, is associated with the very ancient Mysteries. It occurs frequently in the Old Testament, and was given special significance by the Eleusian Mysteries.[260] It is therefore likely that Waite intended to convey the idea that *The High Priestess* is the central core, the unifying factor in all faiths, especially Christianity and Judaism.

Other aspects of the Waite card are more certain, for example, the scroll on which appear the letters T 0 R A. This is the *Scroll of the Law* established by *The High Priestess*. It is also intended to refer to a common, though simplistic, manipulation of the letters into T A R 0 and into R 0 T A, the Latin word for wheel. This means that the Tarot is the Law as well as the very Wheel of Life. In this regard, it is seen that in the Golden Dawn deck the Scroll of the Law is held by *The Hierophant*, who administers that which is proposed by Binah. A scroll in the hands of *The High Priestess* does, however, point out that she is the repository of cosmic memory.

The Marseilles card is the least interesting of the four, with one exception, which is its very title, *The Female Pope*. The card is said to represent *Pope Joan,* described by Stephen de Bourbon in his thirteenth century work. As the story goes, a ninth century English girl fell in love with a monk. In order that they could live together, she dressed herself as a man. After the monk's death, she went to Rome and, retaining male dress, became a priest. Supposedly, she moved up through the ranks of the Church, became a Cardinal, and was finally elected Pope John VIII. She died on the steps of Saint Peter's giving birth.[261] The story is mythical, but is important because it was widely believed during the period when the Tarot cards appeared.

12. THE PATH OF BETH
The Magician
The First Key

   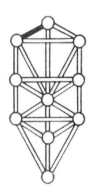

◆ PATH COLOR: Yellow
◆ RELATED SOUND: E-Natural
◆ PLANET: Mercury
◆ MEANING: House
◆ DOUBLE LETTER: Life-Death
◆ ESOTERIC TITLE: The Magus
    of Power.

THIRTY-TWO PATHS OF WISDOM: *The Twelfth Path is the Intelligence of Transparency because it is that species of Magnificence called* Chazchazit, *which is named the place whence issues the vision of those seeing in apparitions (That is the prophesies by seers in a vision).*

The Path of Beth is between Kether and Binah. It is the transition between the One Pure Source of All, energy undefined, and the Great Organizer, a relationship described by the meaning of the letter Beth, which is *house*. It is the "dwelling place" of the spirit descending toward the denseness of manifestation. *The Magician* symbolizes that which builds the house, i.e. directs and encloses the One Spirit which is symbolized by *The Fool*. In this regard it must be appreciated that to consider one card versus another at this level of the Tree of Life is very different from a comparison of cards at the lower levels. The differences between let us say, *The Universe* and the Path of *Judgment* are substantial, if not dramatic. But the higher one works up on the Tree, the more such differences become extremely fluid and subtle. *The Fool* and *The Magician* are separated by only slight degree, a fact not obvious in the anthropomorphized symbolism of the cards.

Scholars dedicated to unraveling the difficult cryptograms of the *Penta-teuch* (first five books of the Bible) are quick to point out that Beth is the first letter to be used. The *Book of Genesis* begins *"Bereshith,"* (בראשית), commonly translated as "In the beginning," but intriguingly rendered by Fabre d'Olivet as "At first, in principle."[263] That which is symbolized by the letter Beth is the first in creation, it is the beginning of the beginning. It is the *First Principle,* or *First Matter* of the alchemists, also called the *Philosophic Mercury.* But to create beginning is to create end. Thus the opposites of life and death, key polarities of creation, are attributed to the letter. The idea is implicit that without the ener-gies of *The Magician,* there would be neither life nor death, neither beginning nor end. *The Magician* initiates this process, a cycle symbolized by the infin-ity symbol *(lemniscus)* as well as the serpent which holds its tail in its mouth *(Uroboros).* Both represent the closed circle of energy in the Universe, begun by the number one (Beth) acting upon the zero (Aleph).

The relationship of Aleph (*The Fool*) and Beth (*The Magician*) to cre-ation are discussed in a section of the *Zohar* which is one of the most charming in all of esoteric literature. We are told that for two-thousand years God had "contemplated" the twenty-two letters of the Hebrew alphabet, and had "toyed with them."[264] And when it came time for Him to create the Universe, the letters presented themselves before Him in reverse order (Tau to Aleph), each asking that they be the first in creation. All were denied until Beth, of whom God said: "Assuredly, with thee I will create the world, and thou shalt form the beginning of the creation of the world."[265] God then wondered why Aleph had not appeared, and called for the letter, which explained: "Because I saw all the other letters leaving Thy presence without any success. What, then, could I achieve there? And further, since Thou hast already bestowed on the letter Beth this great gift, it is not meet for the Supreme King to take away the gift which he has made to his servant and to give it to another." God's response was: "...although I will be-gin the creation of the world with *Beth,* thou wilt remain the first of the letters. My unity shall not be expressed except through thee, on thee shall be based all calculations and operations of the world, and unity shall not be expressed save by the letter Aleph."[266]

It is fascinating to realize that the greatest Mysteries of the Cosmos are such that they are well expressed in the simplest, even most childlike of pictures and words. Indeed, the relationship between *The Fool* and *The Magician* is so subtle and refined that our best hope of even approaching them rests in medita-tion on spiritual text combined with the images of the Tarot cards. It is impos-sible to speak directly of what either the texts or the cards represent. What we try to do is to establish a circle of ideas, each idea giving a suggestion about the nature of the inner truth.

One such idea associated with *The Magician* is that the energies of this card are at once active and passive. The mystery of *The Magician* is that *it is both that which transmits and that which is transmitted.* It is the Life Force (The One) which becomes the *Prima Materia* in the act of transmission.

The Magician is a channel through which the energy of *The Fool* is organized and passes downward. The One Life Energy is directed by *The Magician* as the first step in the evolution of the Universe toward matter. Thus is the Path called the *Transparent Intelligence,* for like light through a glass, energy passes through it from above. The process is especially well represented on the Waite card, where the magician's right arm is raised with the wand pointed downward. This suggests power brought down in a purposeful, willful, way. Moreover, Waite makes some very subtle reference to the activity of all the Supernals here. The inner color of the magician's robe is white, meaning Kether. The outer robe is the red of Binah in Atziluth, and the serpent belt is the blue of Chokmah in Atziluth. Waite's inference is that the *Prima Materia* results from the interaction of all of the Supernal Sephiroth. The God of this Path, Mercury, is the "messenger of the Gods" (especially of his Father, Zeus-Kether) meaning that he is not himself the Creator, only the bearer of its will.

For all practical purposes Mercury (Roman), Hermes (Greek) and Thoth (Egyptian) are the same deity, the amalgam of their qualities having become particularly firm in modern esoteric literature. Of course, since Mercury is the later of the Gods, his attributes depend on those of Hermes and Thoth.

Hermes was very early associated with words, for the simple reason that a messenger must clearly state the cause of the one who sends him .[267] The same meaning essentially applies to the association of words with Thoth who, as the supposed inventor of hieroglyphics, developed that by which the message could be recorded and transmitted. The companion of Hermes, as discussed in dealing with the *Wheel of Fortune*, was the dog-headed Ape, the Cynocephalus, representing the words themselves, as well as the potential for misunderstanding and deceit. It is in this latter sense that Crowley has included the cynocephalus at the feet of his magus.

The relationship of the Hermes energy to words is very profound. Messages are carried by words, but it is also through words of power that the Magician affects his will. Thus is *word* associated with cause and effect. Words transmit ideas from person to person in the same way that *The Magician* transmits the idea of Self-Creation of the One from above.

A word is meant to be spoken (writing is the annotation of spoken thought); it is a sound which carries idea. It is intelligence-laden vibration. Word = vibration. So the idea of *The Magician* is that it is the first vibration through which the One Spirit begins the process of manifestation. It encloses the Spirit and thus encompasses All that is.

This principle is conveyed by a diagram, in the Golden Dawn papers, relating the Mercury symbol to all of the Sephiroth except Kether (Figure 32A).

The horns in this figure spring from Daath (Knowledge) which is not, properly speaking, a Sephira, but rather an experience of passage through the Abyss. [268] And of course, since the days of Lévi The whole Tarot has been fancifully called *The Book of Thoth*.

Pursuant to the idea of Mercury encompassing all Sephiroth except Kether, there is a very interesting diagram showing Mercury on the caduceus (Figure 32B). This is not at all inconsistent with the first symbol, which distinguishes between the creator above, and creation below. The Four Worlds here are not the wand, they are that which is transmitted by the wand of *The Magician*.

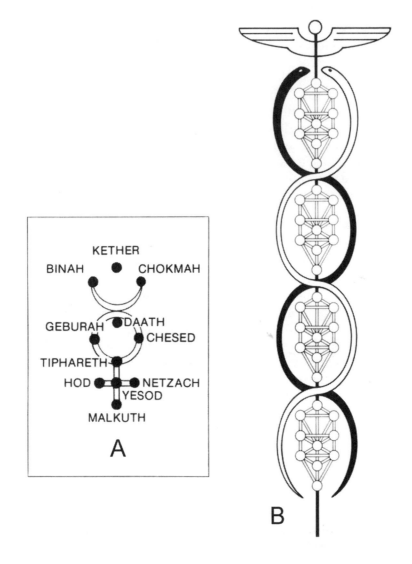

Figure 32. Two Ways of Representing that which is Encompassed by Mercury: (A) The Sephiroth on the Planetary Symbol; (B) The Four Worlds on the Caduceus.

This interpretation of the caduceus and the planetary sign is not common. Astrologers and iconographers usually analyze the Mercury symbol as half-moon, circle and equal-armed cross. These symbolize the moon, the sun and the balance of the Four Elements. The sun and the moon are the dual states of the Cosmos, here in their most refined expression. The Four Elements are first seen, primordially, in Kether, where they are symbolized by the swirling gammadion or swastica. These Elements, potential in *The Fool*, are first differentiated and directed by *The Magician*.

The Magician directs the forces of the יהוה, letters first encountered in the God Name of Binah, יהוה אלהים (YHVH Elohim) at the lower end of the Path of Beth. As it is succinctly expressed in the Golden Dawn documents, the Primum Mobile (First Motion) is acting through the Philosophic Mercury on Saturn-Binah, which is to say that the Supreme Spirit is acting upon the Will to Form. This activity is involved with words, i.e., vibration, and recalls the idea that whosoever can pronounce the יהוה will be Master of the Universe. In this sense "pronounce" means to willfully direct the vibration. So what we have in *The Magician* is the secret to the pronounciation of the Divine Name. This brings us to a very complex idea which is the essence of the Mysteries, an idea emphasized by Case in his *Book of Tokens*. There he says that "all created wills are but reflections" of the will of *The Magician*. Most important Case points out that the individual must allow this Primal Will to act through him or herself.

My superior nature worketh through thee...
...Happy art thou if thou canst grasp this truth.
For then, understanding that not thy weak self,
By my all-knowing Mind,
Looketh out upon the world through thine eyes,
Shalt thou have faith to *let* me see.
Then shalt thou overcome the evil of thy senses
by devoting them wholly to my use.[269]

This is an extremely difficult concept, and one which truly represents the practical core of all religion, mysticism or magic. However the process may be symbolically expressed, the inner direction of the Four Elements by the universal magician, through us, is primary. Waite's card, based on the then secret Golden Dawn card, was the first to show the magician with his wand raised above the actual Elemental Weapons of modern Hermetic Qabalism. On the table are the Wand for Fire (י), the Cup for Water (ה), the Dagger for Air (ו) and the Pentacle for Earth (ה); all are very generalized, but are accurate to the Golden Dawn system.[270]

We have come a long way from the somewhat tentative symbolism of the Marseilles deck. In that Tarot deck, the magician stands at a table manipulating implements germane to the performer-magician of the middle ages, whose stock-in-trade was slight of hand and pleasant deception. Yet the double-ended wand and the hat approximating the form of the infinity symbol suggest something more, as does the very title of the card, *Le Bateleur,* meaning the bearer of the wand.

The wand is, in fact, the only attribute of a magician which has been consistently represented from the ancient world to the present. It is that through which power flows, and by which power is directed with the force of will. It is at least interesting to see that Waite gave his magician of 1910 the exact same wand as that of the Marseilles deck of 1500. Thus did Waite affirm the symbolic value of the early instrument. Presumably, variations on *The Magician* over the years, represent contemporary states of the "magical art."

Judging from magical treatises at the period of the earliest conceivable appearance of the cards, there was no great proliferation of magical instruments. In a work such as the *Heptamaron* of Pietro de Albano (1250-1317)[271] it is clear that magic was an amplification of the priestly art, depending largely on words for its invocations, banishings, and consecrations of talismans. The impetus toward the complex instruments we find on the Golden Dawn card probably begins in the eighteenth century, as is reflected by Barrett's *Magus* of 1801. [272]

Accepting that each version of *The Magician* represents the point of view of an age toward what is called "magic," the Crowley card is provocative. In that version *The Magician* no longer merely holds the wand, he *is* the wand, a conceptual change of no small dimension. Crowley, thus, has accurately represented what we earlier described as the Mystery of the Magician, i.e., that it is at once that which transmits and that which is transmitted. It is the messenger and it is the message.

There is also an important phallic symbolism in this wand of Hermes which transmits power. Even in earliest times Hermes, the messenger of the Gods, carried a staff. Originally it was decorated with white ribbons, later mistaken for serpents (because he was the "Herald of Hades") and turned into what we know today as the Caduceus of Mercury.[273] This is seen on the breast of the Golden Dawn magician.

Time and Victorianism have softened the phallic implication of Hermes' wand, originally very openly represented as *Herms*. These were upright slabs of stone with a bust and a very large phallus curiously attached to the front of the column. So in the ancient world, Hermes was revered as a God of creation, the aspect of *The Magician* which Crowley stresses.

The Magician seems to have been a very difficult card for Lady Freida Harris to paint. Early versions show a central figure with multiple abstract arms, each holding some magical image. The quality of balance is emphasized by the caduceus which rises in the center of the figure .[274] But in the final version, the magician, though centered on an abstract caduceus form, is in a state of activity. The magical instruments seem to float through space, as if they were in constant motion, a continuous creation, something ever changing.

Crowley says that, in fact: "No true image is possible at all, for, firstly, all images are necessarily false as such; and, secondly, the motion being perpetual, and its rate that of the limit, c, the rate of Light, any stasis contradicts the idea of the card"...[275] For Crowley, *The Magician* was the Son and the Word, and "being the Word he is the law of reason or of necessity or chance, which is the secret meaning of the Word, which is the essence of the Word and the condition of its utterance."[276]

11. THE PATH OF ALEPH
The Fool
The Zero Key

   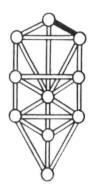

◆ PATH COLOR: Bright Pale Yellow
◆ RELATED SOUND: E-Natural
◆ MEANING: Ox
◆ MATERNAL LETTER: Air
◆ ESOTERIC TITLE: The Spirit of Aether.

THIRTY-TWO PATHS OF WISDOM: *The Eleventh Path is the Scintillating Intelligence, because it is the essence of that curtain which is placed close to the order of the disposition, and this is a special dignity given to it that it may be able to stand before the Face of the Cause of Causes.*

The Path of *The Fool* connects Kether, the Source of All, with Chokmah, the first activity toward manifestation. Aleph is assigned to this Path, the letter designated symbolic of absolute unity by the *Zohar*. As a word (Aleph) means *ox*, which has been interpreted in a variety of ways. Gareth Knight, for example, suggests that for the most earthy of beasts to be applied at this exalted level of the Tree means that "the Spirit's aim is rooted in earth."[227] Paul Case essentially agreed, although his approach was more broad. He called the ox a symbol of the motive power in agriculture, and equated agriculture with civilization. Thus, he described the ox as the life-power, creative energy and "the power at work in all forms of human adaptation and modification of natural conditions."[278] Crowley, on the other hand, concentrated on the letter's shape, said to represent a plow-share: "thus," he says "the significance is primarily phallic."[279] Cynics may suggest that Crowley saw phalluses everywhere he looked, despite the high philosophical tone of his argument. Yet it is true that only by reference to sexuality do we come to the slightest glimmer of understanding of the Universe.

The Fool demands multi-faceted and fluid interpretation. It is certainly the most difficult and profound card of the entire Tarot deck. Emanating from Kether, it borders on the source of the Cosmos, the *Ain Soph,* the Limitless Light which *is not.* Thus, we recognize that whatever can be said about Kether can be said about the subjective effect of its principles on the eleventh Path.

The eleventh Path is the *Fiery* or *Scintillating Intelligence.* It touches a Limitless Light which is darkness to us, that fiery darkness which is at once the *Primum Mobile,* the *possibility* of motion or vibration, and the *first perception* or *will* of the One having the potential for activity. Here, again, we return to the circuitous idea that the Primal Creative Energy of the Universe acts upon itself to emanate the Cosmos. The most concrete way in which this can be described is to say that from nothingness comes the potential for thought. Then thought appears and emanates mind, the vessel which contains thought. *The Fool* is the initial potential for that thought which transcends reason.

Almost everyone has had the experience of feeling that they have touched some special reality in sleep, a lesson which on waking seemed absurd at best. We may recall a few words which, when translated from the sleeping to the waking condition appear absolute nonsense. In fact, any idea which is disconsonant with our waking reality is usually dismissed. Such ideas may be dangerous and disruptive to our perceptions of self and environment, so we put them aside. On the other hand, a great deal of the practical Great Work involves the assimilation of concepts which contradict our mundane ideas of what is "real," and what is not.

Let it be clearly understood that *The Fool, The Magician* and *The High Priestess* (Paths touching Kether) must be approached with a certain good natured whimsy. As we realize that the experience of Kether means the total annihilation of Self as we conceive it, we also see the irony of our attempt to grasp such refined principles from an earthly perspective. We are, as Dion Fortune once noted, little children attempting to spell God. However, once we recognize the impossibility of approaching the highest levels of the Universe directly, we are driven forcibly into the key principle of the Mysteries, *As Above, so Below.* We look into that which is "below" as a mirror reflection of that which is "above."

Every Key is, in fact, fourfold. And while *The Fool* is usually discussed in terms of the highest spirit of Atziluth, it also appears in Briah, Yetzirah and Assiah. Thus, somewhere in our basest and most comprehensible existence, we will find a correlate to the upper activity of *The Fool.* The process is a kind of spiritual detective work. We look deeply into Malkuth and find Kether!

This is the essence of what Teillard de Chardin, the great modern Catholic mystic, was describing. The Divine Spirit is all that we know: we live within it; we breathe it; it is ourselves. Every *thing* is an expression of the energy symbolized by *The Fool*, which is the beginning of all, as Aleph is the beginning of the alphabet.

To Aleph, the first of the maternal letters, is attributed *Air* which, in this sense means the Life-Breath. And while most people believe that the East places more importance on the function of breath than does the West, that is only true of exoteric religion. In Western esoteric techniques, as in the East, breath is everything, both practically and philosophically. In terms of the Tree of Life and Tarot, this may be expressed in another way. We described *The Magician* as relating to "words," meaning vibratory patterns underlying manifestation. It is the power of breath, however, which expels the sound. *The Fool* activates *The Magician.*

Crowley points out another way in which the attribution of Air may be considered. He describes the nothingness which is Air as a *vacuum*, a fascinating concept when related to the Tarot number of *The Fool*, zero. The zero is a vacuum of fertile nothingness; it is the Universal Egg of Spirit, the Egg of *Akasha*. Mathematically, zero is the sum of plus one (male) minus one (female). Thus the egg of the Cosmos is a fertilized ovum of undefined sexuality. It is neither male nor female, but is the potential for both. *The Fool* is the androgenous energy which differentiates into the *dramatis personae* of the other twenty-one keys.

Unfortunately, the correct position of *The Fool* at the beginning of the Keys, has been the subject of dispute. In some works it has been shown placed in the irrational position of next to the last card, i.e., as the card of Shin, letter of maternal fire. However, this placement appears to have been a purposeful attempt to conceal the real mystery of *The Fool* from the profane. Today the sequence of Keys described in the Golden Dawn *Cipher Manuscripts* is generally accepted, as it was by the inventors of the three modern decks illustrated here. *The Fool* belongs on the eleventh Path of Aleph, and nowhere else.

It has been suggested that the key to the function and order of the Cosmos is imbedded in Aleph as it interacts with Lamed. *The Zohar*, which describes Aleph as absolute unity, provides equally interesting material on Lamed. That letter is discussed as central to the word מלכ (Melekh) meaning *King*.[280] This points to Tiphareth as the central, directing force of Microprosopus, the "Lesser Countenance." This is the King over existence as we know it, its interaction of energies being symbolized by the letters Mem, Lamed, Caph and by the corresponding Tarot cards, *The Hanged Man* (מ), *Justice* (ל) and the *Wheel of Fortune* (כ).

The Hanged Man and the *Wheel of Fortune* are the Stabilizing Activating and Stabilizing Formative extremes (see Figure 29) on the Tree of Life between the Personality and the Higher Self. They are exact opposites. *The Hanged Man* is the Water of Universal consciousness, while the *Wheel of Fortune*, Caph-Jupiter, means the very principle of manifestation. Thus, Lamed may be said to effect the perfect balance between the lower creative principle and the consciousness on which it acts. In this we know that Lamed means *ox goad,* the pointed rod which spurs on the ox, i.e., Aleph.

Paul Case offers another explanation. He writes that the word אלף "represents the first outflow of spiritual influence (א), effecting a continual equilibrium of forces in action (ל) resulting in the positive expression of the creative thought (פ) of the Universal Mind."[281]

This is all very complicated indeed, and one can all too easily become bogged down, if not actually deceived by the over-zealous manipulation of letter and number symbols. What seems clear, however, that the sages who produced Qabalistic documents such as the *Sepher Yetzirah* and the *Zohar* expected truth-seekers to go through this process. Thus, we must run the risk of dead-end reasoning in attempting to understand the subtle meanings imbedded in the texts. Is it stretching a point to suggest that implicit in the letters אל is all that is above and below, viewing Aleph as the One, with Lamed as the central balancing energy between the One and that which it projects?

At any event, these are sorts of ideas which, when applied to the Tarot images, are likely to provide special insights. When we know the Qabalistic implications of the letter Aleph and apply it to the image of *The Fool*, the correspondence of picture and ideas triggers something unconscious in us. This may be particularly the case with the Golden Dawn *Fool*, one of the Order's most unusual contributions to Tarot art. The child is intended to be *Harpocrates,* which in the Egyptian *(Heru-p-khart)* literally means "Horus the Child."[282] Heru is also written *Hru* and is referred to by some as the "Great Angel of the Tarot."

There are few Gods which incorporate so many diverse ideas as does Harpocrates: He is the Child God; he is the God of Silence; he is the God of Beginnings, he is the God of the sun at its dawning. He is also the son of Isis and Osiris, although it is not yet in that capacity that he is shown on this Path. He is their child yet to be born. He is all potential. He is the expression of the very meaning of the God Name of Kether, אהיה (Eheieh) which is often translated "I am I, " but which actually means *I will be.* So in the Golden Dawn card, the child is about to pluck the rose. In Waite's card the Fool is about to walk over a cliff. Waite describes his figure as stationary, though it indicates the act of walking.

Because of the importance of Horus-Harpocrates to an understanding of *The Fool* in the Golden Dawn tradition, we must briefly consider the origins of his cult. The Child Horus developed from an earlier God, also known as Horus. This earlier Horus (actually a group of God forms, as was the Child Horus himself) was one of the first Gods to be worshipped generally across Egypt. He was represented with the head of a hawk, suggesting that his nature related to the greatest heights of the Heavens,[283] an idea which would place Horus comfortably on the eleventh Path. But the attributes of the early Horus Gods were assumed in late dynastic times by the Child who represented the beginning of all sequences, including the beginning of the day with the Sun. So Horus was related to Ra, and is most easily placed in Tiphareth. And once more, as in considering the אל, we find that we are moving between the eleventh Path and the sixth Sephira. The correlations are as profound as they are obtuse.

One other interesting point about Horus is that he was traditionally shown as a child with one lock of hair at the side, and a finger on his mouth as an infantile gesture. This gesture was misunderstood by the Greeks to be a "sign of silence," and when the God was given the Greek name Harpocrates, silence was a key attribute.[284] However such attributions may have happened, whether by design or "accident" the symbolism fits remarkably. What could be more perfect than *The Fool* as silence prior to *The Magician* who has been described as the first sound? Here one must believe that symbol systems can evolve in accordance with truly universal principles.[285]

The Fool is, in fact, an archetype, as is the companion animal appearing in every version of the card. The Marseilles deck shows a brown dog tearing a hole in his master's pants leg; Waite represented a small white dog in the same essential pose as the Marseilles dog, though following playfully; Crowley's version, with the tiger "fawning about"[286] the fool, is the most curious. Finally, the Golden Dawn card shows a wolf on a leash being held by the small child whom the fraternity equated with Harpocrates.

All of these cards make a symbolic statement about the relationship of the animal nature to the higher spiritual processes. It has also been suggested that the small dog is the *intellect,* man's faithful companion. The Golden Dawn and Crowley cards, however, offer a more complicated explanation.

The wolf in the Golden Dawn card is perhaps the most explicit in its symbolic statement, for from the earliest times the wolf has been considered a *destroyer.* And in the context of the eleventh Path, it is like the Fenris wolf which devoured Odin, Father of the Gods, what Manly Palmer Hall calls "those mindless powers of nature that overthrew the primitive creation."[287]

The implication is that the Creator's will to self expression holds in check that counter-energy which would otherwise destroy creation as it happened. Yet the wolf must eventually be unleashed, freed back into nature, destroying creation and returning it to the state from which it originally emerged, i.e., the *Ain Soph Aur.*

The child and wolf are the balance of creator-destroyer, and are the first statement in the Tarot of the principle that every *thing* contains its opposite, the real key to esoteric studies. The principle is especially important in relation to *The Fool*, a card of which Waite says "Many symbols of the Instituted Mysteries are summarized."[288]

Waite's discussion of the symbolism in his own cards was very cryptic, and it fell to Paul Case to explain the symbolic complexities woven into the Rider deck. He explains the Wheels of Spirit on the Fool's robe, the wand as a symbol of will, the wallet with an Eye of Horus, the rose meaning freedom from lower forms of desire, and the girdle of twelve ornaments suggesting the Zodiac.[289] On the other hand, it is possible that in his enthusiasm, Case may describe more than Waite intended.

It is at least fortunate that Crowley, being a prolific writer, explained his own deck in great detail. The discussion of his version of *The Fool* is complicated and lengthy, drawing upon a variety of legends. To summarize, these are:

1. *The Green Man*—the very personification of Spring.
2. *The "Great Fool" of the Celts*—this is the inspired madman who is also a savior.

3. *The "Rich Fisherman:" Percivale*—Crowley calls the Parsifal legend "the Western form of the tradition of the Fool." Parsifal represents the foolishness of youth and innocence which, through its purity, achieves the Holy Grail.

4. *The Crocodile*—In ancient Egypt the crocodile symbolized the greatest creative energy, for the rather paradoxical reason that it was not believed to have the means of perpetuating its own species.

5. Harpocrates

6. *Zeus Arrhenothelus*—a deliberate confusion of masculine and feminine; the Divine Hermaphrodite.

7. *Dionysus Zagreus. Bacchus Diphues*—Zagreus was a horned deity torn apart by the Titans. His death symbolized initiation. Bacchus Diphues (meaning double-natured) was a bi-sexual God made mad by intoxication, and thus related to the idea of divine ecstasy.

8. *Bahomet*—according to Crowley, this is a form of the bull-slaying God, Mithras, worshipped by the Knights Templar as an ass-headed deity. He further associates Bahomet with Set, Saturn and Satan.

Crowley has included some reference to all of these ideas in his card, making it one of the most complicated in his deck. The horns on the male figure are those of *Dionysus Zagreus;* his green clothing is that of the *Green Man of Spring;* grapes at his feet refer to the ecstasy of *Bacchus,* the *Crocodile* is at his feet swimming "in the Nile." Other symbols included here are the dove of Venus and the vulture of Maat, both referring to the Godhead. All of these images are linked by the triple egg-shape created by the caduceus in motion, and symbolizing the *Ain Soph Aur.*

Finally, one must call attention to the fact that while Crowley emphasizes Harpocrates on this Path, he represents that God most explicitly on the twentieth Path, *Judgment* (what he calls *The Aeon)*. It is thus implied that Shin-Fire is the fullest expression of that which began with Aleph-Air, and then Mem-Water.

NOTES

1. Gareth Knight, *Experiences of the Inner Worlds*, England, 1975, iv.
2. Richard Cavendish, *The Tarot,* New York 1975, 9. This is the best work yet to appear on the history of Tarot.
3. Louis Réau, *L'Art Chrétien*, Paris 1955, v.I, 163.
4. As is discussed in the section on *The High Priestess*, Waite disagrees with this idea, saying that the Female Pope actually relates to the cult of Astarte.
5. *The Kybalion,* Chicago, 1940, 24 ff. The authors of this work, subtitled "A Study of the Hermetic Philosophy of Ancient Egypt and Greece," are unknown. They have signed themselves only as "Three Initiates."
6. Israel Regardie, *The Golden Dawn,* Chicago, 1940, v.IV, 176.
7. Eliphas Lévi, *Transcendental Magic,* London, 1958, 3.
8. C.G. Jung, *Psychology and Alchemy,* New York, 1968, 101.
9. Israel Regardie, *The Middle Pillar*, Chicago, 1945; also by Regardie, *Foundations of Practical Magic,* England, 1979.
10. It is for this reason that, until the present time, all practical works on the occult contained some purposeful errors.
11. Aleister Crowley, *The Confessions of Aleister Crowley*, New York 1969, 923. This work is modestly subtitled "An Autohagiography."
12. Ellic Howe, *The Magicians of the Golden Dawn,* London 1972, 1-25.
13. Regardie discusses some of his own experiences, as well as his opinions of the Order of the Golden Dawn in *My Rosicrucian Adventure,* Minnesota, 1971.
14. Ella Young, *Flowering Dusk,* New York, 1945, 107.
15. A. E. Waite, *Shadows of Life and Thought,* London, 1938, 184-5.
16. A. Quiller, Jr. (Crowley), "Dead Weight," *The Equinox,* v.I, No.X, 211.
17. Unpublished lecture, addressed to the "Tomorrow Club," in 1945, by Lady Harris.
18. *Ibid.*
19. Israel Regardie, *Golden Dawn*, v.IV,137. "Book T" is also reprinted in *An Introduction to the Golden Dawn Tarot* by Robert Wang, New York, 1978.

20. Gershom Scholem, *Kabbalah*, New York, 1974, 5. Among the more recent scholarly works, which must be considered indispensable, are those of Moshe Idel. His books, include: *The Mystical Experience in Abraham Abulafia*, New York, 1987; *Kabbalah, New Perspectives*, New Haven, 1988; *Studies in Ecstatic Kabbalah*, New York, 1988; and essays in the New York University series: *Essential Papers on Kabbalah*.

21. Rabbi Solomon Ganzfried, *Code of Jewish Law*, New York, 1963, 51.

22. It is also likely that some scholarly purists consider the diagram an unacceptable later development.

23. S.L. MacGregor Mathers, translation of Knorr von Rosenroth's *The Kabbalah Unveiled*, London, 1957, 5-6. See also Christian D. Ginsburg, *The Kabbalah*, London, 1925, 84.

24. Gershom Scholem, *Major Trends in Jewish Mysticism*, New York, 1977,

25. Gershom Scholem, *Major Trends*, 44.

26. Gershom Scholem, *Kabbalah*, 46.

27. Phineas Mordell, *The Origin of Letters and Numerals According to the Sepher Yetzirah*. New York, 1975, first published in the *Jewish Quarterly Review*, new series for April 1912, v.11, and for April 1913, v.111.

28. See: *Sepher Yetzirah*, translation by Wynn Westcott including *The Thirty Two Paths of Wisdom (1877)*, New York, 1975. Westcott was one of the founders of the Golden Dawn, and it is his translation that is most generally used even today by Hermetic Qabalists because it is consistent with Golden Dawn principles; *Sepher Yetzirah*, translation by Isodor Kalisch (1877, first English translation), California, 1954; *The Sepher Yetzirah*, translation and extensive commentary by Carlo Saures, Boulder, 1976. The Saures work is ponderous at best; *The Book of Formation (Sepher Yetzirah)*, translation and commentary by Knut Stenrung (1923), New York, 1970. While Stenrung's translation is generally competent, it is unnecessarily involved and includes a number of nineteenth century misconceptions about the document; *Book of Creation*, translation of the *Sepher Yetzirah* by Irving Friedman, New York, 1977. This is one of the best translations yet to appear, and is particularly valuable for its notes on language.

29. Gershom Scholem, *Kabbalah*, 23.

30. Gershom Scholem, *Kabbalah*, 23.

31. Gershom Scholem, *Kabbalah*, 23.

32. *The Bahir*, translation by Aryeh Kaplan, New York, 1979. This first English translation of the text includes the original Hebrew. Kaplan is out of step with Scholem (who also translated this work into a European language and other major scholars, in insisting that this work is of the 1st century B.C.E.

33. Gershom Scholem, *Kabbalah*, 45-47.

34. Gershom Scholem, *Kabbalah*, 55.

35. Gershom Scholem, *Kabbalah*, 57.

36. Gershom Scholem, *Kabbalah*, 190.

37. *The Zohar*, translation by Harry Sperling and Maurice Simon, New York, 1973. While this well-bound edition, published by Soncino Press, is the best-known, the exact same text is also published by Rebecca Bennett Publications, in a less expensive and somewhat reduced size.

The essential work on *The Zohar* is Isaiah Tishby's three volume, *The Wisdom of the Zohar*, Oxford, 1987.

38. *The Kabbalah Unveiled*, Mathers translation. See note 23.

39. Gershom Scholem, *Kabbalah*, 240.

40. Frances A. Yates, *Giordano Bruno and the Hermetic Tradition*, Chicago, 1964, 12.

41. Frances A. Yates, *Giordano Bruno*, 17.

42. Gershom Scholem, *Kabbalah*, 197.

43. Readers interested in Agrippa are referred to *Agrippa and the Crisis of Renaissance Thought*, by Charles G. Nauert, Jr., Illinois, 1965. This excellent doctoral dissertation has become a standard in its field.

44. Frances A. Yates, *The Occult Philosophy in the Elizabethan Age*, London, 1979, 21.

45. Frances A. Yates, *Giordano Bruno*, 400.

46. Frances A. Yates, *Giordano Bruno*, 402.

47. See "A Note on Dr. Dee and his Occult Researches," an appendix to the 1974 Portmeirion facsimile edition of Dee's *A True and Faithful Relation* of 1659; see also the introduction by Diane di Prima to *The Hieroglyphic Monad*, New York, 1975, an English translation of the Latin work issued in London in 1564. The preface to the original edition of *A True and Faithful Relation* was written by Meric Casaubon, whose father had studied the Hermetic fragments. The standard work on John Dee, a highly readable book, is *John Dee*, by Peter J. French, London, 1972.

48. Frances A. Yates, *The Rosicrucian Enlightenment*, London 1972, 50.

49. "The Fame and confession of the Fraternity of the Rosie Cross," translation by Thomas Vaughan (1652), *A Christian Rosencreutz Anthology*, edited by Paul Allen, New York, 1968, 163.

50. Rudolph Steiner, "The Chemical Wedding of Christian Rosencreutz," *Rosencreutz Anthology*, 19.

51. Frances A. Yates, *Rosicrucian Enlightenment*, 50.

52. Frances A. Yates, *Rosicrucian Enlightenment*, 77.

53. See note 12.

54. Paul Foster Case, *The Book of Tokens*, California, 1947, vii.

55. Israel Regardie, *Golden Dawn*, v.II, 216.

56. Westcott wrote on the Rosicrucians, but he was not much of a scholar. The best work comes from Waite: *The Brotherhood of the Rosy Cross*, New York, 1961.

57. *The Chaldean Oracles,* Edited and revised by Sapere Aude (Westcott's Order name), New Jersey, 1978, xiii.

58. See: E.R. Dodds, "New Light on the Chaldean Oracles," *Harvard Theological Review*, LIV, 1961, 263.

59. Refer to books cited in note 9.

60. Paul Case, *The Tree of Life*, Lesson 4, Figure 4 (no page no.). Page references to Case's study course are generally to the original versions, printed 5½ x 8½ and apparently now in the public domain. Today the BOTA distributes the courses in 8½ x 11, and has added copyright notices.

61. Aleister Crowley, *777*, London, 1955, xxvii.

62. Ben Shahn, *Love and Joy about Letters*, New York, 1963, 5.

63. This, and all comments on the Sephiroth printed in italics preceding the text in

this chapter are from the Golden Dawn "Knowledge Lectures," Regardie, "Concerning the Tree of Life," *The Golden Dawn*, v.I, 191-98.

64. P.D. Ouspensky, *Tertium Organum*, New York, 1927.

65. Dion Fortune, *The Mystical Qabalah,* London, 1951, 299. Dion Fortune was a member of the Order of the Golden Dawn, but broke with Mrs. Mathers to form her own group, The Society of the Inner Light. *The Mystical Qabalah* remains the standard against which all books on the Hermetic Qabalah are judged. The Society established by Fortune has, however, turned toward Christian Qabalism of a sort that Fortune would undoubtedly have disapproved.

66. Israel Regardie, *The Golden Dawn*, v.IV. All quotations preceding the Court Cards and the Minor cards are from "Book T". See note 19.

67. This Lamen is illustrated in full color in *The Secret Temple* by Robert Wang, New York, 1980.

68. "Book T", *Golden Dawn*, v.IV, 143.

69. Manly Palmer Hall, *An Encyclopedic Outline of Masonic, Hermetic, Qabbalistic and Rosicrucian Symbolical Philosophy*, California, 1957, LXXXV.

70. Waite says that his use of the Lion's head above the Caduceus of Hermes is a "variant of a sign which is found in a few old examples of this card." Arthur Edward Waite, Howe, New York, 1959, 222.

71. Manly Palmer Hall, *Encyclopedic Outline*, LIV.

72. Manly Palmer Hall, *Encyclopedic Outline*, LXXXIX. See also T.H. White, *The Bestiary*, New York, 1960, 125.

73. T.H. White, *The Bestiary*, 37-40.

74. Aleister Crowley, *The Book of Thoth*, New York, 1974, 196. This book was originally published as part of Crowley's magazine series, *The Equinox*, v.III, No. V.

75. Manly Palmer Hall, *Encyclopedic Outline*, CXXXII.

76. Manly Palmer Hall, *Encyclopedic Outline*, LXXXIX.

77. Aleister Crowley, *Book of Thoth*, 161.

78. This is an idea with which Regardie disagrees strongly. He views the concept of such "Masters" as having come from the Besant-Leadbeater School, and has stated that this idea "is the way of gross deception." Fortune, however, devotes considerable attention to the masters which she assigns to Chesed. *Mystical Qabalah*, 166-167.

79. Aleister Crowley, *Book of Thoth*, 213.

80. Aleister Crowley, *Book of Thoth*, 191.

81. *Matthew* 8:13.

82. Claudius Ptolemy, *The Centriloquy, or Hundred Aphorisms*, printed as an appendix to Ptolemy's *Tetrabiblos*, California, 1976, 153.

83. *Matthew* 8:13.

84. Aleister Crowley, *Book of Thoth,* 206.

85. Aleister Crowley, *Book of Thoth*, 215.

86. Aleister Crowley, *Book of Thoth*, 167.

87. Karl Baron Von Reichenbach, *Researches on Magnetism, Electricity, Heat, Light, Crystallization and Chemical Attraction in their relations to The Vital Force*, New York, 1974.

88. Aleister Crowley, *Book of Thoth*, 216.

89. Manly Palmer Hall, *Encyclopedic Outline*, LXXXVIII.

90. Manly Palmer Hall, *Encyclopedic Outline*, XXXII. The idea that seamen consider the Swan good luck is mentioned by T.H. White, *Bestiary*, 119.

91. N.G.L. Hammond and H.H. Scullard, Editors, *The Oxford Classical Dictionary*, Oxford, 1978, 472.

92. Quotations here are from the Westcott translation of the *Sepher Yetzirah*.

93. Gershom Scholem, *Kabbalah*, 23-26.

94. Gareth Knight, *Experience of the Inner Worlds*, 146-161.

95. Aleister Crowley, "The Temple of Solomon the King, *"Equinox*, v.I, No. V, 72. Our example is taken from Crowley's quotation from Westcott's *Introduction to the Study of the Qabalah*.

96. Fortune, *Mystical Qabalah*, 43ff.

97. Refer also, on each card to "Notes on the Tarot," by Mathers, *Golden Dawn*, v.I, 141-143 with the "unofficial" discussion of the Tarot Keys, v.IV. ("Book T"), 209. This article, entitled "The Tarot Trumps," is signed by "Q.L.," meaning "Quaero Lucem" the *Stella Matutina* name taken by Mrs. Felkin. She obviously lacked the profound understanding of the Tarot of either Mathers or Crowley, but these descriptions have some utility. They are, surprisingly, the only discussion of the Golden Dawn Trumps. Mathers confined his explanation to those few cards used in the early rituals.

98. This is reproduced opposite the title page to Scholem's *Kabbalah*.

99. The "Magical Images of the Sephiroth" are given in 777, Col. CXX, 25.

100. *Revelation* 4:3. The rainbow as a symbol of God's covenant with Noah appears in *Genesis* 9:17.

101. This is an obscure panel which in 1904 Crowley discovered in the Boulak Museum, an institution now closed, but the collection of which has been taken over by the Cairo Museum. The stele, representing Horus, was of special importance to Crowley, and related to his writing of the *Book of the Law*. This is described in *Confessions*, 395.

102. Aleister Crowley, *Book of Thoth*, 116.

103. Manly Palmer Hall, *Encyclopedic Outline*, CLXI facing.

104. Paul Case, *Thirty-Two Paths of Wisdom*, 16, 4.

105. Aleister Crowley, *Book of Thoth*, 113.

106. Aleister Crowley, *Book of Thoth*, 114. It is anyone's guess how he arrived at this date!

107. Israel Regardie, *Golden Dawn*, v.II, 110.

108. Aleister Crowley, *Book of Thoth*, 111-112.

109. E.A. Wallis Budge, *The Gods of the Egyptians*, v.II, 1969, 379-382. This work is important because it was the standard work on Egyptology at the time the three decks related to the Golden Dawn were produced. It has even been suggested that Budge may have been a member of the Golden Dawn, and had his own secret group within the walls of the British Museum, but this seems unlikely.

110. Israel Regardie, *Golden Dawn*, v.II, 130.

111. Aleister Crowley, *Book of Thoth*, 112.

112. E.A. Wallis Budge, *Gods of the Egyptians*, v.II, 379-382.

113. These manuscripts have never been published, and are in a private collection.

114. Paul Case, *Thirty-Two Paths of Wisdom*, Lesson 16, 1.

115. Manly Palmer Hall, *Encyclopedic Outline*, CXXXII.

116. Aleister Crowley, *Book of Thoth*, 112.

117. "Artemis," *Oxford Classical Dictionary*, 126-27; see also "Artemis," *Larousse*

Encyclopedia of Mythology, New York, 1960, 129-32.

118. E.A. Wallis Budge, *Gods of the Egyptians*, v.ii, 264.

119. This idea appears to have originated with the German poet, Conrad of Wurzburg, who observed that both the lobster and Christ were more beautiful after death. Reau, *L'Art Chrétien*, v.I, 88.

120. Paul Case, *Tarot Fundamentals*, 37.

121. Israel Regardie, *Golden Dawn*, v.II, 135.

122. Aleister Crowley, *Book of Thoth*, 110.

123. Aleister Crowley, *Book of Thoth*, 110.

124. *Zohar*, Nurho de Manhar translation, San Diego, 1978, 62. The Sperling and Simon translation of this passage reads: "Why is this first gate called 'the fear of the Lord'? Because it is the tree of good and evil. If a man deserves well it is good, and if he deserves ill it is evil. Hence in that place abides fear, which is the gateway to all that is good. 'Good' and 'understanding' are two gates which are as one.' R. Jose said: 'The term "A good understanding" alludes to the Tree of Life which is the knowledge of good without evil.'" *Zohar*, trans. Sperling and Simon, v.I.

125. Paul Case, *Thirty-Two Paths of Wisdom*, Lesson 15, 5.

126. Paul Case, *ibid*.

127. Aleister Crowley, *Book of Thoth*, 109.

128. These ideas are also related to the Midnight Sun which, to the Alchemists, represented the Light coming out of Darkness.

129. "Mars," *Oxford Classical Dictionary*, 651.

130. Aleister Crowley, *Book of Thoth*, 108.

131. Aleister Crowley, *Book of Thoth*, 109.

132. *Zohar*, Sperling and Simon, v.I, 97.

133. Aleister Crowley, *The Magical Diaries of Aleister Crowley*, edited by Stephan Skinner, New York, 1979, 37.

134. "Circumcision," *Dictionary of the Bible*, edited by James Hastings, New York, 1963, 163.

135. *Leviticus*, 19:23f.

136. *Genesis*, 7:11.

137. Paul Case, *An Introduction to Tarot*, Lesson 8, 5.

138. Lévi uses the term "Great Magical Agent" interchangeably with the term "Astral Light." *Transcendental Magic*, London, 1958, *passim*.

139. *Oxford Classical Dictionary*, 876.

140. Aleister Crowley, *Book of Thoth*, 105. Notes 273.

141. A work of particular interest is *The Sacred Fire: The Story of Sex in Religion* by B.Z. Goldberg, New York, 1958.

142. Gareth Knight, *A Practical Guide to Qabalistic Symbolism*, Toddington, 1965, v.II, 69.

143. Aleister Crowley, *777*, 40.

144. Hariette and Homer Curtis, *The Voice of Isis*, Washington, D.C., 1946, Introduction.

145. Paul Foster Case, *The Tarot*, New York, 1947, 147.

146. Aleister Crowley, *Book of Thoth*, 102-103.

147. Francis King, *Sexuality, Magic and Perversion*, New Jersey, 1972, 98. Some

Members of the O.T.O. disclaim King's work, particularly his *Secret Rituals of the O.T.O.*, New York, 1973. It is said that he never had access to official O.T.O. documents, and that there are errors in these books. On the other hand, King is a very persuasive and competent scholar, whose work is not lightly dismissed. Pursuant to the claims of efficacy for these sexual techniques, Regardie privately expressed the opinion that Crowley never made much money in this way.

148. Paul Case, *Tarot Fundamentals*, 30.7.
149. Aleister Crowley, *Book of Thoth*, 100, note 1.
150. C.G. Jung, *Psychology and Alchemy*, New Jersey, 1977.
151. Gareth Knight, *A History of White Magic*, London, 1978, 3-4.
152. Walter Lowrie, *Art in the Early Church*, New York, 1947, 74.
153. Saint John of the Cross, *Dark Night of the Soul*, 119.
154. Refer to note 9.
155. This is mentioned by Cavandish in *The Tarot*, 106.
156. Arthur Edward Waite, *Pictorial Key to the Tarot*, 116.
157. C.G. Jung, *Archetypes and the Collective Unconscious*, New Jersey, 1977, 21.
158. Saint John of the Cross, *Dark Night of the Soul*, 34.
159. Jung, *Archetypes*, 22.
160. Aleister Crowley, *Confessions*, 452.
161. Aleister Crowley, *Confessions*, 452.
162. Aleister Crowley, *Confessions*, 840.
163. Aleister Crowley, *Confessions*, 249.
164. *Larousse Encyclopedia of Mythology*, 261.
165. James G. Frazer, *The Golden Bough*, New York, 1958, 413.
166. *Larousse Encyclopedia of Mythology*, 141-43; *Oxford Classical Dictionary*, v.IV, 260ff.
167. The Enochian Tablets are described at length in Regardie's *Golden Dawn*, v.IV, 260ff.
168. Aleister Crowley, *Book of Thoth*, 98.
169. Gareth Knight, *A Practical Guide to Qabalistic Symbolism*, v.II, 116.
170. In the exercise of the Middle Pillar, they are visualized at the right and left shoulders.
171. Paul Case, *Introduction to Tarot*, Lesson 6,6; *Tarot Fundamentals*, Lesson 25, 1ff.
172. E.A. Wallis Budge, *Gods of the Egyptians*, v.I, 417.
173. Aleister Crowley, *777*, 40.
174. Aleister Crowley, *Book of Thoth*, 87.
175. Eliphas Lévi, *The Magical Ritual of the Sanctum Regnum*, translated and edited by W. Wynn Westcott, New York, 1973, illustration facing page 40.
176. Eliphas Lévi, *Magical Ritual of the Sanctum Regnum*, 39-40.
177. "Sphinx," *Oxford Classical Dictionary*, 1009.
178. Unpublished Enochian papers of the Hermetic Order of the Golden Dawn. Here, again, it is necessary to distinguish the historical reality from that which is entirely valid symbolism. Mathers seems to have invented more than one of the "Egyptian Mysteries," though he has done so using sound metaphysical principles.
179. This idea is also expressed in the Enochian papers.
180. *Ezekiel*, 1:4-28.

181. The Middle Ages defined the reasons for the attribution of the animals: Matthew is the *Man* (symbol of Air in the Qabalah) because he wrote about the most human qualities of Christ; Mark is the *Bull* (symbol of Earth) because he wrote about Christ as a beast of burden, carrying the weight of mankind; Luke is the *Lion* (symbol of Fire) because he described the passionate side of Christ and John is the *Eagle* (symbol of Water) because he wrote of Christ in a mystical way, soaring above all heads.

182. Goffredo Rosati, "Symbolism and Allegory," *Encyclopedia of World Art*, New York 1959-68, 815-16.

183. E.A. Wallis Budge, *Gods of the Egyptians*, v.I, 20-21.

184. *John*, 1:1.

185. E.A. Wallis Budge, *Gods of the Egyptians*, v.II, 295.

186. "Typhon, Typhoeus, *Oxford Classical Dictionary*, 1101; *Larousse Encyclopedia of Mythology*, 166, 195; E.A. Wallis Budge, *Gods of the Egyptians*, v.II, 246.

187. Aleister Crowley, *Book of Thoth*, 91.

188. "The Myth of the Going-Forth" as seen by Gnosticism, is discussed by G.R.S. Mead, *Fragments of a Faith Forgotten*, New York, 1960, 186-87.

189. Aleister Crowley, *Book of Thoth*, 89.

190. Paul Case, *Book of Tokens*, 83.

191. *Zohar*, Nuhro de Manhar translation, 303. This passage is not found in the Sperling and Simon translation.

192. St. Jerome was one of the "Fathers of the Church," and the translator of the *Vulgate,* Latin version of the Old and New Testaments. Because of the lion legend, the cat became known as the traditional pet of the scholar. See Réau, *L'Art Chrétien*, v.III, 740-50, also Jameson, *Sacred and Legendary Art*, London 1891, v.I, 285-300.

193. Paul Case, *Book of Tokens*, 91-92.

194. Note 9.

195. Paul Case, *Tarot Fundamentals*, 20.8.

196. *Revelation*, 4.5.

197. Aleister Crowley, *Equinox*, v.I, No. 5, 89.

198. Arthur Edward Waite, *Pictorial Key to the Tarot to the Tarot*, 96.

199. *Ezekiel*, 1ff.

200. Carl Jung made some extremely interesting observations on the vision of Ezekiel and the Chariot, particularly as related to Egyptian thought, in his essay "The Tetrasomia," *Alchemical Studies,* New Jersey, 1976, 278-83.

201. Gershom Scholem, *Major Trends*, 44.

202. Gershom Scholem, *Major Trends*, 46-47.

203. Eliphas Lévi, *Ritual of Transcendental Magic*, 338.

204. Paul Case, *Book of Tokens*, 83.

205. Paul Case, *Book of Tokens*, 87.

206. Aleister Crowley, *Book of Thoth*, 84-85.

207. The fact that this is the only reference to Teutonic mythology in the deck makes the attribution somewhat problematical. What we are calling "Odin" may, in fact represent an error resulting from the cards having been hand-copied over a period of years. Perhaps this figure had a moon helmet of some sort. Nevertheless, the helmet shown in the Golden Dawn deck, as published, is precisely as it appears in Regardie's hand-painted deck.

208. Paul Case, *Tarot Interpretation*, 7.
209. Robert Graves, *The Greek Myths*, New York, 1957, 156: "The Sun's subordination to the Moon, until Apollo usurped Helios' place and made an intellectual deity of him, is a remarkable feature of early Greek myth."
210. Paul Case, *Thirty-Two Paths of Wisdom*, Lesson 10, 1.
211. Paul Case, *Thirty-Two Paths of Wisdom*, Lesson 10, 2.
212. Arthur Edward Waite, *Pictorial Key to the Tarot*, 92.
213. "Andromeda," *Oxford Classical Dictionary*, 63-64.
214. C.A. Burland, *The Arts of the Alchemists*, New York, 1967.
215. Aleister Crowley, *Book of Thoth*, 84.
216. The Vision and the Voice," subtitled "The Cry of the Second Aether which is called ARN" *Equinox*, v.I, No. 5, supplement, 148. This supplement was published as a separate book, *The Vision and the Voice*, Dallas, 1972, with extensive notes by Crowley as well as introductory comments by Israel Regardie.
217. "Vision and the Voice," *Equinox*, 149.
218. Aleister Crowley, *The Vision and the Voice*, note 3, 225.
219. Aleister Crowley, *Book of Thoth*, 80.
220. See: Allen, ed., *Christian Rosencreutz Anthology*; Frances A. Yates, *Rosicrucian Enlightenment*.
221. Arthur Edward Waite, *Pictorial Key to the Tarot*, 88.
222. Paul Case, *The Tarot*, 79.
223. Arthur Edward Waite, *Pictorial Key to the Tarot*, 91.
224. Arthur A. Tilley, "The Renaissance in Europe," *Cambridge Medieval History*, Cambridge, 1969, 790, 791.
225. Henry Cornelius Agrippa, *The Philosophy of Natural Magic*, New Jersey, 1974, 33.
226. See forward to work cited above by Leslie Shepherd.
227. Rudolph Koch, *The Book of Signs*, London 1930, 16.276
228. Aleister Crowley, *Book of Thoth*, 79-80.
229. Paul Case, *Book of Tokens*, 67.
230. Aleister Crowley, *Book of Thoth*, 79.
231. Cavendish, *The Tarot*, 85.
232. Elaine Pagels, *The Gnostic Gospels*, New York, 1979.
233. G.R.S. Mead, *Fragments of a Faith Forgotten*, New York, 1960, 307. Mead was one of the modern pioneers in the study of Gnosticism and while his work has been largely superseded by scholars such as Pagels, his insights remain instructive.
234. Forward to work cited above, by Kenneth Rexroth, xviii.
235. Paul Case, *Tarot Fundamentals*, Lesson 11, 2-3.
236. Jung, *Archetypes, passim*.
237. In his text, *The Emperor* remains on the fifteenth Path, but is assigned the letter Tzaddi. *The Star* remains on the twenty-eighth Path, but is Heh. Yet on his Tree of Life diagram, *Thoth Tarot*, 268, called "The Tarot-General Attribution," *The Star* is actually shown on the fifteenth Path, and *The Emperor* on the twenty-eighth. It will also be seen that in *777*, Columns II and XIV, Crowley uses the standard attributions. One might suggest that Crowley decided late in life that these cards should be transposed, but

remained uncertain about the Path placement. The curious discrepancy between the position of the cards in the text of the *Thoth Tarot,* and on the Tree of Life, suggests that he was at least considering switching the cards as well as the Hebrew letters. The original art of the cards shows *The Emperor* as IV and Tzaddi, and *The Star* as XVII and Heh.

238. Aleister Crowley, *Book of Thoth*, 78.
239. Aleister Crowley, *Book of Thoth*, 77.
240. Frazer, *Golden Bough*, 403.
241. *Larousse Encyclopedia of Mythology*, 214.
242. Graves, *Greek Myths*, 49.
243. Aleister Crowley, *Book of Thoth*, 77.
244. Graves, *Greek Myths*, 49.
245. Aleister Crowley, *Book of Thoth*, 75.
246. Israel Regardie, *Golden Dawn*, v.I, 153.
247. Gareth Knight, *A Practical Guide to Qabalistic Symbolism*, v.II, 145-50.
248. The camel can go long distances without water. This may be taken at one level, to mean a long experience without the reward of contact with the intelligence for which we search on this Path.
249. Aleister Crowley, *Book of Thoth*, 73.
250. Paul Case, *Book of Tokens*, 37.
251. Graves, *Greek Myths*, 124, 348. See also "Hecate," *Oxford Classical Dictionary*, 490, which discusses the confusions surrounding Selene, and points out that no cult of the Moon existed in ancient Greece.
252. Graves, *Greek Myths*, 85.
253. Graves, *ibid.*
254. C.G. Jung, *Symbols of Transformation,* New Jersey, 1976, 323. Notes 277
255. Aleister Crowley, *Book of Thoth,* 74. The A.A., meaning "Astrum Argentum,"or "Silver Star," was the Order founded by Crowley, in 1907, on essentially Golden Dawn principles. In 1909 he began to publish *The Equinox* as the official organ of the A.A. Crowley had apparently joined the O.T.O ("Ordo Templi Orientis") in 1905. This latter, intended as a continuation of the Knights Templar, was founded in 1904. The story of both organizations, and of the Golden Dawn and other such fraternities, is told by Francis King in *The Rites of Modern Occult Magic*, New York, 1971.
256. Paul Case, *Tarot Fundamentals*, Lesson 8, 10-11.
257. Arthur Edward Waite, *Pictorial Key to the Tarot*, 76.
258. Paul Case, *The Tarot*, 52.
259. Arthur Edward Waite, *Pictorial Key to the Tarot*, 76.
260. Manley Palmer Hall, *Encyclopedic Outline, XCV.*
261. Cavendish, *The Tarot*, 71.
262. Waite comments on this card in his *Shadows of Life and Thought,* 188-89: "It is to be noted that though Venetian, Florentine and French packs differ somewhat clearly, of course between narrow limits, Pope Joan has never been termed the Abbess in any, nor can I recall her being so depicted that such a denomination could apply and thus include the design among ecclesiastical estates in Christendom. She comes therefore, as I have intimated, from another region and another order of things...Pope Joan represents not improbably a vestige of the Astarte cultus. I do not pretend to be satisfied with

the explanation...only one point emerges in all certainty: whatever the card may have stood for originally, it was not the mythical Female Pope, an ascription which arose as a leap in the dark of ignorance on the part of people—whether in France or Italy—who knew the Pope Joan Legend but had never heard of Astarte and much less of Isis."

263. Fabre d'Olivet, *The Hebraic Tongue Restored,* part II, 25. His original translation reads: "Premièrement, en principe." D'Olivet is one of those who claimed that there was an early and "pure" form of the Hebrew language which was spoken by the Egyptians and upon which the Greek alphabet was based. The Hebrew spoken by Jews was, supposedly, only a perverted form of this "divine language."

264. *Zohar,* Simon and Sperling trans., v. I, 9.

265. *Zohar*, Simon and Sperling trans., v. I, 12.

266. *Zohar*, Simon and Sperling trans., v. I, 13.

267. "Hermes," *Oxford Classical Dictionary,* 502-3.

268. Israel Regardie, *Golden Dawn, v.* I, 138.

269. Paul Case, *Book of Tokens*, 23-24.

270. See: Robert Wang, *Secret Temple, passim.*

271. Peter de Albano, *Heptameron.* This treatise is section III of *Fourth Book of Occult Philosophy,* by Henry Cornelius Agrippa, London 1978, 73ff.

272. Francis Barrett, *The Magus,* London 1801. The 1967 reprint of this work contains an admirable introduction by Timothy d'Arch Smith.

273. Graves, *Greek Myths,* 66.

274. *Exhibition of Occult and Alchemical Designs for the Cards of the Tarot of the Egyptians,* undated, but probably 1944.

275. Aleister Crowley, *Book of Thoth, 72.*

276. Aleister Crowley, *Book of Thoth, 70.*

277. Gareth Knight, *A Practical Guide to Qabalistic Symbolism,* v.II, 204.

278. Paul Case, *The Tarot,* 29.

279. Aleister Crowley, *Book of Thoth,* 53.

280. *Zohar,* Simon and Sperling trans., v. I, 11.

281. Paul Case, *Thirty-Two Paths of Wisdom,* Lesson 7, 1.

282. E.A. Wallis Budge, *The Gods of the Egyptians*, v.I, 469.

283. E.A. Wallis Budge, *The Gods of the Egyptians*, v.I, 78, 145.

284. Goblet D'Alviella, *The Migration of Symbols*, Wellingborough, 1979. Some may find Carl Jung's work antiseptic and dispassionate, yet the inner process of encountering these archetypes was overwhelming as Jung explains in personal terms, in his autobiographical *Memories, Dreams, Reflections*, New York 1973.

285. Manley Palmer Hall, Encyclopedia Outline, XCII.

286. Aleister Crowley, *Book of Thoth*, 69.

287. Manley Palmer Hall, XCII.

288. Arthur Edward Waite, *Pictorial Key to the Tarot*, 153.

289. Paul Case, *The Tarot,* 29ff.

290. Aleister Crowley, *Book of Thoth*, 53-68.

291. Israel Regardie, *Golden Dawn, I*, 106.

292. These meanings are extracted from several sections of Regardie's *Golden Dawn.* The language is that of MacGregor Mathers.

PRACTICAL WORK AND REFERENCES

"Skrying" With The Cards

Skrying, meaning the projection of oneself into an inner vision, is actually very simple. It involves nothing more than sitting quietly in front of a Tarot card (or other stimulus), closing one's eyes and stepping into that card in imagination. The essential principle is that we create "day dreams," allowing our minds to flow within the given structure of a Tarot card. Soon most students discover that what they experience could not possibly be of their own making. At very least, most are astonished by the vitality and spontaneity of the images which the Tarot cards evoke.

If we make no attempt to directly encounter these images and energies, the whole system of Qabalah and Tarot is utterly useless. It is, as Lewis Carroll's Alice said, "only a pack of cards." Qabalah, Christianity, Hinduism, Buddhism, etc., all reduce to trivia if not applied. This means self-exploration in meditative exercises with the cards, or whatever system we may choose. There is no other way.

A great many people are apprehensive about such exercises. They fear the unknown. But work with the Tarot is quite safe for the well balanced personality. The truth is that meditative exercises are a great deal of work, and may quickly become boring! There is little for most to fear, because we have all sorts of protective mechanisms built into our systems. On the other hand, the person who approaches these materials with a desire to escape from an unpleasant earthly environment runs the risk of disassociation. This means that the fantasy life intrudes on the normal waking consciousness, and it becomes difficult to separate one from the other. It is an illusive feeling of "floating," of being unable to relate to solid things ordinary to our sensory condition. But, again, we are filled with self-protective mechanisms. The person for whom such exercises are not right will quickly give them up, either because they prove dull, or because they prove uncomfortable. Thus, the student should boldly attempt skrying; there is everything to gain. Our own Higher Selves will protect us more than we understand. This is the principle of *The Hanged Man*, that we are not the pursuer, but the pursued. We are also not the protector, but the protected, and a great deal of what we do must be predicated on this article of faith.

The following books are highly recommended for those who wish to understand the skrying process:

The Golden Dawn by Israel Regardie. Attention should be devoted to the Lesser Banishing Ritual[291] and to the sections on Tattva and skrying. These are the historically-important documents of the Nineteenth Century Hermetic Order of the Golden Dawn upon which many occult fellowships today base their practices.
The Inner Guide Meditation by Edward C. Steinbrecher. This book applies Carl Jung's insights on "active imagination" to Path-working. It is an extremely valuable work, though somewhat marred by the author's egocentricity.
Books by Gareth Knight. This distinguished teacher of philosophical and meditative techniques is one of ths most prolific writers of our time. His many books are both readable and reliable, and offer insights into traditional (and safe) techniques of Path working.

Divination

It may come as a surprise to some to learn that the primary reason for divination in the Great Work is not to learn the future. Rather, it is for the development of psychic faculties. The more one uses the Tarot cards to find answers to given questions, the more that person taps into unseen currents. Those who have used the Tarot cards for years will attest to the fact that there comes a point where the cards are not longer necessary to an accurate divination. Answers to specific problems are simply "felt."

Most people tend to consider psychism a natural talent, something with which one is born, and that is true. It is, however, possible to consciously develop psychic abilities. To this end, it is necessary to test these growing abilities fearlessly, by expressing feelings about situations and being willing to be completely wrong! Yet the student of Tarot will find that his "guesses" are increasingly correct, as his friends' responses will corroborate.

Some may find that they develop a psychism which is particularly state-dependent, i.e., they may be more sensitive when using alcohol or other drugs. There are many different methods for using the Tarot cards as divinatory devices, the most complex being that of the Golden Dawn (called by some the "all day method"), as described in Regardie's monumental *Golden Dawn* and in *An Introduction to the Golden Dawn Tarot* by the author of this present book. But one of the best methods is also the simplest, the Fifteen Card

Spread. This method is not so well known as the "Ancient Celtic," ten-card spread, but it has the advantage of depending upon neighboring cards, offering an enormous number of possible card combinations, and being more fluid than other methods.

Before any divination it is wise to invoke some Higher Force. In its simplest form, this may involve visualizing a sphere of brilliant white light over one's head, and a prayer that the Divine Powers may guide the operation of the cards.

Following this invocation, the cards should be thoroughly shuffled. This is the most important step in a divination, and should be done with the mind as clear as possible. All extraneous thoughts should be eliminated, and the mind made completely passive. In the event that the divination is for a person not present, it maybe helpful to visualize the person as the shuffling is taking place.

The cards will then be placed on a table in the following order:

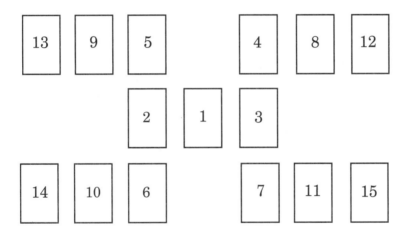

Interpretation

Card One: This represents the Querant, the problems surrounding him, his present situation and primary influences. A Court Card (King, Queen, Prince or Princess) in this position may mean either the Querant or some dominant individual (see general Court Card descriptions in the following section).

Cards Two and Three: These, in conjunction with card One, are the key cards in the spread. They give extended information on the situation and personality of the Querant.

Cards Four, Eight and Twelve (Upper right): These show the direction that the Querant's life will naturally follow, unless some action is taken to change this course.

Cards Thirteen, Nine and Five (Upper left): These are the possibilities for alternative action, which may be desirable or undesirable, depending on the cards in the spread.

Cards Fourteen, Ten and Six (Lower left): These cards will assist the querant in making whatever decision may be necessary. In the case of an older person, one past middle age, they mean past activities which bear on the question. In younger persons they indicate the future.

Cards Seven, Eleven, and Fifteen (Lower right): These show forces operating beyond the control of the Querant, which cannot be changed, but to which one can adapt.

Additional Considerations

The Princes and Queens, when they appear in a reading, almost invariably represent actual men and women connected with the subject at hand. But the Kings sometimes represent either the coming on or going off of a matter: arrival or departure, according to the way in which the cards face. The Princesses may show opinions, thoughts or ideas, either in harmony with or opposed to the subject.

A Majority of Wands: Energy, quarrelling, opposition.

A Majority of Cups: Pleasure and merriment.

A Majority of Swords: Trouble and sadness, sometimes sickness, even death.

A Majority of Pentacles: Business, money, possessions, etc.

A Majority of Trumps: Forces of considerable strength, often Karmic forces beyond the enquirer's controls.

A Majority of Court Cards: Society, meeting with many persons.

A Majority of Aces: Strength, generally, as the Aces are always strong cards.

Outline of Divinatory Meanings

(As taught by the Hermetic Order of the Golden Dawn[292])

THE FOOL. Idea, thought, spirituality, that which endeavors to rise above the material (That is, if the subject which is enquired about be spiritual). If the Divination be regarding a material event of ordinary life, this card is not good, and shows folly, stupidity, eccentricity and even mania, unless with very good cards indeed. It is too ideal and unstable to be generally good in material things.

THE MAGICIAN. Skill, wisdom, adaptation. Craft, cunning, etc., always depending on neighboring cards. Sometimes occult wisdom.

THE HIGH PRIESTESS. Change, alteration, increase and decrease. Fluctuation (whether for good or evil is shown by cards connected with it). Compare with DEATH and THE MOON.

THE EMPRESS. Beauty, happiness, pleasure, success, also luxury and sometimes dissipation, but only if with very evil cards.

THE EMPEROR. War, conquest, victory, strife, ambition.

THE HIEROPHANT. Divine Wisdom. Manifestation. Explanation. Teaching. Differing from, though resembling in some respects, the meanings of THE MAGICIAN, THE HERMIT and THE LOVERS. Occult wisdom.

THE LOVERS. Inspiration (passive and in some cases mediumistic, thus differing from that of THE HIEROPHANT, THE MAGICIAN and THE HERMIT). Motive power, and action, arising from Inspiration and Impulse. THE CHARIOT. Triumph, Victory, Health. Success, though sometimes not stable or enduring. STRENGTH. Courage, Strength, Fortitude. Power not arrested in the act of Judgment, but passing on to further action. Sometimes obstinacy. Compare with JUSTICE.

THE HERMIT. Wisdom sought for and obtained from above. Divine Inspiration (but active, as opposed to that of THE LOVERS. In the mystical titles, this with THE HIEROPHANT and THE MAGICIAN are the three Magi.

WHEEL OF FORTUNE. Good fortune and happiness (within bounds), but sometimes also a species of intoxication with success, if the neighboring cards bear this out.

JUSTICE. Eternal Justice and Balance. Strength and Force, but arrested as in the act of Judgment. Compare with STRENGTH. Also, in combination with other cards, legal proceedings, a court of law, a trial at law, etc.

THE HANGED MAN. Enforced sacrificed. Punishment. Loss. Fatal and not voluntary. Suffering generally.

DEATH. Time. Age, Transformation. Sometimes death destruction, but rarely the latter, and only if it is borne out by the cards with it. Compare also with also with THE HIGH PRIESTESS.

TEMPERANCE. Combination of Forces. Realization. Action (material). Effect either for good or evil.

THE DEVIL. Materiality. Material Force. Material temptation; sometimes obsession, especially if associated with THE LOVERS.

THE TOWER. Ambition, fighting, war, ourage.Compare with THE EMPEROR. In certain combinations, destruction danger, ruin, fall.

THE STAR. Hope, faith, unexpected help. But sometimes also, dreaminess, deceived hope, etc.

THE MOON. Dissatisfaction, voluntary change (as opposed to DEATH). Error, lying, falsity, deception (The whole according to whether the card is well or ill-dignified, on which it much depends).

THE SUN. Glory, Gain, Riches. Sometimes also arrogance. Display. Vanity, but only when with very evil cards.

JUDGMENT. Final decision. Judgment. Sentence. Determination of a matter. without appeal on its plane.

THE UNIVERSE. The matter itself, Synthesis. World. Kingdom. Usually denotes the actual subject of the question, and therefore depends entirely on the accompanying cards.

ACE OF WANDS. Force, strength, rush, vigor, energy. It governs according to its natural various works and questions. It implies natural as opposed to Invoked Force.

TWO OF WANDS. Influence over another. Dominion. Boldness, courage, fierceness, shamelessness, revenge, resolution, generous, proud, sensitive, ambitious, refined, restless, turbulent, sagacious withal, yet unforgiving and obstinate according to dignity.

THREE OF WANDS. Pride and Arrogance. Power sometimes. Established force strength. Realization of hope. Completion of labor, success of the struggle. Pride, nobility, wealth, power, conceit.

FOUR OF WANDS. Settlement. Arrangement completed. Perfected work. A completion of a thing built up with trouble and labor. Rest after labor. Subtlety, cleverness, mirth, beauty, success in completion. Reasoning faculty, conclusions drawn from previous knowledge. Unreadiness, unreliable and unsteady, through over anxiety and hurriedness of action. Graceful in manner. At times insincere.

FIVE OF WANDS. Strife. Quarrelling. Fighting. Violent strife and contest, boldness and rashness, cruelty, violence, lust and desire, prodigality and generosity, depending on whether well or ill-dignified.

SIX OF WANDS. Gain and Success. Victory after strife, success through energy and industry, love, pleasure gained by labor, carefulness, sociability and avoidance of strife, yet victory therein. Also insolence, pride of riches and success, etc. The whole depending on dignity.

SEVEN OF WANDS. Opposition, sometimes courage therewith. Possible victory, depending on the energy and courage exercised; valour, opposition, obstacles, difficulties, yet courage to meet them, quarrelling, ignorance, pretence, wrangling and threatening, also victory in small and unimportant things, and influence over subordinate. Depending on dignity as usual.

EIGHT OF WANDS. Swiftness. A hasty communication. Letter, message. Too much force applied too suddenly. Very rapid rush, but too quickly passed and expended. Violent but not lasting. Swiftness. Rapidity. Courage, boldness, confidence, freedom, warfare. Violence, love of open air, field sports, gardens, meadows. Generous, subtle, eloquent, yet somewhat untrustworthy. Rapacious, insolent oppressive. Theft and robbery, according to dignity.

NINE OF WANDS. Great strength. Power. Health. Recovery from sickness. Tremendous and steady force that cannot be shaken. Herculean strength, yet sometimes scientifically applied. Great success, but with strife and energy. Victory preceded by apprehension and fear. Health good, and recovery, yet doubt. Generous, questioning and curious, fond of external appearances, intractable, obstinate.

TEN OF WANDS. Cruelty and malice towards others. Oppression. Overbearing strength. Revenge. Injustice. Cruel and overbearing force and energy, but applied only to selfish and material ends. Sometimes shows failure in a matter, and the opposition too strong to be controlled arising from the person's too great selfishness at the beginning. Ill-will, levity, lying, malice, slander, envy, obstinacy, swiftness in evil, if ill-dignified. Also generosity, self-sacrifice, and disinterestedness when well-dignified

PRINCESS OF WANDS. A young woman with gold or red hair and blue eyes. Brilliance, courage, beauty, force, sudden in anger or love, desire of power, enthusiasm, revenge. Ill-dignified, superficial, theatrical, cruel, unstable, domineering.

PRINCE OF WANDS. A young man with yellow hair and blue or grey eyes. Swift, strong, hasty, rather violent, yet just and generous, noble and scorning meanness. If ill-dignified, cruel, intolerant, prejudiced and ill-natured.

QUEEN OF WANDS. A woman with red or gold hair, blue or brown eyes. She is steady and resolute, with great power to attract. Kind and generous when not opposed. When ill-dignified, she is obstinate, revengeful, domineering, tyrannical and apt to turn suddenly against another without a cause.

KING OF WANDS. A blond or red-haired man with blue or hazel eyes. Active, generous, fierce, sudden and impetuous. If ill-dignified he is evil-minded, cruel, bigoted, brutal.

ACE OF CUPS. Fertility, productiveness. Beauty. Pleasure. Happiness.

TWO OF CUPS. Love. Marriage. Pleasure, Warm friendship. Harmony of masculine and feminine united. Harmony, pleasure, mirth, subtlety, sometimes folly, dissipation, waste and silly action, according to dignity.

THREE OF CUPS. Plenty. Hospitality, eating, drinking. Pleasure, dancing, new clothes and merriment. Abundance, plenty, success, pleasure, sensuality, passive success, good luck and fortune. Love, gladness, kindness and bounty. According to dignity.

FOUR OF CUPS. Receiving pleasure, but some slight discomfort and anxieties therewith. Blended pleasure and success. Success and pleasure, approaching their end. A stationary period in happiness which may or may not continue. It does not show marriage and love so much as the previous symbol. It is too passive a symbol to represent perfectly complete happiness. Acquisition and contention; injustice sometimes. Some drawbacks to pleasure implied.

FIVE OF CUPS. Disappointments in love, marriage broken off, unkindness from friends (whether deserved or not is shown by the cards with it). Loss of friendship. Death or end of pleasures. Disappointment. Sorrow and loss in those things from which pleasure is expected. Sadness. Deceit, treachery, ill-will, detraction, charity and kindness ill-requited. All kinds of troubles from unexpected and unsuspected sources.

SIX OF CUPS. Beginning of wish, happiness, success, enjoyment. Commencement of steady increase, gain and pleasure, but commencement only. Also affront, defective knowledge, and in some instances, contention and strife arising from unwarranted self-assertion and vanity. Some-times thankless and presumptuous. Sometimes amiable and patient, according to dignity.

SEVEN OF CUPS. Lying, deceit, promises unfulfilled, illusion, deception. Error, slight success, but not enough energy to retain it. Possible victory, but neutralized by the supineness of the person. Illusionary success. Deception in the moment of apparent victory. Lying error, promises unfulfilled. Drunkenness, wrath, vanity, lust, fornication, violence against women. Selfish dissipation. Deception in love and friendship. Often success gained, but not followed up. Modified by dignity.

EIGHT OF CUPS. Success abandoned. Decline of interest in anything. Temporary success, but without further result. Things thrown aside as soon as gained. No lasting even in the matter at hand. Indolence in success. Journeying from place to place. Misery and repining without cause. Seeking after riches. Instability according to dignity.

NINE OF CUPS. Complete success. Pleasure and happiness. Wishes fulfilled. Complete and perfect realization of pleasure and happiness almost perfect. Self-praise, vanity, conceit, much talking of self, yet kind and lovable, and may be self-denying therewith. High minded, not easily satisfied with small and limited ideas. Apt to be maligned through too much self-assumption. A good, generous, but maybe foolish nature.

TEN OF CUPS. Matters definitely arranged and settled as wished. Permanent and lasting success, happiness because inspired from above. Not sensual as Nine of Cups, "The Lord of Material Happiness," yet almost more truly happy. Pleasure, dissipation, debauchery. Pity, quietness, peace-making. Kindness, generosity, wantonness, waste, etc., according to dignity.

PRINCESS OF CUPS. A young woman with brown hair and blue or brown eyes. Sweetness, poetry, gentleness and kindness. Imagination, dreamy, at times indolent, yet courageous if roused. Ill-dignified she is selfish and luxurious.

PRINCE OF CUPS. A young man with brown hair, grey or brown eyes. He is subtle, violent, crafty and artistic. A fierce nature with a calm exterior. Powerful for good or evil, but more attracted by the evil, if allied with apparent Power or Wisdom. If ill-dignified, he is intensely evil and merciless

QUEEN OF CUPS. A woman with gold-brown hair and blue eyes. She is imaginative, poetic, kind, yet not willing to take much trouble for another. Coquettish, good-natured, underneath a dreamy appearance. Imagination stronger than feeling. Very much affected by other influences, and therefore more dependent upon good or ill-dignify than most other symbols.

KING OF CUPS. A man with fair hair and blue eyes. Graceful, poetic, Venusian, indolent, but enthusiastic if roused. Ill-dignified he is sensual, idle, and untruthful.

ACE OF SWORDS. Invoked as contrasted with natural Force; for it is the invocation of the Sword. Raised upward, it invokes the Divine Crown of Spiritual Brightness. But reversed it is the invocation of demoniac force, and becomes a fearfully evil symbol. It represents therefore very great power for good or evil, but invoked. Also it represents whirling force and strength through trouble. It is the affirmation of justice, upholding Divine authority; it may become the Sword of Wrath, Punishment and affliction.

TWO OF SWORDS. Quarrel made up and arranged. Peace restored, yet some tension in relationships. Action sometimes selfish and sometimes unselfish. Contradictory characteristics in the same nature. Strength through suffering. Pleasure after pain. Sacrifice and trouble, yet strength arising therefrom. Peace restored, truth, arrangement of differences. Justice, Truth and untruth. Sorrow and sympathy for those in trouble, aid to the weak and oppressed, unselfishness. Also an inclination to repetition of affronts if once pardoned, of asking questions of little moment, want of tact, often doing injury when meaning well. Talkative.

THREE OF SWORDS. Unhappiness, sorrow, tears. Disruption, interruption, separation, quarrelling, sowing of discord and strife, mischief-making, sorrow, tears, yet mirth in evil pleasures, singing, faithfulness in promises, honesty in money transactions, selfish and dissipated, yet sometimes generous, deceitful in words and repetition. The whole thing according to dignity.

FOUR OF SWORDS. Convalescence, recovery from sickness, change for the better. Rest from sorrow, yet after and through it. Peace from and after War. Relaxation of anxiety. Quietness, rest, ease and plenty, yet after struggle. Goods of this life abundance. Modified by the dignity as in the other cases.

FIVE OF SWORDS. Defeat, loss, malice, spite, slander, evil-speaking. Contest finished, and decided against the person, failure, defeat, anxiety, trouble, poverty, avarice, grieving after pain, laborious, unresting, loss and vileness of nature. Malicious, slandering, lying, spiteful and tale bearing. A busy-body and separator of friends, hating to see peace and love between others. Cruel yet cowardly, thankless and unreliable. Clever and quick in thought and speech. Feelings of pity easily roused but unendurable. As dignity.

SIX OF SWORDS. Labor, work. Journey, probably over water. Success after anxiety and trouble. Selfishness, beauty, conceit, but sometimes modesty therewith. Dominion, patience, labor, etc., according to dignity.

SEVEN OF SWORDS. In character untrustworthy, vacillation. Unstable effort. Journey, probably over land. Partial success, yielding when victory is within grasp, as if the last reserves of strength were used up. Inclination to lose when on the point of gaining through not continuing the effort. Love of abundance, fascinated by display, given to compliment, affronts and insolences, and to detect and spy on another. Inclined to betray confidences, not always intentional. Rather vacillating and unreliable, according to dignity as usual.

EIGHT OF SWORDS: Narrow or restricted. Shortened Force. Petty. A Prison. Too much force applied to small things, too much attention to detail, at expense of principal and more important points. Ill-dignified, these qualities produce malice, pettiness, and domineering qualities. Patience in detail of study, great ease in some things, counterbalanced by equal disorder in others. Impulse, equally fond of giving or receiving money, or presents. Generous, clever, acute, selfish, and without strong feeling of affection. Admires wisdom, yet applies it to small and unworthy objects.

NINE OF SWORDS. Illness. Suffering, Malice. Cruelty, Pain. Despair. cruelty, pitilessness, malice, suffering, want, loss, misery. Burden, oppression, labor, subtlety and craft, lying, dishonesty, etc., according to dignity.

TEN OF SWORDS. Ruin. Death. Failure. Disaster. (Almost a worse symbol than the Nine of Swords). Undisciplined warring force, complete disruption and failure. Ruin of all plans and projects. Disdain, insolence and impertinence, yet mirth and jolly therewith. Loving to overthrow the happiness of others, a repeater of things, given to much unprofitable speech, and of many words, yet clever, acute and eloquent, etc., depending on dignity.

PRINCESS OF SWORDS. A young woman with light brown hair and blue eyes. Wisdom, strength, acuteness, subtleness in material things, grace and dexterity. Ill-dignified, she is frivolous and cunning.

PRINCE OF SWORDS. A young man with dark hair and dark eyes. Full of ideas and thoughts and designs, distrustful, suspicious, firm in friend-ship and enmity, careful, slow, over-cautious. Symbolizes Alpha and Omega, the Giver of Death, who slays as fast as he creates. Ill-dignified; harsh, malicious, plotting, obstinate, yet hesitating and unreliable.

QUEEN OF SWORDS. A graceful woman of grey hair and light-brown eyes. Intensely perceptive, keen observation, subtle, quick, confident, often practical Work perserveringly accurate in superficial things, graceful, fond of dancing and balancing. Ill-dignified: cruel, sly, deceitful, unreliable, though with a good exterior.

KING OF SWORDS. A man with dark brown hair and dark eyes. He is active, clever, subtle, fierce, delicate, courageous, skillful, but inclined to domineer. Also to overvalue small things unless well-dignified. Ill-dignified, deceitful, tyrannical and crafty.

ACE OF PENTACLES. Material gain, labor, power, wealth, etc. It represents materiality in all senses, good and evil, and is therefore in a sense illusory.

TWO OF PENTACLES: Pleasant change. Visit to friends. The harmony of change. Alternation of gain and loss, weakness and strength, ever varying occupation, wandering, discontented with any fixed condition of things; now elated, now melancholy, industrious, yet unreliable, fortunate through prudence of management yet sometimes unaccountably foolish. Alternatively talkative and suspicious. Kind yet wavering and inconsistent. Fortunate in journeying. Argumentative.

THREE OF PENTACLES. Business, paid employment. Commercial transactions. Working and constructive force, building up, erection, creation, realization, and increase of material things, gain in commercial transactions, rank, increase in substance, influence, cleverness in business, selfishness, commencement of matter to be established later. Narrow and prejudiced, keen in matter of gain. Modified by dignity. Sometimes given to seeking after the impossible.

FOUR OF PENTACLES. Gain of money and influence. A present. Assured material gain, success, rank, dominion, earthly power completed by leading to nothing beyond. Prejudiced, covetous, suspicious, careful and orderly, but discontented. Little enterprise or originality. Altered by dignity as usual.

FIVE OF PENTACLES. Loss of profession. Loss of money. Monetary anxiety. Loss of money or position. Trouble about material things. Toil, labor, land cultivation, building, knowledge and acuteness of earthly things, poverty, carefulness. Kindness, sometimes money regained after severe toil and labor. Unimaginative, harsh, stern, determined and obstinate.

SIX OF PENTACLES. Success in material things. Prosperity in business. Success and gain in material undertakings, power, influence, rank, nobility, rule over people. Fortunate, successful, just and liberal. If ill-dignified may be purse-proud, insolent from success or prodigal.

SEVEN OF PENTACLES. Unprofitable speculation and employment. Little gain for much labor. Promises of success unfulfilled. Loss of apparently promising fortune. Hopes deceived and crushed. Disappointment. Misery, slavery, necessity and baseness. A cultivator of land, and yet is loser thereby. Sometimes it denotes slight and isolated gains with no fruits resulting therefrom, and of no further account, though seeming to promise well. Honorable work undertaken for the love of it, and without desire of reward. According to dignity.

EIGHT OF PENTACLES. Skill, prudence, cunning. Over-careful in small things at the expense of the great. "Penny-wise and pound foolish." Gain of ready money in small sums. Mean, avariciousness. Industrious, cultivation of land, hoarding, lacking in enterprise.

NINE OF PENTACLES. Inheritance. Much increase of money. Complete realization of material gain, inheritance, covetousness, treasuring of goods and sometimes theft and knavery. All according to dignity.

TEN OF PENTACLES. Riches and wealth. Completion of material gain and fortune, but nothing beyond. As it were, at the very pinnacle of success. Old age, slothfulness, great wealth, yet sometimes loss in part, and later heaviness, dullness of mind, yet clever and prosperous in money transactions.

PRINCESS OF PENTACLES. A young woman with rich-brown, or red-brown hair, and dark eyes. She is generous, kind, diligent, benevolent, careful, courageous, perservering. If ill-dignified she is wasteful and prodigal.

PRINCE OF PENTACLES. A young man with dark brown hair and dark eyes. Increase of matter, increase of good and evil, solidifies, practically amplifies things, steady, reliable. If ill-dignified, animal, material, stupid. In either slow to anger, but furious if roused.,

QUEEN OF PENTACLES. A woman with dark hair and dark eyes. She is impetuous, kind, timid, rather charming, great-hearted, intelligent, melancholy, truthful, yet of many moods. Ill-dignified, she is undecided, capricious, foolish, changeable.

KING OF PENTACLES. A man with dark eyes and dark hair. Unless very well dignified he is heavy, dull, and material. Laborious, clever and patient in material matters. If ill-dignified he is avaricious, grasping, dull, jealous, not very courageous, unless assisted by other symbols.

Colors on the Tree of Life (from 777)

ASSIAH	YETZIRAH	BRIAH	ATZILUTH	
White, flecked gold	White brilliance	White brilliance	Brilliance	1
White, flecked red, blue, and yellow	Blue pearl grey, like mother of-pearl	Grey	Pure soft blue	2
Grey, flecked pink	Dark brown	Black	Crimson	3
Deep azure, flecked yellow	Deep purple	Blue	Deep violet	4
Red, flecked black	Bright scarlet	Scarlet red	Orange	5
Gold amber	Rich salmon	Yellow (gold)	Clear pink rose	6
Olive, flecked gold	Bright yellow green	Emerald	Amber	7
Yellowish brown, flecked white	Red-russet	Orange	Violet purple	8
Citrine, flecked azure	Very dark purple	Violet	Indigo	9
Black rayed with yellow	As Queen Scale, but flecked with gold	Citrine/Olive Russet/Black.	Yellow	10
Emerald, flecked gold	Blue emerald green	Sky blue	Bright pale yellow	11
Indigo, rayed violet	Grey	Purple	Yellow	12
Silver, rayed sky blue	Cold pale blue	Silver	Blue	13
Bright rose or cerise rayed pale green	Early spring green	Sky blue	Emerald green	14
Glowing red	Brilliant flame	Red	Scarlet	15
Rich brown	Deep warm olive	Deep indigo	Red orange	16
Reddish grey inclined to mauve	New yellow leather	Pale mauve	Orange	17
Dark greenish brown	Rich bright russet	Maroon	Amber	18
Reddish amber	Grey	Deep purple	Yellow, greenish	19
Plum colour	Green grey	Slate grey	Green, yellowish	20
Bright blue, rayed yellow	Rich purple	Blue	Violet	21
Pale green	Deep blue-green	Blue	Emerald green	22
White, flecked purple, like mother-of-pearl	Deep olive-green	Sea green	Deep blue	23
Livid indigo brown (like a black beetle)	Very dark brown	Dull brown	Green blue	24
Dark vivid blue	Green	Yellow	Blue	25
Cold dark grey, approaching black	Blue black	Black	Indigo	26
Bright red, rayed azure or emerald	Venetian red	Red	Scarlet	27
White, tinged purple	Bluish mauve	Sky blue	Violet	28
Stone colour	Light translucent pinkish brown	Buff, flecked silver-white	Crimson (ultra violet)	29
Amber, rayed red	Rich amber	Gold yellow	Orange	30
Vermilion, flecked crimson and emerald	Scarlet, flecked gold	Vermilion	Orange scarlet	31
Black, rayed blue	Blue black	Black	Indigo	32

Every student should paint a Tree of Life. The diagram used for meditation and ritual work has the Sephiroth in the colors of Briah and the Paths in the colors of Atziluth. The preparation of a painting of all four worlds (one above the other) is also recommended. Work is best done on a smooth wooden panel, prepared with gesso. The diagrams should be painted in either oil or artist's acrylic.

Notes on color: The best possible background color for the Tree is metallic gold. This is available in acrylic.

Confusion may exist about some of the colors of Malkuth in Yetzirah and Briah, i.e., citrine, olive, russet and black. The first three are the colors of Hod, Tiphareth and Netzach tinged with the purple of Yesod. Citrine (yellow + small amount of violet) is at the top; olive (emerald green + violet) is at the right; russet (orange + violet) is at the left; black is at the base.

Colors and Sounds on the Tree of Life

The following (Atziluth) color-sound correspondences are taken from the Golden Dawn notebook of Alan Bennett, teacher of both Fortune and Crowley. These correspondences were elaborated upon by Paul Case who developed a system of healing and of invocation still taught by the BOTA.

LETTER	PATH COLOR	SOUND	TAROT KEY
0 Aleph/ א	Bright pale yellow	E	Fool
1 Beth/ ב	Yellow	E	Magician
2 Gimel/ ג	Blue	G#	High Priestess
3 Daleth/ ד	Emerald Green	F#	Empress
4 Heh/ ה	Scarlet	C	Emperor
5 Vau/ ו	Red-Orange	C#	Hierophant
6 Zain/ ז	Orange	D	Lovers
7 Cheth/ ח	Amber	D#	Chariot
8 Teth/ ט	Yellow, Greenish	E#	Strength
9 Yod/ י	Green, Yellowish	F	Hermit
10 Caph/ כ	Violet	A#	Wheel of Fortune
11 Lamed/ ל	Emerald Green	F#	Justice
12 Mem/ מ	Deep Blue	G#	Hanged Man
13 Nun/ נ	Green Blue	G	Death
14 Samekh/ ס	Blue	G#	Temperance
15 Ayin/ ע	Indigo	A	Devil
16 Peh/ פ	Scarlet	C	Tower
17 Tzaddi/ צ	Violet	A#	Star
18 Qoph/ ק	Crimson	B	Moon
19 Resh/ ר	Orange	D	Sun
20 Shin/ ש	Orange-Scarlet	C	Judgment
21 Tau/ ת	Indigo	A	Universe

HEBREW NAMES OF THE ANGELS OF THE DECANS
(Day and Night Angels of the Minor Cards, Two through Ten)

	Pairs of Angels Ruling Wands	Pairs of Angels Ruling Cups	Pairs of Angels Ruling Swords	Pairs of Angels Ruling Pentacles
0	----------------------	----------------------	----------------------	----------------------
1	----------------------	----------------------	----------------------	----------------------
2	דניאל יהואל	חבוי אנעאל	מבהאל יעלאל	ושרי לכבאל
3	עממיה החשיה	יבמיה ראהאל	הקמיה הריאל	להחיה יחויה
4	ביתאל נבאאל	מומיה הייאל	כאיאל לאויה	מנדאל כוקיה
5	יליאל והויה	פהליה לוויה	חעמיה אניאל	פניאל מבהיה
6	עלמיה סיטאל	ייזאל בלכאל	ייזאל רפעאל	יילאל נממיה
7	ללהאל מהשיה	חהויה מלהאל	מיכאל הההאל	מצראל הרחאל
8	האאיה בתהיה	ילהיה וליה	יההאל ומבאל	כהתאל אכאיה
9	שאהיה ירתאל	עריאל סאליה	מחיאל ענואל	הזיאל אלריה
10	אומאל רייאל	מיהאל עשליה	מנקאל דמביה	ההעיה לאויה

THE DIVINE NAMES ATTRIBUTED TO THE SEPHIROTH

Number of Sephira	Divine Names *(Atziluth)*	Archangelic Name *(Briah)*	Choir of Angels *(Yetzirah)*
1. Kether	Eheieh אהיה	Metatron מטטרון	Chayoth ha-Qadesh חיות הקדש
2. Chokmah	Yah יה	Raziel רזיאל	Auphanim אופנים
3. Binah	YHVH Elohim יהוה אלהים	Tzaphqiel צפקיאל	Aralim אראלים
4. Chesed	El אל	Tzadqiel צדקיאל	Chashmalim חשמלים
5. Geburah	Elohim Gibor אלהים גבור	Kamael כמאל	Seraphim שרפים
6. Tiphareth	YHVH Eloah Vedaath יהוה אלוה ודעת	Raphael רפאל	Melekim מלכים
7. Netzach	YHVH Tzabaoth יהוה צבאות	Haniel האניאל	Elohim אלהים
8. Hod	Elohim Tzabaoth אלהים צבאות	Michael מיכאל	Beni Elohim בני אלהים
9. Yesod	Shaddai El Chai שדי אלהי	Gabriel גבריאל	Kerubim כרובים
10. Malkuth	Adonai ha-Aretz אדני הארץ	Sandalphon סנדלפון	Ashim אשים

THIRTY-TWO PATHS OF WISDOM

SEPHIROTH

1 Kether/ כתר   The Admirable or Hidden Intelligence
2 Chokmah/ חכמה   The Illuminating Intelligence
3 Binah/ בינה   The Sanctifying Intelligence
4 Chesed/ בסד   The Measuring, Cohesive or
                    Receptacular Intelligence
5 Geburah/ גבורה   The Radical Intelligence
6 Tiphareth/ תפארת   The Intelligence of the Mediating Influence
7 Netzach/ נצח   The Occult Intelligence
8 Hod/ הוד   The Absolute or Perfect Intelligence
9 Yesod/ יסקד   The Pure Intelligence
10 Malkuth/ מלכות   The Resplendent Intelligence

PATHS

11 Aleph/ א   The Scintillating Intelligence
12 Beth/ ב   The Intelligence of Transparency
13 Gimel/ ג   The Uniting Intelligence
14 Daleth/ ד   The Illuminating Intelligence
15 Heh/ ה   The Constituting Intelligence
16 Vau/ ו   The Triumphal or Eternal Intelligence
17 Zain/ ז   The Disposing Intelligence
18 Cheth/ ח   The House of Influence
19 Teth/ ט   The Intelligence of all the Activities
                    of the Spiritual Beings
20 Yod/ י   The Intelligence of Will
21 Kaph/ כ   The Intelligence of Conciliation
22 Lamed/ ל   The Faithful Intelligence
23 Mem/ מ   The Stable Intelligence
24 Nun/ נ   The Imaginative Intelligence
25 Samekh/ ס   The Intelligence of Probation
26 Ayin/ ע   The Renovating Intelligence
27 Peh/ פ   The Exciting Intelligence
28 Tzaddi/ צ   The Natural Intelligence
29 Qoph/ ק   The Corporeal Intelligence
30 Resh/ ר   The Collecting Intelligence
31 Shin/ ש   The Perpetual Intelligence
32 Tau/ ת   The Administrative Intelligence

INDEX

INDEX

D

E

S

Sacrificed Gods, 16, 88, 91
Sagittarius, 76, 106, 111, 117, 131, 129
    175-179, 235
Salamanders, 66, 74
Salt, Alchemical, 73, 224; *Empress* as,
    234-231; Chokmah as, 231
Salt, Sulphur, Mercury, 198, 205,
    231, 234
Sammadhi, 186
Samael, Ruler of Volcanic Fire, 151
sandals, 108, 111
Sangrael Foundaton, 14
Sattva, Rajas and Tamas, 198
Saturn, 36 (Fig. 6), 48, 61, 69, 70, 72,
    85, 90, 93, 102, 106, 107, 117
    127, 143, 163, 164, 166, 172,
    173, 182, 191, 192, 204, 208;
    devours its children, 61
scales of Justice, 190, 191
scarabaeus (dung beetle), 157
Scarlet Woman, 207, 221
sceptre, 78
Scholem, Gershom, 1, 5, 20, 23, 209
Scorpio, 66, 86, 92, 101, 129, 180, 184
scorpion, 183
scourge, 83
Secret Chiefs, 11, 12, 186
Secret Paths, 37, 38 (Fig. 8)
Sepher Yetzirah, 9, 21, 22, 29, 30, 41, 77,
    126, 128-131, 144, 146, 148,
    153, 157, 178, 193, 198, 201,
    220, 226, 246
Seraphim, 53, 83, 124, 151
serpent, 66, 68, 96, 109, 117, 122, 147,
    151, 161, 167, 179, 183, 184, 188,
    193, 198, 201, 202, 204, 206, 207,
    216, 238, 242; with tail in its
    mouth, see: Uroboros;
    Nechesh or Leviathon, 207;
Set as, related to Saturn, Satan and
    Bahomet, 248
Sevens, 93-103
Seven Palaces of Assiah, 146
sexual love, Yod, 129, 199, 200,

Shahn, Ben, 44
Shemhamaphoresch, 72; Names of
    God, 146
sight, Heh, 223-227
Signs of Zodiac on Tree of Life,
    130 (Fig. 22)
silence, sign of, 246
Simon Magus and Simonian Gnost-
    ics, 201
Simon and Sperling, translators of
    Zohar, 22
Sixes, 91-94
skeleton, 181-183; mounted and
    in armor, 185
skrying, 50, 98, 115
sleep, Qoph, 129, 156, 157, 160
smell, Zain, 213, 216
Smith, Pamela Colman, 13
snake, Teth, 203-205
Solar Logos, 161, see: Logos
Solar and Lunar currents, 214
Solomon, 171; temple of, 165, 212, 235
solve et coagula, alchemical formula,
    216
spear, 83, 85, 167, 189
speech, Cheth, 208
Sphinx, 197, 198
Spiritual Self, 52, 54, 77, 135, 139, 140,
    (Fig. 29), 152, 167, 200, 205,
    209, 211, 212, 215, 219, 228
St. John of the Cross, 183, 186, 233
St. Theresa, 109, 176
stag, 68
Star, evening, 164
Star, Tzaddi, 160-164
Steiner, Rudolph, 26
"Stele of Revealing," 151, 207
Stella Maris, 67, 183
Stella Matutina, 12
Stoics, 201
Stone of Adam, 164
Strength, Teth, 203-208
Sulphur, *Emperor* as, 224, 231
    Binah as, 231
Sulphur, Salt, Mercury, 224, 234
Sun, subordinate to Moon, 214